The Pink Line

ALSO BY MARK GEVISSER

Lost and Found in Johannesburg: A Memoir

A Legacy of Liberation: Thabo Mbeki and the Future of the South African Dream

Portraits of Power: Profiles in a Changing South Africa

As Coeditor

Defiant Desire: Gay and Lesbian Lives in South Africa

PRAISE FOR THE BOOK

'In this masterful recounting of sexuality and identity around the globe, Mark Gevisser achieves an almost shocking empathy. His accounts are riveting, brilliantly researched, liberal, and forthright. He talks to people with and without privilege, of every race and of every nationality, limning the aspects of queer experience that are universal and those that are local. In intimate, often tender prose, he brings to life the complex movement for queer civil rights and the many people on whom it bears. Whether recounting suffering or triumph, Gevisser is a clear-sighted, fearless, and generous guide.'

– **Andrew Solomon,** author of *Far From the Tree: Parents, Children, and the Search for Identity*

'Mark Gevisser's *The Pink Line* is a book I've been waiting a long time for: a global geography of queer struggle, a wide-ranging, open-hearted, beautifully told account of the radically various state of LGBTQ rights in the world. This is a book that should be very widely read – and not only read but acted upon.'

– **Garth Greenwell**, author of *What Belongs to You* and *Cleanness*

'*The Pink Line* is a deep diagnostic account of the ways in which queer lives and queer loves cross the fraught frontiers of race, rights, discrimination, and denigration to transition from agony to agency, and isolation to community. Mark Gevisser has given us a rare piece of writing in which the quotidian confrontations and consolations of everyday life build into an encyclopedic vision of the global frontiers of the queer condition. This is politics and poetry all at once. Gevisser occupies the frontlines of sorrow and struggle with his informants who, in becoming his friends and comrades, together define an activism of defiant desire unafraid of the ambivalences and contradictions of the human condition. *The Pink Line* is a remarkable narrative of resilience, romance and realism.

– **Homi K. Bhabha**, author of *The Location of Culture*

'*The Pink Line* traces a planet-spanning fissure that runs through the most intimate dimensions of life, documenting the sometimes literally war-torn rift zones where so-called 'traditional values' are being mobilized by states to combat trans, queer and feminist social movements. A smart and sobering book for our times.'

– **Susan Stryker**, author of *Transgender History: The Roots of Today's Revolution*

'Mark Gevisser's sensitive yet firmly broad book coheres the concept of a 'pink line': the difference between the wish of queer individuals for autonomy, versus the increased manipulations of gay and trans identities to shore up power systems. His book is both enlightening and disturbing in a world where the wish to be understood can become a commodity of domination.'

– **Sarah Schulman**, author of *The Cosmopolitans*

'No one understands queerness from an armchair – and few have captured that truth better than Mark Gevisser. *The Pink Line* is a vital exploration of queerness around the globe, searching and intimate but also expansive in its scope. Like all the best writing about LGBTQ lives, this book clearly changed its author. It would be impossible not to be transformed by the reading of it.'

– **Samantha Allen**, author of *Real Queer America: LGBT Stories from Red States*

Mark Gevisser

The Pink Line

Journeys Across the World's Queer Frontiers

HarperCollins *Publishers* India

First published in India in 2020 by
HarperCollins *Publishers* India
A-75, Sector 57, Noida, Uttar Pradesh 201301, India
www.harpercollins.co.in

2 4 6 8 10 9 7 5 3 1

P-ISBN: 978-93-5357-803-9
E-ISBN: 978-93-5357-804-6

Typeset in 10/16 Berling LT Std
Manipal Technology Ltd, Manipal

Printed and bound at
Thomson Press (India) Ltd

MIX
Paper
FSC FSC® C010615

This book is produced from independently certified FSC® paper to ensure responsible forest management.

To Dhianaraj Chetty

An identity is questioned only when it is menaced, as when the mighty begin to fall, or when the wretched begin to rise, or when the stranger enters the gates, never, thereafter, to be a stranger: the stranger's presence making you the stranger, less to the stranger than to yourself. Identity would seem to be the garment with which one covers the nakedness of the self: in which case, it is best that the garment be loose, a little like the robes of the desert, through which one's nakedness can always be felt, and, sometimes, discerned. This trust in one's nakedness is all that gives one the power to change one's robes.

—James Baldwin, *The Devil Finds Work: An Essay*, 1976

CONTENTS

AUTHOR'S NOTE

ON TERMINOLOGY

I like the word *queer* because of its double valence. As well as having been reappropriated by people across the world to describe themselves, *queer* means *different* or *skewed*: to see things from a "queer perspective" is to look at the world askance, to see it afresh. But frankly, it is also convenient: it is a catchall that can hold (well, most of) the *Ls*, the *Bs*, the *Gs*, the *Ts*, and everyone else on the expanding alphabet. For this reason, however, it has sometimes lost its "queer" meaning, particularly in the United States. If everyone is queer, no one is. I hope to get the right balance here.

Also, in some parts of the world, including the United Kingdom, African American communities, and my native South Africa, *queer* remains awkward. This is because it is still so often used as a slur. It is also rejected by some transgender people who are very clear, like Liam, whom you will meet in these pages, that they are "straight."

I have done my best to use the language the people I write about feel most comfortable with. I describe Liam as a straight transgender man because this is how he describes himself. Sean, who was also assigned female at birth, is genderqueer and prefers the "they" pronouns: so this is how I identify them, too, despite the grammatical infelicity. I have endeavored to abide by this principle even though this leads to inevitable inconsistencies in the text. Some people speak of "LGBT" rights and communities, some of "LGBTI" ones, some of "LGBTQ," of "LGBTIQ," "LGBTQ+," etc. In the 2010s, the accepted convention in human rights discourse was "LGBT" and so this is my default. But if Tiwonge calls herself an LGBTI, that's what I call her too. If Pasha calls herself transgender, that's what I call her; if Charlotte calls herself a transsexual, ditto.

On that note: *cisgender* is a word developed by the trans community itself to describe people like me: those whose gender identities and expressions are congruent with the bodies they were assigned at birth. I share the philosopher Kwame Anthony Appiah's skepticism about the need to begin every sentence: "As a white, gay, cisgender, middle-class, middle-age South African man …," or whatever one's identity markers happen to be. In a 2018 *New York Times* op-ed, Appiah makes the point: "Because members of a given identity group have experiences that depend on a host of other social factors, they're *not* the same."[1] I speak for myself, and not for any group. But I speak from a certain vantage point and new debates about "cultural appropriation" notwithstanding, I want you to know where I'm coming from, as I ask you to accompany me on this journey.

I hope that some of you, reading this book, will be able to see yourselves in these pages and to identify with the people I write about. I hope that for all of you, there is the thrill of the new, too—as there was for me. In the very paragraphs above there are words or phrases you might not be familiar with: *cisgender*, *gender congruent*, *assigned gender at birth*. Is it *sex change surgery*, *gender reassignment surgery*, *gender affirmation surgery*, or *gender confirmation surgery*? These are shifting sands, as the lexicon of a long-misunderstood group of people establishes itself as common usage, outside of the pathologizing discourse of medicine. There is not agreement: some people use *transsexual* to differentiate those who have had surgery; others reject it because of its derogatory or eroticized history. Once more, I have tried to steer a course using the way people describe themselves—and the accepted conventions of the moment—as a guide.

A key precept of the contemporary transgender rights movement, particularly in the West, is to draw a line between *sexual orientation* and *gender identity*. A few nifty slogans from the transgender movement itself have helped me understand this, and I hope they help you, too:

"My gender is between my ears, my sex is between my legs";

"My gender identity is who I go to bed as, my sexual orientation is who I go to bed with";

"Sex is what I do with my clothes off, gender expression is what I do with my clothes."

These work well in an American context but do not begin to capture the complex swirl of sexualities and gender identities in other places. If this book has one overarching agenda, it is to show that there is not only one way to be in the world.

ON TRANSLATION

This book tells the stories of many people who do not speak English at all, some who speak it well as a second language, and some for whom it is the mother tongue. In Malawi and South Africa, Egypt, Russia, India, and Mexico I worked through Chichewa, Arabic, Russian, Tamil, and Spanish interpreter-researchers. This means that the people whose stories I am telling are refracted through this extraordinary cohort of go-betweens, who worked double time with me: always having to listen to me, and to our subjects, while I could zone out a little after asking the question and waiting for the translation, and doing much fixing, digging, and cultural translation, too. Every one of them was invaluable, but they covered a range of fluency in English, and had their own linguistic idiosyncrasies, due to where and how they learned the language. In some instances, given the fact that I was in touch with my subjects over six years, I was compelled to use more than one interpreter, and my subject's voice would thus change in the transcripts, from visit to visit. Pasha, from Russia, sometimes speaks the more British English of my interpreter Margret, and sometimes the more American one of my interpreter Zhenya.

If, in Tamil Nadu, Sheetal's mode of expression seems coarser than that of her protégé Lakshaya, this might not just be because of their respective personalities: it is because Sheetal chose to speak to me in English, of a sort, while Lakshaya could not, and is therefore filtered through the more standard English of my interpreter Lavanya. Even when there was no interpreter present, these possible discrepancies present themselves. Is Nadav, the Israeli, more articulate than his boyfriend Fadi, the Palestinian? I doubt it, but Nadav lived in Australia as a child, while Fadi learned English online.

Sometimes, too, I was speaking in imperfect French or Spanish to people for whom these were native or second languages: I can state with certainty that things got lost in the transfer. Still, despite all these limitations, I have worked hard to bring to you people in their own voices, with translations that are as close as possible to what my subjects said to me. But translation is a screen, and not a translucent one.

ON ANONYMITY AND SECURITY

Several people asked for pseudonyms or to be disguised. Given the danger that queer people face, particularly in environments such as Egypt or Nigeria, I promised anonymity to whoever sought it. I always indicate when I have done this. Curiously, it was in the United States more than anywhere else that people asked for their names not to be used, or that only first names be used so that they could not be tracked online. This might be a function of the fact that this book is published, first, in the U.S.; that Americans are particularly media savvy and wired; and that my primary subjects there were all just coming of age and thus were legitimately worried about what might follow them into adulthood. But I think it says something else, too: how fraught the debate is in the U.S. and how fragile and intemperate the cultural discourse around transgender identity in particular has been despite the relative safety and freedom that people enjoy compared to other parts of the world.

PROLOGUE

A DEBT TO LOVE

"GAYS ENGAGE."[1]

This was the front-page headline of the *Nation* newspaper, from the central African country of Malawi, on Sunday, December 28, 2009. Above it was a photograph of two people, bleary and uncomfortable in matching his-and-hers outfits cut from the same patterned wax print: "Gay lovebirds Tiwonge Chimbalanga and Steven Monjeza on Saturday made history when they spiced their festive season with an engagement ceremony (*chinkhoswe*)," the article read, noting that this was "the first recorded public activity for homosexuals in the country." Down the left side were some helpful "fast facts": Homosexuality was "illegal in Malawi" and carried "a maximum sentence of five or 14 years imprisonment ... with or without corporal punishment."

Four and a half years later, in May 2014, I looked at this page with Tiwonge Chimbalanga: she had brought it into exile with her, across three thousand kilometers and four countries, and tacked it onto the corrugated-zinc wall of her shack in Tambo Village, a township outside Cape Town. Although she displayed it, she objected to it, too: "I am not a gay, I'm a woman," she said to me in English, before reverting to her native Chichewa: "They told me I was gay when they arrested me. They told me that I was paid to do my *chinkhoswe* by LGBTs from overseas. But the first time I heard the word *gay* was when I saw it next to that picture and when the policemen came and took me away."

When I had arrived earlier, Aunty—as Chimbalanga was universally known—had been waiting for me on the street in an elaborate purple ensemble with full skirts and turban, the kind of confection usually reserved for a *chinkhoswe* back home. I thought she might have made the effort because she was receiving a visitor, but it turned out this was how she always dressed, so very much at odds with the Lycra-Leggings style favored by local women in this sand-swept proletarian place. Aunty was tall and very dark with broad features and would have stood out anyway, even if she did not wear thick foundation to cover her facial hair, which gave her skin a silvery sheen. She was brittle, and regal, with a studied haughtiness, but I saw how quickly this could evaporate into a kind of girlish bashfulness when she was more relaxed, or when she had cause to remember her life before people told her she was gay and took her away.

Aunty moved in the determined manner of someone who might collapse if she did not keep her chin forward. In her low-heeled silver pumps, she led me along a sodden narrow path between shacks to her own, one of several in the yard behind a big house on Joe Slovo Street. Aunty's was the nicest by far, thanks to the relief aid she received from Amnesty International as a released "prisoner of conscience." She had a large television, a sound system, and a coterie that included her "husband" of about a year, Benson, an unemployed Malawian compatriot who lived with her. Neighbors popped in constantly to cadge a tomato, or to buy some of the beer she sold on the side. "Aunty! Aunty!" they exclaimed, somewhere between affection and mockery, as they passed her locked security gate.

I had brought a meal: a bucket of Kentucky Fried Chicken and a magnum of Mountain Dew. Benson was a small, mild man, quietly inebriated, and seemingly dominated by Aunty. She ordered him to unstack some plastic chairs and she smoothed, it seemed to me, an imaginary cloth out over the table that filled one of her two rooms. Taped somewhat randomly along the wall alongside the "Gays Engage" page were photographs of her with people who appeared to be her lovers and friends, and other articles detailing her imprisonment and release back home. These were interspersed with adverts carefully cut from South African magazines, tending toward a girlie-on-a-sports car hyperfemininity. A code had been carefully written with black marker across the front of the oversize fridge: "ROMA 13 8."

I asked what this meant.

Aunty reached across the table for the tattered green Bible she had been gifted by her most regular visitor in jail back in Malawi: a priest who urged her to repent. She opened it to Romans 13:8, and read the verse aloud, with some difficulty: "'Let no debt remain outstanding, except the continuing debt to love one another, for whoever loves others has fulfilled the law.'"

Why had she chosen to write those words on her fridge?

"These are the words that were printed on the card at my engagement ceremony," she said in Chichewa, through her friend Prisca, another Malawian refugee; Aunty struggled with English even after four years here. "I want all visitors to my home to know what love means. Then they will know I did nothing wrong."

WHEN CAROLINE SOMANJE, the journalist responsible for the "Gays Engage" piece, received a tip-off alerting her to the public *chinkhoswe* of two men, she knew she had a scoop. She told me this over the phone from Malawi when we spoke in 2014. Before that, the only time the country's media had ever covered homosexuality was, occasionally, when a man was charged with raping a minor. But word was spreading about the issue even here, in one of Africa's sleepiest, most underdeveloped countries.

A South African network provided satellite TV to Malawi, as to all over Africa, and the soap *Generations* had just introduced a black gay character. The news channels carried frequent items about gay marriage in the West, particularly in the United States, where the issue had caught fire following the debate over Proposition 8 in California. And the AIDS epidemic was forcing an unwelcome discussion about homosexuality: this was at the increasing insistence of international donors. In response, the allegation that gay rights as a Western imposition had taken root. As had the power of this topic to create scandal and sell newspapers: Somanje's editors may well have noted this effect in Uganda, where the tabloids regularly named and shamed alleged homosexuals.

After receiving the tip-off, Somanje rushed to Mankhoma Lodge along the airport road in Blantyre, Malawi's biggest city: here Aunty had been working as a cleaner and cook. The scene Somanje found was edgy: "There was a huge crowd. People were hostile; they had come to satisfy their curiosity, not to celebrate a wedding. Tiwonge was in tears."

The tip-off had in fact come from Aunty's employer, a prominent local politician and businesswoman who had actually paid for the *chinkhoswe*: she had thought it would attract business, but had then panicked when things seemed to be getting out of hand. During the ensuing trial the woman, Jean Kamphale, would tell the court that Aunty had deceived her into believing she was a woman: Aunty had allegedly explained her masculine facial features away by saying she had been born a girl but was bewitched as a child.

Aunty confirmed to me that she did indeed offer that explanation—I came to understand that she believed it herself—but Kamphale was lying to the court: she had known all along that Aunty had a male body. This was clear to me when I interviewed her and her family in Blantyre, later in 2014. Kamphale's daughter Rachael told me that she had pleaded with her mother to hire Aunty despite the fact that "he" was "gay": "These days, us younger people, we're more open to it. It's not something new anymore. We've been modernized, we're growing up in a world that keeps changing, so when we meet someone who happens to be gay, big deal!"

The authorities felt differently. When the police arrived at the lodge the next morning, a copy of the *Nation* in hand, they forced Aunty to strip. Once they ascertained she had male genitals they arrested her and Monjeza on suspicion of being in contravention of Section 153 of the Penal Code, a colonial British hangover that forbade homosexual sex as "carnal knowledge against the order of nature."[2] The two were charged, although the provision had never previously been used against consenting adults, and there was no evidence of intercourse. After a humiliating trial that brought Blantyre to a standstill, they were found guilty and sentenced to the maximum punishment of fourteen years' hard labor: "a scaring sentence," as the magistrate put it: the public needed to be "protected from others who may be tempted to emulate their [horrendous] example."

The ensuing international outrage included an online petition initiated by Madonna, who had two adopted Malawian children, and culminated in a mercy mission to the country by Ban Ki-Moon, the United Nations Secretary-General. At a joint press conference with Ban in June 2010, the Malawian president Bingu wa Mutharika announced that he would pardon Chimbalanga and Monjeza. But he made it clear he was bowing to international pressure: the two had "committed a crime against our culture, our religion and our laws."[3]

After their release, Steven Monjeza was paid by *The Nation* for an interview in which he denounced Aunty for having bewitched him. He announced his happy engagement to a local sex worker and was back in jail within months for stealing a cell phone. I tried to find him when I visited Malawi in late 2014, but he was apparently inside again.

Aunty eventually sought asylum in South Africa, on the basis of the persecution she suffered in her native land after her release, when her notoriety made it impossible to be in public. But her life in South Africa was not easy. She had a ravaged body that she exposed to me, scar by livid scar, to illustrate this: they were the results of attacks she sustained since moving to Cape Town in 2011.

One magazine page, taped to Aunty's wall, startled me each time I visited: a photograph of James Small, South African rugby's sexy bad boy, covered in blood on the playing field, beneath an Afrikaans headline that translated as, "He Takes No Shit." Aunty told me that when her husband, Benson, wanted to go to the shops she needed to accompany him, to protect him from the insults arising from his relationship with her. She clearly had learned to use her fists, and I would learn that she was not shy to do so. But when she curtsied in greeting and failed to meet my eye, or swayed gently to prayer in church on a Sunday morning, I remembered who she was: a devout rural girl from a small village beyond the tea plantations on the Thyolo escarpment in southern Malawi, far, far away.

THIS BOOK IS AUNTY'S STORY, and that of others from different parts of the world who have found themselves on what I have come to call the Pink Line: a human rights frontier that divided and described the world in an entirely new way in the first two decades of the twenty-first century. No social movement had caught fire so quickly as the one that came to be known as "LGBT": the worlds Aunty and I inhabited in 2014 were unimaginably different from how they had been for each of us, from such very different places, even a decade previously.

Aunty's home in Tambo Village is not twenty kilometers from the handsome century-old bungalow, overlooking the ocean, where I wrote this book. My husband, C, and I bought it in 2012; we were married three years earlier, in 2009, the same year that Aunty held her *chinkhoswe*. But while her commitment ceremony brought her abject humiliation, a fourteen-year jail sentence, and a life in unwanted exile, mine got me a much-desired few years in Paris, spousal benefits from C's job, and the same rights as any other married couple in our home country, South Africa. Our post-apartheid constitution was famously the first in the world to guarantee equality on the basis of sexual orientation; ten years later, in 2006, South Africa became the fifth country in the world to legalize same-sex marriage. Here we were, a married gay couple, the beneficiaries of rights in a way I could not have imagined when I was a young man.

Three decades previously, a steely defiance cloaking my terror, I had come out to my own parents at the age of nineteen. They were supportive, but my father could not hide his concern: Would I ever know the joys of family? Would I lead a lonely life? I had fought my corner: of course I could have children; of course I would find love. But it was 1983—there was not yet even an Internet to provide me with the ammunition of information and the solace of a virtual community—and I struggled to convince myself. Then, as I was opening into adulthood, the AIDS epidemic descended, with its cruel confirmation of everything gay men had been taught to believe about ourselves: we were sinners and we were being punished; our sexuality was morbid and we would die.

Through all of this I came to believe, fervently, that I and others like me had the same right to live openly as anyone else, and I did my bit to fight for this. As an undergraduate in the U.S. in the 1980s, I took on the mantra of Harvey Milk, the gay San Francisco politician assassinated just a few years previously, in 1978: "Gay brothers and sisters, you must come out!"[4] The only path to full participation for gay people in society, the only path out of the shame and secrecy of my own adolescence, was through being visible, so that others—our colleagues and classmates, our children and neighbors, our parents and priests—would know we were there. Returning home in 1990 after South Africa's liberation movements were unbanned and Nelson Mandela freed, I wrote publicly about my sexual orientation and co-edited a book on gay and lesbian life in South Africa. At the same time I had a prominent career as a journalist, which was in no way damaged by being out of the closet.

Two decades later, in 2013, C and I were living in France when that country finally legalized same-sex marriage, upgrading the status from the Pacte civil de solidarité (Pacs), a form of civil union. On a Sunday in May, hundreds of thousands of people descended on Paris for the Manif Pour Tous, a rally against same-sex marriage and in favor of "the family," supported by a Catholic Church trying to maintain relevance in a rapidly secularizing society.[5] Many of the participants wore T-shirts showing a pictograph of four little stick figures: a mother, a father, and two children. Together with a South African friend, a white woman who with her wife had adopted two black children, I watched the crowds: their indignation seemed, to us, to be born of confusion more than anger, confusion at what had become of the certainties of their world. It seemed as if *they* were the new outsiders to a burgeoning social consensus: despite their numbers they were a minority of French people, according to the polls.[6] Even in the United States, where "gay rights" had long been a casus belli for the culture wars, the annual Gallup poll showed that by 2016, 61 percent of Americans favored same-sex marriage.[7]

Gay men or lesbians marrying and raising children; openly lesbian heads of state and openly gay multinational corporate executives; puberty-blocking medication that helped children who planned to change their gender; presidential orders liberating transgender kids to use the toilets congruent with their gender identity. Such things were unthinkable when I had participated in New York Pride parades in the 1980s and helped organize the Gay and Lesbian Awareness Days at Yale.

Now, in my middle age, as the twenty-first century unfurled into its second decade, this change was happening in progressive enclaves of the world, in places such as the Bay Area, or Buenos Aires, or Amsterdam, or Cape Town. But the planet was spinning faster than ever before: due to the unprecedented movement of goods and capital and people and especially ideas and information—what we have come to call "globalization"—people all over the world were downloading these new ideas, often acquired online, and trying to apply them to their offline realities. Thus were they beginning to change the way they thought about themselves, their place in society, their options, and their rights. Even in places as far-flung as Blantyre, where Aunty held her *chinkhoswe*, age-old conventions around sexuality and gender were being disrupted. There were new negotiations over what was private and what was public, what was illicit and what was acceptable by society.

From 2012 to 2018—the high-water years of this new global phenomenon—I traveled extensively, trying to understand how the world was changing, and why. I did not go everywhere. Rather, I chose places where I felt I could meet people who could best tell the story of how the "LGBT rights movement" was establishing a new global frontier in human rights discourse—in the way that the women's rights movement, or the civil rights movement, or the anti-colonial movement, or the abolitionist movement, had done in previous eras. I wanted to understand how this new struggle was a consequence of these prior—and ongoing—ones, but also how different it was, too, in this era of digital revolution and information explosion, of consumerism and mass tourism, of mass migration and urbanization, of global human rights activism.

I tracked Aunty's journey back from Cape Town—which advertises itself as "the gay capital of Africa"—to her remote home village in Thyolo. I followed a gay Ugandan refugee from Kampala to Nairobi in neighboring Kenya, and then on to resettlement in Canada; I hung out with trans and non-binary kids from an LGBTQQA (Lesbian, Gay, Bisexual, Trans, Queer, Questioning and Asexual) youth group in Ann Arbor, Michigan, and I followed them as they fanned out across the U.S. I spent time with a group of *kothis*—"women's hearts in men's bodies"—who ran a temple in a South Indian fishing village outside Pondicherry, and also with transgender software engineers working for multinational corporations in nearby Bangalore; with lesbian mothers in Mexico and transgender mothers in Russia; with queer Palestinians in trendy cafés in Tel Aviv and Ramallah and queer Egyptians at sidewalk cafés in downtown Cairo; at Pride marches in Tel Aviv and Delhi, London and Mexico City. And I followed the new international elite of activists and funders as they traveled the world in a never-ending circuit of meetings and conferences, forging the networks that advocated for this new global agenda.

I witnessed a troubling new global equation come into play: while same-sex marriage and gender transition were now celebrated in some parts of the world as signs of humanity in progress, laws were being strengthened to criminalize such actions in others. In 2013, the same year that the United Kingdom passed the Marriage (Same Sex Couples) Act, Nigeria promulgated its antithesis: the Same Sex Marriage (Prohibition) Act. Even the parentheses were reactive: this was *meant* to provoke the former colonial oppressor, and the title was cynically preemptive, drawing a rhetorical line in the sand against the West by promising to inoculate African society against future "infection." Nigeria's was the harshest anti-homosexuality law in the world outside of Islamic Sharia: it prescribed mandatory sentences of fourteen years not just for sex but for any kind of "homosexual behaviour," including attending gatherings or associating with people thought to be homosexual.

Thus was a Pink Line drawn: between those places increasingly integrating queer people into their societies as full citizens, and those finding new ways to shut them out now that they had come into the open. On one side of this Pink Line were countries that had undergone social changes due to their own women's rights and gay rights movements; these countries supported "LGBT Rights" as a logical application of the UN's 1948 Universal Declaration of Human Rights. On the other were those that condemned the idea as a violation of what they would come to call their "traditional values" and "cultural sovereignty."

Some countries—such as Russia and Uganda—used anti-gay legislation to erect moral barriers against the unstoppable energy flow of globalization. Others, like Egypt, Turkey, and Indonesia, attempted to demonstrate their righteousness by cracking down on transgender women, the most visible face of this immorality from the West even if, as in Indonesia, third-gender *warias* had long been part of their own society.[8] The crackdowns were often done using laws forbidding prostitution or "debauchery" or "vagrancy," but as Aunty's case so ably demonstrated, such laws were not needed in countries that enforced or strengthened their anti-sodomy laws, as these could be applied to anyone officially male, regardless of gender identity.

In 2018 the World Health Organization amended its International Classification of Diseases (ICD), which provided the global codes for diagnoses, so that *gender incongruence*—the new term for *gender identity disorder*—would be moved out of "mental disorders" and into "sexual health conditions." Some countries—led by Argentina and Denmark—had already begun to make it possible to change one's gender legally by "self-determination," meaning that you no longer needed any kind of external diagnosis or certification. In South Asia, where there have been third-gender communities for centuries, activists were energized by the new global transgender movement and used their country's constitutions to gain victories in gender recognition.

But along the way, a new Pink Line had been drawn, with new battlegrounds opening up new frontiers of the culture wars.

In the United States, this line ran right through children's bathrooms, as school boards and parents fought legal battles to prevent transgender children from using the facilities consistent with their gender identities. In early 2018, Donald Trump tried to ban transgender people from serving in the military—a sign, *The New York Times* said, of the American president's "cruel determination to transform America into a country that divides and dehumanizes its people."[9] Later, Trump's government would moot restricting the rights and opportunities of transgender people by defining gender as "biological" and immutable.

In many parts of the world, the staking of a Pink Line along LGBT Rights disrupted age-old ways of dealing with sexuality and gender variance. As had happened in the West in the late twentieth century, homosexuality came to be increasingly understood in Latin America, Asia, and even Africa as an identity deserving of rights and recognition rather than simply a sexual behavior to be kept on the down-low. And having a gender identity different from the one you were assigned at birth came to be seen as a human right, something medicine and surgery could facilitate.

This offered opportunities for upliftment on the one hand, but shut down space on the other, as Western notions of the gender binary settled in societies where gender was often permitted to be more fluid. Suddenly, age-old transgender categories, such as Indonesian *warias* or Senegalese *goor-jigeen*, came to be pinked with the new LGBT brush. In many parts of the world, men walk arm in arm or hand in hand: in countries like Egypt and Nigeria, where there was moral panic against a new category of people demanding space and rights, even these gestures of affection became suspect.

If you had satellite television in Dakar or Lagos—or Cairo or Kabul—you could flip between *Transparent* or *Orange Is the New Black* on one network, and Wahhabi tirades against all sorts of Western infidel activity, including homosexuality and transgenderism, on another. You and your kids could fight over whether to watch homophobic rants on the Christian Broadcasting Network—or a Brazilian telenovela with a gay subplot. On BBC or CNN or even Al Jazeera you could watch reportage of gay pride parades in an increasing number of countries, including India and Turkey, or of children changing their gender in America. And you could also see mass protests by Catholics in France and Latin America against the new foe, *gender ideology*, a catchall term that covered sexuality education, same sex marriage, and gender transition.

In the age of digital technology and social media, previously isolated people suddenly found themselves part of a global queer community, able to connect with others first in chat rooms and then on hookup sites or social media platforms; to download ideas about personal freedom and rights that encouraged them to become visible; and to claim space in society. But so, too, through some of the same platforms, could members of faith groups forge networks—and access ideologies and strategies—far beyond their individual parishes or mosques. Religious identity, like sexual or gender identity, became globalized, and a clash between the two was inevitable.

There was a cultural bifurcation in some places. In Malaysia, conservative Islamism seemed to be gaining purchase: through the new adoption of Sharia laws that banned, among other things, "posing as a woman"; through raids on gay bars and the censorship of exhibitions; and even—in 2018—through an unprecedented sentencing of two women to public caning for lesbianism when they were found with a dildo in a car. But at the same time, younger and more urban Malaysians supported LGBT rights—as they did in many other places—as a way of branding themselves as part of the global village. When a prominent nationalist group called for a boycott of Starbucks in 2017 because the company supported gay rights, this made young urban coffee drinkers even more passionate about the "global space" the chain provided. A Malaysian acquaintance told me: "We go to Starbucks because it's great coffee, but also because it's part of the bigger world." In India, middle-class professionals identified themselves as global citizens through their support of the decriminalization of homosexuality; in Mexico and Argentina, they did so through their support of same-sex marriage.

Mass migration had much to do with these shifts in consciousness: from the countryside to the city, and across national borders from one part of the world to another. People suddenly found themselves in worlds with mores utterly different from the ones in which they had been reared, beyond the reach of their clans or congregations. Perhaps fleeing persecution or struggling for economic survival, or perhaps taking advantage of the ability to travel or study that upward mobility brought, many experienced what is called "personal autonomy" for the first time: the power to make their own decisions about their lives. They then carried such notions about sexual orientation or gender identity back home, to shake things up there. Traveling alongside them on the journey South or East, or from the city to the countryside, were Western aid workers and public health officials, activists, and tourists.

All this movement—across borders real and virtual, on land and in cyberspace created a new sense of space and identity for people the world over. It also created a new set of challenges, as people attempted to toggle between the liberation they experienced online and the constraints of their offline lives, or between their freedom in the city and their commitments back home.

It created new categories of people demanding rights—and also moral panic.

It created new horizons, as societies began to think differently about what it meant to make a family, to be male or female, to be human—and also new fears.

The Pink Line ran through TV studios and parliaments, through newsrooms and courtrooms, through bedrooms and bathrooms, through bodies themselves.

It cleaved Aunty's life, and many others', too.

Writing about it seemed, to me, to be my debt to love.

1

THE WORLD'S PINK LINES

"Mr. President ... did you press President Sall to make sure that homosexuality is decriminalized in Senegal?"[1]

"And, President Sall ... You just said you embrace democracy and freedom. As this country's new President, sir, will you work to decriminalize homosexuality in this country?"

THESE QUESTIONS WERE PUT by an American journalist to Barack Obama and his host, the Senegalese president Macky Sall, at a press conference after the two had met in Dakar on June 27, 2013.

The question was inevitable: while they were flying over the Atlantic the previous day, Obama and his staff had erupted into cheers when they heard that the U.S. Supreme Court had overturned the Defense of Marriage Act (DOMA), paving the way for same-sex marriage across the country.

The case had been brought to the court by an octogenarian widow named Edith Windsor, whose life partner of forty-four years, Thea Spyer, had died in 2009. DOMA barred recognition of same-sex marriages by the U.S. federal government, and Windsor had sued because this meant she could not collect spousal tax benefits after Spyer's death. It was a perfectly telegenic test case, and in the majority judgment Anthony Kennedy ruled that DOMA had stigmatized same-sex couples by enshrining a "separate status" for homosexuals into law.

In 1996, when President Bill Clinton signed DOMA into law (under duress, he insisted), 68 percent of Americans opposed same-sex marriage, and only 27 percent supported it.[2] By 2009, just fifteen years later, this ratio had flipped, and Obama would later describe the "marriage equality" movement as "the fastest set of changes in terms of a social movement that I've seen [in my lifetime]."[3] His own public turning point had been in May 2012: not uncoincidentally, just days after a Gallup poll revealed that, for the first time, more Americans supported same-sex marriage than opposed it. Now, a year later, on his way to Senegal, the president issued a statement from Air Force One: "The laws of our land are catching up to the fundamental truth that millions of Americans hold in our hearts: when all Americans are treated as equal, no matter who they are or whom they love, we are all more free."[4]

This was not the case in Senegal, where the penal code outlawed homosexual acts as "improper or unnatural," a law now being applied after having been dormant for many years. In what had been a perfect storm, the centripetal world-shrinking energies of globalization had brought aggressive new strains of Islam from the Arab world to this West African Muslim country at exactly the same time as the global

AIDS epidemic hit; it was a storm made only more severe in the following years as word spread—through the increasingly penetrating channels of online media and satellite news—of LGBT rights and same-sex marriage in the West.

In December 2008, the Senegalese government hosted a pan-African AIDS conference. The new jargon was "men who have sex with men" (or MSM): this formed a prominent part of the conference program, as did Senegal's own MSM organization, AIDES Sénégal. The event caused an outcry from Senegalese clerics and Islamist politicians already inflamed by sensationalist media coverage of a "gay wedding" (an eerie premonition of what would befall Tiwonge Chimbalanga in Malawi a year later). The authorities responded by raiding an AIDES Sénégal meeting and arresting those present. Nine men were sentenced to eight years in prison, found to be guilty of using their HIV outreach work as "cover to recruit or organize meetings for homosexuals."[5] They were eventually pardoned after five brutal months in jail, on the basis of no evidence of actual sexual congress. But their lives were ruined. Many fled the country.

The situation was little changed when Barack Obama arrived four years later, trailing liberal Americans' euphoria about the Windsor decision in his wake. I had visited Dakar a few months previously, and met leaders of the LGBT movement living underground and in fear. A prominent male journalist was in jail, as were several women: like almost half of the sodomy laws the world over, the Senegalese one criminalized lesbian sex, too.

Obama's government had made the global protection of LGBT rights an American foreign policy priority in December 2011, when Hillary Clinton, the Secretary of State, had famously declared to the United Nations that "gay rights are human rights, and human rights are gay rights."[6] Obama instructed state agencies "to combat the criminalization of LGBT status and conduct" and "to respond swiftly to abuses against LGBT persons." As a consequence, the State Department began reporting regularly on the matter, and Obama was surely briefed on the department's 2012 Senegal finding, which was that "LGBT persons often faced arrest, widespread discrimination, social intolerance and actors of violence" in the country.[7]

Now, at the grand colonial Palais de la République in Dakar, Obama told the reporter who asked him about LGBT matters that he had personally called Edie Windsor from Air Force One to congratulate her; the judgment was "a victory for American democracy."[8] The topic of decriminalizing homosexuality had not come up in his meeting with the Senegalese president, Obama said. He tried to respond with delicacy toward his host by drawing a line between personal beliefs and customs and traditions, which had to be "respected," and the state's responsibility, which was to treat all people equally. He explicitly linked his advocacy of LGBT rights to his country's own history of racial discrimination: "We had to fight long and hard through a civil rights struggle to make sure that [people are treated equally]."[9]

When it was his turn to speak, the Senegalese president Macky Sall made the point often advanced by those who set "traditional values" against the notion of "universal human rights": "We cannot have a standard model which is applicable to all nations … We have different traditions." He put the issue into a time frame: while he insisted (incorrectly) that his country did not persecute homosexuals, his society had to take time to "digest" these issues: "Senegal … is a very tolerant country … but we are still not ready to decriminalize homosexuality."

In fact, Sall was a liberal with a human rights background who had previously made positive statements about decriminalization. And compared to other African leaders his comments were mild, even encouraging, in that they suggested a path to reform. But he was under pressure from the Islamist lobby and could also not be seen to be pandering to the West. He would later voice his frustration in an interview with the German magazine *Zeit*: "You have only had same-sex partnerships in Europe since yesterday and now you ask it today from Africans? This is all happening too fast! We live in a world that is changing slowly."[10]

The phrasing was revealing. No one—not the *Zeit* journalist, nor Obama nor even the Senegalese human rights movement—was calling for his government to legitimize same-sex partnerships. Rather, Sall was being asked to reform his country's penal code and decriminalize homosexual sex, given the way the law had been applied as a discriminatory tool in the country.

But there were two other assumptions in Sall's statement that caught my eye, and that have helped frame the questions of this book. The first was that "we live in a world that is changing slowly," and the second was that the people asking for change in Senegal were outsiders: the West, "you"; *not* Senegalese citizens themselves.

Was he correct?

AS I PONDERED MACKY SALL'S ASSUMPTIONS, I thought about another country where the Pink Line was being drawn, traced in this case over the disintegrating old marks of the Iron Curtain: Ukraine. In the precursor to the Maidan revolution and Russia's invasion of Crimea, the country was wrestling in 2013 over whether to continue its application to the European Union, or to join Vladimir Putin's new "Eurasian" customs union. This was the year that Putin took aim at the EU and its eastward spread, and the way he did so was by claiming to protect the "traditional values" of Orthodox Slavic society against a decadent secular West. The dog whistle for this strategy was to call Europe "gayropa."[11] A Kremlin proxy erected billboards all over Kiev showing same-sex stick figures holding hands, with the slogan: "Association with the EU means same-sex marriage."[12] And there was even a popular punning rhyme on the Russian television many Ukrainians watched: "The way to Europe is through the ass" ("*v Evropu cherez zhopu*").

Accession to the EU did indeed require an embrace of "European" values, which included the protection of LGBT people against discrimination and violence. Ukraine and Russia had both abolished the crime of sodomy for consenting adults (in 1991 and 1993 respectively), a precondition to joining the Council of Europe. Now, as a new religious and political elite sought to establish itself in countries disoriented by the collapse of the Soviet Union, the new legal status—and visibility—of gay people could stand in for the general lawlessness of the post-communist era.

This was a trend in the region, as nativist nationalist politicians began to use LGBT rights as a way of reestablishing a sovereignty they felt had been subsumed into Europe. In Poland, the Kaczynski twins built their anti-European Law and Justice Party in no small part through the demonization of that country's budding LGBT movement. In Hungary, Viktor Orbán's Fidesz did the same, including through a 2012 constitutional amendment that outlawed same-sex marriage. In Poland and Hungary as in Russia, public homophobia was part of a greater project of asserting a national identity against migrants, another perceived negative consequence—along with gay visibility—of open borders.

At the same time that Russia began cracking down on migrants—particularly from Central Asian countries—it developed and passed its federal law "for the Purpose of Protecting Children from Information Advocating for a Denial of Traditional Family Values": the "gay propaganda law" as it became known. The law outlawed any mention of homosexuality in the presence of minors, or in a medium where they might read it or hear it. This unleashed a wave of violent aggression, from witch hunts of teachers to brutal online entrapment and torture to violent attacks on public demonstrators. It had a particularly harsh effect on transgender women, who were seen to be the most visible—and freakish—face of Western debauchery.

Europe's criticism of the law only went to prove its moral bankruptcy, President Putin said in a December 2013 tirade: the West's trend of recognizing "everyone's right to the freedom of consciousness, political views and privacy" meant an acceptance of "the equality of good and evil."[13] The primary evidence of this trend was the normalization of homosexuality: "a direct path to degradation and primitivism, resulting in profound demographic and moral crisis," he had said in a speech three months previously.[14]

It was in the context of all this that I met the Ukraine's leading LGBT activist, Olena Shevchenko. She told me how she and her comrades were fighting for a much lower bar than marriage equality: to stave off a copycat anti-propaganda bill currently in parliament, promoted by Russian proxies and right-wing Ukrainian nationalists alike, and to seek protection from the burgeoning public violence against queer people, a function—as in Senegal—of their own increased visibility. But some of Shevchenko's allies in the Ukraine civil society movement remonstrated with her: it was not the right time to talk about these issues at all. Ukrainian society was not ready, and it might play into the opposition's hands about being European pawns.

Shevchenko was a lawyer in her thirties who would become a leader of a female-only volunteer military unit during the February 2014 revolution. "Yes," she said to me, "Yes, they are right. Ukrainian society is *not* ready for LGBT rights. I agree. But

Ukrainian LGBTs, themselves, they cannot be restrained anymore. They go online. They watch TV. They travel. They see how things can be. Why should they not have similar freedoms? Why should they be forced to live in hiding? The world is moving so fast, and events are overtaking us in Ukraine. We have no choice but to try and catch up."

WHO WAS CORRECT?

Senegal's president Macky Sall, who believed that "we live in a world that is changing slowly"?

Or the Ukrainian activist Olena Shevchenko, who insisted that "the world is moving so fast ... We have no choice but to try and catch up"?

Both, actually.

The Pink Line, in the twenty-first century, is not so much a line as a territory, a borderland where queer people work to reconcile the liberation and community they might have experienced online or on TV or in circumscribed spaces, with the constraints of the street and the workplace, the courtroom and the living room. It is a place where queer people shuttle across time zones each time they look up from their smartphones at the people gathered around the family table; as they climb the steps from the underground nightclub back into the nation-state. In one zone, time quickens, in the other it dawdles; spending your life crossing it could make you quite dizzy.

Like Aunty in her new Tambo Village home, the people I met while researching this book were subject to a whole range of influences, from the pulpit to the smartphone. But like Aunty, who came up with the idea for her *chinkhoswe* all by herself and was making her own life in Tambo Village, they all had agency. In this respect at least, Olena Shevchenko understood something that Macky Sall could not or would not see: the call for change might be supported by external players such as Barack Obama or the European Union, but it was being made by Senegalese and Ukrainian people themselves.

THIS BOOK IS primarily a collection of stories, then, with very singular protagonists making very personal decisions, in very specific places. These people drive their own stories; the rest of us—activists and policymakers, scholars and scribes and readers—try to catch up.

But this book is also an argument: about one way the world has been changing in the twenty-first century, and why this is happening.

It was no coincidence that the notion of LGBT rights was spreading globally at the exact moment that old boundaries were collapsing in the era of globalization. The collapse of these boundaries meant the rapid global spread of ideas about sexual equality or gender transition—and, at the very same time, a dramatic reaction by conservative forces, by patriarchs and priests, who feared the inevitable loss of control that this process threatened. These were the dynamics along the Pink Line, particularly in places where people came to be counted as gay or lesbian or MSM or transgender for the first time. In most societies, they had always been there, albeit in ways that were sometimes circumscribed or submerged or edgy, but now they claimed new status as they took on new political identities.

And they became enmeshed in a bigger geopolitical dynamic.

In the French presidential election of 2017, the National Front candidate Marine Le Pen said the world was no longer divided into "left wing" and "right wing," but rather into "globalists" and "patriots"; Le Pen lost the election to Emmanuel Macron (who insisted he, too, was a "patriot"), but elsewhere in the world leaders with similar views scored major victories. Donald Trump came to power in the United States in 2016, using the word *nationalist* and alleging that those who embraced globalization were unpatriotic. The United Kingdom voted to leave the European Union the same year, and the new prime minister, Theresa May, famously said, "If you believe you are a citizen of the world, you are a citizen of nowhere."[15] Both the Trump revolution and the Brexit one—and others in Europe, too, such as the populist victory in Italy in 2018—sought to reassert national borders against the free movement of trade, capital, and people most of all. The new politics was not only about erecting walls, but also about making claims that these walls had previously been taken down too quickly.

Particularly in Europe, these new-look nationalist movements sometimes bolstered their agendas by claiming they were protecting not just jobs and citizens but values, too; by the time Le Pen was running for office in 2017 these values included the rights of LGBT people. The man who wrote this script had been the crusading Dutch anti-immigration politician Pim Fortuyn, assassinated in 2002: openly gay, Fortuyn attracted mass support when he claimed that Muslim intolerance of homosexuality posed an existential threat to European civilization. His far-right successor, Geert Wilders, drove the agenda hard. When a troubled Muslim man killed forty-nine people at the Pulse gay nightclub in Orlando, Florida, in June 2016, Donald Trump—then on the campaign trail—slammed "radical Islamic terrorism";[16] Wilders, fighting his own election campaign back home, capitalized on this in his own statement: "The freedom that gay people should have—to kiss each other, to marry, to have children—is exactly what Islam is fighting against."[17]

Wilders lost the Dutch election but he influenced the agenda to such an extent that even the liberal incumbent, Mark Rutte, publicly conceded the growing Dutch "unease when people abuse our freedom ... [when they] harass gays, howl at women in short skirts or accuse ordinary Dutch people as racists ... If you reject our country in such a fundamental manner, I'd rather see you leave."[18]

In France, Marine le Pen played both sides: she opposed same-sex marriage but would not participate in the massive protests against it. In a television interview during a 2013 Russian visit she agreed enthusiastically with her new Kremlin comrades that "homophilia is one of the elements of globalization."[19] But her deputy and chief strategist was the gay Florian Philippot, and she openly courted the gay vote in 2017 with the message that her policies were all that stood between them and Islam's "hatred of homosexuals," as she put it in a televised debate with Macron.[20]

Other right-wing European parties followed suit. In 2018, a spokesman for the Flemish nationalist Vlaams Belang said that his party was the country's most gay-friendly, because all the others were "willing to import thousands of Muslims who have very violent ideas against being gay or transgender."[21] And although the anti-immigrant Alternative for Germany (AfD) opposed same-sex marriage and wanted to limit sexuality education in schools, it had an openly lesbian leader—Alice Weidel—and a gay grouping within the party that insisted action against "Islamic orthodoxy" was necessary for the "survival" of LGBT Germans.[22] In 2016 the AfD's Berlin branch put up billboards stating: "My partner and I don't want to get to meet Muslim immigrants who believe that our love is a deadly sin."[23]

In Western Europe, LGBT rights was being staked as a Pink Line against the influx of new migrants. At the same time in Eastern Europe it was being staked as a Pink Line against decadent Western liberalism. In both instances, queer people themselves came to be instrumentalized politically as never before. They acquired political meaning far beyond their own claims to equality and dignity. They became embodiments of progress and worldliness to some, but stigmata of moral and social decay to others.

IN 2013 THE SWEDISH MEGA–HOME store IKEA published a story in its online magazine about two women from Dorset in the west of England, Kirsty and Clara, making a home with the company's furniture: "We're two mums bringing up our baby boy in Clara's mum's loft," says Kirsty.[24] "We're not your average family in your average home, but if my nan can raise two sons in a tiny caravan, we can make it work in our little loft."

The article was part of a global campaign by IKEA that reimagined the kind of families inhabiting its warm, Nordic interiors. But in a neat illustration of the way new global trends come up against local realities, IKEA pulled the story from its Russian catalog because it worried its publication would fall foul of the new gay propaganda laws. There were rumblings in gay communities internationally about IKEA's self-censorship, and some threats of a boycott; the following year the company made the decision to stop publishing its catalog entirely in Russia rather than compromise its "values."

At exactly the same time that IKEA pulled Kirsty and Clara from its Russian campaign, a program was aired on Russian national television purporting to be an investigation into LGBT rights but actually articulating, very crudely, the Kremlin's position on the matter. The program was titled *Play Actors*, to suggest that crafty Russians "played" at being gay to attract foreign funding. It set out to answer the following question: "Is Russia threatened by [foreign] homosexuals trying to infiltrate our country to organise a protest movement on the pretext that our state is oppressing gays and lesbians?"[25]

When a panel of "experts" on the program hear that athletes of the same sex might hold hands in the opening ceremony of the upcoming Sochi Winter Olympics in solidarity with LGBT Russians, some respond with gasps of outrage. The celebrated feminist writer Maria Arbatova—the only sensible person on the panel—chides them: "If sportsmen holdhands in the Olympics will something happen to the Russian federal budget? Will our sports records plummet?"[26]

Vitaly Milonov, the country's most outspoken anti-gay politician, explodes on air: "[If athletes hold hands] I'm not going to let my children watch TV."[27]

"*Throw* your TV away!" jeers Arbatova.[28] "*Let* your children remain completely ignorant [about the world]!"

In this interchange was encapsulated the terms of the battle being fought, all over the world, along the Pink Line. If Arbatova saw Milonov as a fearful provincial, Milonov saw Arbatova as a rootless cosmopolitan. If she embraced the inevitable process of globalization in the name of progress and "human rights," he was trying to protect his children from the consequences of this process, in the name of faith and "traditional values."

This conversation, of course, is as old as the concept of modernity. Around sexuality in particular, it reaches back to nineteenth-century Europe, when scientists started codifying sexual behavior and societies began talking about it. It was a conversation that animated the discourse around the rights of homosexuals and "transvestites" in Berlin, and the Oscar Wilde indecency trials in 1895. And Stalin used it to trigger a moral panic against homosexuals in the Soviet Union in the 1930s, when he recriminalized sodomy after a raid on several homosexual venues in Moscow (it had been decriminalized after the revolution). Explaining the move in *Pravda,* Stalin's propagandist Maxim Gorky declared that it was time for the proletariat to "crush, like an elephant," such symptoms of capitalist disease emanating from the West.[29]

How different is this language, really, from that of people like Vitaly Milonov, or the African leaders who, in the early twenty-first century, sought to criminalize homosexuality further? Listen to David Mark, the leader of the Nigerian Senate, and the man responsible for that country's anti-gay legislation, talking in 2013: "There are many good values we can copy from other societies but certainly not this one"; the new law would "prove to the rest of the world, who are advocates of this unnatural way, that we Nigerians promote and respect sanity, morality and humanity."[30]

Both the Russian Gorky and the Nigerian Mark were setting themselves up, across the expanse of the twentieth century, as custodians of tradition and morality, against the juggernaut of Western liberal capitalism. And one of the most effective ways of doing this was through the staking of a Pink Line. This was a strategy increasingly deployed in the twenty-first century, as information about "gay rights" and "gay marriage" proliferated. At his ruling party's 2003 congress, the Malaysian president Mahathir Mohamad said that Europeans wanted to impose an "unlimited freedom" on the world, one that included "the practise of free sex including sodomy as a right ... Our way of life must be the same as their way of life.[31] Asian values do not exist for them." There was no more potent way to define "Asian values"—or "African values," or "Slavic values," or "Muslim values," or "Christian values" or "proletarian values"—than to set it against this abomination now being embraced by the secular West.

But even if this construct was not new, what gave it force in the twenty-first century was the speed with which ideas blew across this planet. "There is always backlash when people come out," the veteran American LGBT activist Julie Dorf said in 2014, "but what makes this era different is that what happens in the USA today is known in Azerbaijan tomorrow. And what the right wing and conservative forces fear, is true: rights are rights are rights. When you do start to fight for the equality of LGBT people, it will at some point lead to calls for marriage equality, and that's terrifying, even if marriage equality is not what activists are asking for today in, say, Nigeria or Russia. They are simply asking to live in peace and not be killed, to have the same basic protections as everyone else."

The twenty-first-century conversation about sexual orientation and gender identity is a global one, although—like IKEA's campaign—it has local or regional accents. In Russia and many African states it has been about the most basic rights to freedom of association and safety for some people, and about protecting children for others. In countries ranging from the United States to Mexico and France, the conversation has been about what a family looks like and who has the right to make one. In the Catholic countries of Europe and Latin America, the Pink Line became part of a broader conflict over "gender ideology," and the accusation that humanity is meddling with a divine plan. In the Middle East the conversation blossomed as a result of the Arab Spring, as a budding queer movement made tentative first steps toward public visibility—and was described, too, as a negative symptom of this opening up. In much of Asia the conversation was carried on the winds of new social media, and also by rapid urbanization and industrialization, which meant vast new young populations away from their families for the first time. In different ways all over the world, the conversation now encompassed discussion about gender identity, and about a person's right to change the categories of male and female, or to live between them. What these different Pink Lines had in common was the way they set something called "tradition" against something called "modernity." The work of queer people along the Pink Line was often to reconcile these: to embrace a liberating notion of modernity while remaining part of their societies and communities.

All over the world, precisely because the conversation was new in many places, it was vibrant and often violent, as conservative forces blew back against the inevitable consequences of a newly globalized world and the ideas that it generated. It is too simple to call this backlash "homophobia" or "transphobia," although it often deployed, or provoked, such fear or hate. It mobilized moral panic in which homosexual or gender-variant people became scapegoats, or bogeymen, or excuses to rally law and order, or evil forces against which nationhood was defined. In most instances, these campaigns purported to protect "traditional values" or "natural order" from the depredations of modern society; ordinary people from a global or cosmopolitan elite.

Having been personally moved by the Tiwonge Chimbalanga case,the UN Secretary-General Ban Ki-Moon used the platform of the African Union in Addis Ababa, in 2012 to call on African countries to repeal sodomy laws. The ranking African in the Vatican, Cardinal Robert Sarah, responded harshly: "You cannot impose something stupid like that. Poor countries like Africa [*sic*] just accept it because it's imposed upon them through money, through being tied to aid."[32]

This was the great shibboleth of the global anti-gay discourse, from Maxim Gorky and *Play Actors* in Russia to Cardinal Sarah and Aunty's persecutors in Malawi: homosexuality was a commercial transaction, a form of material exploitation or "recruitment" that set out to exploit poor people, or young people, or dark people, and to compromise the values in which they were reared.

IF THIS WAS a script that reached back into history, its first modern application, in the era of "gay rights," was in Iran's 1979 revolution: the fierce condemnation of homosexuality, including the death penalty under Sharia law, was one of the ways the new rulers differentiated themselves from the Western decadence of the Shah's regime (another, of course, being the severe constraints on women). There are no reliable figures for how many alleged homosexuals have been executed since 1979, but thousands have gone into exile.

Now, in 2015, the Iranian leader Ayatollah Khamenei issued a statement about how Iranian youth were exposed to threats more dangerous than ever because of "communications media that can spread a wrong thought or comment."[33] Iran was "not involved in the military war" anymore, but "in political, economic and security wars—and, above all, the cultural wars." Khamenei was not talking, specifically, about homosexuality, but about the broader diffusion of Western values into the country. In other statements, he made it clear that homosexuality—and same-sex marriage in particular—were the prime avatars of this "stampede on human values," as he once put it.[34]

Such notions took root even in the more tolerant parts of the world, in the second decade of the century. Indonesia, the world's largest Muslim country, had always been one of the world's more easy-going ones, but during an uncharacteristic crackdown on queer people in Indonesia in 2016, the minister of defense, Ryamizard Ryacudu, branded the LGBT movement more dangerous than even a nuclear war, because "we can't see who our foes are, but out of the blue everyone is brainwashed."[35] He called this "a proxy war" in which "another state might occupy the minds of the nation without anyone realising it ... everything we know could disappear in an instant—it's dangerous." Like Khamenei, Ryacudu was acknowledging the ineffectiveness of conventional warfare—of borders themselves, really—against this new threat. It was a moral war, and it needed to be fought on moral terms, along bandwidth and airwaves rather than physical borders.

In May 2017, the conservative Hungarian president Viktor Orbán hosted a global initiative called the World Congress of Families, led by American Evangelicals and Russian Orthodox conservatives. In his opening speech, Orbán linked his severe anti-immigrant policies with Christian "traditional values," and boasted about how his country's fences had changed history by stemming the tide of migrants entering Europe.[36] In another part of the world, at exactly the same time, Donald Trump was campaigning for the presidency by expressing a similar faith in walls.

But another keynote speaker in Budapest underscored the unfixed nature of these new battles. The speaker's name was Jack Hanick, and he was a Fox News founder who had moved to Moscow to help set up Tsargrad TV, "God's TV, Russian Style" as the *Financial Times* called it.[37] Hanick projected an image from *The Brady Bunch* onto a big screen: The 1970s American show might have had a male patriarch and a stay-at-home mom, he said, but with its "blended family" it represented nonetheless the beginning of an inexorable moral slide into *Modern Family*, the twenty-first-century sitcom that "idealizes same-sex marriage."[38] "This is a war," Hanick said, "but it is not a war to be waged in the physical world." If television was "at the centre of a spiritual war," as Hanick put it, so, too, was the Internet.[39] Hanick's employer at Tsargrad TV was Konstantin Malofeev, a right-wing oligarch-activist who had set up Russia's Safe Internet League: in the name of child protection the league set out to patrol cyberspace by learning lessons from China. The architect of "the Great Firewall of China," as it became known, was a man named Fang Binxing. At a forum on the subject in 2016 hosted by Malofeev, Fang insisted that "if borders exist, they exist in cyberspace too"; he also alleged that the American government directly controlled the companies that dominated cyberspace.[40] Google, Facebook, and Twitter are, of course, barred from China.

China had decriminalized homosexual sex in 1997 and depathologized homosexuality in 2001. But as the country's queer population became increasingly visible through Western media and online, its cyber-marshals soon turned their attention to it. In 2016 and 2017, the government put out a list of "abnormal sexual relationships" banned from television and the Internet: these included "same-sex relationships" along with "incest," "sexual perversion," and "sexual abuse."[41] In 2018, Sina Weibo—the Chinese Twitter—announced it would remove any graphic material that was pornographic, bloodily violent, or homosexual, in order to comply with government policy. This prompted the largest protest China had yet seen over LGBT issues. The hashtag #IamGay was posted over 500,000 times, and viewed more than 530 million times; tens of thousands of people tweeted their own stories about being queer or having queer family or friends. Weibo retracted quick time.

In different parts of the world, people found community and information—and sex—online, but the increased connectivity also brought new threats to security, from cyberbullying and unanticipated exposure to online entrapment. At an international LGBT conference in 2012, I heard how opponents of the Assad regime in Syria were blackmailed with evidence of their activity on gay hookup apps. In the years following, dozens of Egyptian men were entrapped by the vice police through Grindr, and the company disabled its global positioning function in the country in response.[42]

In Russia, a journalist named Elena Klimova used social media to provide resources for queer youth with an initiative called Children 404: 404 being the error number on the Web for a page that no longer exists. "One family in 20 has an LGBT child in it, and those children are society's invisible 'Children-404,'" Klimova wrote.[43] Hundreds of youths participated, joining a closed group on VKontakte, the Russian social media platform, or sharing their portraits and stories on open pages. At the very same time, another group called Occupy Pedofilia used VKontakte to entrap gay men, and then post horrific videos of their torture and assault.

Thus were the Pink Lines of the twenty-first century staked: by IKEA and Grindr, by *Modern Family* and Weibo, as much as by the policy makers in the U.S. State Department or the Kremlin, the technocrats at the UN Commission on Human Rights, and the activists on the frontlines on both sides.

ON DECEMBER 18, 2008, the fiery French human rights minister Rama Yade drew the first Pink Line across the floor of the United Nations General Assembly when she introduced a declaration, on behalf of the European Union, condemning "violations of human rights and fundamental freedoms based on sexual orientation or gender identity."[44] Sixty-six states supported the declaration. Fifty-seven others immediately signed a counter-declaration, protesting that the move interfered illegally in their domestic affairs and could result in "the social normalization, and possibly the legitimization, of many deplorable acts including paedophilia."

Later, Vladimir Putin's Russia would come to lead this countermovement at the UN, but at this point Russia stayed out of the fray—it did not sign either statement, and almost all the signatories of the counterdeclaration were from the Muslim world or from Africa. But the Pink Line's frontiers were not as predictable as one might have imagined: the sixty-six supporters of the Yade initiative demonstrated a fascinating new global geopolitics. The United States was not a signatory—yet. George W. Bush's Republican administration was still in office and the debate over marriage equality was raging domestically: the Americans seemed to think that to support the declaration would influence states' rights to decide such matters for themselves. Soon after Barack Obama was inaugurated a month later, the U.S. would sign on.

And while the Yade initiative might have been driven by European trailblazers, ten of the signatories were from Latin America and an astonishing fifteen from Eastern Europe. This would lead to the nationalist backlash in the years to come, but at this point an official embrace of LGBT rights was seen in Eastern Europe as a mark of modernity, of membership in the new global post–Cold War liberal consensus—and, of course, most significantly, as a ticket into the European Union.

In Latin America, too, new post-totalitarian democracies were coming to embrace "*la diversidad sexual*"—"sexual diversity"—as a symbol of their new openness, in defiance of their autocratic predecessors and the powerful Catholic Church, often seen to be in collusion with the dictators. In 2002, Buenos Aires had become the first jurisdiction in Latin America to offer same-sex couples the same benefits as straight ones, and in 2009, Mexico City passed a raft of laws making it the most progressive place in the Americas outside of Canada: same-sex marriage was legalized, as was adoption by same-sex couples, and the voluntary legal changing of gender identity. What was remarkable, in Latin America, was the way the struggle for gay rights vaulted over that for reproductive rights. By 2017, same-sex marriage was legal in Argentina, Brazil, Colombia, Ecuador, Uruguay, and much of Mexico. But abortion on demand was legal only in Uruguay, in Cuba, and in Mexico City. The victory of the LGBT rights movement, across the region, was to brand same-sex unions as being about love and family; in this way it could counter the Catholic Church's influence in a way that abortion rights activists struggled to do.

Although the discussion at the United Nations was initiated by European countries and—in the Obama years—godfathered by the

United States, it was increasingly led by Latin American countries, to counter the "cultural imperialism" allegation. The African and Islamic states refused, even, to discuss it. The issue came to a head in 2016, when—after four years of fierce debate—the UN's Human Rights Council voted by the slimmest of margins to appoint an "independent expert" to investigate violence and discrimination against LGBT people; a watchdog, in effect.

The African Group of states went to the General Assembly to object, and the former U.S. ambassador to the UN Samantha Power later told me that she and her team spent an inordinate amount of time trying to fend off efforts to kill the initiative. In the end the African Group's gambit failed by a narrow margin, 77 votes to 84: the watchdog could start his work. Presenting his 2019 report, the expert, Victor Madrigal-Borloz, stated that in much of the world, a "criminal" ignorance arising from prejudice made it impossible to estimate the number of LGBT people affected by violence and discrimination.[45] In the absence of data, "policymakers are taking decisions in the dark, left only with personal preconceptions and prejudices."

Almost all of Africa and the Muslim world voted to stop the appointment of the expert; almost all of Europe, North America, and Latin America voted for him to continue. There were some surprises among Muslim countries—Albania and Turkey voted for the initiative to proceed, but the swing region, it turned out, was East Asia.

In 2008, the only Asian country to sign the Yade declaration had been Japan. But in the years following, South Korea, the Philippines, Thailand, and Vietnam signed on too (Taiwan, not a member of the UN, became the first Asian country to legalize same-sex marriage, in 2019). With the exception of the Philippines, these countries were outside of the theocratic influence of Christianity and Islam; ideologically as well as economically, they seemed to have less to fear from globalization, and were influenced by arguments about the economic benefit of being open to LGBT rights, from tourism and multinational corporations. Also, like the countries of Latin America, their distance from their former European colonizers, if this had happened at all, was sufficient that there was no political capital to be gained from staking a Pink Line against neocolonialism, as there was in Africa.

"SHOULD SOCIETY ACCEPT homosexuality?"[46]

This question was asked by the Pew Research Center in its quadrennial Global Attitudes & Trends survey, in July 2013. Of the 39 countries polled, tolerance levels were much higher than anticipated in Europe and North America: Spain, 88 percent; Germany, 87 percent; Canada, 80 percent (the U.S. was far behind, at 60 percent). But they were so low as to be negligible in Africa: Nigeria, 2 percent; Uganda and Senegal, 4 percent. So, too, the Muslim world: Pakistan, 2 percent; Egypt and Indonesia, 3 percent. Latin American and Asian countries ranged across the spectrum. Pew called its survey *The Global Divide on Homosexuality*, and its overarching conclusion was that there was "greater tolerance" toward homosexual people "in more secular and affluent countries," although Russia and China were exceptions: 16 percent and 21 percent respectively.

However limited such polling might be, it offers the only empirical comparative indicator of global attitudes toward homosexuality, and the correlation between these and the law. Scholars have defined a useful "ladder," when it comes to homosexual rights.[47] On the lowest rung are "basic rights": to live without fear of discrimination and harassment. Higher up are "sex rights": the repeal of anti-sodomy legislation. And on the top rungs are "love rights": to cohabit, to marry, and to make families. The countries that are highest on the legal ladder are generally those highest in the Pew tolerance rankings—

although it was not always clear which was the chicken and which the egg: Does a tolerant society create just laws, or do just laws forge a tolerant society?

There are some outliers to the equation, however, and one of the most notable is my home country: although South Africa was at the very top of the rights ladder given that "love rights" were entrenched by marriage equality, it notched only 61 percent on the Pew Center's 2013 tolerance index.[48] Brazil and the United States were the other outliers, also near the top of the rights ladder, but both with middling tolerance levels. What these three countries have in common is that they are worlds-in-one-country, multiethnic societies with high inequality rates: at the time of Pew's 2013 survey South Africa had the second-highest Gini coefficient—which measures inequality—in the world; Brazil, the 19th; and the U.S., the 39th, out of 157 countries.[49]

A 2016 survey on South African attitudes painted a more complex portrait.[50] Of those polled by the state's Human Sciences Research Council, 72 percent said they disapproved of homosexual activity. Nonetheless, 51 percent felt that homosexuals deserved the same rights as all other South Africans, and should not be discriminated against. The Other Foundation, which commissioned the research, consequently named its report *Progressive Prudes*, as if to suggest that we South Africans carried the Pink Line inside us: even if we accepted that these people deserved rights, we disapproved of what they did.

Was this the legacy of a post-apartheid human rights dispensation that had vaulted ahead of social attitudes? And if so, did this data confirm Macky Sall's complaint about being asked to move too quickly in Senegal? I felt the opposite: if anything, it was a measure of South African "tolerance," insufficient though this might be, that so many people respected the rights of those they disapproved of. It also suggested that you could indeed change attitudes by changing the law, or providing moral leadership, even if backlash complicated the process.

I had seen this, personally, very early in the South African democracy—in 1997, when I had reported the story of a young Soweto couple. When Sbongile Malaza's grandfather found out about her relationship with Pretty Robiana, he turned a gun on Pretty and assaulted them both, calling their relationship "satanic" and "un-African"; they fled Soweto and sought refuge in a women's shelter.[51] When Pretty laid charges of attempted murder, she received an unexpected response from the newly appointed local police commander, a black woman: "The constitution is here now," she said. "You people have decided you want to lead this life and it comforts you, so let's call the family together and ... make peace." The commander convened a meeting with both families and made Pretty, in her mid-twenties, sign an affidavit taking responsibility for nineteen-year-old Sbongile, still at school.

When the commander told Sbongile's family that "there's nothing illegal about this relationship," Grandfather Malaza changed his tune: he started negotiating with Pretty for the payment of bride-price.[52] It was, I wrote at the time, "a startling example of how people change their ideologies to fit in with new hegemonies." I cited Tsietsi Thandekiso, the gay pastor who married them: "Homophobia in the townships is superficial ... We are living through a time where it's actually not such a big deal to be gay ... There are gays on the streets, gays in the taverns. It's become part of life."

He might have been overly sanguine. Asked by the *Progressive Prudes* survey two decades later whether they found lesbians to be "disgusting," 64 percent of the black respondents agreed (as opposed to 44 percent of the white respondents).[53] Asked whether they found cross-dressers to be "disgusting," 71 percent of the black respondents agreed (compared to 49 percent of the white ones). But given the commonly held assumption (one I realized I shared) that a Pink Line divided pale people from dark ones in my country as elsewhere, these discrepancies were not nearly as great as I had anticipated: 29 percent of my white compatriots found me disgusting, but 61 percent of my black compatriots did not. Indeed, compared with the Pew Center's figures for other African countries, and given the levels of religious devotion in black South African communities, the tolerance level of the black South Africans surveyed was remarkably high: 57 percent said they would accept a gay or lesbian family member.

In 1996, when South Africa adopted its post-apartheid constitution specifically protecting people on the basis of sexual orientation, the digital revolution was expanding its reach in the country. Rights and information arrived at the same time, and in their wake an urban black queer subculture asserted itself, on the streets and in popular entertainment. Pretty and Sbongile were part of a vibrant scene in Soweto, and there was a thriving black gay bar and club scene in Johannesburg. In 2004 black activists launched Soweto Pride and there were queer black celebrities all over television. In these same years South Africa's black middle class mushroomed, due to the African National Congress government's policy of Black Economic Empowerment. More black people than ever before received university educations and became professionals. *Progressive Prudes* confirmed that educated South Africans—black or white—were more likely to be tolerant toward homosexuality and gender-fluidity than uneducated ones.

But there were some very disturbing findings, which suggested how much more challenging life was for Tiwonge Chimbalanga than for me, even though we were both, supposedly, in the same LGBT basket. I was stunned to read that 73—there was an actual number—of the 3,115 respondents said they had physically assaulted "men who act like women."[54] Another 218 said they might do so in the future. Seventy-nine respondents—there was another number—said they had physically assaulted women who "dressed and acted like men in public." Another 143 said they might do so in the future. The percentages were small, but the numbers said something about how quickly fear or ignorance turned to hate and violence in South Africa, a country where there were unacceptably high levels, anyway, of interpersonal and gender-based violence, linked to high unemployment and alcoholism rates.

This helped to explain the fact that I lived with little fear of hate-inspired violence, while just twenty kilometers away Aunty was the frequent victim of assault. And why one of her neighbors in Tambo Village had started a shelter for black working-class lesbians, given how many had become the victims of what is called "corrective rape" since a black lesbian subculture began asserting itself in the townships. This violence, particularly against butch women, was a lashing out by some young men, at a time of intense economic instability, at a new category of putatively empowered people whom they believed had usurped them and were stealing their jobs and their women.

I was a white gay man, living on the "secular and affluent"—as the Pew report put it—side of a Pink Line that divided not only the world but also my new home city of Cape Town; Aunty was a poor black transgender woman, living on the other. There were many components to this Pink Line between us: I lived behind walls, drove a car, and was gender normative; she lived in a crowded yard, was a pedestrian, and was gender nonconforming. I was painfully aware that I crossed this Pink Line every time I drove just twenty kilometers along the False Bay shore, from my seaside bungalow in Kalk Bay to her shack in Tambo Village.

2

AUNTY'S STORY

CHIMBALANGA VILLAGE—BLANTYRE—CAPETOWN

Tiwonge Chimbalanga—"Aunty," Malawian refugee, office worker and informal beer seller, Cape Town, late thirties. Pronouns: she/her/hers.

Benson—Aunty's husband, Malawian migrant, unemployed, Cape Town, forties. Pronouns: he/him/his.

Blackie Chimbalanga—Aunty's uncle, village chief, Chimbalanga, seventies. Pronouns: he/him/his.

Annie Manda—Aunty's cousin, homemaker, near Chimbalanga, fifties. Pronouns: she/her/hers.

1

In September 2014 I traveled from Cape Town to Malawi, to try to understand more about Aunty Tiwonge Chimbalanga's life there, before her *chinkhoswe*; before she had heard the words *gay* or *transgender* or *LGBTI*, or been arrested and jailed and forced into exile in South Africa.

Aunty wanted me to carry some gifts to her family back home, so I stopped by her Tambo Village shack before I left. She had selected a couple of framed studio photographs that had been hanging on her walls: Aunty and her husband, Benson, set serenely against waterfalls, perched on gilded gazebos in fantastical parks. These she wrapped in the layers of the old clothes I was to distribute to her relatives. I took out my phone to film a message to the family. The couple snuggled against each other to fit into the frame, Aunty in a rather grand black sun hat and her favorite pink neon plastic beads over a frilly black blouse, Benson with his walnut face and swimming-away eyes. In her message, Aunty said that she had been through difficult times but that her family was not to worry. Benson was bashful and taciturn: "I am Aunty Tiwo's husband and everything is fine." A few days later I bumped down a steep rutted track to a village, also named Chimbalanga, about an hour south of Blantyre, Malawi's biggest city. It was poor and remote: no electricity or running water and not another vehicle on the road. The whole village gathered on the hard red ground beneath the stately mango tree outside the chief's mud-brick home: word had spread that Aunty herself was coming and everyone wanted to see her. Two plastic chairs were brought out from the chief's house; on these he and I sat, with about fifty people at our feet. I passed around the framed photographs, which the villagers accepted, with gasps, in Aunty's stead, as evidence of a fabled life abroad.

The chief, Blackie Chimbalanga, was Aunty's maternal uncle, and her adoptive parent. He had taken her in at age five, after her mother had died. "My uncle accepted me as a girl," Aunty had told me. "This is because I was active among other children—cooking, taking care of kids, and when a baby got sick I was the one who knew he had fever." When others insulted her, "My family made a complaint, and the culprits were taken to traditional court." Aunty recalled that this happened three times; the culprits were chastised, and fined some chickens.

The chief confirmed to me that there had been at least one such trial. He was now in his late seventies but with the startling briskness of old country folk. We trotted up the hill to an empty clinic with no supplies so we could have some privacy, and he told me that when he took Aunty in he had been living with his wife and children in another village. But when his marriage broke down and he returned to Chimbalanga alone, he brought Aunty with him. Aunty was still a child, but "I saw nothing wrong in him doing all the female tasks," he told me, "because someone had to do it, either him or me." His niece's gender role suited the chief, and so he pragmatically accepted it. This confirmed Aunty's memory: "At some point my uncle said to me, 'You are a real woman, you are not a man anymore, because of the female work you are doing.'"

But Aunty felt that her uncle was exploiting her, and fought with him. As a teenager she ran away to live with her cousin, the chief's daughter Annie Manda. Aunty always dressed as a boy, Mrs. Manda told me, but everything else about her was feminine: so much so that she was frequently the object of derision. Mrs. Manda noticed how Aunty would put up her fists to defend herself, and tried to persuade her, unsuccessfully, to ignore the slights and slurs.

Aunty left the Manda family after some years in school, when she was about seventeen. Why she went is unclear, but it seems linked to bewitchment, which was in turn linked to her gender identity. Aunty's version is that she had severe headaches and nosebleeds and suspected that those bewitching her wished to kill her, so she fled north and found a traditional healer who might help her. Mrs. Manda told me, however, that the family thought Aunty was bewitched because "he grew up as a man but never had any interest in women.

He went to the north to be assisted, so he could act as a man and have feelings for women."

If this was the family's intention, it backfired. When Aunty returned two years later, she was dramatically different: living entirely as a woman, dressing in traditional twinsets known locally as "Nigerians," and with a new name. She now claimed she was a member of the northern Tumbuka tribe, rather than of the Lomwe, the people of her home district. Because "Tiwonge" is gender-neutral and pronouns in Malawi are gender-neutral, too, she encouraged people to call her "Aunty," even though this is usually a term of respect reserved for older women.

Aunty believed that the healer up north released her from her bewitchment. Perhaps it was a release from the constraints of gender that society had imposed on her: away from home, she was able to find the courage to reinvent herself in such a way that her exterior could begin matching how she felt inside.

But she needed liquid courage, too. After her time in the north she had settled in Blantyre and found work—and when I was in the city in 2014, I met her former employer, a retired bank manager named Vaida Kalua. As we admired the roses in her manicured garden and drank Cokes procured from the informal shop she operated from her home, Mrs. Kalua told me that she linked her employee's deepening alcoholism to an increasing insistence on presenting as a woman: "Maybe it's the stress of always having to defend yourself," Mrs. Kalua volunteered. She had initially retained Aunty as a houseboy, but "little by little, he started wearing feminine clothes. First the *chitenje* wrap and then the matching top and trousers. It was not a problem for me, but I wanted to protect him, because he was being mocked and insulted. I tried to talk to him about stopping. He would not listen."

Mrs. Kalua still ranked Aunty as one of the best houseboys she had ever employed, but after seven years of employment they had a disagreement—about drink, and bringing men onto the property—that led to Aunty's departure. Aunty established herself in a shack, living by selling *kachasu*, Malawi's potent home brew. One of her customers was the man who would become her first serious partner. He had a wife and children, but Aunty accepted the polygamous situation—until she was needled one too many times by the man's wife. Aunty retaliated with her fists and knocked out two of her rival's teeth. The man left her. When her shack burned down two years later, she arrived at the nearby Mankhoma Lodge, on the fringes of Blantyre, carrying all her possessions, including a huge teddy bear. "I felt sorry for Aunty Tiwo," Rachael Kamphale told me, "and besides, we needed a maid. My mom was on the road all the time, there were kids to look after, and I had schoolwork to do."

The person back home to whom Aunty was closest was the village teacher, her brother-in-law Simon Wangiwa. "Aunt Tiwo never wanted to be criticized about her dressing and her actions," Mr. Wangiwa said to me when I visited Chimbalanga village. "She would start a fight with whoever did that." Mr. Wangiwa thought this was reasonable: "Everyone can be temperamental when pushed so far. Even you, sir, when someone steps on your shoes, you will react. It's not that different." He also had a neat, and logical, way of describing how he came to accept Aunty, and why he had never clashed with her: "Of course I knew Tiwonge was born a boy. But her character made me accept her as a woman. I stopped seeing her as anything else."

When I first met Aunty, she told me that all her five older siblings had died—perhaps as a consequence of the same curse that had claimed her parents. But when I visited the village, I discovered that two of them still lived there: a brother, who came rushing up to greet me in excitement, and a sister who stayed away. I heard that Aunty had had a violent physical altercation with this sister just before leaving for South Africa; the sister, a fervent Christian, believed Aunty deserved to go to jail and should change her ways.

Although Aunty's family history was complex, she drew solace from a narrative of family support. This narrative was not inaccurate: even if they did not attend the *chinkhoswe* (they had not been invited), members of her family rallied when she was arrested, they supported her during the trial (Mrs. Manda was frequently in court) and embraced her when she came back to live in the village after her release. Aunty joined the women's group of the village church, and became an enthusiastic member of its choir. "I got more strength when I came out of jail," she told me. "My family advised me never to change."

Perhaps the last word on the matter belongs to Chief Blackie Chimbalanga himself, who told me that his position was hereditary, and that he was preoccupied with selecting a successor from among his nephews.

"Why only your nephews?" I asked. "Why not Tiwonge?"

"Why not indeed?" he twinkled back. "There are many villages which now have women as chiefs!"

THE PERSON WHO took me to Chimbalanga village was a strapping Blantyre man-about-town named Dunker Kamba, who had been the first person to visit Aunty in jail after her arrest on December 28, 2009.

Kamba had been one of the founders of CEDEP, the deliberately vague Centre for the Development of People, set up in 2007 to provide Blantyre's small but growing homosexual community with AIDS education and services. As elsewhere in the continent, funding had become available for MSM (men who have sex with men) outreach work, and this provided cover for gay men to begin to mobilize, in organizations such as CEDEP. "When you go the human rights route, they shut you out," Kamba explained to me as we drove out to Chimbalanga. "But when you go the public health route and you have statistics to prove your existence, then they'll listen to you."

The confluence of the AIDS epidemic and a global LGBT rights movement meant that local gay people were beginning to make themselves heard in the early twenty-first century, even here in Malawi. By the time of Aunty's *chinkhoswe* the small country had been ravaged by AIDS, globalization, and bad governance. Dependent on tobacco, tea, tourism, and development aid (which accounted for 40 percent of its budget) it was one of Africa's poorest, most beautiful, most conservative backwaters: until 1994 women were not allowed to wear trousers in public.

But after its relatively late conversion to multiparty democracy in 1994, Malawi had found itself with an exemplary constitution, which the savvy CEDEP activists were now attempting to use to decriminalize sodomy. In the very months preceding Aunty's arrest in 2009 CEDEP had mounted—with Dutch funding—a public campaign to revise the laws. This antagonized the government: quite apart from its Christian conservatism and its links to the ideologies of American evangelism, it was chary of any kind of civic challenge to its political authority. Just weeks before Aunty's *chinkhoswe*, CEDEP's offices had been raided, Dunker Kamba detained, and a whole lot of its safer-sex materials confiscated as pornography.[1] Now, after the arrests of Aunty and her fiancé, Steven Monjeza, the authorities seemed to think that CEDEP had deliberately staged the *chinkhoswe* with foreign backing—to test the waters, or to challenge the government.

In truth, the first time Dunker Kamba and his boss Gift Trapence heard about *chinkhoswe* was when they picked up *The Nation* on the morning of December 28 and read the "Gays Engage" story. They had never previously met Aunty, or even heard of her. But because

CEDEP itself had just been raided, the men knew immediately that Chimbalanga and Monjeza would be arrested. And so they rushed to the Limbe Police Station, where the couple was detained. They were the first visitors, and they struggled to get access: "We were told, 'Why do you want to see these *animals*?'" Kamba remembered—and were eventually given five minutes with them.

"If I had known this would happen, I never would have done it," Aunty told Kamba and Trapence. She claimed she did not know that what she was embarking upon was illegal: "She believed she was a woman, not a homosexual man, and she thus would not have seen any problem with the event," Kamba said to me.

Aunty had told me that she had already done one *chinkhoswe*, with her previous partner, but it had been quiet and private. Why, then, did she decide to go public with Monjeza? At different times she gave me different reasons: "It's our culture," she said in one discussion. "You can't just one day wake up and decide you are married. You have to introduce the families to each other." But although Monjeza's family was present, hers was not, and she hired local "dancing girls" to play their role in the ritual. The custom is that guests at a *chinkhoswe* contribute to the nuptial coffers. "I was well-known," Aunty said another time. "I attended a lot of weddings and funerals. This was a way for people to give back to me." On one point she was totally consistent: "I *was* doing it to be visible, because it's everybody's right to get married. But I was not doing it for others, for the LGBT so they can come out. *I was doing it for myself.*"

Perhaps more than if she had been assigned female at birth, Aunty needed public affirmation of her female place in the world. Her employer had egged her on, either out of naiveté or greed, and spread the word all over Blantyre. Now, after the arrests, the country was inflamed. "No one could talk about anything else," Gift Trapence told me. "It was in the newspapers, on the radio shows, in the taxis, on the pulpits." Sodom had been exposed, and "it was as if Malawi itself was coming to an end." Blantyre came to a standstill every time Aunty and Monjeza appeared in court, and the streets around the court were clogged with curious and often very hostile onlookers.

Trapence, a serious moonfaced man, in his late thirties when we first met, was a highly effective political operative: he had been skillfully steering the discourse in Malawi away from the "gay marriage" headlines dominating the LGBT struggle in the West and toward basic security and health-care provision. But now, with Aunty and Monjeza in the dock, "everyone thought we were trying to get marriage in through the back door. It was a deeply traumatic period for us. There was a witch hunt. We had to go underground as an organization, and so did the gay community. We shut down our office."

While I was in Blantyre in 2014 I met Amanda, a university-educated "queen" (her own choice of words). Before the arrests, Amanda told me, she felt "quite free" dressing as a woman in Blantyre at night. "I loved doing it, to attract men, although of course I realized I could get into trouble if I was disclosed." But immediately after Aunty's arrest, "I stopped. I was afraid. Even now, so many years later, our whole gay life in Blantyre has come to a stop. I still won't dress as a woman in public. The one or two times I have done it, people shout at me, 'Aunty! Aunty!' They haven't forgotten."

During their trial in early 2010, Aunty and Monjeza were subject to humiliating physical examinations and sent for mental observation; much of the media coverage of all of this was both salacious and contemptuous. Monjeza, bewildered, dissolved into a weeping wreck. Aunty, usually wearing a *chilenje* wrap and a feminine blouse, stood her ground: television footage shows her slapping away hands trying to touch her as they are transported to court in an open truck. One day she collapsed vomiting with malaria, and was left to lie in her own mess in the dock, before being forced to clean it up herself.

CEDEP coordinated the legal defense, and an international solidarity campaign. A British lawyer who came to work on the defense team, Richard Bridgland, told a documentary crew during the trial that Aunty was "an inspirational character.[2] Tiwonge is in a cell for twelve hours a day, two poor meals, and this is a guy who still looks immaculately dressed. Not a trace of bitterness, not a trace of anger." In the early days of Aunty's celebrity, her gender identity was not understood: "In the UK we would call Tiwonge gay and proud," her lawyer said.

Bail was denied on the grounds that the couple needed protective custody, and Malawi's chief justice refused to refer the case to the Constitutional Court for adjudication. Finally, in February 2010, the court handed down the maximum sentence of fourteen years' hard labor. For a brief moment, Malawi became headline news. Western aid agencies threatened to cut programs. The British gay activist Peter Tatchell led a solidarity campaign from London, and Madonna's petition drew thirty thousand signatures. At the United Nations, Ban Ki-Moon had been persuaded that the discrimination faced by LGBT people was indeed one of the greatest human rights challenges of the era, and had decided to make it one of his legacy projects. He flew to Malawi himself, where he addressed parliament and called for the repeal of anti-sodomy laws worldwide; he had his meeting with President Mutharika that led to that grudging pardon. Madonna, for her part, thanked the thirty thousand who signed her petition for the role they had played: "I have always believed that love conquers all," she wrote in a public letter.[3]

After their release, Aunty and Monjeza were taken by their supporters to Lilongwe, Malawi's capital, four hours' drive north: it was thought that they would be safer here. CEDEP set up a secure house for them, but Aunty and Monjeza fought violently and Monjeza left after two weeks, returning to Blantyre to denounce Aunty.

Without sustained psychological counseling, Aunty found ballast in heavy drinking: "It helped me to forget all my problems," she told me.

At the time, Gift Trapence and Dunker Kamba were also living in the safe house. They were in hiding, too, largely because of the growing role Trapence was playing in a broad-based anti-government protest movement. He co-led a national two-day protest during which the state killed nineteen protesters. In response to this and other clampdowns—including an extension of the penal code to criminalize lesbian sex too—the American government suspended a 3.5-billion-dollar power infrastructure grant to the country. At the same time, Malawi's economy collapsed, the ripple effects of the 2008 global crash, exacerbated by bad governance. "People were angry," Kamba told me. "Aid was frozen, people were not eating, not drinking, there was no fuel, no soft drinks. People were trying to find a scapegoat, and the gays were blamed. We were the ones who were cutting off aid from the West!"

In this context, the rules of the CEDEP safe house were very strict: Aunty had to be inside by nightfall, and could not bring strange men home. But she struggled to adhere, and returned at least once having been beaten and robbed. "It was a terrible responsibility for us," Kamba told me. "What if something happened to her? What would we tell her family?"

A religious group had offered to sponsor her emigration to Canada but nothing came of it, and so Amnesty International suggested South Africa: because of its constitutional protection of sexual minorities, because of its proximity, because there was a local transgender organization willing to host her, and because Aunty would not need a visa. Even this was a challenge, though: the state dragged its heels issuing her a passport. While Aunty waited, CEDEP and Amnesty felt it too risky for her to stay in Lilongwe, and sent her back to her home village.

When Aunty finally got her passport a year later she was told she had a week to prepare for departure. Dunker Kamba drove down to the village to fetch her, and Amnesty International put her up in a Blantyre guesthouse, flying in her South African hosts to meet her and accompany her back. "I really want to get out of here, so I can wear my miniskirts the way I want to," she told one of them. Such was her sense of possibility, and liberation, in her new home.

On the day of her departure she arrived at the CEDEP offices dressed for her flight fully accessorized, in a very feminine skirt and blouse. "Aunty," Dunker Kamba said to her, "do you want to leave Malawi? You know you are not going to get through the airport if you go out in public like that!" Eventually they compromised on a "more unisex" alternative, a traditional outfit of matching pants and shirt. "I don't think Aunty was being difficult or defiant at all," Kamba recalled. "Because she feels herself so strongly to be a woman inside, she does not understand that she does not look like one."

2

Accompanied by Dunker Kamba, Aunty boarded a South African Airways flight in October 2011. Just over two hours later, they landed at Johannesburg's O.R. Tambo International Airport, across the Pink Line. The authorities were waiting for her when she asked for asylum at passport control: The South African government had already been lobbied by Amnesty International and had agreed to give her refugee status. She thus became one of the country's first refugees granted asylum on the fear of persecution because of sexual orientation or gender identity.

Aunty was destined for Cape Town, where she would be hosted by a transgender advocacy organization called Gender DynamiX (GDX). But while her asylum application was being processed she stayed at the Johannesburg guesthouse of a gay pastor, Paul

Mokgethi-Heath, who remembered that she arrived "traumatized," but that the possibility of a new life in South Africa thrilled her. He recalled, particularly, scenes at his church where "all the queens gathered and clucked around Aunty, and gave her tips about her hair and her nails, how to be a *real* woman!"

The phrase *LGBT refugee* had been used since around 2005, when refugee service organizations in Turkey had begun noting a significant influx of gay, lesbian, and transgender refugees from Iran, fleeing fear of imprisonment or pressure to undergo sexual reassignment surgery.[4] According to the 1951 UN Refugee Convention, a "refugee" was anyone who had "a well-founded fear of being persecuted for reasons of race, religion, nationality, membership of a particular social group, or political opinion." In 2008, the UNHCR ruled that the term "particular social group" could apply to "LGBT individuals."[5] Some countries were already granting asylum on this basis, but the UNHCR decision made it a matter of international policy. By the end of the Obama administration in 2016, the United States took, by far, the largest number of such refugees; an estimated seventy-five to one hundred annually.[6]

Five years previously, when Aunty moved to South Africa, Northern European countries were leading the way. Belgium, for example, accepted 441 such refugees out of 1,298 prospective applicants between 2007 and 2010.[7] The very high number of rejections, here and elsewhere, reflected concerns about "credibility": how were authorities to verify whether applicants had legitimate fears of persecution—and if they were gay in the first place?

Some countries, like the Czech Republic, were accused of conducting invasive sexual arousal tests on asylum applicants.[8] In others, like Australia and the United Kingdom, there was spirited jurisprudence on whether the state could deport applicants on the grounds that they had not exercised enough "discretion" about their sexual orientation back home.[9] In the United Kingdom, two such applicants—from Iran and Cameroon—were denied refugee status on the basis that they could escape persecution back home if they concealed their identities: the men took the case to appeal, and in 2010 they won. In a passage from the Supreme Court judgment that has entered the queer canon, one of the judges, Lord Rodger, insisted that " just as male heterosexuals are free to enjoy themselves playing rugby, drinking beer and talking about girls with their mates, so male homosexuals are to be free to enjoy themselves going to Kylie concerts, drinking exotically colored cocktails and talking about boys with their straight female mates."[10]

Notwithstanding Lord Rodger's stereotyping of gay men (would a gay refugee be "credible" if he liked rugby and drank beer?) the decision shifted the debate decisively, and was affirmed by the UNHCR: it was not acceptable to deny asylum on the grounds that LGBT people could escape persecution by concealing their identities.[11] Still, in 2019, a U.K. immigration judge rejected the asylum claim of a man because he did not wear "lipstick" and behave in an "effeminate" manner, the way other claimants did, the claimant's lawyer said.[12] British data showed that between 2016 and 2018, the country refused at least 3,100 asylum claims from countries where homosexuality is illegal—1,197 from Pakistan alone.[13] The Lib Dem party slammed what it called "the Home Office's culture of disbelief."

Obviously, given the high profile of Aunty's case, she had no "credibility" problems in her application for asylum in South Africa; neither would it have been reasonable to expect her to conceal her identity. Her application was processed in Pretoria in a record thirty days: usually only temporary asylum was granted, and the process of getting permanent refugee status took an average of three years for most applicants. Aunty told me that the Home Affairs officials were "very fine, very nice": a far cry from the blunt discrimination, bureaucratic stalling, and naked extortion to which most asylum seekers in South Africa are subject.

In Cape Town, Aunty was given a self-contained flat in a shelter for abused women and children in the "colored" township of Manenberg, and was enrolled in English classes at a nearby school for refugees. Aunty excelled at the first two levels of English classes but struggled with the third, and eventually stopped attending class: her teachers were convinced this was because she was afflicted by untreated post-traumatic stress disorder. One, a perceptive young woman named Chivonne Africa, felt that Aunty was upended by the kind of pride that comes from a lifetime of having to be on the defensive: "She did not take well to any kind of correction, because she was so keen on expressing herself the way *she* wanted to express herself." Once the coursework moved from basic literacy to math and social science, she began to play truant.

This withdrawal coincided with the time when she stopped living at the shelter—and when she became involved with Benson. Although Aunty told me the shelter was a "good place," her lawyer Lusungu Khanyama Phiri remembered that it was "very lonely for Aunty. She really struggled. Here she was, trying to start a new life, being who she wants to be, going out and meeting a man, but she's confined … with no men allowed and a curfew. And when she does sneak out to get herself something to drink and have some company, she finds herself recognized by Malawians who abuse her."

Within four months of arrival in Cape Town, Aunty was assaulted violently on two occasions, both times left unconscious, and hospitalized. She showed me the knife-wound scars on her leg and her back: in both attacks, she said, her assailants were Malawians. In the first she was told she was "shaming Malawi," in the second that she would be taught a lesson because she had "too much pride." Meanwhile, the shelter was struggling with her non-adherence to rules. Her hosts at GDX decided it would be better for her to have her own space, and settled on a flat in nearby Tambo Village; this was where Martin, the outreach worker assigned to her, lived. Martin would help her integrate while keeping an eye on her.

But Aunty's new landlord began complaining almost immediately about his tenant's carousing, and told her to leave. GDX decided to use some of the Amnesty grant to buy her a *zozo*, as prefabricated shacks are known in South Africa: she would have her own place at last. By this point, her relationship with GDX had broken down almost completely. "There were trust issues," Amnesty's Simeon Mawanza told me. "We had to mediate many times. She was convinced other people were eating the money destined for her. This is one of the traps of development aid: 'Other people are taking our money.'"

Liesl Theron, the founder of GDX, had been instrumental in bringing Aunty to South Africa. "The problem has its roots in the way we coochy-coochied Tiwonge at the beginning," she told me. "She stayed on the premises [GDX shared a converted school with the shelter], and at one point we had six staff members running after her. We realised that Tiwonge couldn't be our only project, and so we started withdrawing some of that very visible, intensive support we initially gave her, not least because we felt she needed to start looking after herself while there was a little bit of money left in the Amnesty grant. We wanted her to spread her wings while there was still a safety net beneath her. But I think she must have experienced this as abandonment."

Theron's successor, Sibusiso Kheswa, was more blunt: "The biggest barrier to her integration is the money she has received. It doesn't push her, like all other foreigners are pushed, to interact with the locals, to learn the language and find something to do."

Simeon Mawanza, who managed her relocation grant at Amnesty, recalled walking with her through a shopping mall one day, and pointing out hawkers selling fruit and vegetables. "I suggested she consider doing something like that. She was indignant: 'Me? Tiwonge Chimbalanga? Selling vegetables on the street? Never!' I responded, 'My sister, at some point we all have to do what we have to do to go up again.'"

Tambo Village is on the fringe of Guguletu, a lively, dense township filled with churches and schools and children on the streets, but also with shebeens—as illegal taverns are called—and with risk. Aunty came to South Africa to be free but she was, Martin—the GDX outreach worker—said to me, "*too* free for a South African township." He tallied the damage that celebrity had done to her: not only that it gave her airs and graces, but that people recognized her. "'Oh, we saw you on TV, Aunty! Let's meet! Let's drink!' Then the money's finished." Martin spent two years in almost full-time service to Aunty, much as Dunker Kamba had in Malawi. He took her to school every day, he tried to help her save money, he rushed out to rescue her when she was attacked, he shrugged it off when she turned on him.

Short and thickset, Martin hailed from the Eastern Cape and had the polite diffidence and laconic charm of a rural man. He had been assigned female at birth, and had come to Cape Town in large part to undergo his own gender transition; he lived in Tambo Village with his girlfriend and her toddler child. He did not want to talk much about his own experiences, save to say that "people are still so ignorant, and it takes a brave person to say 'I'm trans.'" Still, the very fact of his existence, knitted into the life of the Cape Flats, was evidence of a significant phenomenon in urban South African queer culture in the second decade of the twenty-first century: the number of young black people who had come out as butch lesbians but who were now taking hormones, binding their breasts, and living as men.

Martin had left GDX about a year before we met, but had still kept an eye out for Aunty, rebuilding the shack for her when she had to relocate once again—this time through no fault of her own. But although Martin still professed a great affection for her, he had recently withdrawn entirely. The final straw had been Aunty's interruption of a Sunday afternoon *braai* (barbecue) at his house with accusations that his friends had stolen her cell phone—when, in fact, she had left it somewhere while drinking. If she could get her drinking under control, Martin told me, "Aunty will fly."

The problem, he felt, was that Aunty was living a lie: "She's telling herself that she's in '*that* class.' 'I can pay for anything! I can pay for *you!*' She's not living her life, she's living someone else's life. But she's not working, she's not qualified to do anything." Martin shrugged. "Maybe it's a gay thing, you know. I've got another gay friend who is wearing things that I could never dream of buying…"

Despite the thirty dollars a week from Amnesty—a decent amount in a South African township—Aunty never had enough. She collected her allowance every Tuesday in the presence of Benson, and made a show of giving a chunk of it directly to him. Sibusiso Kheswa of GDX understood that Aunty was parlaying her Amnesty income into a bid for protection, "to build a community around her, including securing lovers, who don't have incomes for themselves." Kheswa, himself a transgender man, told me that he had noted, too, that "particularly in relationships, if you are a transwoman, you're likely to compromise a lot: here's a person who says, 'you're my *woman!*' You'll let go of everything to hold on to that."

As I traveled the world researching this book, I met people in such relationships, from India to Russia, from Mexico to the Philippines. Indeed, Aunty's previous man, a Zimbabwean, had beaten her up and forged her asylum papers so that he could work. Benson was "a good man," Aunty insisted. "He does not beat me, and he loves me."

But of course such relationships will lend themselves to abuse: they can turn, literally, on a penny, from protection to threat. I witnessed this myself, not with regard to Benson but another friend, when I went to visit Aunty one day. She had invited two neighbors over: a Malawian man named Bernard and his South African wife, Asanda. The couple was expansive with Saturday-afternoon drink: They loved Aunty, they told me, and defended her against slurs: "I *shout* at people if they start with her," Asanda told me. "I give them *hell*, in Xhosa, and that shuts them up."

Bernard told me that he had been in South Africa for ten years, "so we know about these people [gays], we are used to them." But then, a few hours after I had left, I received a hysterical call from Aunty. Bernard had been at a shebeen and was now outside, slashing at her shack with a knife, threatening to kill Benson because he had come upon the notion that I had paid him for an interview (I had not). Bernard wanted some of the action, too, for having spoken to me.

A FEW DAYS after the incident with Bernard, I went back to Tambo Village. It was about 10:30 on a Thursday, the morning after a public holiday, and as I pulled up outside Aunty's shack for our scheduled appointment, I heard loud music. A neighbor, walking past my car, cursed aloud, and I realized the music was coming from Aunty's place. I looked through the security gate and saw her sitting at the big table with Benson and three other men, a video of Malawian music playing on the TV. One of the men was slapping cards on a table littered with glasses of beer, and there was much animated chatter. When I was spotted the men evaporated, and their hostess hastily cleaned up. As we settled down she explained that the men had come to "console" Benson because of an altercation the previous day: the very neighbor whom I had heard cursing had insulted Benson, by accusing him of having AIDS and being on antiretroviral medication, and Aunty had been provoked into physical retaliation. As she told the story, she began weeping uncontrollably. What seemed to trigger her distress was the hardship her husband had endured by being linked to her—and the consequent possibility that he might abandon her.

While we were talking, Aunty's friend Bernard wandered in, the previous dispute seemingly forgotten. He was blind drunk, and had an inadequate Band-Aid covering a nasty fresh wound on the side of his neck; he had been slashed with a broken bottle the previous evening. He was always getting stabbed in shebeens, Aunty said, because "he gets drunk and starts shouting, and people get angry with him. Shebeens are dangerous places. That's why I don't go to them anymore. Now I only drink at home."

By now her tears had become quite desperate. Tambo Village was too dangerous for her and Benson and she wanted to leave. She planned to sell the shack and rent a room in town. We also spoke, that morning, about her plans for medical gender transition. Although she told me that she very much wanted to begin taking estrogen, the GDX staff had mentioned to me that she had twice missed her initial appointments at Triangle Project, an LGBT health service that referred transgender people into a free, state-funded hormone-therapy program. When I asked her why, she said: "There was no one to take me. I don't know my way around."

Language, of course, must have been a barrier, particularly when it came to the prospect of intimate consultations with a doctor or therapist.

But the issue lay elsewhere too: she did not think of herself as "transgender," a term she only heard for the first time when she was introduced to GDX in Cape Town.

Ronald Addinall-Van Straaten, the gender specialist who ran the program at Triangle Project, told me that this was a phenomenon not uncommon among his clients: "Sometimes you want to say to a person, 'Let's get real here. This is what you need to do to survive.' But when you're talking about someone who has fought so hard to have their own identity, constantly having to fight people telling them that they are not what they know themselves to be, that sense of self needs to be respected."

As I sat with Aunty that Thursday morning, I wished she would find her way to the Triangle Project, so that she could hear those words herself.

3

In July 2016, nearly two years after our first meeting, Aunty headlined an event called Colours of Cape Town, held on a Saturday at the Nest, a trendy venue for "young African creatives" in downtown Cape Town.

"Join us for a night of solidarity with the LGBTI refugee community," the Facebook invitation read. It was put out by PASSOP, People Against Suffering, Oppression and Poverty, the refugee support organization where Aunty volunteered twice a week. Over a hundred people responded, piling into the Nest's upstairs rooms and spilling out onto the wrought-iron Victorian balcony that hung over the action on Darling Street, just off the Grand Parade. The crowd was unusual for Cape Town, a city that was still more racially segregated than Johannesburg: there was a large group of the refugees I had come to know—people from Zimbabwe and Uganda, from the Democratic Republic of Congo and Burundi—scattered among the queer kids who had found out about the event on social media. There were young lesbians from Khayelitsha with buzz cuts and attitude, and there were older activists whom I had not seen in twenty years. A choir opened the proceedings with heavenly gospel: it was from the newly established local branch of a Nigerian LGBT church called House of Rainbow.

I had arrived late, but I spotted Aunty immediately. She looked radiant and regal in an elegant purple "Nigerian": a long skirt and blouse with extravagant gold and silver brocade, crowned with a lavish turban. Benson was at her side, all smiles and nods, swallowed up in a matching suit. When Aunty rose to take the mike, her voice was tentative but unfaltering, each word spoken with the care it must have taken her to write it: "My name is Tiwonge Chimbalanga and I am a Malawian currently residing in Cape Town, South Africa." After describing her involvement in "the first gay marriage in Malawi," she told of her "very painful experience" in prison, and her difficulties in South Africa, the assaults and the unemployment. And she made a big point about gratitude, thanking seventeen organizations and individuals by name and "all the people who came to see me and support me during that time [in prison]. As people we must all help each other during difficult times, like I was helped."

A pamphlet was distributed at the event: "African LGBTI people who face extreme danger in their home country flee to South Africa to find refuge, as [South Africa's] constitution is the most progressive in the region. However, the lived reality after arrival is far from desirable. LGBTI refugees face extreme challenges after relocating to South Africa." The pamphlet outlined these: a "double marginalisation" because queer people were not "accepted into their own refugee communities because of their sexual orientation/gender identity nor are they accepted into LGBTI communities because they are foreigners," and an inability to find work or shelter because of both homophobia and xenophobia.

Since the end of apartheid, other Africans had been pouring into South Africa by the millions, and in a society where there was both severe unemployment and crime, foreigners were blamed for both: a wave of xenophobic violence in May 2008 left sixty-two people dead and thousands displaced. PASSOP had been founded the previous year, and by the time Aunty became involved it had established an LGBTI Network numbering about forty, although only a handful of these had actually—like Aunty—applied for refugee status on the basis of their sexual orientation or gender identity. The rest "either did not know they could apply on the basis of being LGBTI, or feared they would be persecuted again or outed in their communities if they did," I was told by the coordinator, an exiled Congolese human rights lawyer named Guillain Koko.

Koko dedicated much of his time to helping members of the network get resettled out of South Africa, to countries like the United States: the UNHCR would do this if you could prove you were as vulnerable in the country to which you had fled as you had been back home. One of Koko's prime candidates for resettlement was Aunty, given the violence she had endured in Cape Town. But she did not want to move again, largely because of Benson: she could not bear to lose a man again.

IT WAS AT PASSOP that I had first met Aunty, in early 2014. The organization was housed at the time in a somewhat decrepit suite above a storefront in Wynberg, in Cape Town's southern suburbs. The top floor, an attic space, was given over to the LGBTI Network, scattered with mismatched furniture and strung with rainbow banners the PASSOP crew had made for a recent Pride march. It had the feel of a student common room, and there was a constant trail of people passing through, sleeping off a rough night on the couch, hopping on to the free Wi-Fi, or consulting Koko on their cases. Always buzzing about, too, were a handful of international interns: American or European volunteers, often graduate students, who had come to roll up their sleeves to do fieldwork with this newly recognized marginalized group in a conveniently accessible city.

But Aunty was seldom to be found there, up in the LGBTI loft. She far preferred to be downstairs "with the other women," she told me, helping out the caseworkers as they assisted disoriented walk-ins far away from home and looking for a way to stay. This is how Aunty met her friend Prisca, who acted as interpreter for me: "Aunty Tiwo is polite and courteous to everyone, unlike many of the other people," Prisca told me. "So we don't even think about who she is. We just see her as someone helping us."

I watched Prisca's eyes widen as she translated Aunty's story for me. Prisca was a staunch Christian who had not really processed the reality of her friend's identity. At first she managed this by exceptionalizing Aunty: there was her friend, whom she loved, and there were others, who were sinners. But Prisca—a fashionable young woman who worked as a nanny for a white family—had an open mind and a big heart, and by the last of our meetings, a few weeks later, she was full of outrage at the hardships that had befallen her friend, "just because of who she loves."

Like everyone at PASSOP, Prisca only knew Aunty sober. Tendai, the Zimbabwean receptionist and another of Aunty's friends, was uncomprehending when I asked about Aunty's drinking. She thought about it for a while, visibly distressed, before answering: "You must understand, Mark. When you sit at home, bored, that's when you drink. That's why Aunty needs a job."

I took these words to heart.

When I first started visiting Aunty, she routinely hit me up for a handout. I had responded at first by arriving with groceries, or paying for her transport costs if she was coming into the city to see me, or helping out with a dentist when Benson was doubled over with the pain of a toothache. This is where conscience takes me, on the job, when I find myself asking people in distress to share their stories with me. But after listening to Tendai and Prisca, I began to see another way for Aunty. PASSOP lost its funding in 2015: it had to lay off most of its staff, and could no longer afford to pay the small stipend—about fifteen dollars a day—it offered "volunteers." PASSOP needed staffers as much as Aunty needed the stipend: it was a first port of call for asylum seekers arriving in Cape Town. And so I gave the organization enough funds to retain Aunty for two days a week. Not only would this offer Aunty a reason to go to work, and much-needed income now that her Amnesty grant was finally coming to an end, but it would also give PASSOP an extra hand, and the organization would continue to expose refugees to a transgender person helping them, thus breaking down their own prejudices, as it had done Prisca's.

Having set up this arrangement, I stayed away. I had not seen her for about a year when I made contact with her and PASSOP again, in early 2016, to invite Aunty to participate in a panel at the University of Cape Town's Summer School. The staff told me that even though she was only paid for the two days, Aunty came in almost every day and had become an indispensable part of the team. As well as doing her basic cleaning duties she had learned how to use the computer and was helping walk-ins with their "newcomer letters." Aunty came to the university event with me: so moved by her was an older gay British man that he offered to fund PASSOP to employ her for a further two days a week. I retreated: first the British man took up the slack, and then a German foundation.

Through PASSOP and its computer, Aunty discovered social media. By the time she headlined the Colours of Cape Town event, she was on Facebook with over seven hundred friends: most were also Malawians, or members of the Cape Town refugee community, but they included a couple of prominent American activists and several African leaders of the movement, from Uganda to Zimbabwe. She was wired now, even though her status updates were in Chichewa and the images she posted were always selfies: Aunty sitting industriously at a computer in the office; Aunty striking a pose against the merry-go-round in a public park. By the time I saw her at the Nest that evening she was mainlined to her smartphone: "Facebook bad," she told me. "Too many Malawians. Talk shit to Aunty. Too much shit. WhatsApp better." She often sent me messages, keeping in touch in her telegraphic way, which suited the medium perfectly.

I went back to visit her at Tambo Village. She and Benson proudly showed me the stall they had built abutting the shack: she had finally gotten off her high horse and taken the last of her Amnesty grant as start-up capital to build it, and to stock it with cabbages and tomatoes, apples and onions. Benson ran the stall while she went to work at PASSOP. She soon realized, though, that she did much better selling beer, and expanded that part of her business; the demand was higher, as were the profit margins, and it didn't spoil. She stopped selling vegetables, and her shack became another township shebeen.

Aunty seemed to have become more at one with her environment. Rather than her elaborate "Nigerian" outfits she would, on an average weekday, wear a tight faded denim miniskirt and a T-shirt, with sneakers threaded with bright pink laces that matched the plastic beads around her neck. She had decided not to take any hormones, she told me: she now spoke about this quite emphatically, without the previous excuses about access. But the small orbs under her tight T-shirt suggested she might be using a breast-enlargement cream.

She also seemed to have made her peace with her neighbors, and she introduced me to a new friend, a Xhosa woman in the yard with whom she went to church. There was also an older Malawian simply known as Madala (Old Man), who told me he was from Aunty's home village and had been sent by the family to find her. Despite her assaults at the hands of compatriots, she had finally managed to forge a community of them around her. There were many Malawians in Tambo and she lived, largely, in a Chichewa world.

NOW, AT COLOURS OF CAPE TOWN, I watched Aunty receive a standing ovation following her speech. I was immensely proud of her. And I was also gratified that I had been able to play some part in helping her find her feet. This was not just out of a sense of pity or justice but also—I realized—out of kinship. I, too, had been asked to say some words at the event at the Nest and I had focused them on the "double marginalization" bind. Refugees usually sought work and shelter in their own ethnic or national networks when they arrived somewhere, I explained, but if they were queer, they did not have access to this resource, ostracized as they were because of their sexual orientation or gender identity. "*We*, as LGBT Capetonians who benefit from the freedoms of this society, are their family now," I said, "and we have an obligation to them."

Much as I believed this, I was troubled by my own feelings of pride and gratification. I remembered the words of her other benefactors, about the dangers of the dependency trap. Was I contributing to it, too? I did not think so, as my contribution was funneled through PASSOP where she was earning it. But I had not gone to enough effort to be anonymous, and she had discovered that I was her benefactor. Why had I allowed this to happen? Had I fallen victim to the white man's savior complex? Was I tearing up, listening to Aunty speak publicly about a year after I had started funding her, because I believed I was playing some role in her redemption with my paltry thirty dollars a week?

I ruminated on something that had challenged me throughout my years of research into the Pink Line. If the new twenty-first-century "conversation" about sexual orientation and gender identity was being disseminated across the globe by the vectors of globalization—by the digital revolution and mass migration, by a transnational human rights movements and popular culture—then surely I needed to understand myself as one of these vectors, too. I carried my own ideas and my own experiences in my rucksack, not to mention in my wallet (or the perception of it) and even in my own struggle as a gay man, and I unpacked these each time I encountered someone like Aunty.

I was particularly conscious of this as an Open Society Fellow: my own benefactors were among the world's largest funders of the new global LGBT movement, and this undoubtedly opened doors for me. This forced me to think about how I might be introducing ideas that weren't there before, or in some way influencing the way people and their communities thought about themselves and the world. I might have played a small role in helping Aunty settle into a more stable and integrated life, and done my bit as "queer family." But I had to accept that I had become part of a dynamic of solidarity and dependency that was intrinsic to the staking of the Pink Line, and to the global queer politics of these times.

Even if I embraced and accepted the agency of people such as Aunty, I had to grapple with the fact that my very presence in her shack in Tambo Village, or under the tree in her native village of Chimbalanga, fueled the notion that people like me paid people like her to be gay or LGBT—or, at the very least, that there was a funding stream, a passage to upward mobility, attached to such novel identities.

There had been much of this discourse around Aunty in Malawi. Commentators repeatedly accused her of having staged her *chinkhoswe* for financial gain, and alleged that her few Malawian supporters had all been "bought" by Western money. It was openly stated by the Malawian president Bingu wa Mutharika that the only reason he pardoned Aunty and Monjeza was to unfreeze development aid from the West. And of course once Aunty went into exile, this became proof of her payout: her *chinkhoswe*, and her alliance with her global supporters, was a ticket to all the riches that South Africa offered. My visit to her home village, and the outlandish studio backdrops to the photographs I brought, would have underscored this.

Shortly after Aunty's release, in May 2010, the *Daily Times* of Malawi published a widely circulated story headlined "NGOs Cash in on Gays": unnamed donors, it was alleged, were offering local organizations five hundred thousand dollars to promote homosexuality in the country.[14] Certainly, when I visited Malawi five years later, I encountered a booming micro-economy: lawyers, journalists, and priests, all allegedly straight, jetting off to Geneva to talk about LGBT rights at the UN Human Rights Council, or being funded to run sensitization workshops, or even to place articles in the local media. This was raising eyebrows—even though, of course, the amounts circulating were negligible compared to those in other development aid sectors, such as public health or education. I was not surprised that I, too, was frequently shaken down for a fee in Blantyre: several people—including the pastor who married Aunty, and a prominent gay activist—would only speak to me if I paid them. I did not.

All over Africa, the "recruitment" canard was fervently advanced by those who feared or disapproved of this new social phenomenon. It had a corollary, of course: homosexuality was a form of exploitation—or the consequence of it—rather than an innate characteristic. These ideas have always been part of Western anti-homosexual discourse, where—in Britain, for example—upper-class homosexuals were accused of exploiting and corrupting working-class men by paying for their services. This line of thinking holds a particular place in anti-colonial theory, too: Frantz Fanon, the Caribbean psychiatrist whose works became primary texts of black emancipation, wrote that the black homosexual compatriots he encountered in Europe were not "neurotic" as Freud had described, but were doing it as "a means to a livelihood, as pimping is for others."[15]

Now, in twenty-first-century Africa, "recruitment" had a plethora of applications. In Senegal, the lucrative AIDS industry was seen as the honeytrap; in Nigeria, the devil was at work; in Zimbabwe, "recruitment" was deployed as an anti-Western nativism. And in Uganda, where the discourse was the most intense, all the above dynamics were at play. The rhetoric was equally strong in Russia and other countries of the former Soviet Union, where gay propaganda legislation was expressly formulated to prevent such recruitment, and where there was a similar nationalist discourse about insulating citizens from the corrupting effects of Western liberal capitalism.

Aunty's gender identity was manifestly not a strategy for getting out of poverty: it drove her deeper into the poverty cycle because of the way it stigmatized her. Still, it is undeniable that her embrace of an LGBTI identity was connected to the capital this label carried in a new global economy where the wealthy West—people like me—valued such identities and understood people like her as vulnerable, and deserving of our help, or at the very least our solidarity. Aunty knew exactly what she was doing when she told the audience at Colours of Cape Town that her *chinkhoswe* was "the first gay marriage in Malawi," and when she ostentatiously thanked her seventeen benefactors at the end of her speech, before taking her standing ovation.

She was singing for her supper along the Pink Line.

LATER IN 2016, I went to visit Aunty in Tambo Village. It was a Monday morning and, as always after the weekend, the township was bleary. Both Aunty and her home were in disarray. I noticed immediately that the television above her fridge—her most prized possession, usually pumping out Malawian music videos—was shattered.

She grimly told me that she had gone to church as usual the previous day, but that Benson had decided to stay home. She had returned, later in the day, to mayhem: Benson had spent the day drinking beer and smoking *dagga*, and by evening was on a deranged bender, shouting at customers and trashing the shack. Aunty's neighbors—including her long-suffering landlord—tried to help, to no avail, and eventually she called Benson's family, who told her to turf him out. All her neighbors agreed: it was time to give Benson the boot. As Aunty told me this story, Benson sat next to her looking contrite, or perhaps just drunk. He remembered nothing of the previous day's events.

I drove her to work and, later, took her to lunch at a Nando's near the PASSOP offices. She was downcast. "I will give my husband one more chance," she said.

"Why?" I asked. "He is drinking your money and chasing away your customers. Now he has broken your television. Why don't you listen to your neighbors and friends?"

She was silent.

"Because you love him?"

"Too much."

3

A NEW GLOBAL CULTURE WARS?

IN MARCH 2009, the year before Tiwonge Chimbalanga was arrested in Malawi, a prominent pastor sent out an invitation to a seminar to expose "the Homosexuals' Agenda" in a country to the north: Uganda. "Today," wrote the pastor, Stephen Langa, "the well funded and well organized homosexual machinery is taking one country after another by de-criminalizing homosexual practices in those countries and legalizing gay marriages in some of them.[1] Uganda is now under extreme pressure from the same group to de-criminalize homosexuality."

Langa's seminar promised to help Africans "protect themselves" from this juggernaut, and was headlined by three American Evangelical speakers.[2] The first two were Caleb Lee Brundidge and Don Schmierer, the United States' most notorious conversion-therapy practitioners. The third was Scott Lively, whose 1995 book *The Pink Swastika* alleged that a homosexual plot to take over the world began in Nazi Germany, and that gays worldwide now connived to foment "social chaos and destruction" through gay marriage, divorce, child abuse, and AIDS.[3]

An African cleric named Kapya Kaoma, based in Boston, responded to Langa's invitation, and traveled to Uganda to attend the seminar. Kaoma was an Anglican priest from Zambia, deeply troubled by what he saw as the American religious right's "exporting of homophobia" to his native continent, and the subsequent hate-mongering this engendered.[4] Kaoma had first noticed this in his own church, when American Episcopalians opposed to the ordination of gay priests and to same-sex marriage had made common cause with African Anglicans in the 1990s. Now Kaoma was focused, specifically, on the way American evangelists were trying to influence public policy in African countries, according to a culture wars script they had honed back home.

And so Kaoma—a married heterosexual man with children and the disarmingly solicitous manner of a parish priest—went undercover to Stephen Langa's anti-gay seminar. In the paper he published after his visit, Kaoma cited Scott Lively's keynote address, in which the American pastor compared the decriminalization of homosexuality to legalizing bestiality and child molestation. He reported on his conversations with participants who spoke of how they had been awoken by the American speakers to the need, as one put it, to "stand firm to fight homosexuality." And he confirmed that, while in Uganda, Scott Lively met with the parliamentarian who had authored the country's proposed anti-homosexuality legislation, which included the death penalty for repeat offenders. Kaoma called his report *Globalizing the Culture Wars*, to capture the way the American religious right was taking its mission abroad, having lost the battle back home.

The term "culture wars" was first used, in the United States, to describe the division over "moral" issues activated by conservatives in the Republican Party in the late 1970s, to mobilize voters and influence policy in an increasingly secular and liberal society. American electoral politics subsequently cleaved along social issues: "blue" Democrats might believe in spending on social welfare and government, but they were increasingly defined by their secular values and social liberalism; "red" Republicans might want small government or fiscal conservatism, but they were increasingly defined by their belief that religious faith should set national values, and by their social conservatism. Beginning with a pushback against *Roe v. Wade*, the 1973 Supreme Court decision that legalized abortion, American culture warriors staked battlegrounds over reproductive rights, over sex education and science education, and then, of course, over gay rights. These battles came to a head in the early twenty-first century, over marriage equality.

But by the time Kapya Kaoma was listening to Scott Lively in Kampala, the polls were showing, clearly, the trend among Americans toward supporting same-sex marriage. The religious right had "spent decades demonizing LGBT people and working to keep them in the closet," wrote the Southern Poverty Law Center in a 2013 report.[5] But this religious right now found itself "on the losing side of a battle that it now seems incapable of winning. As a result, these groups and individuals have increasingly shifted their attention to other nations, where anti-gay attitudes are much stronger and violence against the LGBT community far too common."

This project might have found advocates on the lunatic fringe, like Scott Lively, but it had very establishment roots. It was empowered by the White House itself, during the tenure of the Evangelical George W. Bush, and specifically his Emergency Plan for AIDS Relief (PEPFAR). PEPFAR prioritized "faith-based" HIV programming, including the preaching of abstinence over the distribution of condoms. What David Kuo, the key architect of Bush's Evangelical policies, said about American domestic policy applied to global AIDS policy, too: "We knew government couldn't feed Jesus to people," wrote Kuo later, "but if we could get money to private religious groups—virtually all of whom were Christian—we could show them to the dining room."[6] American Christian organizations obtained PEPFAR grants and established surrogates in the region, many of whom worked off the American culture wars script. With their American funding, they gained significant institutional power, and came to influence national politics in countries like Uganda and Malawi.

At the same time, a group of American politicians and clerics known as "the Family" became involved in helping set social policy in several countries: their existence was first exposed by the journalist Jeff Sharlet, who labeled them as "America's secret theocrats."[7] They saw the opportunity in Uganda, where their point person was David Bahati, a Wharton-educated legislator who would author the country's anti-homosexuality bill. "We are *going* to get the bill through, now or later," said Bahati to Sharlet when they met in Kampala in 2009.[8] "And when we do, we will close the door to homosexuality, and open society to something larger." That, wrote Sharlet, "was the crux of the matter for Bahati. To him, homosexuality is only a symptom of what he learned from the Family to be a greater plague: government by people, not by God."

The African continent was fertile ground for such dogma, since "government by people" had not turned out so well in much of it. Like Islamists, Christian evangelists had a social mission *and* the funds to provide services—such as health and education—that failing states were increasingly unable to deliver. They were also syncretic and ecumenical, taking on indigenous modes of devotion and integrating them into worship. And perhaps most important, they promised a path to prosperity through devotion, and could be joyous and exuberant oases in a very difficult world. There were some powerful converts, including Uganda's first lady, Janet Museveni, a devotee of the Saddleback Church's Rick Warren. Warren would say on a 2008 visit to Uganda that "homosexuality is not a natural way of life and thus not a human right."[9]

It would take four years for David Bahati's Anti-Homosexuality Act to be passed in December 2013 and then to be struck down, seven months later, by the country's Constitutional Court for procedural reasons. In the intermediate time a wave of violent homophobia swept Uganda: a prominent activist was killed, many others were outed by a sensationalist media, and many fled into exile. The United States applied sanctions against the country, and Scott Lively stood trial in his hometown in Massachusetts for "crimes against humanity." When the judge finally ruled in 2017 that he could not take the case because it was outside his jurisdiction, he nonetheless said he believed the American pastor had violated international law by having aided "a vicious and frightening campaign of repression against LGBTI persons in Uganda."[10]

These global culture wars played out elsewhere, too. In Belize, a tiny former British colony on the Caribbean coast, an activist named Caleb Orozco went to court in 2013 to get the country's law against buggery (the British legal word for sodomy) declared unconstitutional. Orozco's major opponent was one Scott Stirm, an in-country Texan missionary whose funding and legal support came from two large right-wing American Christian organizations. Orozco eventually won his case in 2016, represented in court by Lord Peter Goldsmith, the former UK attorney general, and supported by international human rights organizations.

As in Uganda, both sides claimed they were victims of a proxy war, alleging undue interference by outside players with their own global agendas. The Southern Poverty Law Center accused the American Christian organizations of "fanning the flames of anti-gay hatred" with "vicious propaganda, born and bred by American ideologues";[11] Stirm hit back that his American supporters were only assisting Belizeans against "the homosexual global attack on morality and family values."[12] The following year, after past and present U.S. ambassadors to Belize called on it to repeal the law, Stirm's Belize Association of Evangelical Churches retorted that "no nation, large or small, has the right to manipulate, coerce, or interfere in the processes of another nation."[13]

In the end, of course, the Belize Supreme Court decided the matter according to its own constitution, and ruled in Caleb Orozco's favor. He became something of a local hero, and was given several assignments not related to LGBT rights by the government. Belize moved on.

THE SAME BROAD set of American Christian actors were busy in another part of the world where a Pink Line was being drawn against the alleged cultural imperialism of Western liberals. Here the imperial "aggressor" was the European Union, accused of meddling in the affairs of the countries of the former Soviet bloc. The fact that there was a demographic crisis in these countries—populations were plummeting—meant that the "pro-family" culture wars agenda fell on fertile ground here: the fight against abortion, contraception, and homosexual families. As early as 1995, American religious conservatives came to Moscow to hatch the World Congress of Families (WCF) with their Russian counterparts.[14] By 2015, the WCF was "one of the most influential American organizations involved in the export of hate," according to the leading U.S. LGBT rights organization, the Human Rights Campaign.[15]

The "family values fervor" that swept through Russia at the time can be traced to two 2010 WCF encounters, according to the *Mother Jones* journalist Hannah Levintova: a Sanctity of Motherhood conference in Moscow, at which the WCF's Larry Jacobs was a keynote speaker; and the presence of a Russian Orthodox Church emissary, a former nightclub owner named Alexey Komov, at a WCF meeting in Colorado the same year.[16] Later, Vladimir Putin and Hungary's Viktor Orbán took up the "family values" baton and ran it as a political agenda, but its seeds were germinated by this relationship between American Evangelical and Russian Orthodox Christians.

Alexey Komov was by no means the only or even the most powerful advocate for Russia's "gay propaganda" legislation, but he was the primary link between Russian and American conservatives. The WCF helped him set up a Russian group called FamilyPolicy.Ru, which provided Russian lawmakers with data and strategy from the American experience. This, after all, was a script originally written in the United States, starting with Anita Bryant's 1977 Save Our Children campaign in Florida, which sought to expunge all references to homosexuality from curricula, and which resulted in several "no promo homo" laws across the country. In 2017, seven American states still had these laws on the books, which long predated the Russian ones, as did Margaret Thatcher's notorious Section 28 amendment, which forbade local authorities from "promoting" homosexuality in schools. The Thatcher amendment was only repealed in 2003.

After Russia passed its federal gay propaganda law, its author Yelena Mizulina successfully introduced a law banning the adoption of Russian children by foreign homosexual couples. To make her case, Mizulina used the controversial research of the University of Texas sociologist Mark Regnerus, which claimed very negative outcomes for children of homosexual parents, including increased vulnerability to abuse. Homosexual parents would teach their children to be gay just as alcoholics would be more likely have children who drink, Mizulina told a 2013 State Duma meeting. This was the kind of "social experiment that the West is conducting on its own children," and Russia had had enough of such experimentation, "where the family was destroyed."[17]

If American right-wing Christians were sharing a culture wars playbook with their Russian brethren, the Russians believed they were educating the Americans, in turn, about what Alexey Komov called "the dangers of this new totalitarianism," on the basis of their prior experience of communism.[18] Komov told *Mother Jones* in 2014 that there were "influential lobbies" seeking "to promote an aggressive social transformation campaign using LGBT activists as the means. We see it as the continuation of the same radical revolutionary agenda that cost so many lives in the Soviet Union, when they destroyed churches. This political correctness is used … to oppress religious freedoms and to destroy the family." This idea ignited a new ecumenical movement of Orthodox, Catholic, and Evangelical opponents to the new red under the bed, "gender ideology," in which marriage equality and an acceptance of transgenderism were examples of the gravest threat yet to humanity since communism: a denial of God-given nature. The movement ranged from Latin America (where it was embraced by Jair Bolsonaro) through Donald Trump's United States and back to former communist countries themselves: not only Russia, but Hungary and Poland too. The archbishop of Krakow,

Marek Jędraszewski, encapsulated these new geopolitics in August 2019 homily when he said that while Poland was "no longer affected by the red plague," there was a "new one that wants to control our souls, hearts and minds ... not Marxist, Bolshevik, but born of the same spirit, neoMarxist. Not red, but rainbow."[19]

In Poland, opposition to marriage equality was a plank in the 2019 electoral campaign of Kaczynski's ruling Law and Justice Party, and at a party rally Kaczynzki praised the archbishop for his stand: "[We must] live in freedom," he said, "and not be subject to all that is happening to the west of our borders ... where freedom is being eliminated."[20]

MEANWHILE, ON THE other side of the Pink Line:

In October 2012, I sat in the medieval gilt-and-velvet chamber of the House of Lords listening to a historic first-ever debate on LGBT issues in the British Parliament: the Conservative peer Lord Lexden had used his privileges "to ask Her Majesty's Government what assessment they have made of the treatment of homosexual men and women in the developing world."[21] There was consensus from all—to the left and to the right of the Speaker's scepter—that the United Kingdom should advance and protect the rights of homosexuals globally.

The Labour Party's Lord Chris Smith—formerly Britain's first openly gay British cabinet minister under Tony Blair—lauded the progress made in his country over the previous fifteen years "in securing the rights and liberties of lesbians and gay men." But it was "particularly shaming" that this was not true in much of the rest of the Commonwealth, where homosexuality remained illegal in forty-two of the seventy-eight member-states—including Malawi, Uganda, and Belize. The "bitter irony" was that these laws "have been inherited from us. I believe that that gives us a special responsibility to do whatever we can to help to change things."

When Britain's Buggery Act—which originally carried the death penalty for homosexual acts—was first passed in 1533, it was staked along a Tudor Pink Line. It was introduced by Henry VIII as a pretext for raids on the Catholic Church, whose monasteries were seen as hotbeds of homosexual activity—and also harbored the gold the Protestant king craved. "The desire of the king for the wealth of the Church had turned sin into a crime," writes Peter Ackroyd.[22] The death penalty was dropped in 1861, but in 1885 the law was amended to criminalize any sexual contact between men—or intention of sexual contact—as "gross indecency." It was this provision that saw Oscar Wilde jailed, and thousands of other men, too, until homosexual acts between two consenting adults in private were finally decriminalized in the United Kingdom in 1967, long after everywhere else in Western Europe.

The same Victorian era that expanded buggery into "gross indecency" also extended sodomy as a crime to the British colonies, through Lord Thomas Babington Macaulay's Indian Penal Code of 1860, which provided the basis for most of the laws across the empire. Clause 377 proscribed "carnal knowledge against the order of nature," and arose out of two very particular colonial preoccupations, the legal scholar Alok Gupta has written: the fear of "moral infection" from the natives, and the mission of "moral reform" among these new subjects.[23]

Britain shed most of its empire before it decriminalized homosexuality in 1967, and this meant that homosexual acts remained illegal in almost all the newly independent countries of the Commonwealth—although this was seldom enforced before LGBT rights began to be asserted in the twenty-first century. In his speech at Westminster, Chris Smith was right about the irony here: some in these countries used this colonial legislation to back up their claims that homosexuality was unacceptable, and that the demand for its decriminalization was a neocolonial slight on their sovereignty.

Still, the notion that Britain had a "special responsibility" to advocate for the decriminalization of laws it had introduced to the world suggested a new civilizing mission, or at least a new ideological project for the liberal West. A year previously, in October 2011, the British prime minister David Cameron mooted that British aid to countries be conditional on their decriminalization of homosexuality. The response was rage: in a typical comment, the Tanzanian foreign minister fumed that "We are not ready to allow any rich nation to give us aid based on unacceptable conditions simply because we are poor."[24] African activists reported that there was a significant uptick in homophobic violence following Cameron's statement, and almost all the continent's LGBT organizations and leaders signed a letter condemning an approach that could only make life more difficult for queer Africans—who were, of course, the beneficiaries of aid alongside the rest of their compatriots, and who would, as had already happened in Malawi, be further scapegoated if aid was withdrawn on their account.[25]

What happened in Uganda perhaps best expresses the effect of the threat of such international pressure, and the bind in which Western countries (and some African leaders) found themselves. In a 2010 meeting with the American ambassador, the Ugandan president Yoweri Museveni actually condemned David Bahati's anti-homosexuality bill, calling its harsh penalties "unacceptable" and saying it would be shelved.[26] A leaked State Department memo offers a key clue to why Museveni might have changed his mind four years later and signed the bill into law: "The President twice referred to a recent local political cartoon depicting him on this issue as a puppet of Secretary Clinton [and other Western leaders], and asked international donors to stand down to give him room to deal with the anti-homosexuality legislation his own way."

In the years following this meeting, the sponsors of the Ugandan bill promoted it to murderous effect, David Cameron made his comments on conditional aid, Hillary Clinton made her "gay rights are human rights" speech at the United Nations, and the Obama administration declared the promotion of LGBT rights a foreign policy priority. The U.S., Britain, and other countries threatened sanctions if Uganda passed the anti-homosexuality bill into law. By 2014 Museveni's attitudes had hardened, and—faced with his first serious political opposition in twenty-three years in power—he felt he could not afford further allegations of being a neocolonial stooge. The West's concerted opposition to the bill, he said upon signing it into law, was "an attempt at social imperialism, to impose social values."[27]

By signing it, he was performing a gesture of anti-colonial self-determination against such "imperialism," no matter that the ideas powering the bill had come from the West, too.

THE POLICIES THAT Hillary Clinton announced at the United Nations in December 2011 had an almost immediate effect. American embassies provided much-needed sanctuary and relief funding for persecuted locals, and the U.S. opened its doors to LGBT refugees as never before: even well into the Trump era, after 2016, American missions remained vital refuges for persecuted queer activists in Africa and Asia. But inevitably, this human rights policy became entwined (or at the very least associated) with America's military agenda. In July 2011, even before the Clinton speech, the U.S. embassy in Pakistan decided to host an LGBT Pride event at its Islamabad compound—just two months after Osama bin Laden had been assassinated nearby in an American airstrike on Pakistani sovereign territory. Anti-American locals were quick to capitalize on the connection: "We condemn the American conspiracy to encourage bisexualism in our country," said Mohammad Hussain Mehnati, a leading establishment cleric, at a rally to protest the event.[28] "They have destroyed us physically, imposed the so-called war on terrorism on us and now they have unleashed cultural terrorism on us."

In 2010, President Obama had passed the Don't Ask, Don't Tell Repeal Act, allowing openly gay men and lesbians to serve in the U.S. Armed Forces. By 2013, there was even a Kandahar LGBT Pride event at the U.S. military base in the beleaguered Afghan city, and a Department of Defense promotional video about it. One of the gay American soldiers interviewed said: "I think it's very important that we are here representing the United States of America, and we hope that when we leave here, we have left all positive qualities, and what America is like, and that we are an equal country, which treats all our citizens equally."[29]

Some LGBT activists began to critique the way that homosexuals had become part of the establishment in countries like the U.S. by gaining the rights to marry and serve in the military. One of the implications was that gay people were beginning to be enlisted to buttress—and to justify—nationalism and racism, as had happened in the new right-wing politics of Western Europe exemplified by Pim Fortuyn and Geert Wilders in the Netherlands. This was termed "homonationalism" by the scholar Jasbir Puar.[30] Israel was cited as a prime example, accused of "pinkwashing" its human rights abuses against Palestinians by embracing LGBT rights to brand itself as an oasis of liberal freedom.[31] Indeed, the Israel Defense Forces had welcomed openly LGBT conscripts long before Obama repealed the Don't Ask, Don't Tell policy.

Some activists and scholars questioned the value of a Western identity-based approach to the extension of sexual freedom in parts of the world without the liberal Western tradition that spawned the contemporary LGBT movement, societies that had their own histories and customs for accommodating difference. The most eloquent, if extreme, proponent of this view was the Palestinian academic Joseph Massad, a professor at Columbia University.

In 2002, Massad had published a provocative and influential essay in which he argued that Western human rights activists and tourists alike had disrupted age-old modes of homosexual activity in the Arab world by foisting the "gay" label onto them.[32] This, he maintained, had forced an unspoken but widely accepted practice into the light of day, and demanded that a set of rights be attached to them. Massad pointed the finger at Human Rights Watch and Amnesty International, as well as specifically LGBT-focused groups such as the New York–based International Gay and Lesbian Human Rights Commission; he called this nexus "the Gay International." Their advocacy provoked unnecessary cultural conflict, he wrote, and a new awareness of homosexuality that actually shut down space rather than opened it up, by forcing the fluid sexuality of Arab men into the "Western binary" of "gay" or "straight." Suddenly the customs that provided cover for homosexual activity, such as holding hands in public or washing one another in a *hammam*, become suspect.

Certainly, I found many examples of this dynamic in my travels, from the way holding hands did indeed become suspect in Nigeria after the new 2014 law criminalized any "public show of same sex amorous relationship," to the disappearance of the *goor-jigeen*—an age-old transgender community in Senegal—after the moral panic of 2008.[33] But while Massad's reading is helpful in understanding this complex dynamic, it retreats into a kind of willful nostalgia: like Macky Sall, who expatriated the call for LGBT rights in Senegal ("*you* are asking this from us"[34]) or Cardinal Robert Sarah, who believed that the poor were being "bought,"[35] or the Ukrainian president Leonid

Kravchuk, who in 1999 blamed "foreign movies" for homosexuality in his country, Massad imagined natives thoroughly insulated from global influences before the Gay Internationalists come along, and unable to think—and dream—for themselves.[36]

SOMETIMES, DURING THE YEARS I was researching this book, I closed my eyes and saw a Red army thundering across the African savannah—or the plains of Eastern Europe—led by Vladimir Putin waving a "traditional values" flag, with phalanxes ranged behind him of American right-wing evangelists, Catholic anti-"gender theory" warriors, imams and priests and nativists, and authoritarian leaders fearing democracy. Coming to confront them from the West was a Blue army behind Barack Obama, commanding international human rights organizations, Western development agencies, the international AIDS agencies, globalizing multinational corporations, and LGBT activists. I was in the Blue army, of course.

The image was misguided. It must have been formed, somewhere in my brain, by overexposure to the ideas of Samuel Huntington's *Clash of Civilizations*, so prevalent around the turn of the millennium, but critiqued for their geographic determinism and a monolithic sketching of the world into an increasingly democratic "west," versus a "rest" destined for dictatorship.

The world was more complicated.

In *Globalizing the Culture Wars*, Kapya Kaoma writes about how African clerics became "proxies in a distinctly U.S. conflict," following the great battle in the American Episcopalian Church over the ordination of the openly gay priest Gene Robinson as bishop of New Hampshire in 2003.[37] Kaoma reviews the way American dissidents funded African Anglicans and provided them with anti-gay doctrine, and he cites a researcher who concluded that "what has long been portrayed as the authentic voice of African Anglicanism is, manifestly, not African, and perhaps never has been."

But you could look at it another way.

The Nigerian bishop Peter Akinola commanded a flock of seventeen million, the biggest by far in the Anglican Communion, and at the 1998 Lambeth Conference he led the campaign against the ordination of gay priests and the blessing of same-sex unions, achieving the stunning victory of 526 votes to 70.[38] The Africans had the numbers and they had the doctrine, and it became a matter of pride for them that they were holding the line, no longer the savages but now actually the bulwark against a new barbarian at the gate. Taking up the cudgels against homosexuality "offered African clergy a way to symbolize the inexorable reality," the political scientist Rahul Rao writes, "that power was shifting within the [Anglican] Communion towards the more populous African constituencies."[39] Even if the African churches had become beneficiaries of their American brethren (or perhaps because of it), there was a redemptive energy to the African defense of biblical proscriptions against homosexuality. Whatever people in the West might think, it was, for them, an *African* position.

ONCE, IN WASHINGTON, D.C., in 2013, I heard Kapya Kaoma give a lecture about the impact of the American religious right. He insisted that homophobia was a Western import to his native Africa, brought first by Victorian missionaries in the nineteenth century and then by American evangelists in the twenty-first.

He was challenged by another African present, the Cameroonian activist Joel Nana, who led a continent-wide coalition of LGBT organizations dealing with men's health. Nana, of course, was in the

Blue army, and he spoke frankly of his own personal growth and development while working for the International Gay and Lesbian Human Rights Commission. He wanted to know if he was any more or less "authentic" than the bilious Pastor Martin Ssempa, the leading Ugandan homophobe in the Red army, trained in Texas and a beneficiary of much of the American religious right's largesse, or Pastor Stephen Langa, trained in Canada, the man who brought Scott Lively to Uganda.

Nana worried that if you treated homophobia solely as a Western export, you were viewing Africans once more as the passive receptacles of Western ideas—which was exactly the way the evangelists viewed Africans when they accused them of being corrupted, or bought, by an international gay agenda. "If we truly believe that Africans are human, we should also be able to understand that they can make their own decisions," he later said to me. "These decisions may be influenced by the need to protect or to violate rights, for real or perceived personal or collective good, but they remain African decisions. They are owned and defended. Denying them the agency that allows them to do that is similar to stripping them of their humanity."

4

MICHAEL'S STORY

MBARARA—KAMPALA—NAIROBI—VANCOUVER

Michael Bashaija—Ugandan refugee in Nairobi, high school student, late teens. Pronouns: he/him/his.

Pius—Michael's boyfriend, Ugandan refugee, high school student, late teens. Pronouns: he/him/his.

Robert "Changeable" Mulinde—Michael's "mother," Ugandan refugee, primary school teacher, late thirties. Pronouns: he or she.

Shane Phillips—Michael's American "big bro" and benefactor, from Arizona, casual worker and human rights activist, forties. Pronouns: he/him/his.

1

After my meeting with Michael Bashaija in July 2015 I dropped him on the Ngong Road to get a *matatu* back to Rongai, outside of Nairobi, where he lived in a communal house with twenty other Ugandan LGBT refugees, all of whom had fled across the border to Kenya. I watched him tuck his luxurious braids back into his woolen red beanie and manoeuver his slight frame, rendered even skinnier by his tight green jeans, into the rhythm of the street. He arranged his eloquent features into a blank mask of maleness and disappeared into the rush-hour throng.

If asked a question by someone on the road he would try to mutter something in Swahili, a language he barely spoke; if he answered in English, he would be identified as a foreigner. If there were a policeman, he might be asked to show his papers. And that, he had said to me, "is when the trouble will begin. There's no war in Uganda, so when someone sees that I am asylum seeker here, they know there can only be one reason: *sin!*"

A few hours earlier I had watched Michael pull the beanie off and shake out the braids, parted in a line along the top of his crown so that they fell down the sides of his head and made a heart of his fine-boned face. I had not seen him in a year, and I noted immediately how he was both more feminine and more assertive than the shy eighteen-year-old I had met in Kampala a year previously. There was something in his manner, even in the way he threw his tote bag down in rage and frustration, that told me he had stepped into himself.

Michael had come to meet me straight from the offices of the United Nations High Commissioner for Refugees, where he had needed to get new documentation: his papers had been torn up by Kenyan policemen when he had refused to pay a bribe. At first, he told me, the guards at the UNHCR had mocked him and denied him access: "You Ugandans are bringing sin to Kenya!" Finally he had been granted access, but when his new papers had been issued he had been told he would have to repeat the refugee-eligibility interview he had done a few weeks previously.

This had thrown him into a panic. "They don't believe me, that I'm a real LGBTI," he said as we met, dissolving into tears. "*I know it*. They must think I'm one of the fraudsters. Or maybe they are punishing me because I was part of that protest [against UNHCR]."

I had first met Michael in the Ugandan capital, Kampala, in June 2014, the day before he was to go to court to testify against the man who had entrapped him via Facebook, extorted him, beat him up, and tortured him sexually. The attack had happened the previous February, just after Uganda's president, Yoweri Museveni, had signed the country's Anti-Homosexuality Act into law. Although the death penalty had been withdrawn for what was called "aggravated homosexuality"—having sex with minors or while infected with HIV—life imprisonment remained the mandatory sentence for anyone who "touches another person with the intention of committing the act of homosexuality."[1]

From the very beginning I had been struck by how carefully and thoughtfully Michael spoke, given that English was not his first language and that he had been unschooled for the previous two years. He had told his story dispassionately, as if he were looking at his violated self from far away. But now, in Kenya, he was different, aggrieved and anxious. Without a successful refugee-eligibility interview, he could not move forward: he could not get an Alien Card from the Kenyan authorities, which would give him more protection, and enable him to work and begin the process of applying for resettlement in the United States. "I don't think I can make it here. Let me go back to Uganda to die." It was a teenager's plea, a threat, a cry for help. "It's better than staying here. Nobody cares for me here."

MICHAEL HAD FLED Uganda six months previously, one of about seventy Ugandans claiming asylum on the basis of sexual orientation or gender identity in December 2014, an all-time high. He was registered, housed in a transit center for a few days, and given 12,000 Kenyan shillings ($120). He went off to find a friend he had made contact with, and who had invited him to share a room near the airport.

A week later, on Christmas day, while shopping for the festive meal, Michael was shoved by three men: "Why you acting like a girl?" They threw him to the ground and kicked him. He returned home with bruises and a swollen eye, horrified that no one had intervened to help him. The words of his assailants haunted him, in the way they sliced through his fantasies of the security that asylum would bring: "Museveni chased you from your country, and now you've come here, also to spoil it."

Michael moved to a building in a more central district, where several other refugees lived. A few weeks later, he was arrested in a police raid on the building after neighbors lodged a complaint about a raucous party. He and thirty-four other Ugandans were taken to holding cells at the local police station, where Michael was roughed up by the cops when he was found to have concealed a cell phone with which he was trying to call for help. After twenty-four hours inside he suffered a panic attack and passed out; he was taken to a hospital, and when he was discharged he learned that he and his fellow refugees had all been evicted from their lodgings. With not enough funds in the middle of the month to find a new place to live, the released refugees gathered at the UNHCR's offices but were denied entry. They staged a protest at the compound gates, sleeping there over three nights. When the group engaged in what the UNHCR described as "violent behaviour," the agency felt compelled to call the Kenyan police to disperse them.[2] A Ugandan Catholic priest living in Nairobi named Father Anthony Musaala stepped in. He rented two properties in Rongai and called these "the Ark Communes"; here he gave shelter to Michael and the others.

This is where Michael was living when I traveled to Kenya to meet him in July 2015.

TO GET TO THE ARK COMMUNES, I had to drive twenty kilometers out of Nairobi and through the town of Rongai before turning off at a local bar to bump down a steep dirt track that deposited me at a steel gate, set in a high cinder-block wall. Behind the gate was a large old settler house; there was a netball pitch cleared in the dust (the Ark team apparently competed in local tournaments) and a big old couch on the veranda, leaking its upholstery. I would later be interviewed on this couch for "Ark TV" by a kid named Kenneth who had been a "radio personality" in Kampala before being forced to flee; he would do the job in a snappy navy blazer and pair of retro frames with no lenses, filmed by another communard with a smartphone.

The house had no running water or oven—cooking was done on an open fire in the kitchen—and a few pieces of mismatched furniture scattered about the common areas. A chart of officials was neatly tacked up: the "President" was Father Anthony, the Ark founder; there was also a "Chief Justice" and a "Minister for Ethics and Integrity," a dig at the Ugandan ministry of the same name, responsible for leading the official anti-gay campaign back home. Michael—at nineteen the youngest resident—was "Deputy Minister for Education"; his job was to seek out training opportunities, and he and two others had recently enrolled in a computer course but had dropped out due to lack of funds.

Also posted on the entryway wall was a daily schedule and a set of injunctions: "Be Clean and Orderly!"; "Be Friendly and Hospitable!"; "Be Enterprising!" [twice]; "Be Happy!" A table of "Rules and Regulations" listed the punishments for various infractions: a fine of five hundred Kenyan shillings for not maintaining "self-discipline and presentability at all times"; a fine of having to fetch five jerry cans of water from the village communal well for spending the night in someone else's bed without official permission.

At the time I visited there were around twenty residents, some sharing bedrooms, some in the partitioned double garage or burrowed into outdoor storerooms. A few rooms had signs of more permanent settlement—carefully made curtain-dividers, photos on a mantelpiece, neat racks of clothing—but most reflected the transience of their inhabitants. Michael's room, a pantry off the kitchen, was dark and sparse: there was a mattress on the floor, and a padlocked duffel bag beside it. I had brought provisions, and as Michael's boyfriend Pius supervised a lunch team, the other residents gathered in the communal area to tell me about their lives.

Tony, the laconic matinee-idol director of Ark's dance troupe, had collapsed recently due to the high blood pressure condition he could not afford to treat, but had fled the hospital when the attending doctor realized he was gay and threatened to call the police. Alex was an anxious older man who had been one of the first Ugandans to seek refuge in Kenya, and had endured hell in the Kakuma refugee camp in the desert up on the Ethiopian border: he was despondent because the United States had denied him resettlement on the grounds of credibility. Yasin, an articulate professional in his thirties, was one of the more recent arrivals: he had been forced to leave his place of residence a week previously, when it had been surrounded by a mob who had discovered the residents were homosexuals. The village chief and local police commander had come to the refugees' aid, but it was not possible, of course, to return.

Here, too, in Rongai, the Ark Communes had begun to arouse the suspicions of the neighbors. In response to the terrorist attacks of 2014 and the influx of Somali refugees from the north, the Kenyan government had initiated a program called Usalama Watch: all Kenyans were to become acquainted with their neighbors, and to report anyone they did not know, or found suspicious. Inevitably, this triggered xenophobia, and made life even more difficult for the Ugandan refugees, too. A complaint had been lodged with the authorities in Rongai about these "strangers" living at the house, and the local police had come to investigate. The residents had insisted they were political refugees, as they had been coached to do by the UNHCR, but neither neighbors nor the authorities were convinced.

This dissembling created an almost impossible dilemma. "We are told to be on the down-low and even lie about why we are here," Michael said. "But we're also told we need to integrate into Kenyan society and be enterprising so we can support ourselves. How is it possible to do both?" The group was still smarting from a communication issued by the UNHCR's Nairobi office a few weeks previously: "It is essential for LGBTI persons in Kenya to act in an inconspicuous and discreet manner for their own security … It is therefore of utmost importance that applicants keep a low profile." Michael said that he was trying hard not to "gay it up." But, he said, repeating a maxim that the refugees had taken on as some kind of motto, "Nature obeys no law."

Many felt that being in Kenya put more constraints on them than living in Uganda. Back home, they knew the lay of the land and could negotiate it. "I've changed the way I dress completely," Kenneth told me. "I've cut my hair, I've taken out all my pins [piercings]. In the world I look as if a man. But I will not say I keep a low profile in speaking and movements. It is imbued in me. I've tried, I've really tried, but even when I dress like this, people think me girly."

Did he dress more flamboyantly back home in Kampala? "Of course! Over there, we were much more *swaggerlistic*!"

Michael's mentor at the communal house was in his early forties, a primary school teacher named Robert, known universally as Changeable, fired when his sexuality had been revealed. "Michael is my daughter," Changeable told me. "Since he has come to Nairobi, he is so much more comfortable with himself. He is realizing that he is not just gay, but actually transgender. That is why he gets slapped so often in the streets. For walking girly."

Michael seemed to agree with this assessment, although not, it seemed to me, with much conviction. Anyway, this would have to wait until he was resettled in America—he was dead set on being placed in the U.S.—he told me. For now, he needed to hold his femininity in check if he was going to survive.

Why, then, did he get the braids?

"I did it because, huh! I just felt I needed to be myself. In Uganda there were rules, but here I'm independent. No one can tell me, 'Don't do this, don't dress like that, Michael, don't braid your hair.'"

Michael needed the braids, and he needed the beanie: the former as part of his process of self-actualization and the latter to keep that very process in check, given where he found himself. It would be a difficult balancing act for anyone to maintain, let alone an impetuous nineteen-year-old just discovering his agency in the world. He had left Uganda on a journey toward being himself, after a violent and oppressive adolescence where his very survival was at risk because of who he was. His crossing the border to Kenya was the first step toward this imagined freedom, to the life that he believed awaited him in the United States. And he was living with a group of other people with exactly the same expectations. How, in such a context, do you temper such expectation? How do you gather up your hope, particularly after such abjection, and pile it back into the beanie?

MICHAEL'S LIFE HAD been extremely tough in Uganda. But like most of the other Ugandan refugees I met in Nairobi, he had been drawn to Kenya by what the UNHCR itself would admit was a "pull factor for young Ugandans."[3]

In December 2013, the first twenty-three refugees had presented themselves at the Kakuma refugee camp, in the arid north of the country, once it became clear the Bahati bill was going to be signed into law. Usually, refugee resettlement to a third country took between three and five years, but the UNHCR saw immediately how vulnerable these new refugees were, particularly in an environment such as Kakuma, filled with conservative Muslim Somali and Sudanese refugees. The agency was lobbied intensively by the U.S. State Department, which had now made the protection of LGBT people a foreign policy priority, and so it streamlined the process to an unprecedented six months. By mid-2014, the twenty-three were in the West, mainly in the United States.

The UNHCR had also agreed to give the LGBT refugees at Kakuma their own special encampment right next the police station. But this backfired: the group was immediately rendered more visible and perceived by others to be favored. The attacks on them intensified, and when a second group of Ugandan refugees staged a protest at Kakuma the UNHCR decided to permit them to live in Nairobi, and to give them the financial assistance of six thousand Kenyan shillings (sixty dollars) a month in lieu of the shelter and food they would have received at the camp.

These, then, were the "pull factors": quick resettlement and a monthly stipend. Unsurprisingly, the agency was overwhelmed with applicants, even after the Anti-Homosexuality Act was nullified. A year later, when I visited, there were five hundred Ugandan LGBT asylum seekers registered in Kenya, but the UNHCR estimated that at least a hundred of those were fraudulent. The agency had been alerted by the refugee community itself that a busload of new applicants had been told by their traffickers to play the gay card, and that other applicants were actually still living in Uganda and just popping over the border at the beginning of each month to receive their stipends.

The UNHCR put the brakes on, and reverted to standard procedures. Now hundreds of refugees expecting quick resettlement found themselves stuck in Nairobi, an environment where, as the agency's Moore put it to me when we spoke in late 2015, "The environment for them, in a legal sense, is just the same as in Uganda. And in a social sense it's not so different either. It's just that Kenya has not received as much attention as Uganda. But the barriers are all there, in Kenya, for LGBTI refugees: against local integration, finding employment, accessing livelihood, being safe from violence, enjoying a meaningful life. The reality of this homophobic society makes their situation very difficult indeed."

The Ugandan refugees were quite unlike any other population the agency had dealt with: young, urban, educated, and fully aware of their rights. Unlike abject Somali or Congolese villagers fleeing war, they had left their home country with the clear understanding that these rights had been violated, and the expectation that they would be respected elsewhere. And not least because of the homophobia they encountered in Kenya, they had no intention of staying: "They don't want to be here, they want to be in the West," a Kenyan woman who ran a church-based integration program told me. "And there is this perception that if you learn Swahili and get a job and fit in, then the UNHCR will be less likely to resettle you, since resettlement to a third country is only granted if you can prove you are unsafe in the country that gave you asylum."

And so here they were, these worldly young people mainly from cosmopolitan Kampala, now in a society at least as intolerant as the one they had left, easily identifiable and therefore frequently harassed, intimidated, extorted, and even attacked or arrested. When I came to Nairobi in July 2015 to meet Michael and his fellow refugees, I found a group of mainly young men—there were a handful of lesbians and a few transgender women among them—who were aggrieved, dissatisfied, and seemingly unable and unwilling to integrate into Kenyan society. Even Nairobi's own LGBT community viewed them with suspicion. One Kenyan friend came back from a work trip to Kampala extolling it as "the San Francisco of East Africa" and wondered why Ugandans needed to leave at all; he called them "professional gayfugees," using his country as a stepping stone to the West.

Word was out: Michael and his crew were hustlers, they were trouble.

2

"I will tell you, Mark, my problems began with love."

These were Michael Bashaija's first words to me, when I turned my recorder on in my hotel room in Kampala in June 2014, a year before I would see him again in Nairobi. I was not the first person to whom he had recounted his story, and he understood how to craft it: a British journalist had interviewed him the previous day, and his kidnapping and assault had featured prominently in a Human Rights Watch/Amnesty International report, which is how I had found him in the first place.[4]

At the age of fifteen Michael had begun a relationship with a classmate, in the military barracks in the west of the country where he was raised. The boy got drunk and told his family about the relationship; the family blamed Michael and went to his parents. Michael's father was a career soldier and his mother a preacher: his father sent the military police home to rough him up, and his mother banished him from church. He was forbidden from being in the presence of his siblings in case he contaminated them. His parents stopped providing meals to him and paying his school fees. He left home.

This happened at the height of the government's public campaign to drum up support for the Anti-Homosexuality Act in early 2012. If Michael had been a few years older and his teenage romance discovered a few years earlier, his misdemeanor would probably have been ignored—or, at most, dealt with through a thrashing and a warning. Michael might have been one of the very few to find his way to Kampala and into the city's burgeoning *kuchu* community (*kuchu* is the Luganda word for *queer*, reappropriated by the Ugandan LGBT movement); more likely he would have taken heed of the warning and worked harder to keep his sexuality covert. But Michael had the mixed fortune of being born on the Pink Line: the years of his childhood were, coincidentally, those when public discourse about sexuality spread due both to the AIDS epidemic and the digital revolution, alongside the parallel global dissemination of a Christianity inflected with American-style anti-gay ideology.

Uganda was largely Christian, traditionally divided almost evenly between Catholics and Anglicans, but in the first decades of the twenty-first century, the number of Evangelical Protestants rose dramatically—to 11 percent in 2014. This was in no small part due to the influence of American missionaries: Michael's mother herself had been reborn into an Evangelical church. We can conjecture that even if Mrs. Bashaija knew about the "abomination" of homosexuality from Leviticus 18:22, she probably only became well-versed in it around the time of Michael's birth, in 1996. This was the time when the worldwide Anglican Communion was gearing up for its Lambeth Conference battle over homosexuality, and the issue began to be preached about from pulpits across the continent as the African Anglican church rallied its supporters against the ordination of gay priests and against same-sex marriage.

This new rallying point was especially potent in Uganda because of the singular history of homosexuality and the church here. The Baganda kingdom had been one of the most sophisticated in precolonial Africa; in the 1880s, at the time of colonization, the *kabaka* (king) was a young man named Mwanga, addicted to "the practice of homosexuality," according to the Christian narrative about the conquest of Uganda, and presiding over a court rotten with "abominable vices" and "shameful passions."[5] The *kabaka* was not a convert himself, but at a time when different religions were competing for souls in his kingdom, he maintained a balance of power by retaining both Catholic and Protestant courtiers. When—according to the Christian narrative—some of these men resisted his sexual advances, he executed at least thirty of them, most in one public burning, in March 1886. This led to a coalition of Christians and Muslims who gained the assistance of the British in deposing him in 1888 and, ultimately, to the colonization of Uganda.

In the very act of staking out modern Christian Uganda, then, was the expulsion of the abomination of homosexuality: Mwanga's victims, crusaders against vice, are claimed as martyrs by the church, and the site of their massacre is the country's most hallowed pilgrimage site. And so, of all the African countries, Uganda was particularly predisposed to the wave of political Christianity that was heralded by the battle within the Anglican Church and entrenched by the burgeoning Evangelical movement. As in so many places in the world during these years of the staking of the Pink Line, this radical new form of Christianity began to take root at exactly the same time that a gay subculture developed in the country, giving anxious patriarchs and priests a potent new proselytizing tool.

Due in no small part to the savvy networking of Ugandan activists, the country attained global notoriety as one of the world's worst places to be gay. But my Kenyan friends were right: before the promotion of the anti-homosexuality legislation, it had indeed been home to the most open scene in East Africa. In 2004, a group of activists founded Sexual Minorities Uganda (SMUG), the first such organization on the continent outside of Southern Africa. As with Senegal, this had much to do with the way AIDS was tackled in Uganda: The country, one of Africa's most devastated by the epidemic, had been one of the first to confront the crisis. This meant that organizations like SMUG could access funding for MSM work, and begin to grow institutional roots, at the same time that right-wing Christian organizations were doing the same thing by accessing American PEPFAR funding for "faith-based" initiatives. The clash was inevitable.

As talk about same-sex marriage became louder in the West and the Ugandan movement grew stronger back home, the evangelists lobbied lawmakers to criminalize same-sex marriage through a constitutional amendment: in 2005 the Ugandan parliament voted overwhelmingly to do this. Michael Bashaija was nine at the time and he already knew he was "not like other boys," he told me, and that he "preferred to do girly things." But whereas previously this might have been seen simply as an abnormality, it was now becoming evidence of an abomination.

We can speculate that Michael's parents read the coverage around the constitutional amendment, including detailed descriptions of the dens of vice where such abominations were practiced. The day after the constitutional amendment, the government-owned *New Vision*—the largest newspaper in the country—published an editorial calling on the state to "visit the holes mentioned in the press, spy on the perverts, arrest and prosecute them."[6] Two weeks later, the chairman of a local council in Kampala obliged, with a raid on SMUG's founder, Victor Mukasa. The men confiscated items without a warrant, arrested Mukasa and a friend, and hauled them to the police station where they were roughed up and sexually assaulted.

Mukasa was transgender: assigned female at birth, he had been subject to a horrific exorcism in his church when his "lesbianism" had been exposed. He was fearless and canny and, by the time of this arrest, already plugged in globally. With the help of international organizations he sued the Ugandan state. It took four years for judgment but in 2009 a judge ruled that the arrest of Mukasa had been in breach of the constitution. Mukasa was awarded damages of about seven thousand dollars, but the judgment only spurred the anti-gay evangelists in Uganda to redouble their efforts, aided by their American supporters. It was a few weeks later that Stephen Langa sent out his invitation for the meeting with Scott Lively and the other Americans.

Then in October 2010, just after Michael Bashaija turned fourteen, the Ugandan magazine *Rolling Stone* (no connection to the American one) ran the headline "Hang Them" on its cover, and published the names, photographs, and addresses of one hundred prominent alleged homosexuals.[7] The harassment of those named began almost immediately. Once more, the SMUG activists used Uganda's independent judiciary to seek legal relief; they gained an injunction to prevent any further such publication, and ultimately won a ruling that the publication was in violation of their rights to dignity and privacy. The damages awarded were high enough to shut down *Rolling Stone*, but its editor was unrepentant: "The war against gays will and must continue. We have to protect our children from this dirty homosexual affront," he said.[8]

Three months later, SMUG's director David Kato was murdered in his home. His assailant was caught and convicted, and although the motive was found to be robbery, the heightened public discourse had undoubtedly rendered Kato more vulnerable to violent assault—and his murder further inflamed the anti-gay discourse in the country. Michael Bashaija did not recall any of this, from his youth in a barracks town. But it was around this time, just as he was beginning to understand his attraction to other men, that Ugandan clerics, and perhaps his mother, too, began preaching routinely against the sin of homosexuality.

In February 2012, almost exactly when Michael's relationship with his classmate led to his expulsion from the family home, there was another spike in the media coverage of homosexuality: David Bahati reintroduced his bill in parliament. A few days later, the minister for ethics and integrity Simon Lokodo raided and shut down an LGBT training workshop at a hotel, claiming it to be an "illegal assembly." Lokodo later defended his actions by saying: "You cannot allow terrorists to organize to destroy your country."[9] He accused Westerners of "recruiting people to go out and divulge the ideology of LGBT" in his country, where "the culture, tradition and laws do not support bestiality and lesbianism."

IT WAS IN this toxic environment that Michael Bashaija, age fifteen in 2012, left home and made his way to Kampala where, he reckoned, he might find others like him. This was on the basis of the barest shreds of information from a couple of covert sessions in a local Internet café. A man found him, weeping, at Kampala's central bus station. He took him to the east of the country and gave him a job in a hotel. But after a month Michael was retrenched. He had saved enough now for a smartphone and this mainlined him into the Ugandan capital's gay community. "It was Facebook that saved me, and Facebook that hurt me," he told me.

Through social media Michael found a man who housed him for a couple of weeks, had sex with him, and then chucked him out. Michael found shelter in a mosque for a while until the imam discovered he was a "Christian dog" and turfed him out, too. On the street, disoriented and hungry, he was picked up by a Christian crusade that took him in and put him up at the Destiny Orphanage and Boarding School. At the end of the year, the Destiny pastors took Michael back to his home, where his drunken father confronted them with a machete and the words "Are you the ones who are teaching my son homosexuality?"

Discovering the reason why Michael was on the streets in the first place, Destiny's crusaders decided to put him back there. When my Ugandan researcher, posing as a concerned fellow Christian, contacted the school's head pastor Eve Murgerwa over Facebook, the pastor explained: "We could not be with someone who was a gay person, there was fear that he will spread it among other students." When my researcher suggested that this might have been an "irrational decision," the pastor shot back: "Why would a born-again Christian even think that we did something wrong to let a homosexual go???"

And so, sixteen years old, Michael was homeless again. Through Facebook, he met a series of men who let him down or exploited him, wanting to fuck him or pimp him, until he landed up in the care of an older student activist named Apollo who took him in, in early 2014, and provided something of a haven for him.

Shortly thereafter, just after the passage of the Anti-Homosexuality Act, Michael received a friend request on Facebook, from one "John Doe." Mr. Doe told Michael he had read his story on his timeline and wanted to help put him back in school. He asked Michael to come over so that he could document his story. Michael agreed, because "he had a kind, quite gentle face, and was talking like he was gay." On arrival, he was led into a bedroom where, he told me, he was confronted by "a gay guy, stripped naked on the floor, being kicked and beaten by two other men." Michael turned to flee, but the "kind" man stopped him, threw him to the ground, forced him to strip, and started beating him, too. He was held there for about eight hours: during this time he was told to masturbate with cooking fat mixed with red pepper, he was urinated on, he was burned with hot water, he was tied up, he was kicked and beaten to the point of coughing up blood, and he was coerced into sex with another hostage, a third, older man.

"All the time they were asking me, 'Who made you gay? Why are you gay? Who paid for you to be gay?'" Michael recalled. They took his wallet and his phone, and released him—with heavy threats—when he promised he could get more cash. He managed to contact his friend Apollo, who connected him with a Ugandan organization that provided legal services to the LGBT community. A lawyer accompanied him to the police station to lay charges: here he encountered one of his assailants, who had been identified by another victim. The process of reporting his attack traumatized Michael further, from the way the police officers shouted at the lawyer, "You human rights organizations are helping gays," to the fear of reprisal once his assailant was released on bail. Indeed, about a week later, a group did arrive at Apollo's door: "We will deal with you, we know what you do, we'll hunt you down," they said. Although they did not harm him and Apollo this time, Michael became paranoid that people were following him. With the help of Apollo and others, he enrolled at a boarding school and got out of Kampala, coming back only whenever he needed to testify in court.

3

On December 27, 2014, six months after I met Michael and he testified against his assailant, I received the following Facebook message from him:

> *Hi Mark. I'm sorry I'm disappointing u but for my wellbeing I have to. I flees [sic] to Kenya. Its two weeks now … [a]fter the guys who blackmailed me were after me. Their friend was released hence they were hunting me. I feared for my life. I'm now in Kenya and a registered refugee under UNHCR … I'm now struggling in Nairobi as a refugee. I was beaten up on Christmas by some Kenyan's for walking girly. I do need all*

support as I know u will not let me alone … I love u so much n I'm sorry about school. happy new year

I had been one of those who had helped Michael go to school in Uganda. I had felt compelled to contribute when I heard there was a plan by elders in the community to get him back. I could not but think back to my own coming-of-age difficulties as a gay man, living in financial comfort and not rejected by my family: How could Michael even begin to accept himself in his current situation? I had paid two hundred dollars to enable him to register to complete Form 3 and did a go-around with friends, gathering commitments from others for him to proceed further should he pass the year.

The funds went directly to Michael's boarding school, but while he was there—and particularly when he was on school holiday back in Kampala—he would message me from time to time with pleas of poverty or hunger. My dominion seemed to extend over his personal life, too. At one point, trying to open up a channel of intimacy, he messaged me to ask if he was permitted to have a boyfriend. I tried to be light about it—"You are an adult, Michael, you can do what you like"—before warning him somewhat sanctimoniously to use condoms. By this point he was calling me "big bro" and telling me how much he loved me. But then he would fire a salvo of fury because he was not getting any pocket money. If it did not materialize, he threatened, "I will leave this school! I cannot stay." It was unbearable that "the other students will think I do not have family to look after me."

My reply was harsh: "Michael, you *don't* have family to look after you. They threw you out. That's your reality. I'm so sorry. It's not fair. But that's how it is."

Then he did leave, for Nairobi.

I RESPONDED TO the message he sent informing me of his departure, wishing him luck and telling him that the funds I had found for him were only available for his continuing education. He seemed keen, and spent some time investigating school options in Kenya, but had left all his documentation in Uganda, and so he would need to start again in Form 1 (the equivalent of eighth grade)—an impossibility, given his age. Anyway, he had other more pressing needs, and I found myself releasing funds as a form of emergency relief. To tide him over during a period when the UNHCR stopped paying its financial assistance to refugees as it investigated fraud, I sent him two hundred and fifty dollars. This was meant to be for food and shelter but, having heard that his mother had been in a road accident, he chose to send a large part of it to her: like so many of the rejected queer kids I have met on my travels, he was trying to buy his way back into his family. At this point I stepped away: I put the remainder of the money I had raised for him in the trust of Neela Ghoshal, the Human Rights Watch researcher who had introduced me to him in the first place, and empowered her to make the decisions about it.

When Michael and I met in Nairobi, he told me that he was under terrible pressure to send money home to his ill mother now that he was working in Kenya.

"But you are not working here, Michael," I said. "You are an unemployed asylum seeker with a tiny UNHCR grant. You're not even allowed to work in Kenya yet."

He looked sheepish. "My family think I am here because I have a job." "Why didn't you tell them the truth?"

"Because when I sent my mother that money I didn't want her to know it was gay money."

"What's gay money?"

It was a leading question, and Michael got it immediately. He shot his eyebrows up in a characteristic arch and nodded his head forward, in my direction, by the slightest of degrees.

THE TRUTH IS, my presence in Michael's life gave tinder to the prejudices of people like Michael's father, who shouted, "Go to those people who taught you to be a homosexual for your tuition!" or like Michael's assailants who demanded to know, "Who paid you to be gay?" When the Anglican archbishop of Uganda, Henry Orombi, told a researcher in 2009 that "the activists that are promoting gay relationships have attracted people financially" and that "where a boy needs school fees … and you offer him money[,] temptation is very strong," he was talking about people like me.[10]

It was this very "recruitment" bogeyman that justified the strengthening of anti-homosexuality proscriptions beyond anti-sodomy laws in Uganda. Perhaps it was easier for many "traditional Christian" Africans to understand homosexuality as a material relationship than to accept it as natural, and somewhat inexplicable, human behavior—or as an offense against God. If I am gay because of my desire, then the world no longer makes sense: what becomes of all I have learned in church about sin, and what will happen to my family's bloodlines and wealth?[11] But if I am gay because I am needy, or because I am greedy, it is somehow understandable.

As with Aunty's female identity, Michael's homosexuality was manifestly not a strategy for getting out of poverty. But as with Aunty, it could be said that his assumption of an LGBTI identity—which is what he and all the other refugees called themselves—was connected to the capital this label carried in the new global economy, where the wealthy West valued such identities: they were deserving of our help, or at the very least our solidarity.

When Michael found himself orphaned, the LGBTI ticket became his surest means of survival. But even if the initial connections he made on Facebook were transactive, they were also emotional. Over time and over space, from the molly houses of London to the voguing houses of Harlem or the third-gender *hijra* houses of Mumbai, there has been a constant to communities of sexual and gender outlaws: alternate families form, intergenerationally, and bonds are cemented by the way people become "mothers" and "daughters," or "brothers" and "sisters."

When Changeable claimed Michael as his "daughter," in Nairobi's refugee community, he was taking on a responsibility, but also laying claim to a relationship that he hoped would sustain him, emotionally and materially, in the absence of the family that had rejected him. Likewise, when Michael called me "big bro" and told me he loved me, it might have been the expedient deployment of affection, but it was also a hankering for the family that had been lost to him: with, of course, this family's support, emotional as well as material.

In the digital era, where these new families are virtual as well as physical, and where social media allows for a dizzy fast-tracking of intimacy, it was inevitable that Michael would acquire an American "father," too: his name was Shane Phillips and he lived in Phoenix, Arizona.

Phillips was a gay man in his late forties, a devout Christian, who told me his story in a Skype conversation in September 2015. He had been bothered by the Evangelical right wing's role in Uganda since hearing about it in 2009, and had felt compelled to show Africans a different face of Christianity. An itinerant construction worker and pizza-delivery man, he set up an organization called One World Voice, the goal of which, he told me, was "to save more lives than anyone has on the planet, because nobody tries in the world anymore." He wanted to set up a "safe space" for resettled refugees in Phoenix. He offered himself as Michael's "anchor host" in the United States should he be resettled there, and his dream, he told me, was for Michael to be the center's first resident.

Phillips told me that he was increasingly horrified by the stories he was reading about Uganda, and the prospects of what he called, on his website, an imminent "genocide" against gays in the country. He raised five hundred dollars from a local pastor "to get a few people out," and began connecting with Ugandan networks on Facebook: "I was delivering pizzas for Papa Joe's at the time. Every bit of extra money I made went towards getting people out of Kampala."

Immediately after Museveni signed the Anti-Homosexuality Act into law in February 2014, Phillips was online, looking for people to help. He found Charles, a man Michael was staying with at the time. Phillips sent enough money to get both men to Nairobi to apply for asylum, but when Charles stole the money and left Michael in the lurch, Phillips and Michael began messaging each other online. "When Michael told me his story," Phillips told me, "I said to him, 'I promise you I'll be a father to you for the rest of your life, no matter what it takes. I will never leave your side.'" Michael was one of three young men with whom Philips forged such a bond. And indeed, Michael did talk about Phillips as a lifesaver. As I listened to both their accounts, I heard the strains of many father-son relationships, in the guilt trips and manipulations, but Phillips was true to his word: they messaged almost daily, and had regular audio conversations. They met, finally, when Phillips visited Africa for the first time in February 2015, and spent a few days in Nairobi: both men wept, and in the photographs posted online, Phillips—bald and bulky and full of expansive American bonhomie—towers over his beaming, slender ward.

Phillips's material contributions to Michael's welfare were small: he was overextended already with the support he gave to others and he was not a man of means. But when Michael began messaging him in early December 2014 with increasingly panicky messages, stories of nightmares, and threats of suicide, Phillips felt compelled to act. "It was clear that he had to get out," Phillips told me. "I sent him the funds for a bus fare and told him to get to Nairobi."

Phillips had been inspired, in his newfound activism, by the solidarity work of other Americans, primarily the activist and blogger Melanie Nathan, who launched a program called Rescue Fund to Help LGBT People Escape Africa.[12] Nathan offered "Ultimate Savior" status to donors who gave over three thousand dollars, "Elie Wiesel Special Coins" (she was inspired by the solidarity of Jews toward Holocaust survivors and Soviet refuseniks) to those who donated enough for an airplane ticket, and "Nelson Mandela Coins" (she was South Africa–born) to those who donated enough for a passport. Her objective was "to help persecuted LGBT Africans escape from their countries, as well as supporting safe housing, and quests for asylum."

Nathan received much recognition for her efforts. But her approach—and by implication Phillips's, too—had its staunch critics. The South African activist Melanie Judge wrote in *The Guardian*: "Promoting an 'escape' from Africa to 'greener US pastures,' without simultaneously addressing the underlying conditions that force this migration, is dangerous and opportunistic."[13] Such interventions, Judge said, were "at best palliative and patronising [and] at worst they reinforce the victimhood of Africans and the saviour status of westerners. This is part of the logic that keeps the 'homosexuality is un-African' discourse in play."

Such initiatives were also slammed by some of the leaders of the Ugandan LGBT movement who felt that they created precisely the kind of situation Michael found himself in, stranded in Nairobi. But when I put this to Phillips, he countered with emotion that every person he had helped personally—he estimated there were about forty—had been in a "life and death" situation, and suicidal.

Richard Lusimbo, a SMUG leader who had arranged a small grant for Michael in Uganda told me he was "shocked" when he heard about Michael's departure. "He had, of course, been thrown out of home, and he was the victim of this terrible assault, but everything had seemed to be working since then. The police had found his attacker and the courts had prosecuted him. The community had rallied around [Michael], he was back in school. His story seemed to be moving towards a positive resolution, and we need those stories, to balance out the 'Worst Country in the World for Gays' stereotype."

Why, I asked Michael, did he leave?

He confirmed that Shane Phillips had counseled him to do so, but he insisted that he really did have no other option. Even if he went back to boarding school, where he was sponsored, he would have to look after himself for six weeks before it opened again. He was eighteen, and without any work or any marketable skills, and could not countenance sex work. Apollo was demanding a cut of his SMUG grant, and they had fallen out. Despite his relief funding, he had nowhere stable to stay and, to exacerbate his insecurity, he had heard that his assailant had been released from jail: "I felt it was only a matter of time before they would come and get me."

4

On my last day in Nairobi, in June 2015, I went to watch Michael perform with the Ark dance troupe at a club in the Ngong foothills; the kind of place people with a little money to spare might drive out to for a drink and a barbecue lunch, or a swim, on the weekend. Brightly painted in blues and yellows with exclamatory Swahili slogans on the walls, it consisted of a series of open thatched pavilions set around a huge, sparkling blue pool. It was not far from the Ark Communes, and a group of the Ugandans had become friendly with the owner. They had been rehearsing their troupe to participate in a dance competition on World Refugee Day (they would win), and they proposed to the club's owner that they provide entertainment on Sunday afternoons. The troupe raised funds for costumes, and rehearsed diligently: they were a huge success, and the club paid them fifteen thousand Kenyan shillings (a hundred fifty dollars) a gig.

Michael was one of the dancers—in the "contemporary" rather than the "traditional" category, he told me. He, like all the others, was passionate about the project: "It gives us a chance to express ourselves, as Ugandans and as LGBTIs. To be proud of being Ugandans, too!" It also created a space where they could connect with local Kenyans rather than living in fear. The way they could express themselves "as LGBTIs" was by using the cover of dance to "gay it up a bit"; and, in the traditional dances, to make space for those members who were girly to play the female roles, on the pretext that they were an all-male troupe.

I noticed, however, that as the Ugandans arrived at the club, there were several women, too. Sockie, the group's "public relations officer," explained to me that the club owners had not invited them for several weeks: in fact, they were performing for free this afternoon, just so they could show me what they did. Sockie worried that the owner—or the patrons—might have begun to suspect the troupe was gay: for this reason, they had decided to corral a group of female Ugandan refugees to join them, as cover.

Sockie was MC. "Representing!" he shouted into a microphone from a DJ box, his sunglasses glued to the back of his head. "Rep-REEEE-SENTING!!!!!!" He pumped the gerund along with the beat a few more times before he finally came to its object: "Rep-re-sen-ting UUUUUUUUUGan-da!" and the dancers emerged in a line, led by Eddie, the hunky lead whose ability to transform the traditional

Baganda hip-swing into a rapidfire twerk stole the show. The men were bare-chested, with cinched traditional skirts hitched high up the thigh; the three women were decidedly more modest.

The program ran through traditional dances from across the country, and threw in some stirring gospel numbers, too. The crowd was thin that afternoon, just a handful of punters who giggled occasionally and applauded politely, seemingly enjoying themselves. No matter: the Ugandans had brought their own home crowd, and each dance was enthusiastically documented by a battery of smartphones: vlogs would be all over social media that evening. The troupe was loving it, and so was I: I felt the rain of relief after so many long, dry days of complaint.

The troupe's showstopper was a song from the north of Uganda, in which a prospective groom bargains a bride-price with his betrothed's family. The strapping Eddie played the groom, of course, mugging burlesque; Michael's boyfriend Pius was the bride's father, his lanky charm sheathed in a long robe. One of the women played the bride, and another her mother. Both women were exceptionally—and no doubt accurately—diffident in their roles, and I wondered, with a giggle, whether the guys had restrained themselves similarly when they played these female parts, before they had felt compelled to bring these shy beards into the show.

In another song, a mother counsels her betrothed daughter about the pleasures of parenthood. There was something achingly poignant about the satisfaction these queer outsiders took in performing such familymaking rituals, given the way that most of them had been cast out of their own.

Michael had participated in these traditional dances, his braids held in check by the knitted red beanie. His expression was more earnest, more interior, than most of the others, and he chose to keep his T-shirt on. He reemerged, during the costume change, in his skinny green jeans, the beanie still in place, to dance the "contemporary music" interludes, either alone or with one other guy. His moves seemed carefully planned at first, and were striking in the way they fused a macho hip-hop staccato style with more feminine swirls. As the speakers pumped hectic bass into the hills, Michael closed his eyes and allowed himself to be shaped by the beat. His movements became less structured and more fluid. The earnest expression he had worn in the traditional dances released itself into a beatific smile.

A FEW WEEKS LATER, Michael left the Ark Communes house because it was beginning to feel unsafe. Soon after, the remaining residents called the UNHCR to help evacuate them when they were faced with the imminent threat of attack by a mob. The agency put them up in a hotel for four days until they could find alternate accommodation, and advised them to live in smaller and less conspicuous groups. Ark collapsed amid the resettlement of its older and more responsible members.

Several of the guys I had met in Nairobi began messaging me from their new homes: Alex from Amsterdam, Roy from Columbus, Changeable from Philadelphia. But things became more insecure in Nairobi for those not yet resettled. At the end of 2015, the UNHCR announced that it would be stopping its monthly stipend to the LGBT refugees and replacing the funds with an enterprise development scheme, more sustainable long-term but far less dependable. Some made a go of it, but they were the minority: others simply threw up their hands and returned to Uganda, became increasingly dependent on sex-work, or even relinquished themselves to the Kakuma refugee camp. Michael and a friend submitted a plan for a street-food stall but by the end of 2016 nothing had come of it. Anyway, Michael had proven more adept at another form of entrepreneurship: he survived through the network he had developed, of individual benefactors like Shane Phillips, and another in the Netherlands, whom he had also met online. This was not much but it kept him alive, and he was generous with what they gave him, supporting others, too.

In September 2016, Michael finally had his refugee-eligibility interview, and was given formal asylum status in Kenya. He went for his resettlement interview, and was told that he was being recommended for Canada: with its social services, this was a better option than the U.S., given his youth and vulnerability. Perhaps, too, the UNHCR's resettlement officers were reading the winds of the 2016 U.S. presidential campaign correctly, and predicting the radical change in policy toward migrants and refugees under Donald Trump.

Michael's Facebook posts became feistier, even joyous, and he appeared like any cocky teenager, showing off a new shirt or a new head of short dreads, or just celebrating the pleasure of being out with his bae on a Saturday night. Still, his life remained extremely unpredictable. When he came down with pneumonia in November 2016, he was admitted to the Nairobi Women's Hospital on the UNHCR's instructions. But for reasons not clear, the agency refused to pay the bill of two thousand dollars when it was time to release him, and the hospital detained him. This meant he missed his resettlement interview at the Canadian embassy. Finally, through the intervention once more of Human Rights Watch's Neela Ghoshal, who watched over Michael like a guardian angel, the UNHCR settled the bill. But by the end of the year—the second anniversary of his flight to Kenya—he was again in despair: he was very ill. It turned out he had tuberculosis, and would not be permitted to resettle until it was cleared. It would take until 2018 for his resettlement papers to be signed: he would be going to Vancouver.

ON SEPTEMBER 9, 2018, Michael flew from Nairobi to his new home in Canada, via Amsterdam. Wearing a bright red hoodie, he documented the journey on social media, raising his fingers to the camera in selfies that projected bemusement and anxiety. "Thanks to everyone," he wrote to his "Kenyan friends and family": "I wish to see you again."[14]

"Ive arrived safely," Michael posted from the arrivals hall in Vancouver the following day.[15] He was given temporary accommodation at the Welcome Centre of the Immigrant Services Society of British Columbia and assigned a caseworker. He attended an orientation, went for checkups at the in-house clinic, and was helped to set up a bank account, into which $2,200 (Canadian) was deposited. He would be given $1,000 a month for a year, to help him on his way, divided into benefits for food, shelter, communication, and transportation. There was also a clothing allowance of $550, particularly for winter wear.

Michael's Facebook posts in his first few weeks in his new home suggested the random and somewhat alienated life upon arrival in a place of promise, if not—yet—of ease: a close-up of a pizza slice ("feeling the meal"); a photograph in a mall with bags ("Shopping"); a selfie lighting up and getting stoned ("Beautiful BC"); videos of an Evangelical preacher in a hall; an underground club featuring a teen punk band; a karaoke evening; and—was it possible?—a Beyoncé concert.[16] There were also several photographs of slips showing that rent had been paid on properties in Nairobi: he devoted much of his time to helping other refugees back in Africa, and promoted his Michael Bashaija Foundation online. He had left several people behind in the room he had rented in Nairobi, and he sent them between thirty and fifty dollars of his own funds every month, he told me when we spoke in January 2019.

The messages Michael reposted from other Ugandans still stuck in Kenya suggested that life was not getting easier, not least because the world had turned its gaze away from Uganda and its LGBT problems and the Trump administration had slowed down the resettlement of refugees in the U.S. And in May 2019, a well-argued case brought by Kenyan activists to decriminalize homosexuality was rejected by the high court, in a judgment that claimed, astonishingly, it saw no evidence of discrimination—and that decriminalization itself would be unconstitutional, as it would lead to "same-sex persons living together as couples," in "direct conflict" with the constitution's stipulation that marriage was between a man and a woman.[17]

Across the world from this all, Michael's first months in Vancouver had clearly been tough, and he was somber and circumspect. Some misunderstanding over a cell-phone contract had left him in debt already and without a phone; his caseworker seemed to have abandoned him; the LGBTQ refugee organization with whom I had put him in touch seemed flaky and unresponsive; his first landlord had asked him to leave because the rent had been late due to a delay from the resettlement agency; his second landlord was nice—a black gay man he had met on Grindr—but he had no privacy, in a city called Surrey some distance from Vancouver. He had met other Ugandan LGBT refugees, and spent Christmas with them, but did not see much of them: distances were great and people busy.

"I have anxiety issues," he told me. "Everyone I try to talk to is avoiding me." He had gone to a youth meeting at Qmunity, Vancouver's LGBTQ community center, but the others attendees had shied away when he tried to strike up a conversation; "Even on the train, people move away from me. So I'm keeping to myself. I'm scared talking to people. The ones I do talk to are just pushing me away." His link to the outside world was Grindr, not the most affirming of environments.

He did make two friends through Grindr: a Chinese Canadian, and a Nigerian one. The former helped him find a stacking job in a drugstore—he quit when he moved to Surrey—and the latter took him to church, where Michael enthusiastically joined the choir. But he only lasted a couple of Sundays. "That pastor does no preaching without speaking ill of LGBTI people and how they ruin the world. I could not sit there." He felt this was for security reasons as much as anything: "You know I am girly, Mark. What if they suspected?"

In the grim trough between Christmas and New Year Michael found a Facebook post for pastoral counseling. He e-mailed up a flare for help. One Jim Jardine responded, from the Port Kells Church, and when Michael said it could not wait until the new year, the pastor came to see him immediately. Although it was clear to Michael from the visit that the counseling would take the form of getting him to renounce his homosexuality, "I kept it going," he told me when we spoke a few weeks later. "He promised me a job, he said he would help with accommodation, I felt desperate."

Following some Canadian provinces, the city of Vancouver had just tabled a bylaw prohibiting businesses from providing conversion therapy. Surrey was a different city, though, and Pastor Jim might argue he was not running a business. Still, what transpired was an egregious replay of the abuse Michael had experienced from Evangelical Christians when he first fled to Kampala. I have a record of all their online communication: after receiving several messages, prayers, and scriptural readings about "sexual immorality" from Jardine, Michael felt he could not proceed. "I'm glad that you've tried to help," he wrote to the pastor, "but I can't betray myself. I'm gay and that won't change. I'm sorry."

The pastor fought back: "Well that's simply not true Michael. You were taken advantage of. It is important that you become filled again with the Holy Spirit … Trust me bro I almost lost it myself. If you want freedom I can help you through … [but] if you love the sin and the shame there is very little I can do for you."

When that did not work the pastor upped his game: "So I guess you are not interested in my friend's job. No problem. Where will you live my friend?"

"I am sorry," Michael wrote back. "I am not going to change so I don't want a friend bind [bent] on changing me. I am so in love with my nature until God will judge me. I don't want to be straight."

And so Pastor Jim dumped him, adding that he would always be there for Michael if he changed his mind: "My heart is for anyone caught as a slave to find freedom in God's kingdom."

AT AROUND THE SAME TIME, Michael noticed that a stranger on Facebook was liking all his Facebook posts. Once more desperate for a connection, he made contact, since the liker seemed to be of the same age, and was from Vancouver. They chatted for a while and traded a couple of links, and then the kid said, seemingly unprovoked, "Stop talking to me."

"Ok sorry," wrote Michael. "Thought you wanted to talk. Have a great evening."

"Get the fuck out of my country you nut," came the response.

For the first time in his life, Michael encountered a new phenomenon, and he started using a new word: *racist*. His Chinese friend from Grindr "turned out not to be such a friend. He had these racist ideas. In his mentality, it was as if black people are pets, poor things, to do what you like [with]."

I was struck—and saddened—by Michael's stoicism. It seemed to me that his current situation, six months in to the place that was meant to be his sanctuary, had exacerbated rather than ameliorated his anxieties, tilting them into the direction of paranoia. But there was none of the old rage, none of that indignation. I felt awkward about pushing him to talk about his new life—I could tell he was holding it together by a thread—and so I let him take the lead. "It's not what I expected, Mark," he volunteered in one conversation: "I thought people would be welcoming. They seem to be welcoming, but they push you away indirectly. I thought people were going to be all happiness." He paused. "But it's okay. It's okay, it's okay. Really, it's okay."

We spoke once or twice in the following months, and I followed him online. He told me he had a job working as a busboy in a famous seafood restaurant at the Vancouver Marina. By mid-2019 he was posting exuberant selfies, gesturing over the skyline from a high-rise condo or sitting at a café table looking smart and worldly in a collared shirt and thin black tie. In one image, he crouched on a war memorial statue in imitation of the bronze soldier behind him, pointing a gun at the future.

THE PINK LINE THROUGH TIME AND SPACE

"WE ARE SORRY TO SEE THAT YOU [in the West] live the way you live. But we keep quiet about it."[1]

The Ugandan president Yoweri Museveni said these words to the international media when he signed the country's Anti-Homosexuality Act into law in 2014. It was a perspective significantly different from the "homosexuality is alien" dogma of other African leaders, such as Zimbabwe's Robert Mugabe, who understood homosexuality as a Western import, or even those of Uganda's own sponsors of the bill, such as David Bahati. Museveni, rather, was drawing a line between the Western way, where sexuality became part of a public identity, and thus deserving of recognition and rights, and the African way, where it remained private. He was right in his basic premise: while homosexuality is an inherent component of human behavior across time and cultures, the notion of gay identity or LGBT rights comes from the West, as a result of a very particular social, political, and economic history.

This context frames the Pink Line, which was drawn through space as well as through time. The line through space could be seen as a geographical border: between those parts of the world that had come to the point of accepting the existence (and equality) of people who deviated from sexual or gender norms, and those parts of the world that continued to deny it. The line through time could be seen as a progression of eras, from an oppressive past to an egalitarian future. It would be more accurate, though, to understand the Pink Line—in space as well as in time—as a border between different knowledge systems: the first understood sexuality as something you *did*, wrong or right ("I sleep with men," "I sleep with women") and the second came to understand it as something you *were*, a mark of identity: "I am gay"; "I am straight".

From the late nineteenth century onward, people—first in Europe and then worldwide—took on this second understanding, assuming sexual and gender identities that were both social and political; initially as *urning* or *shwul* (in Germany) and then as queer, homo, gay, lesbian, transgender, and queer again, or now LGBTI, as Tiwonge Chimbalanga and Michael Bashaija would come to call themselves. By the twenty-first century, words were being coined in some parts of the world to signify these new identities, and to name their bearers as something other than perverts or deviants: *mithli* in Arabic, *tongzhi* in Chinese. In other places, age-old third-gender identities—such as *hijra* in India or *'yan daudu* in Nigeria—began to shift meaning, or status, as they came into contact with the newer political identities of transgender or gay.

ALL SOCIETIES HAVE, of course, their ways of understanding sex and sexuality, gender and gender identity. The European way—which provided the template for what would later be understood as LGBT—had its roots in the eighteenth century, when industrialization and urbanization were reshaping society and modern nation-states began to develop.

The great French theorist of sexuality Michel Foucault has shown how, as a function of this modernity, there was the emergence of "a political, economic, and technical incitement to talk about sex."[2] This was largely because governments began to understand that they were no longer simply ruling subjects, but managing populations. The new understanding required an engagement with birth and death rates, with issues like marriage, fertility, and contraception, and hence with a discussion about sex and sexuality. By the nineteenth century, the study of sex had become a reputable scientific endeavor. From Charles Darwin to Sigmund Freud, scientists explored sex and codified it. The actual words *homosexual* and *heterosexual* were coined by an Austro-Hungarian journalist named Károly Mária Kertbeny, in 1869, in an attempt to find scientific language to describe people attracted to the same sex—as he was. When Richard von Krafft-Ebing published his groundbreaking *Psychopathia Sexualis* in 1886, he imported these terms into the lexicon of science.

Of course, there already existed religious codes for sexual behavior, drawn from the Judeo-Christian scriptures; these had been the basis for European law. But now new binaries were developed to stand alongside—or even to challenge—the religious division of human behavior into "virtue" and "sin." Sexual behavior was now apportioned scientifically into that which was normal and that which was abnormal; that which was public and that which was private; that which was healthy and that which was pathological. Although it might not seem so from a twenty-first-century perspective, this was a huge step forward toward the rights later claimed: homosexuals were to be helped and healed or at the very least *studied*, rather than jailed or demonized or ignored. They came into the light in an entirely new way—and even found a measure of public recognition and qualified acceptance, particularly in Germany.

Much earlier, the French Revolution had established the principle that non-procreative sex between consenting adults was legal, and this was adopted into the Napoleonic Code, which formed the basis for the law of much of Southern Europe and Latin America. But sodomy—sometimes defined as "non-procreative sex"—remained illegal in most of Northern Europe, including Germany, and in 1897 the sexologist Magnus Hirschfeld founded a visionary proto–human rights movement to fight Paragraph 175 of the German penal code. Hirschfeld's Scientific Humanitarian Committee failed to change the law: homosexual acts between consenting adults would be illegal in West Germany until 1969. But Hirschfeld's campaigning did manage to introduce into the public domain the notion that homosexuality was a natural variance rather than an illness or a sin. A homosexual culture thrived in Berlin until the Nazi clampdown of the 1930s, largely due to this activism, and to the policies of a progressive police chief.

Hirschfeld oversaw the first rudimentary sex-change surgeries and lobbied successfully for "transvestites" (he coined the term; *transsexual* and *transgender* would come later) to have official identity cards permitting them to present as the other gender. Thirty years previously, a Bavarian lawyer named Karl Heinrich Ulrichs had coined the word *urning—uranian*—to describe a female soul within a male body, often understood to be so because of his attraction to other males. There was not the distinction that would later develop between gay and transgender: although he would come to change his views, Hirschfeld, too, initially understood homosexuals to be a "third sex."

Beginning in Germany in the late nineteenth century, then, "homosexuality" and "transvestitism" were fixed into a public identity and politicized in a process that spooled out across the Western world through the course of the twentieth century, culminating in the gay rights movements of the 1970s. With such an identity marker you could not only form bonds with others like you, but you could also claim rights on this basis: if enough of you banded together, you could even wield political power, in the way that other minorities and special interest groups already did, particularly in the United States.

There was a dark flip side to this dynamic, too, one that played its own role in the formation of sexual and gender identity as we understand it today. Once the notion of a homosexual identity entered the public domain, the accusation of homosexuality—sinful in Christian Europe—could be martialed to fight other battles. In a precursor to the way queer people would be targeted in some parts of the world in the twenty-first century, there were a series of public exposés of alleged homosexuals in late-nineteenth-century Germany. In the most sensational of these, a nobleman named Philipp von Eulenburg was "outed" by left-wing journalists to discredit his close friend (and possible lover) Kaiser Wilhelm. Publicity of the subsequent trial did more than even Hirschfeld's efforts to popularize the notion of an innate homosexual identity, even if not in the way the sexologist might have intended.

And then, of course, there was the catastrophe of the Third Reich, which played its perverse role, too, in the formation of a modern political gay identity. Once the Nazis came to power in 1933, the very first book burnings were of Hirschfeld's library; Hitler branded him "the most dangerous Jew in Germany."[3] A year later, the Nazi leader Ernst Röhm was assassinated along with his homosexual coterie and many others, in "the Night of the Long Knives." Heinrich Himmler had masked a power struggle by claiming the moral cleansing of the party. The purge marked the beginning of the Nazi persecution of homosexuals as a group: thousands were forced to wear the inverted pink triangle, and were rounded up and sent to concentration camps, where around fifteen thousand would die.

It was for good reason that the pink triangle later became the symbol of the gay movement: if you were oppressed because you were a member of a minority, you could claim restitutive rights on the same basis. After World War II, the modern human rights regime was codified in the 1948 Universal Declaration of Human Rights, and the work of the movement from then on was to ensure that these rights applied to those discriminated against on the basis of their sexual orientation or—later—of their gender identity.

The first modern gay rights organization, the Dutch COC (Culture and Recreation Center), was established in Amsterdam in 1946. In the decades following, certain cities in the West became the fulcra of this movement, which sometimes emerged out of violent protest, as with Stonewall in New York City in 1969. From Amsterdam and London through New York City and San Francisco, to Mexico City and Rio de Janeiro, Pink Lines also came to describe urban peripheries. They came to divide the city from the countryside more than they did one country—or era—from another.

BY THE TWENTY-FIRST century there were queer communities in Istanbul and Beijing, in Moscow and Mumbai, at least as substantial, relatively, as those in the cities of Western Europe or the Americas. Across the world, even in countries that were hostile to LGBT rights (like Russia or Egypt) or indifferent to them (like China or Turkey), there was the unprecedented growth of urban gay populations in the first decades of the twenty-first century as millions of young people flocked to the world's booming megacities, particularly in rapidly industrializing Asia. What was happening in these cities mirrored a process that the historian John D'Emilio described in his groundbreaking 1983 essay "Capitalism and Gay Identity."[4]

D'Emilio provides a key understanding, alongside Foucault, as to how modern gay identity was forged in Europe through the Industrial Revolution. As people moved out of the countryside and into the city to find work, they began to practice "personal autonomy": they were no longer bound in the same way to family and fealty but were now individual workers, valued as much for their productivity as their reproductivity. And they were away from home. They earned the space—literally as well as figuratively—to assert their rights to privacy and to choice. In the immigrant and peripatetic New World the effect was even more intense: young people, far away or even across the oceans from their families, experienced an unprecedented amount of personal freedom in cities such as New York and San Francisco.

In her book *Transgender History*, Susan Stryker uses D'Emilio's theory to imagine what the same forces of capitalism and urbanization might have meant specifically for lesbians (for whom personal autonomy was harder to win but more significant, given their obligations to marry, bear children, and look after elders) and for gender-variant people: if you were assigned female at birth but could successfully pass as male, you "had greater opportunities to travel and find work "; if you were assigned male at birth but felt yourself to be a woman, you had "greater opportunities," too, to realize independence, in the faraway cities where you could reinvent yourself.[5]

In the twenty-first century, a version of the dynamics described by D'Emilio and Stryker was happening in rapidly urbanizing societies across the world. It was boosted this time around by the Digital Revolution, which disseminated information and brought people together as never before. And, of course, by the kind of consumer culture that made "gay" a global brand, from hook-up sites to fashion styles to music and clubs and even drugs.

Young men partied in their thousands at gay clubs in Moscow and St. Petersburg every weekend, for example, even at the height of Russia's "gay propaganda" clampdown—although they had to be discreet, or undercover, almost everywhere else in these cities. On that 2013 Russian television program *Play Actors*, the cultural journalist Elena Yampolskaya said that "when people come to Moscow from provincial cities, they would act as real men at first but then, several years later, you see something created by stylists."[6] This afforded her a punch line: "Gays are created by stylists, not by Mom and Dad."

The "stylist," of course, was the city itself: a place where you could slip out of the grasp of your clan and find your own way. In Indian cities, new workers in the call centers or tech industries found themselves away from home for the first time, working night shifts and sharing accommodation with other young people, able to explore their sexuality or gender identity away from the prying eyes of family, and to stave off arranged marriage for a little while longer. Cities were also places to which you could flee—for anonymity or even sanctuary. By 2011, runaway brides had become such a problem in the huge new industrial hub Gurgaon that a court decided to make the precedent of accepting the marriage of a lesbian couple as a way of protecting them legally from the dangers of honor killings from their respective families. Armed with this judgment attained in the city, the couple later returned to their rural district, where—they later reported—they found acceptance from their families.

Becoming a breadwinner in the city brought you some independence, and also some status and space: through remittances home you could parlay your earnings into respect and acceptance. But being a breadwinner carried obligations, too—and, compelling though John D'Emilio's ideas are, they cannot capture the complexity of non-Western societies in the twenty-first century, as queer people struggle to balance family commitments with newly acquired urban notions of personal autonomy. China offers a striking example. By the second decade of the century, Blued, the largest gay app on the planet, had *forty million* users, many able to hook up and form communities or couples because they were urban migrants living without their families. Still, because they were products of China's one-child policy and obliged to keep the family line going, a large number of them were also signing on to apps that specialized in gay *xinghun*, or marriages of convenience, so that a grandchild could be presented during the annual trek home to the countryside. The largest of the *xinghun* web-sites, Chinagayles.com, had over four hundred thousand users in 2018, and claimed to have matched over fifty thousand couples.

And while urbanization opened up space for upwardly mobile queer people, it sometimes had a negative effect on poorer ones. Sandeep Namwali, an Indonesian activist and medical doctor, explained to me how this happened in his native Jakarta, in the years following the Suharto dictatorship in the early twenty-first century: "urbanization and gentrification intertwined with Islamic modernity in a project to cleanse the cities," he said, describing a project that had both moral and material agendas. Third-gender *waria* had been part of the city's life for decades: they earned their livings on the street through sex work and busking, but now vagrancy laws were being used to clear them out, and—particularly after a 2016 moral panic—they lost much of their space, and thus their ability to earn a living. Those who could afford to went online; the rest became increasingly destitute.

IN OTHER PARTS of the world, city governments sponsored and sometimes even ran Pride events. This was true for Sydney's Mardi Gras, as well as—controversially—Tel Aviv Pride, which the city itself organized, with national government funding, as a way of encouraging "pink" tourism, and promoting Israel as an oasis of tolerance in a hostile part of the world. The Mexico City government ran that city's Pride, too: I was struck, when I attended in July 2016, by the way the parade's focal point, the statue of the Ángel de la Independencia, was draped with official bunting declaring, *Ciudad de Diversidad*, City of Diversity.

With over half a million people, Mexico City's Pride was the third largest in the world, after São Paolo and Rio de Janeiro in Brazil. It extended for miles along the Paseo de la Reforma, rolling out according to the standard grammar of these processions the world over: first the activist groups and community organizations chanting slogans, then the corporate-affinity groups with cleverly branded logos, then the party trucks belonging to the nightclubs and bars, pumping bass into the morning as go-go boys and drag queens threw condoms to the crowds. There were, as everywhere, the local inflections: the mariachi bands here rather than the whirling dervishes you might see at Delhi Pride; brightly embroidered tunics and ponchos rather than lederhosen and dirndls in Munich; the adorable float of gay vaqueros (cowboys) the real deal rather than macho camp.

But what was most striking to me were the more nondescript participants: not just their number, impressive alone, but their demographics. Certainly, all the expected subsets of a global twenty-first-century Pride culture were there: the older couples, the families, the home-stitched performance artists, the battalions of gym boys in muscle vests, the biker girls and the transgender sex workers, the queer kids with their piercings and their shavings, the lone old queens taking their annual bows. But the surprise came in the number—the tens of thousands, really—of working-class youths from *la periferia*, the exurbs of this megalopolis, marching quietly between the disco trucks, seemingly in awe of the event, present but not quite sure what to do (it seemed to me), until the evening party in the Zócalo—the city's fabled central square—gave them a more familiar script: drinking and dancing to the music of a stellar lineup, including the pop-singing icon Alejandra Guzmán.

I trailed a group of three of these young men, dressed in globalized branded sportswear somewhat scuffed by the street. They seemed a bit disoriented as they traipsed behind a disco truck. Every now and then, they would break into a gesture of exuberance—twirling around a beat or waving to an onlooker—but would then reel themselves back into a somewhat sullen masculinity. When I went over to chat to them, I noticed that one—he introduced himself as Jaime—kept his hands clenched in fists. I mistook the fists for a kind of defensive aggression, but at a certain point in the conversation, Jaime sprung them open into jazz hands: his nails were painted, alternately, violent magenta and milky mauve. Then he pulled them shut again, and laughed about how he would need to be sober, and stripped of such adornment, for church with his family the next morning.

Mexico Pride was the strongest image I had seen, in my travels, of the way the city functioned as a place of possibility for queer people who might otherwise lead more constrained lives. And it was a powerful indication of the way the forces of globalization—not least the Information Revolution, and urbanization, of course—were shifting societies like this, pulling an increasing number of young people from the periphery into a public identity, even if just for a day.

Jaime and his friends came from Iztapalapa, the dense working-class neighborhood to the east of the city notorious for its crime rate. They told me that they knew some transgender girls from the barrio who worked the street, and an older lesbian couple who ran a restaurant, but they associated with neither: back home they were straight boys, and crossing the Pink Line, for them, was the forty-minute metro ride between Iztapalapa and the Zona Rosa—the "Pink Zone" that is the city's traditional gay neighborhood.

THREE AND A HALF YEARS before I attended Mexico Pride, I was in Bangalore—India's tech hub in the south of the country—for its Pride events, in December 2012. I was struck here, as I would later be in Mexico, by the mix: in particular the way that branded employees from American multinational corporations join the *hijras* and the radical queer activists in a vibrant and somewhat anarchic parade. The procession, culminating on the broad stone steps of the Bangalore Town Hall and diligently martialed by police officers, offered a sense of how quickly life in India's cities was changing.

Bangalore Pride was, at the time, one of eleven such events across India. Three years previously, in 2009, the Delhi High Court had ruled that Section 377 of the Indian penal code was unconstitutional in the case of consenting adults, the result of an inspired eight-year-long campaign. Shortly after I visited India the Supreme Court reinstated Section 377, and it took until 2018 for the matter to be settled, finally. "History owes an apology" to members of the LGBT community and their families, Judge Indu Malhotra said at the beginning of her ruling, "for the delay in providing redressal for the 'ignominy' and 'ostracism' they have suffered through the centuries ... The members of this community were compelled to live a life full of fear of reprisal and persecution."[7]

By this point all India's political parties supported decriminalization, save the ruling Bharatiya Janata Party (BJP), which stayed silent on the matter. From Bollywood movie moguls to Bangalore tech magnates, "modern" Indians scrambled to support the decriminalization of homosexuality as a marker of the country's progress and thus its rightful place in the new liberal global economy. "India has now entered the 21st Century," newspapers blared in 2009, when the Delhi High Court first "read down" Section 377;[8] the editors of a book about the campaign and the judgment wrote that the judgment had become "a metaphor—straight out of the imaginary thesaurus that lists new meanings in the New India."[9] Bollywood had finally found the gay character, and newspaper columnists joked about the day that Indian parents would start placing matrimonial ads to find grooms for their gay sons.

At Bangalore Pride, in December 2012, I met a group of young transgender men from the neighboring state of Kerala. I struck up a conversation with one of them, Dev, who worked in a Bangalore call center servicing North American clients. At work Dev was understood to be a tomboy "or maybe even a lesbian" and could get away with wearing "pantshirt," as Indians say: "It doesn't matter how I look, as long as I sound good. No one even minds if the callers think I'm a man. I can even use my male name."

With an asymmetric short haircut and piercings, Dev did indeed look like a hip—if slight—young man on the streets of cosmopolitan Bangalore. But back home in Kerala he was—incontrovertibly—a daughter and a sister, and a prospective bride. The border between Karnataka—Bangalore's state—and Kerala was his Pink Line, and he laughed about how he had become adept at crossing it, changing into female clothes in the tight space of a bus station toilet cubicle before setting out to his family home. On the Kerala side of the Pink Line an arranged marriage seemed inevitable, which Dev staved off "for now" with monthly remittances back home: the fact that he was helping support the family could be used as an explanation for why he was not yet married. He dreamed of running away to Hong Kong for surgery—or, more realistically, for a work transfer to Delhi, farther away from his family.

CRISSCROSSING THE PINK Line—and the double life such crossings entail—has always been a factor of queer identity, the world over. The dissonance can be severe: at home, disclosure might result in expulsion or even violence upon you, while on the other side of the Pink Line you might be fetishized as a symbol of tolerance and diversity.

Starting in 2007, Mexico City's crusading progressive mayor, Marcelo Ebrard Casaubon, had used startling new laws legalizing abortion and same-sex marriage in order to attract young and forward-looking people—and pink-dollar tourists—to the metropole, branding his city *La Ciudad de las Libertades*, the City of Freedoms.[10] Buenos Aires used Argentina's progressive policies to brand itself similarly, as the city's official website put it in 2018: "The top destination in Latin America for LGBT travelers" because of its "atmosphere of tolerance, diversity, liberty and respect."[11]

This was a key dimension of cities with visible queer communities in the era of mass travel: from Buenos Aires and Rio de Janeiro to Tel Aviv and Cape Town and of course Bangkok, cities became significant pink tourism destinations. Gay populations even came to be seen as a predictor of economic growth, as the urban planner Richard Florida claimed in his influential 2002 book, *The Rise of the Creative Class*.[12] "To put it bluntly," Florida said presciently about San Francisco, "a place where it's OK for men to walk down the street holding hands will probably also be a place where Indian engineers, tattooed software geeks, and foreign-born entrepreneurs feel at home."[13]

Florida's ideas had an impact on cities across the world, but perhaps nowhere more so than Singapore, a modern and cosmopolitan city in the twenty-first century that still had a sodomy law on its books and an authoritarian government. In 1998, the premier Lee Kuan Yew had criticized the West for accepting homosexuality, but by 2007 he had changed his tune: he now argued that homosexuality needed to be decriminalized if his booming city-state was to realize its potential as "part of the interconnected world": "If we want creative people we [have] got to put up with their idiosyncrasies as long so they don't infect the heartland."[14]

As it turned out, the Singapore Supreme Court disagreed with Lee: It upheld the law after a 2014 challenge. Homosexuals might be necessary for economic growth, but the heartland needed nonetheless to be shielded from infection by them. The dichotomy demonstrates, acutely, the way that urban queer folk remain subject to the repressive regimes of their families or churches or governments, even if they seem freer than ever before.

In *Transgender History*, Susan Stryker notes that the first North American laws to criminalize cross-dressing coincided with the rapid urbanization of the 1850s because of the emergence of gender-variant people in the cities.[15] This mirrors the way Mexican and Brazilian authorities began using public order bylaws to clamp down on the growing homosexual scenes in their cities in the mid-twentieth century and then, in the twenty-first century, the way anti-sodomy laws were being applied for the first time and new legislation promulgated to rein in urban gay communities in Africa and the former Soviet Union.

But even in a city like Lagos, in very homophobic Nigeria, there was enough bandwidth in the atmosphere and enough gaps in the urban fabric beneath it—a beach, a hotel bar, a theater lobby—to enable queer people to connect online and then find a way of meeting. Just how vulnerable this space was, however, was made manifest in August 2017, when a weekly party at the Vintage Hotel north of Lagos was raided after a complaint: forty men were arrested and charged under the Same Sex Marriage (Prohibition) Act. In a country where no one was out of the closet despite large urban gay populations, their photographs were published in the mainstream media. "HIV Epidemic Looms," blared the national *Sun*, reporting that almost all the men had tested HIV-positive in jail "and now roam freely in the society" as a result of having been granted bail.[16] The paper worried—literalizing the infection metaphor used by Singapore's Premier Lee—that the accused could be "infecting new persons by the day" given the "propensity among some of them to suddenly go on an infection-spree mission."

A year previously, I had visited Nigeria and spent some time in Ibadan, the university city an hour's drive from Lagos in southeast Nigeria. While there, I attended Sunday services at an LGBT church called House of Rainbow, which met in a nondescript apartment in a gated compound at the end of a market street on the edge of the city. I watched the way the twenty-odd congregants arrived: dressed in ordinary male street wear and carrying sizable bags, they knocked on the locked gate of the unmarked apartment. Having been appraised through the keyhole, they were granted access. But before settling themselves into the makeshift pews of white plastic chairs set around an altar beneath a rainbow-colored banner, they made their way to the back of the apartment to change. The bathroom was a busy place before prayers, as parishioners did themselves up—sometimes with no more than a frilly vest or a little mascara or a pair of sling-back heels—to meet their Lord "as I really feel myself to be," one of them told me. At the end of the service, the pastor, Onwambor—a furniture salesman by day—reminded his flock to remove the makeup and change back to their street clothes, and to "comport yourselves decently" upon leaving the premises, "as you arrived."

The Pink Line might be a frontier between countries, or between different parts of the world governed by clashing ideologies, or between the suburbs and the city, or between the past and an imagined future, but in the minds of queer people themselves, it is often a security gate: between fear and vulnerability on the one hand, and sanctuary and affirmation on the other.

IN THE EARLY twenty-first century, some cities developed reputations as safe havens for queer people: tourists and shoppers and economic migrants and political refugees alike. In 2013 I attended a support group for LGBT migrants in downtown Johannesburg: they had all come here from other African countries to work or because of political turmoil back home, and not because of their sexual orientation. But now that they were experiencing the relative freedom of being able to live a gay life, despite the constraints of xenophobia and crime, none had any intention of returning home.

Beirut occupied a similar place in the Arab world. It had long been the "Paris of the Middle East," and as it reconstructed itself after the conflicts of the late twentieth century, queer people from all over the region began visiting as tourists, along with others seeking pleasures not available back home. Many from the huge Lebanese diaspora returned home after the war—from the cities of Europe and North America—and they had much to do with Beirut's tolerant, cosmopolitan vibe. So, too, did the city's diverse population and its privileging of entrepreneurship and commerce. If Beirut became famed for its gay nightlife, it also became a magnet for people seeking refuge from violence and persecution in other countries.

Although sodomy was still illegal in Lebanon, Beirut was the home of the region's first open LGBT organization, Helem, founded in 2004. By 2016, Helem had opened a community center and spawned an important international queer network, the Arab Foundation for Freedoms and Equality (AFE). In 2019, though, the country's intelligence service attempted to shut down's AFE's annual conference: the names of all participants were recorded, and those from other countries were banned from reentering Lebanon. The intelligence service justified this on the grounds of "protecting society from imported vices" that disrupted "the security and stability of society" and violated "the Lebanese public order."[17] Tangled among all the frontiers criss-crossing this divided little country, here now was another one: a Pink Line.

The region's other "open" city was Istanbul, a consequence of Turkey's keenness to join the European Union in the first decade of the century. As Istanbul exploded into a conurbation of fifteen million people, a vibrant LGBT community became part of its fabric: queer people flocked there from across the country, as did queer refugees from Iran in particular. From 2003 there were Pride marches setting off from Gezi Park in Taksim Square, the first in the Muslim world. By 2013 there were over ten thousand participants, but the march was banned in 2014 in the aftermath of the Gezi Park occupation, in which LGBT activists played a significant role. Still, repeated bannings and police intimidation could not stop Istanbul Pride: in 2019, thousands gathered, despite a huge police presence and the use of tear gas and plastic bullets to disperse the crowd.

But in Turkey as in so many other countries, there was significant backlash to this new visibility, from the banning of all LGBT events in the capital city of Ankara to a spike in the murders of transgender women, reportedly the highest rate in Europe. Some leaders began reciting the global culture wars script. When the interior minister Süleyman Soylu complained in September 2019 about how the U.S. was funding the Syrian Kurdish insurgency, he added that it was also giving $22 million in aid to an LGBT organization in Ankara: "Is it necessary for me to say that the real goal here is [the U.S. asserting] its belief, identity and existence in this land?"[18]

In dramatic ways, the region's other great metropole, Cairo, magnified the Pink Line dynamics of Beirut and Istanbul. As would happen at Gezi Park, many young Egyptians came out on Tahrir Square during the 2011 revolution. An activist I will call Murad told me how he had moved to Cairo from Port Said to study. Before the revolution, he had lived "the gay life" offered by the city, remaining the respectful son of a devoutly religious family back home. But his Cairo coming out had been "online and in private space," as he put it. "The revolution changed all this," he told me, in words that described what happens—in theory at least—in cities. "It gave me this sense of unity, this urge to get out of my safe bubbles within the new platform of activism. We were all in the square: straight, queer, Sunni, Shi'a Muslim, Copt. I was aware that the square was very diverse. Why couldn't society be the same?"

We were talking in 2015, after the Egyptian military's coup the previous year, and the clampdown that followed.

6

MAHA AND AMIRA'S STORY

CAIRO—ISTANBUL—AMSTERDAM

Amira—owner and manager of the Girls' Café, late thirties. Pronouns: she/her/hers.

Maha—Amira's wife and an accountant and LGBT activist, early thirties. Pronouns: she/her/ hers.

Nawal*—Feminist activist and revolutionary, late thirties. Pronouns: she/ her/ hers.

Zaki*—Professional and intellectual, late fifties. Pronouns: he/him/his.

Ayman Sirdar—Pop star, early twenties. Pronouns: he/him/his.

Abdel Rahman—University student, early twenties. Pronouns: he/him/his.

Murad*—Activist and graduate student, mid-twenties. Pronouns: he/him/his.

Amgad*—Regular customer at the Girls' Café, early twenties. Pronouns: she/her/hers.

***Pseudonyms**

1

Ahwet el-Banat it was called: the Girls' Café.

The name was painted onto a banner by Maha and Amira and hung over the entrance to the converted shop front that they leased in June 2012. On a decaying pedestrian street in downtown Cairo, the girls' red plastic chairs jostled with the black or white or orange ones of neighboring cafés, the waiters of each establishment pulling them periodically back into line, a rippling quilt of competing territories along the street's chipped flagstones. Downtown Cairo had been remodeled in the late nineteenth century to evoke the cosmopolitan modernity of Paris: regimented facades with Art Nouveau detail and wrought-iron barriers around green islands. As night fell a century later, in the dying weeks of the Egyptian revolution that had overturned the country, the elegant streetlamps flickered on unexpectedly (everything else was in a profound state of disrepair), in a play of light with the glowing coals in the *shisha* pipes being lit in dozens of sidewalk cafés. Around one table would be clustered long-haired university students; around another, office workers playing backgammon or shopkeepers on break. It was the sweltering summer of 2013.

In the later years of the Hosni Mubarak regime, Cairo's *wust-el-balad* (downtown) had been the site of ever-increasing protests, and *downtown* became a byword for freedom and modernity, for a place where women might sit in public and smoke *shisha* without a veil, where men and women could sit together or even hold hands. Although the scene was still largely male, mixed groups were more common here, as were fervent late-night debates about politics and society. This was the revolution's liberated zone, and the Girls' Café seemed part of it.

The Girls had their regulars, like the well-dressed older man who settled in every evening with his newspaper for an hour or two, or the immaculately coiffed legless woman who rolled over in her wheelchair at six on the dot to smoke her *shisha*. There was also, always, smoldering on the periphery, the muscular local thug who had appointed himself the Girls' protector. As the night drew in, fragrant young men in sharply pressed shirts and tight jeans would wander over, alone or in little groups, pulling chairs up to ever-expanding tables. Many of them identified as "ladyboys"—the queer Egyptian vernacular for transgender—and although they wore male clothing on the street, their female selves escaped: in a shriek that would pierce the street's steady thrum, in an arm shot skyward, an extravagant greeting, or even a catfight. These would be alarm bells to Amira, who would come rushing over to shush them before returning to her *shisha* at the "bosses' table" by the door, around which were often gathered a group of lesbian women, quieter and less concerned than the men with physical appearance.

Amira was brisk and butch and had a stern manner that brooked no dissent but broke easily into laughter. She tucked her shoulder-length hair into a baseball cap, and wore jeans low on the hips. Maha, her wife (they had married privately—and obviously illegally—the previous year) was a little younger, buxom and warm, with an inviting smile under hair that fell down one side of her face. Maha worked at a foreign embassy and came over to the *ahwa* after work in the evenings to help out. In the months following the revolution, she had helped found Egypt's first LGBT organization, Bedayaa (the word means "beginnings"), and although she was not out of the closet she was passionate about this new cause in her life.

As you sat at the Girls' Café you could discern, as the night wore on, the song lines of post-revolution queer Cairo: down to the El-Horreya bar or the Greek Club on Talaat Harb, both of which sold alcohol, over to Tahrir Square to cruise, if that's what you were looking for. You could spend the night flitting between tables at the Girls' Café and another queer-friendly *ahwa* around the corner, burrowed out of the lobby of a grand but derelict old block with tables spilling onto a busy street. The traffic never really stopped but in the early hours of the morning, once it had calmed down a bit, customers would commandeer the thoroughfare itself, the late-night taxis dodging tables bubbling with *shisha* and gossip. "After the revolution, everyone was on the streets, as never before, the gays more than anyone," Maha said to me. "One evening, it was April 2011, a big group of us were sitting at that café over there"—she pointed to a more formal establishment—"there were some very feminine gays with us, wearing makeup and women's clothes, and laughing loud. The waiters went and called the military police who came over and wanted to search the bags of the boys." The police found makeup in a handbag, which the women tried to insist was theirs. We giggled at the notion of the butch Amira pretending to own makeup, and the police were similarly unconvinced: they admonished the group for inappropriate behavior, and left.

"But the workers at the café were not happy," Maha continued. "They started cursing the boys and a violent fight broke out. Two of our friends were held hostage." The military police returned, and everyone dispersed, but Maha and her friends were certain they had been followed home. This was two months after the Tahrir Square revolution, which had forced the resignation of Mubarak, and the military was clamping down in an attempt to restore order; Maha and Amira and their friends panicked, particularly after Maha started getting phone calls from a man "asking creepy questions." The friends hunkered down in Maha and Amira's downtown apartment, not going out to public places until about two months later.

"We realized, 'This is crazy. We didn't fight a revolution to stay inside,'" Maha remembered, and out of this realization was hatched the *ahwa*. The notion, midwifed by the revolution, was simple, yet revolutionary itself. As Amira put it to me: "Gay people deserve a place like everyone else. A place where they can sit outside, safely, without harassment or being bothered."

It would take a year for them to make it happen, and then a year again before it was shut down.

ONE AFTERNOON, MAHA came to meet me at the Girls' Café after she had finished work. I was in Cairo to understand how the Pink Line was being staked here, in this great city seemingly liberated by the Arab Spring and the 2011 revolution. I knew I wanted to write about the Muslim Middle East, and my shortlist also included Istanbul and Beirut, but I chose Cairo precisely because being out in the open was so new here, and because the Mubarak regime had been so repressive. Maha and Amira and their clients were the very first Egyptians to be open in public, despite the fact that there had always been a discreet scene in the country: in private homes and some discreet restaurants for middle-class people and in the *hammams*, the public baths, for poorer ones. And gay sex tourism had always been one of Cairo's draws, in a society where male homosexual sex was a more acceptable alternative to pre- or extra-marital affairs, so long as it was on the down-low and you were the active partner. Partly for this reason Egypt had already been a Pink Line frontier, during the horrendous crackdown following the raid of a floating club on the Nile called the Queen Boat in 2001.

Maha and I settled in at the bosses' table, sipping cold hibiscus tea, and watching Amira, hands on hips, dressing down a supplier.

"She's tough!" I laughed.

"That's why I like her." Maha laughed back. "She *has* to be tough. She is the only woman who owns an *ahwa* in the whole of downtown. I think this causes as much trouble for us as our gay customers. It drives the other owners crazy that there's a woman here on the same level as them, it's like we are taking not just the customers but the authority from them, too. They sometimes even taunt Amira that she must be sexually frustrated because all her customers are *khawalat* (the Egyptian word for *faggots*, derived from the word for traditional transvestite dancers).

Amira had been threatened so many times—or the *ahwa*'s property broken—that the women frequently thought of closing the place down. They were also becoming increasingly exasperated by some of their customers who just could not seem to tone down the camp, perhaps intoxicated by the possibility of being themselves out in the open for the first time. The provocation for a fight was often a customer's inappropriate cruising of other men.

I thought of a line I had just read in Shereen El Feki's book about sexuality in the Arab world, *Sex and the Citadel*—"The *ahwa* is an intensely masculine place, you'd swear they put testosterone in the *shisha*"—as Maha told me the story of the worst incident yet.[1] "It was some months ago. Two of our male customers, very feminine, were getting some pizza from the restaurant over there and some of the local thugs came to our workers and said, 'It will be good for everyone if these people stop sitting here. If we see them here again, we will beat them up.' Of course, we did not tell our customers to go away, and later in the evening, a group of workers came over from the next-door café"—she gestured to the chairs across an invisible line just a few feet away—"they hit one of the gay guys, but the other ran away. Amira was trapped inside."

Amira, who had joined us by this point, picked up the thread: "One guy started to tease the [gay] boy with a laser. When the boy asked him to stop, he started beating him, and called the others. They came with sticks. They broke up everything, they threw broken chairs around, they beat up my workers. When they stopped breaking everything, I picked up a chair from the inside, and I walked outside. I kicked aside some of the broken chairs, and I put my chair down. Right here, where we are sitting now. I asked my workers to prepare me a *shisha*."

Amira looked her assailants in the eye and dared them: "So. Is there anything else you would like to do?"

2

"Amira and I were the first lesbians on the square on January 25," Maha told me, with an unusual burst of exuberance, as we sat at the bosses' table one afternoon. Like millions of their generation, they were accidental revolutionaries: they found their public voices—and each other—during the fabled "Eighteen Days of Protest" on Tahrir Square.

Maha had just ended a long-distance relationship with a foreign woman and was in a funk. She had seen reports on social media calling for a "Day of Revolt" and, off work, she had gone downtown with the vague idea she might check things out. She settled in to an *ahwa* for her morning *shisha* and by lunchtime she was part of a large table that included Amira, whom she vaguely knew, as reports started to pulse through of the large numbers gathering at the square. She said she wanted to check it out and Amira—sweet on her—volunteered to come along.

When they got there, there were already thousands gathered: in the center, a core of fervent radicals and students waving banners and chanting; around them many more, watching to see what would happen. "Suddenly, for no apparent reason, the first [tear] gas bomb landed right at our feet," Maha remembered. The two women raced back to their friends at the café, and after mulling it over for a while, decided to return to the square: "And we did, every day for eighteen days, until Mubarak fell."

They were there for the March of the Millions to the Presidential Palace on February 1; they were there three days later when two million Cairenes took to the streets on the Friday of Departure. They did not pitch tents in the square and move in, but they watched the battles between stone-throwing revolutionaries and the security forces outside the Egyptian Museum, they saw blood being spilled, they held up their open hands chanting "One hand!" along with millions to evoke the unity of the Egyptian people, and the experience changed their lives.

When Mubarak's resignation was announced on February 11, some of the women in Maha and Amira's circle of friends proposed a celebration. The first plan was to go to the beach at Alexandria, but it was not safe to travel. And so instead they rented an apartment in downtown Cairo for two days, on the weekend of February 19, and about fifteen women moved in. "It was *horrible*!" Maha remembered with a little shriek. "It was crazy! It was the craziest two days the whole group ever had. Drama, drunk girls, beer, alcohol, weed, drama, drama, drama! We didn't leave the apartment. It was one of the best things we've ever done in our lives. I got drunker than I have ever been. I was sitting on a chair with all the bottles next to me, drinking, drinking, drinking. There was music. People were dancing."

Through her inebriation, Maha became conscious that someone was asking her, repeatedly, to dance: "Who is this crazy girl? Can't she see I can't get up?" The crazy girl was Amira. The two had bonded on the square, and Amira was now making her move. Maha tried to get up, and passed out. She vaguely remembers that Amira helped her to a room, put her to bed, and stayed with her for a few hours. When she came to, Amira was there, wiping her face with a wet towel. This was the beginning of their relationship.

When I asked Amira about it she let rip a ribald laugh. "We *did* it!" she exclaimed. "The Egyptians did it, and *we* did it, too!"

THREE MONTHS LATER, the couple rented an apartment together on Talaat Harb right in the very center of the city. It was in an early-twentieth-century block much like the nearby Yacoubian Building at number 34 on the same street, made famous in Alaa Al-Aswany's novel. The apartment had a faded grandeur, with balconies and high ceilings and a big living room overlooking the city's high street. This was exactly at the time of the incident with the military police, after which the women and their friends decided to stay inside for a while, and so the apartment became something of "our private, indoor café," as Maha put it: the salon of a circle of women (and one or two guys) who now called themselves Banat Wust-el-Balad, "the Downtown Girls."

"We were called the 'downtown people' almost as a form of insult—as if we were arrogant," Maha remembered. "This was even how other LGBT people saw us. People who were not open-minded, who were religious, discreet about their image. *They hated us.* But for us, being called 'downtown people,' we loved it. We're open-minded, we're liberal, we're *downtown*."

Amira had been living downtown in her own flat, since 2008. She had been discovered with a girlfriend by her mother, and had left home after a family fight. She was the daughter of a comfortable mercantile family, and had begun working in her father's shop at the age of fifteen. She had been financially independent ever since, working in real estate and running an *ahwa* in Heliopolis. "But when I left home and moved downtown I became more open about myself. More proud of myself, coming out as I had done in a very closed-minded part of Cairo."

Even though Maha shared the rent with Amira at Talaat Harb, she was only able to stay over for a night or two a month, by lying to her parents about needing to travel for work. She lived in an outlying district of Cairo with her family, also prosperous merchants, and would typically stop over at Talaat Harb for a few hours on her way home from work, or come in to spend the day on Fridays. She loved cooking, and making meals rather than sleeping over would be the activity that bonded her to her new shared home with Amira. After six months Amira moved to a bigger place, also downtown, and it was here that the couple held their wedding in January 2012: fifteen friends watched as they exchanged vows and rings with the date of the wedding inscribed on them, before sharing a feast.

In a good month Maha could contrive to spend maybe four nights in the arms of Amira. She was frustrated by her double life, but did not really see a way out of it unless they left Cairo, a city they loved. But "Yes," Maha said, "if we can't live a life like any two normal people, a normal relationship, a loving relationship, then, yes, we are actually thinking of leaving the country."

BOTH MAHA AND AMIRA had been using the words *lesbian* and *gay* to describe themselves since about 2007, when the Internet became easily accessible in Egypt. They had been part of intersecting networks of women who had found each other in chat rooms online, as the digital revolution and globalization meant that Egypt underwent its own version of the culture wars: between a mainstream that turned, in droves, to a Saudi-style Islamism the state could no longer suppress, and an increasingly restive generation of young people connecting with one another online in the region.

Maha felt this bifurcation acutely in her own home. Her parents had been secular and worldly liberals; she was sent to co-educational Catholic schools and raised to be a professional. She was desperate to study history, but her father laid down the law: she was to become an accountant, as he was, so that she could support herself.

But in 2000, her mother started attending mosque and wearing hijab for the first time, along with millions of other Egyptian women. Her well-traveled father followed suit, and Maha found herself, to her surprise, in a devout home. In these years it became the fashion at university to be veiled and Maha joined the trend. But a conflict with her mother in 2006 changed her: "We were watching a TV talk show about Baha'i people, and my mother agreed with those panelists insulting the Baha'i participant. When I challenged her, she said, 'You're not a true believer!' and I said to her, 'If you think that because I have an opinion I'm not a believer, then you're right: I'm not a believer in your religion anymore.'"

Maha had already recognized her sexual orientation. Her parents had been early adopters of satellite television, and the family loved American dramas. When she was about fourteen, "there was a girl kissing another girl [on one of the shows], and while my sisters were disgusted, I thought it was somehow nice." This would have been in the mid-1990s. She shelved this early teenage response until, following her conflict with her mother, she began surfing online, picking up information not only about homosexuality but about freedom and democracy, too. Finally, in 2008, she was "awoken," she told me, by a serious illness, and she decided to stop dating men, and typed the words "Lesbian in Egypt" into the search bar on MSN Chat.

She was twenty-two, and her world exploded: "It was my wild times. From the summer of 2008 until I met Amira in 2011, I had *eight* girlfriends. *Eight!*" She became part of a group of women who would meet in cafés or at restaurants. The habit of women smoking *shisha* in public had, peculiarly, come to Egypt from the Gulf at the same time as Wahhabi Islam, and "it wasn't unusual at all to see groups of women together in public, so no one suspected we were lesbians. And there's no problem with women being affectionate with each other in public."

After a while, several gay men joined the women's tables. Maha and Amira liked to ham it up about "how much simpler life was when we were just women in our group, when there were no men making trouble by being too loud," as Maha put it. But what attracted them to their new male friends was, precisely, their courage: "They're more visible," Maha said. "They know how to claim space. Women don't fight back enough."

FOR MAHA, LIFE before the revolution was about fear: "Fear of society, fear of parents, fear of everything. But after the revolution it was, like, 'Well, this is just who I am.' Freedom. I don't think this was only for the gays. It was for everyone. 'I can do whatever I want, now. No one can stop me.'"

When I visited Cairo in 2013, everyone I met had a way of explaining the sudden visibility of queer people in Egypt following the 2011 revolution. Zaki, an intellectual and a veteran of the gay community, spoke of a new courage: "People understood that they only had one life, and it can finish any time, so they better live it now. They are taking more risks. It's a dare-or-die game."

Abdel Rahman, a student, had beautiful words to describe the way people now occupied public space: "People started floating in the streets with their thoughts, and their feelings, rather than leaving these behind when they went outside."

Being on Tahrir Square, Amira told me, not only bonded her to Maha, but increased the number of queer people she knew: "There were *so* many, and we would meet, first it would be eye contact, but you would just know! Then we would introduce ourselves. We became close friends in those eighteen days. The circle became wider and wider."

One of those the couple met on the square was a feminist activist, whom I will call Nawal. The number of queer people on the square was a revelation to her, Nawal told me: "I saw not only intellectual gay men and those activists in the feminist movement like myself, I saw transgender women in smallish groups, sex workers I knew from the Ramses [Station] public toilets, gays, lesbians, intellectuals, non-intellectuals. I couldn't believe it. *Yanni,* I wanted to kiss each and every one of them."

It was also a bellwether: "I thought to myself, if all these people are coming onto the streets, it's not just another demonstration. For these people to have the guts to come out like this, definitely, something big is going to happen." For Nawal, "the Eighteen Days was almost a utopian communal society … People who in everyday life would be harassing me were being nice and cooperative, offering me food, offering me protection."

But visibility and safety seemed to be mutually exclusive, and Maha and Amira's own disillusion was swift. On March 8, 2011, International Women's Day, they heeded a Facebook call to attend a march on the square: to demand the constitution be changed to allow a woman to stand for the presidency. The few hundred women who participated found themselves confronted by a much larger counter-protest of angry men, and the couple could not believe the insults lobbed by some of the very men who had protested alongside them just six weeks previously: "Stay at home! Stay in the kitchen! Do you think you can be president? It's not going to happen!" They tried to protect a foreigner from being sexually harassed, eventually forming tight circles of women to stave off what had transformed into an angry molesting mob. Maha was pushed off a high curb and hurt her knee badly; as Amira pulled her away from the chaos they saw about thirty men pounce on the woman who had been standing next to them. Two years later, they remained haunted by this image and their inability to assist her. "In the Eighteen Days no one did anything to us," Maha said to me. "People were respectful and supportive. Now the truth hits you again. It's a long process. You do not just suddenly become free. You have to work hard. We did not go back to the square."

Instead, they began thinking about their *ahwa*.

3

One of the reasons why the visible presence of queer people on Tahrir Square seemed so significant to the feminist activist Nawal was because of the way any kind of public display of a queer identity had been forced underground by brutal repression a decade before. Nawal remembered, in particular, a conversation on the square with three young men. "They were very sweet, smiling, touching, and they said to me, 'We're young, and we haven't seen what you have seen. But we know we must be careful, because of Queen Boat.'"

"Queen Boat" loomed, like a funeral barge, over queer identity in Egypt in the twenty-first century. The floating club had been popular with expatriates and gay men, and on May 11, 2001, it was raided by the Vice Squad of the Egyptian police in collaboration with its State Security Investigations division. The raid had been preceded by several arrests of homosexual men; in total, fifty-two suspects were charged with participating in a "homosexual cult."[2]

Egypt does not have an anti-sodomy law, but since 1951 it had criminalized *fujur*, or "debauchery"—a Qur'anic sin—which initially referred to prostitution, but which was extended by a 1975 court decision to homosexual conduct even when money was not exchanged. Now, by adding conspiracy charges to the *fujur* ones, the State was able to send the Queen Boat case to a State Security court. This led newspapers to announce, as one did, "Perverts declare war on Egypt!"[3]

The primary accused was a wealthy thirty-two-year-old businessman, a political foe of the president Hosni Mubarak. Many believed the raid had been ordered primarily to rake in more suspects so as to be able to make conspiracy charges against him stick. The co-accused ranged across class, from street vendors to professionals. They were tortured and abused for three weeks in jail before being brought to trial; beseeched by their families to hide their faces, they fashioned masks from white prison clothing which they wore in court, a potent symbol of their shame. There was no hard evidence of either conspiracy or sexual conduct against any of them, besides the notorious "forensic" anal examination the Egyptian authorities did, using a discredited diagnostic protocol developed in nineteenth-century France. Still, twenty-three were found guilty, and given sentences of two to twelve years. Those acquitted were released into another kind of prison. Most were shunned or disowned by their families; those who were married lost their wives, and their access to their children. Some managed to flee into exile; others burrowed underground.

The Queen Boat raid was only the beginning of a clampdown that would last several years. The Egyptian police state was adept at surveillance, and the sudden arrival of social media in Egypt may well have alerted the authorities—and in particular the Vice Squad—to a gay subculture in Cairo, and to the popularity of the floating nightclub in particular. For several years the squad conducted a series of entrapments, using blackmailed informants from within the gay community to set up parties that would then be raided. The police also lured lonely people from chat rooms to assignations, usually at Tahrir, whence they would be spirited up to Vice Squad's offices on the thirteenth floor of the foreboding State Security building over the square, to be interrogated and charged. Human Rights Watch recorded at least forty-seven prosecutions arising out of these kinds of online entrapments between 2001 and 2004, but believed this to be only "a fraction of the whole."[4]

Scott Long, who conducted the Human Rights Watch investigation, has described online entrapment as "exploiting solitude."[5] Fearful of meeting people on the street any longer, or unable to do so in the public places closed by the clampdown, men sought solace and company in the new technology available, which gave them "a dangerous simulacrum of security. You believe you're safe, because you can hide who you are. You're not safe, because others can do the same."

A perceptive report by Howard Schneider in *The Washington Post* situated the Queen Boat raid and its consequences in a "broader cultural struggle between religious traditionalists and advocates of a more secular and tolerant society."[6] Schneider noted how, after suppressing a violent Islamist uprising in the 1990s, "The Egyptian state is ever more willing to ban books, jail dissidents and prosecute those seen as deviants in an effort to undermine fundamentalist arguments that the country is becoming too Westernized."

The state was using the gay issue in another way too: to telegraph to human rights activists and their supporters in the West, as Murad—a queer activist—put it to me, "'This far and no further! You will not dictate to us who will have rights and why.' Meanwhile, Mubarak was saying to Egyptians, 'You see? This is what the international community wants when they talk of democracy, and this is what we are going to protect you from: sodomy, debauchery, perversion.'"

And so the Queen Boat episode was an early plotting of the Pink Line, between a West-oriented "globalized" world view in which homosexual desires were affirmed into a "gay" identity and subculture, and a patriarchal Muslim society determined to hold its ground against this onslaught and all it represented. After a group of American legislators condemned the Queen Boat trial in 2001, the semi-official *Al-Ahram al-Arabi* magazine ran the following headline: "Be a Pervert, and Uncle Sam Will Approve."[7] The state-owned *Al-Akhbar* spoke of "the globalization of perversion."

Scott Long of Human Rights Watch described the crackdown as a "moral panic," one of several that the Mubarak regime unleashed at the time to divert "the media from the mounting crises of a political system mired in inaction and … unable to address growing poverty or popular discontent"; to create "scapegoats"; and to "recast itself as defending [religious] orthodoxy" even as it violently suppressed the Islamist Muslim Brotherhood.[8] His report claimed, with evidence, that there were more men imprisoned for homosexuality in Egypt at that time than in any other country in the world.

AT A SMALL drinks party of moneyed gay professionals in the uppermiddle-class district of Zemalek in the summer of 2013, I mentioned that I had been spending time in the downtown sidewalk cafés. The other guests mimed horror. Certainly this was about class: "I went once," a law professor said, "and I was interested in a very handsome young man—until he opened his mouth. *The teeth!*" But it was also about visibility: "Have these children forgotten the lessons of the Queen Boat?"

Zaki, the older man who had told me that it was now "dare-or-die" in post-revolutionary Egypt, had decided at the last minute not to go to the Queen Boat on the night it was raided. What happened to his generation after the raid and the trial, he said to me, was "a dive back into the closet. We disappeared for years." He had been in a close-knit group of nine gay men: the other eight rushed into marriage and made families.

The period of repression and surveillance following the Queen Boat raid lasted about five years, abating around 2006. Still, when I visited Egypt six years later, the rupture was still palpable: between the Queen Boat generation, and those children of the revolution, like Maha and Amira, who had discovered their public identities on the square and in downtown Cairo later in the decade.

Zaki seemed to be one of the only links between these two generations. A man of some means, he made his flat available for meetings of Bedayaa, the new LGBT organization, and the downtown kids would make their way out to his wealthy suburb to sit amidst his extensive collection of antiquities and oddities to talk about issues like security, faith, and visibility. As I sat in that living room myself one afternoon, Zaki drew me an extensive map of Cairo's queer spaces over the years, from the Nile Hilton's Tavern to more recent clubs and restaurants. Most had closed their doors to gay customers, and Zaki believed this had played a big role in the growth of the sidewalk queer scene: "They won't have us inside, so we sit outside."

Still, when Zaki's older middle-class friends went downtown, they stayed well away from the sidewalk cafés. These days, their preferred place was an expensive "continental-style" restaurant that was welcoming to gay customers. Zaki's routine was to hunker down there with his older friends for a drink or two (there was, of course, no alcohol available on the sidewalks), leaving to make several forays to the sidewalk cafés as the night wore on, to check in on his younger, more open friends.

AS I WAS sitting with Zaki in his apartment that afternoon, he showed me a Facebook post from that morning by a young acquaintance: "I have an announcement to make," it began, in Arabic. "I'm attracted to men and women equally … I hope that now that I am known for who I really am, that I'll be accepted by all of you. But if you don't accept me, kiss my ass." Zaki messaged the kid in private: "I'm proud of you. But if you need any advice, come back to me. It won't be easy." The public responses ranged from joshing disbelief ("give me part of the hash you are smoking, *habibi*") to horror and condemnation. While we were scrolling through these, we watched in real time as the young man recanted: "For those of you who believed me, I have to tell you, this was a game. I was forced to do it because I lost at poker last night."

"This is the age we live in!" Zaki said. "The digital world gives space for people to imagine themselves as something and then"—he clicked his fingers—"once you write it or say it, you become it and live it."

In a society such as Egypt, this could create extreme dissonance. Zaki and I discussed a transgender woman I had interviewed the previous day, who juggled three Facebook profiles: a "straight male" one for her family and school friends; a "straight female" one through which she could explore being a woman; and a transgender one, through which she interacted with the online community of people like her. Through the last channel, she found an online black market source for estrogen, and began taking it. Her changing appearance worked wonders for her "straight female" online profile, but was beginning to attract negative responses on the streets of the city, and problems with her family, too. Some elders in the community prevailed upon her to limit her transgender explorations to her room and her webcam.

"We are the children of the revolution," the student Abdel Rahman said to me, sitting at the *ahwa*, "but more than that, we are the children of the Internet." Abdel Rahman was typical of his generation in that he had discovered his identity online (his portal, as with so many, was through gay porn) and had entered the gay community through the hookup sites: first Manjam, and then Hornet and Grindr, with their global positioning technologies. He had been robbed twice by hookups emerging from online contacts, but he had also met his boyfriend, Fadi, when Grindr told him there was someone online just two doors down the street. He was as deeply committed to the app as his community space as Zaki's generation would have been to the Tavern Bar or the Queen Boat, in another era.

While I was in Cairo I met someone else who had come out on social media. His name was Ayman Sirdar, and he was a pretty-boy pop singer with long curly hair and a dedicated following of young, largely female fans. Ayman had come out on his Facebook fan page in late 2012, "because this is the revolution, and we must be who we are," he told me, as I sat with him in the Heliopolis McDonald's. He had received some negative feedback, he said, particularly from his broader family, but his new status did not seem to have made much difference to his popularity with his fans.

I went to one of Ayman's concerts with a group of people including Zaki and Maha. We watched teenage girls in hijab bouncing around beneath the stage to their idol's signature tune, an Arabic boy band version of "I Am What I Am," with lines such as "The rainbow needs your eyes to love difference, for them to be able to see its colors."

"Do they know what this song's about?" I shouted over the music to Zaki. "Do they know he's gay?"

"Perhaps they just think he's just a modern young guy," said Zaki. "What do you call it in Europe? Metrosexual." As for the song: "He always introduces it by saying that he dedicates it to each person who feels different. And since *everyone* feels different, particularly young people, they can take it at that meaning."

But Ayman's online coming out remained part of his digital fingerprint, even after the military coup in July 2013 and the anti-gay clampdown that would ensue as part of a broader repression and reassertion of military power in Egypt. Ayman received death threats following his participation at a large concert at the pyramids in 2014 and he decided to go into exile. When I found him again in 2017, he had received asylum in the United States on the basis of feared persecution because of his sexual orientation.

He made his living as a subway busker.

4

When Maha and Amira's *ahwa* was trashed in February 2013, a few months before I met them, Amira had called the police while still trapped inside the shop. "But of course nobody answered," she told me. This was the double edge of the revolution: "We *do* have more freedom as gay people, but the outlaws, they have more freedom, too."

This state of lawlessness was a new and shocking feature of post-revolution Egypt. In the disorder that followed the Muslim Brotherhood's election to power in 2012, the police force evaporated. Unlicensed enterprises such as the Girls' Café could spring up anywhere. And gay people could claim public space, as never before. But they were also at personal risk, like all Egyptians, as never before. Cairo had been a famously safe city, but now there were assaults and muggings on the streets, even home invasions. And since, in the eyes of most people, gay people were outlaws anyway, their new visibility only served to indicate further the collapse of Egyptian society since the revolution.

Visibility itself was a double-edged sword, "the hell-heaven," as Amgad, a habitué of the Girls' Café, put it to me: "The heaven is [that you are] finally able to be yourself on the streets and part of a community. The hell is harassment, like you never got when you just stayed inside."

Amgad was gingerly experimenting with a transgender identity, and Amira, who was close to him, told me that her friend "now actually finds it harder to go out as a woman. Before, no one would notice, but now everyone knows us, and when people are on their way to Tahrir Square to protest criminality, they see a ladyboy and they shout, '*These* are the criminals we need to get off the streets!'"

JUST DAYS AFTER I LEFT CAIRO, on June 30, 2013, Maha and Amira joined about twenty million Egyptians in what was probably the largest public protest in the country's history, calling for the removal of Mohamed Morsi, the Muslim Brotherhood president.

There were two main counts against Morsi: his imposition of an Islamicized constitution that also gave him near-dictatorial powers, and the dysfunction of his government, particularly the breakdown of law and order. The protest was convened by a mass civil society movement called Tamarod (the word means "rebellion"), and Zaki was passionately involved.

Exploiting the Tamarod protests, the military under General Abdel Fattah al-Sisi deposed Morsi and seized power, with massive popular support. A few weeks after this coup, the new government crushed an Islamist insurgency. Sisi declared a state of emergency with a 7:00 p.m. curfew. At the *ahwa* Maha and Amira found themselves caught between the curfew and the extortions of the local thugs, now working in cahoots with a police force once more visible.

The final straw was an incident in October 2013, when Amira became involved in a battle with a thug who had beaten up one of her waiters. In the argument that ensued, she broke her assailant's penknife, a small but emasculating act: "They didn't like a woman breaking their weapons," she told me. "They told me they were going to do something big to me. Steal all my things. Then they went to my sister and threatened to throw acid in her face." The costs of running the Girls Café had become too high for Maha and Amira. They shut it down.

At around the same time that they closed their doors, there was a highly publicized raid on a gym in a working-class district of the city.

Fourteen men were arrested, publicly exposed on television, beaten and abused in detention, and found guilty of *fujur*. So began Egypt's second round of intense persecution of homosexuals, twelve years after the Queen Boat raid. By November 2016, one source tallied that at least 274 people had been the targets of police action, prosecution or violence, in 114 criminal cases and 21 documented hate crimes.[9] Once more, Egypt was imprisoning more people for homosexuality than any other country in the world. "Every week we received a phone call that someone we knew was arrested," Maha told me. "Every time, you felt the circle getting smaller, either because of arrest, or someone leaving the country."

In September 2014, there was an ominous echo of the Queen Boat when eight men were arrested and found guilty of *fujur* after attending a purported same-sex wedding ceremony on a boat on the Nile. Three months previously, a video of this event had been leaked onto YouTube and gone viral, eventually making its way onto television. This generated outrage, not least from the ousted Muslim Brotherhood: one of its leaders tweeted that "for the first time in Egypt we hear of gay marriage. The coup leaders embrace the Western agenda of demolition and the decay of religion, and Egypt is converted into a brothel."[10]

In this context, the authorities seemed to have felt compelled to respond. As one foreign ministry official told *BuzzFeed*: "Egypt and the rest of the Arab world, in this post–Arab Spring moment, are all watching each other carefully. Nobody wants to be accused of secularism or Western values—that is not what this post-Arab-Spring, post-Islamism moment means. We are still traditional societies, and the leadership today has to show this to the nation."[11]

The new regime seemed intent on hauling out the weapon of *fujur* as part of a broader crackdown that included new regulations against all protest; against nongovernmental organizations that played a watchdog role over state repression; and against any political activity that challenged the state. The jails were filled with alleged dissidents, mainly Islamists, but also some human rights lawyers and activists from the left. In this context, said the human rights lawyer Dalia Abdel Hamid, "the police want to show that they have a strong grip on society [through the arrest of] LGBT people";[12] clamping down on debauchery was an easy way, too, she said, for the military to demonstrate that it was "more Islamic than the Islamists" it had removed from power, and to win skeptical Muslim Egyptians over to its side.[13]

In Senegal in 2008, the exposé of a "gay wedding" in a celebrity magazine snowballed into the arrests of nine HIV activists; in Malawi the following year, Tiwonge Chimbalanga and Stephen Monjeza were arrested and sentenced to fourteen years' hard labor after the front-page coverage of their engagement. So, too, in Egypt, was the anti-*fujur* clampdown of the Sisi era the result of a toxic dance between sensationalist media houses and a repressive and anxious state.[14] If the commercial media was exploiting the local angle to a growing news story about "gay rights" and "same-sex marriage" that consumers would have been following anyway online or on satellite television, then the authorities were using the clampdown to perform their ability to maintain control of a citizenry that was increasingly aware of the larger world, and of other ways of being.

And so the Pink Line first staked by the Queen Boat raid thirteen years previously was reasserted in Egypt, this time intensified not only by the Digital Revolution and mass media, but by the Arab Spring itself. The tragedy of this was the way that young Arabs who had come out during the revolution—who had internalized the messages of personal autonomy and independence carried by it, and by their access to a global marketplace of ideas—were caught on the frontiers of the Pink Line, finding themselves to be the provocation for the ensuing clampdown. This time around, though, the specific targeting of transgender women (or gender non-conforming men) was becoming a prominent component of the state's campaign. Visible as never before since the revolution, "ladyboys" were perhaps the most easily identifiable symbol of the downtown "debauchery" against which the Sisi dictatorship had set itself.

By 2014 the police started to use online entrapment again, this time with more sophistication. Hookup apps like Grindr, with their global positioning technology, made the job that much easier; in response, Grindr disabled its GPS function in Egypt in September 2014, sending out a standard warning to all users and even providing a link to an information page about how to become an asylum seeker.

One of those entrapped online was a former waiter from the Girls' Café, sentenced to three years in jail after an online entrapment. So, too, a volunteer at Bedaaya, the LGBT organization that Maha helped lead: Bedaaya's leaders panicked and shut down their activities. Lesbians had not yet been targeted, but Maha and Amira felt increasingly isolated and vulnerable. In July 2014, while Amira was sitting at an *ahwa* in downtown Cairo, a café owner came rushing over to tell her to leave the district quickly as police were going door-to-door with a photograph of her, asking owners if they knew where to find the proprietor of the *ahwa alkhawalat*—the faggots' café.

Amira took fright, and was on a flight to Istanbul three days later.

A FEW WEEKS LATER, Maha told me, a TV show broadcast an "investigation" into the threat that atheists allegedly posed to Egyptian society. A reporter was sent to interview the denizens of a downtown *ahwa* universally known as "the atheists' café," as it seemed to have soaked up the remaining revolutionaries who still hung out downtown. Maha shared the link with me. Clearly visible in one shot were Maha and Amira (who had not yet left Cairo when the footage was taken): Amira was playing backgammon with a male friend while Maha was looking on, *shisha* pipe in mouth. Maha translated the voice-over for me: "The opinions of people about atheists vary. Most call them perverted, ignorant and corrupt [and] think they should be banished from society."[15] (In Arabic, the word for pervert is *shaz*: it has its derivation in the word for "different," but has come exclusively to mean "gay" or "homosexual.")

Maha's parents happened to be watching. They hit the roof. Maha had never mentioned her sexuality or her activism to anyone in her family, although they knew Amira and liked her. But now, following the broadcast, one of Maha's sisters had a word with her: "She told me that she knew I was working for LGBT rights. She had all the information. She knew *everything*." Maha was terrified because her sister's closest friend was a senior operative in the police intelligence services: "Either he told my sister about me, or she told him. Either way, it was creepy." She took three months' unpaid leave from her job and bought a ticket to join Amira in Turkey.

The women stayed with friends made through the LGBT and feminist movements of the region. When Maha's leave period expired, they found themselves at a crossroads. Maha decided to return to Cairo: "I knew things would be the same, perhaps even worse, but I wanted to be home. I wanted my job back, too." Amira disagreed: although she was less worldly—she spoke little English—she had always been keener to leave. She would stay in Turkey and seek asylum.

But then once Maha was back, Amira's resolve dissipated. She followed her wife back to Cairo. By this point the downtown scene was completely extinguished. Amira found a place near the pyramids, a long trek from Maha's family home on the other side of town. Without their downtown haunts and across the city from each other, the women struggled to find their space, as a couple and in their ever-diminishing community. Lesbian friends married men and had kids. One of Maha's closest gay friends was seeking asylum in the Netherlands, another in Germany. Amgad had undergone gender reassignment surgery, in large part to avoid conscription, but never left her house for fear of harassment. Amira's sister, also a lesbian, had joined a boatload of Syrian refugees in Turkey, beached in Greece, and made her way to Belgium to seek asylum.

In July 2015, Maha was invited to participate in a global LGBT rights conference in the Netherlands, sponsored by the Dutch government. It took place over Amsterdam Pride, and she returned to Cairo blissed out, "feeling freedom like never before, feeling safe for the first time, too." This time being home sent her spiraling into depression: she quit her job and bought another ticket to Amsterdam in September 2015. She consulted an asylum lawyer on arrival, and just before her Schengen visa expired a month later, she presented herself to the authorities with the words she had been rehearsing: "I would like to seek asylum in the Netherlands on the basis of my fear of persecution as a lesbian in Egypt."

Amira stayed behind in a Cairo that seemed increasingly bleak, desperately trying to get a visa that would allow her to follow Maha to Europe.

"AMIRA AND I have not seen each other for one year and four months," Maha told me when we spoke on WhatsApp in March 2017. "It's been a rough time but we have a strong relationship. We tried not to be together, but we failed. So now we are together again. Together, apart."

Maha gave me a video-tour of her new apartment, assigned to her by the Dutch authorities, on the sixth floor of a 1970s social housing complex in an immigrants' quarter. It had a neat kitchen, a small bedroom, a living room with two couches and a *shisha* of course. There was also a generous balcony over a canal, "my little Nile." Maha's life was full again, the scene in her flat reminiscent of the Talaat Harb glory days. She showed me the produce laid out on the kitchen counter in preparation for the *merhaba* chicken she was preparing to feed visitors that evening. I noticed the piles of luggage everywhere: "Refugees. Other Egyptians. There are so many here. They're still staying in the refugee reception centers, and they don't feel safe leaving their stuff there, so I keep it all here for them." Maha had met at least ten Egyptians housed in these centers; she had known some of them, vaguely, back home.

Maha had been in one of these centers herself when she arrived, but she moved out pretty quickly to stay with friends because of the homophobia of the other refugees there. She also struggled with what she perceived to be the homophobia of her interpreter in her first asylum seeker's interview, she told me: "He kept on using *shaz* [pervert] for 'gay.' So I said I would prefer to speak English in my second interview, and if no one was available then I would prefer a female interpreter." When she arrived for her second interview, she saw that there *was* a female interpreter—but she was veiled. "Oh my *God*," Maha remembered, "how am I going to tell her I am gay? But once we started she was so nice, and I felt really guilty for judging her."

Maha also felt awkward about the "anti-immigrant vibe" in the Netherlands, in particular the growing support that the anti-immigration politician Geert Wilders was gaining by, as Maha put it, "using the gay community to make a point about Muslim immigrants. It feels like it pits one half of me against the other half of me."

The electorate rejected Wilders's PV V party in the March 2017 elections, but this tension was very much part of the Dutch life Maha encountered: the spark was rekindled a few weeks after the election when a gang of Moroccan teens violently assaulted a gay couple holding hands in Arnhem. In protest, many Dutch men—including political leaders in their sober suits and ties—responded by being photographed holding hands in public.

The Netherlands was famously the world's most gay-friendly country: same-sex partnerships had been recognized since 1998, and discrimination on the basis of sexual orientation had been outlawed since 1994. When Maha arrived, in 2015, the notion of

LGBT equality was deeply embedded in Dutch society. Ten years previously, the Dutch government had released a controversial video, to be viewed by prospective immigrants, including footage of two men kissing and a woman bathing topless, as examples of Dutch culture. Prospective immigrants were tested on attitudes toward homosexuals in their naturalization exams. One of these—found in a sample online test from 2005—offers the following question: "You're on a terrace with a colleague and at the table next to you two men are fondling and kissing. You are irritated. What do you do?"[16] The answers available were:

a. You stay put and pretend you don't mind.
b. You tell your colleague in a rather loud voice what you think of homosexuality.
c. You tell the men to sit somewhere else.

The assumptions were revealing: the possibility that you might not be irritated at all was not anticipated.

Maha was impressed, initially, with the support she was getting from the Dutch authorities. Once she had her refugee status, they found her accommodation and subsidized her rent. She met other queer refugees—mainly from Syria—in the integration program she was compelled to attend, and these became her circle of friends. She was taking the compulsory free Dutch lessons provided by the state and hoped to enroll in a master's program in gender studies at the University of Amsterdam. She had just come out of the hospital after emergency surgery following a burst appendix: the entire procedure was free, and she was amazed at the quality of the care.

Still, she said, her first year was "very hard. I knew I was safe and everything but I was missing Egypt terribly. I was moving from one place to another, it was tiring me, and I kept on thinking, 'Should I go back and try again, or do I stay here?'" The deception to her family was particularly challenging, and her father had stopped speaking to her: "I told them I was tired of Egypt and my job, and they keep on asking when I'm coming back to see them, and I have no answer for that." But in the end, she decided to tough it out. The plan was to apply for a partner visa for Amira when she became eligible, in about a year's time.

I FINALLY GOT to speak to Amira, too, in late 2017. We chatted on the phone over three consecutive nights, between 2:00 and 3:00 a.m., Egypt time (and my time, too, in South Africa). It had been logistically complicated. This was because she kept hours that anywhere else in the world would seem insane, because we needed an interpreter whom she could trust, and because she lived in a far-flung quarter of Cairo that took time for the interpreter to get to, "far, far from downtown," Amira said wistfully.

How was she, I asked? "Still alive."

I wanted to know how her life was different from when I had last seen her. She let out a cry. "I live my life inside."

She explained that she no longer went downtown—"I'm too well-known there, and it's not safe"—and, besides, there were no cafés where gays could sit anymore: "I'm depressed, I'm lonely, I'm just waiting to find a way to leave Egypt."

Her friend Noor was interpreting for us, and reported to me that Amira broke into a huge smile when I asked her for "good memories" of the Girls' Café.

"It was a lot of effort," Amira said. "A huge effort, managing it, and we ended up shutting it down. The people downtown called us 'Café *Khawalat*' but we challenged everything. I made something for the community. I challenged society by doing that."

It was a bad connection. There was a long silence after Noor had finished translating, and some strange clicking sounds. Was somebody listening in? "Hello!" I yelled into my cell phone. "*Hello? Noor, are you still there?*" "We are still here," Noor said in her calm, deliberate English. "Amira is saying that she will open a café again, in Amsterdam. We will drink tea and smoke *shisha*. It won't be Cairo, but it will be Cairo."

EARLIER THAT EVENING, at a slightly more civilized hour, I had also spoken to Zaki. "I was hopeful about three years ago," he had said to me. "Now I understand the situation will never change. So I have decided to have a normal life, a hidden life. The fight is over." Perhaps, he allowed, "the hopelessness is so extreme because the expectations were so extreme. I have no expectations anymore." Still, unlike Amira, he had no plans to leave Egypt: "When I go to Paris, I see these beautiful men, out of the closet, but sitting alone at cafés. Here, at least, I am never alone."

In these Cairo nights of long-distance catch-up, I also managed to pin down Murad, the activist, who was trying to get into a graduate program in the United States.

"It seems like the Queen Boat era all over again," I said, but he disagreed emphatically: There might be a retreat from political activism or public life, "but among the younger generation there is no retreat from gay identity and activity. On the contrary. This is a result of the Internet, and perhaps the revolution. They are out, and they can't go back in."

AMIRA'S PARTNER VISA came through in late 2017, and she moved to Amsterdam. By this point the couple had been in the turmoil of trying to live outside Egypt for nearly four of their seven years together, and had not seen each other for two. Their differences had become irreconcilable: This and the strangeness of Amsterdam made Amira's time there unbearable. The couple split up, and Amira returned to Cairo after six months. She deeply regretted having left Amsterdam, she told me when I contacted her a few months later: she was working on another plan to get out of Egypt.

When Maha and I spoke at around the same time, in mid-2018, her criticism of life in Amsterdam had set into bitterness. "There's a lot of discrimination in this country," she told me. "It looks beautiful on the outside, but going through it, the system is horrible. It doesn't give you the space to make progress as a refugee. You might have been a doctor where you come from, but you'll be working in a supermarket here." She disliked, particularly, the "whitewashing," as she called it: the way the politicians "use asylum to show Netherlands is a great, secure country, but the system is really fucking people up." Despite the government grant to refugees, "we are not even considered as second-class citizens."

Maha was a coordinator of a "queer refugees group" called SEHAQ "the word is pejorative for *dyke* in Arabic and we wish to reclaim it"—and when we spoke she was helping organize a memorial service for a member, a Lebanese man, who had recently taken his life: "his departure is a reminder of the vital need to be supportive of each other and build a community, in this violent oppressive system that actively works to exclude us and to drain us," read the notice on the group's Facebook page.[17]

Sehaq hosted regular parties at Vrankrijk, the "political café" on Spui Street. "Our form of dancing, our form of socialising, is political in itself because we are creating a space that doesn't exist," another of the group's founders, Nisreen, told *The Guardian* in 2019.[18] "It is very subversive to gather and have fun, to not only ask for services. Asylum seekers don't need services—they need freedom."

But Maha struggled to define what freedom even meant anymore. She knew it was prudent to remain in the Netherlands for the two more years it would take to get Dutch papers, she told me when we spoke in 2018, but she lived her life on the verge of buying a plane ticket to Cairo: "I feel I've been in transit these last three years. As if I've been on a long travel. I think of going home every single day."

7

PINK FOLK-DEVILS

IN SEPTEMBER 2017, the hugely popular Lebanese alt-rock band Mashrou' Leila played at Cairo's Music Park Festival. The lead singer Hamed Sinno was openly "queer," one of the only such celebrities in the Arab world, and during the concert two fans waved a rainbow flag. It was not the first time this had happened in Cairo. "A rainbow flag, in public, in Cairo," Sinno had written on Facebook after a concert the previous year.[1] "I'm … fucking proud. Whoever you were, your courage is bloody inspiring.'"

But this time, after images of the flag-waving went viral on social media, Egypt's chief prosecutor announced that he was launching an investigation. By January 2018, over eighty-five people had been arrested and at least forty had served time in jail, including the two young people who waved the flag, charged with promoting an illegal organization.

Six years previously, Iraqi kids feeling liberated by the winds of the Arab Spring found themselves to be victims of a far more brutal clampdown, when the minister of the interior labeled the emo subculture a "Satanist" foreign influence.[2] Emo was an androgynous global youth style, and in Iraq it became associated not only with Western decadence but with homosexuality. An anti-emo moral panic rippled through Iraqi media, and militias went on purges: the United Nations Assistance Mission in Iraq (UNAMI) reported an estimated fifty-six to ninety deaths and was able to directly verify at least twelve, "most likely motivated by negative attitudes to 'emo' fashion or perceived sexual orientation."[3]

There was a precedent for crackdowns of this sort in Iraq. In April 2009, as American troops began to withdraw from the country, a squad of assassins in black masks swept through Baghdad, picking out men who seemed effeminate, exposing them to their families as "perverts," abducting them and killing them in gruesome ways. A thirty-five-year-old man named Hamid escaped: "They came into my house and they saw my mother, and one of them said: 'Where's your faggot son?'[4] There were five men. Their faces were covered. Fortunately I wasn't there but my mother called me after they left, in tears. From then on, I hid in a cheap hotel for two weeks. I can't face my family—they would reject me. I can't go home." Hamid fled Baghdad, and when a Human Rights Watch researcher interviewed him several weeks later, he was still so traumatized he struggled to speak. His partner of ten years had been one of the victims, pulled out of his family home: "They had thrown his corpse in the garbage. His genitals were cut off and a piece of his throat was ripped out."

A source at UNAMI estimated that hundreds of men were killed this way in early 2009, in the chaotic months of the American withdrawal. One executioner told a reporter he believed he was tackling "a serious illness in the community that has been spreading rapidly among the youth after it was brought in from the outside by American soldiers."[5] The death squads were aligned to Muqtadar al-Sadr's Mahdi Army, and several informants told a Human Rights Watch investigation they believed these Shia militias sought to reestablish themselves after the American occupation, "by appearing as an agent of social cleansing," as HRW put it, aiming "at popularity by targeting people few in Iraq would venture to defend."

There are scholars in both the Sunni and Shi'a traditions who dispute the orthodox Qur'anic position on homosexual activity, or who even argue that the Qur'an is silent on the issue. Whatever the case, there is little evidence it was punishable by death in precolonial times, because of the way the guardians of religious law turned a blind eye to people's private lives. But with the rise of political Islam in the late twentieth and early twenty-first centuries—just as queer people were tentatively claiming some public space—the censure of homosexuality became part of a broader political project across the Muslim world, from Senegal to Chechnya, from Egypt to Indonesia. It had a particular effect: it could be used to signal the need to erect barriers against "the ravaging moral decay, which has been coming out of the West to the rest of the planet," as Iran's Ayatollah Khamenei said about homosexuality in a 2016 speech.[6]

In 2018, six countries explicitly carried the death penalty for homosexuality under Sharia, as did the Muslim states in northern Nigeria. In others, it was part of a broader prohibition against any sex outside of marriage. Few enforced it but one entity that did, emphatically and even performatively, was ISIS. From 2012 onward, the caliphate boosted its global online profile by disseminating footage of suspected homosexuals being killed, often thrown to their death off buildings. By 2018, Human Rights Watch had evidence that suggested over forty men had been executed.[7]

In July 2017, after the male actor Karar Nushi was murdered in Baghdad (allegedly for the crime of having long hair) the British Iraqi commentator Amrou Al-Kadhi wrote in *The Independent* that it was "not a coincidence" that "violence against LGBTQI+ people in Iraq has escalated dramatically since the Western invasion in 2003."[8] Homosexuality had "become imaged as a Western export." "Disdain for the West is potent on Iraqi soil—what did we expect after destroying a civilisation for no *actual* reason?" Whether extrajudicial or legal, these killings were all Pink Line murders in that they set out to kindle moral panic about homosexuals, seen to be a demonic foreign threat to "pure" Islamic society.

THE CONCEPT OF "moral panic" was first fleshed out by the anthropologist Stanley Cohen in his classic 1972 book *Folk Devils and Moral Panics*, to describe moments when "a condition, episode, person or group of persons emerges to become defined as a threat to societal values and interests."[9] In her prescient 1984 essay "Thinking Sex," Gayle Rubin described the way moral panics are often about sex: "The media become ablaze with indignation, the public behaves like a rabid mob, the police are activated, and the state enacts new laws and regulations. When the furor has passed, some innocent erotic group has been decimated, and the state has extended its power into new areas of erotic behavior."[10]

Rubin was writing about twentieth-century America, but her description could be read forward to parts of Africa, Russia, and the

Middle East in the twenty-first century, or back to one of the first documented panics over homosexuals, the routing out of "molly houses" in eighteenthcentury London. Although buggery was a capital offense in Britain, the law was seldom applied—until a group called the Society for the Reformation of Manners used a crusade against mollies to headline its campaign to clean up London.[11] "Mollies" were effeminate men (or transgender women, according to today's definitions); the molly houses that were drinking establishments and brothels were relatively unhindered, and generally unknown to the broader population. But after the society's undercover investigations provoked a 1699 police raid, mollies became a matter of public scandal, with sensational newspaper coverage, dozens of arrests, trials, and even executions under the buggery law. In a way that prefigured the moral panics of the twenty-first century, the campaigns were led from the pulpit and often blamed on baleful foreign influences: one Reverend Bray preached from St Mary's Le Bow in 1708 against "an evil force invading our land"—from Europe, of course.

There was another way that this early moral panic anticipated what would happen later, in Senegal and Egypt, in Russia and Uganda and Indonesia: It was disseminated by the winds of an Information Revolution. What social media was to the early twenty-first century, mass newsprint media had been to the early eighteenth. As the historian Rictor Norton puts it: "The massive publicity that followed sodomitical trials in early eighteenth-century England, France and the Netherlands—in poems, broadsides, pamphlets—was made possible by advances in cheap printing technology and an increasing public appetite for 'news.'"[12]

Norton offers an assessment of the effect of this sudden publicity that also resonates with the early twenty-first century. The moral panic about mollies "outed" them not only to modern historians and contemporaries, but to one another: the Society for the Reformation of Manners "was itself responsible for stimulating the growth of the gay subculture," which "coalesced under the pressures of this reforming environment."[13]

IN EARLY 2016, *Republika,* a conservative Islamist newspaper in Indonesia, ran a headline that "LGBT Is a Serious Threat";[14] at the same time the minister of higher education responded to a brochure for an "LGBT Peer Support Network " at the University of Indonesia by saying that gay organizations should be banned from campuses.[15] Over the next months, provoked by headline-seeking tabloid journalism, a moral panic caught fire in the country, as politicians, clerics, and government agencies railed against LGBT rights. There were raids throughout 2016 and 2017 on saunas, nightclubs, hotel rooms, hair salons, and private homes—and the arrests of at least three hundred people in 2017. With the exception of the tourist island of Bali and a couple of bars in Jakarta, public queer life shut down. "When America sneezes, the world catches a cold," is how the founder of the country's LGBT movement, Dede Oetomo, put it to me—his explanation of why the 2016 moral panic happened when it did, a few months after U.S. Supreme Court legalized gay marriage. Islamists seeking to gain political power in a country renowned for its secular and pluralistic society exploited the news in an environment where LGBT organizations had mushroomed, in part because of HIV funding. Once the new pink folk-devil was named, even members of Joko Widodo's liberal technocratic government were compelled to add their voices to the new moral panic—particularly in the run-up to a 2019 election that conservative Muslims hoped to win, in coalition with Widodo's challenger, a former military general.

"You need to look and sound religious if you want to survive in mainstream politics here," given the spread of Islamism here, Oetomo said to me. The secular Joko won handily, but this was in no small part due to the running mate he selected, the conservative cleric Mar'uf Amin. As head of the country's Ulama Council, Amin enthusiastically had supported *fatwas* that, Human Rights Watch reported, "have been used to legitimize increasingly hateful rhetoric by government officials against LGBT people and in some cases fuelled deadly violence by militant Islamists against religious minorities."[16]

In countries prone to sex panics, queer folk know to lie low and take care in election seasons. In the run-up to Senegal's 2019 presidential election, the MSM organization AIDES-Sénégal made the decision to have no public profile whatsoever, even though its work was largely around public health. And during the moral panic linked to Indonesia's election, Sandeep Namwali—a medical doctor who had set up an organization providing services to *waria* in Yogyakarta—went to see the police to ask for extra protection for this community.

Namwali was astonished at the response: the commanding officer was more than happy to provide protection to this "minority" community with which his force very familiar, so long as they were not part of the new "LGBT threat." "It hit me that they had no idea what LGBT was," Namwali told me. "They just knew it was dangerous, a threat to society." From the dictatorship's purges of communists in the late-twentieth century, these invisible "enemies from within" had long been a trope of Indonesian politics, and "LGBT was just the latest manifestation."

The LGBT crisis in Indonesia was "only indirectly about children or Islam," wrote the anthropologist Tom Boellstorff.[17] "It is really about national belonging, about who will have a place at the table in Indonesia's evolving civil society." Two decades previously, Boellstorff had coined the term *political homophobia,* writing about an earlier series of attacks on perceived homosexuals in Indonesia, to describe the way that "male–male desire can increasingly be construed as a threat to normative masculinity, and thus to the nation itself."[18] Boellstorff showed how the Indonesian state was using a crackdown on gay men who were tentatively coming out for the first time to flex its muscles against broader opposition to its rule. This would be exactly how Vladimir Putin in Russia and African leaders like Uganda's Yoweri Museveni and Malawi's Bingu wa Mutharika would deploy political homophobia in the twenty-first century.

A narrower but more potent application of political homophobia took place in Malaysia in 1998, when the premier Mahathir Mohamed dispensed with his former deputy and opponent Anwar Ibrahim by charging him with sodomy and jailing him. The previous year, Zimbabwe's Robert Mugabe used similar charges to end the career of Canaan Banana, the former president of the country, and in Egypt Hosni Mubarak used "debauchery" charges to jail a troublesome opponent through the Queen Boat raid of 2001. State-aligned Russian media tried to smear the Ukrainian boxer-turned-politician Vitali Klitschko in the same way, in 2013.[19]

In all these instances, the allegation of homosexuality did double time. First, it was not only immoral but illegal, too, and could thus be used to tarnish your enemies and to rally supporters. And second, particularly given the messages about it being beamed over from the West, it was a potent way to suggest a threat to sovereignty by liberal globalized commodity culture. In Malaysia, Mahathir Mohamed exemplified this with two steps: first by imprisoning Anwar, and then by taking up the cudgels against the European promotion of "hedonism" and "sodomy" as a violation of "Asian values."[20]

In Nigeria and Uganda, the two African countries that sought to strengthen the censure of homosexuality by passing new laws, the process was driven by ambitious politicians who happened to be fervent Christians: David Mark and David Bahati. Given the sensationalist media interest in the gay issue, their aggressive promotion of political homophobia established their religious credentials and also grew their careers, expanding their constituencies through mobilizing against an unpopular and feared community, and the imagined threat of same-sex marriage. As populist politicians, they were also asserting a national identity—an *African* identity—against the neocolonial onslaught.

There were certainly examples of a Western high-handedness on the issue, or a confusion of human rights agendas with more imperial intentions, but these claims were usually a stand-in for the more abstract anxieties about a loss of control in the age of globalization over one's subjects and territories. The AIDS epidemic and the 2008 global economic crash had only heightened the dependence of many African countries on the West, and in this context there was a new impetus to fight the "neocolonialism" of development aid. And so, as many African leaders in particular became increasingly uncomfortable with such dependency, they looked to find a place to put their pride; they might be poor, but at least they had values! In all the world's global indicators of well-being, they could at least lead in one: morality. What better way to maintain popular support than through the scapegoating of an unpopular minority in the name of a battle against Western decadence?

HOMOSEXUALITY HAS LONG been a convenient scapegoat for perceived social ills, or a convenient way to slur enemies, or against which to define one's own righteousness.

In Nazi Germany, Heinrich Himmler blamed it, along with abortion, for the low birth rate among Aryan Germans; this was one of the foundation stones of the official homophobia of the Third Reich. Vladimir Putin took a leaf out of this script when—in his December

2013 speech on the subject—he described the normalization of homosexuality as a sign of "the loss of the ability to self-reproduce" in Western countries.[21] The countries of the West were "implementing policies that equate large families with same-sex partnerships," Putin said; this was like equating "belief in God with the belief in Satan." Of course, Russia's demographic crisis had little to do with same-sex partnerships and families, but political homophobia became a significant weapon in its pro-natalist arsenal, a campaign that included reviving the Soviet tradition of awarding medals and monetary prizes to large families.

As in the African countries, the most aggressive proponents of the Russian gay propaganda legislation were ambitious regional politicians using the issue to build their constituencies through the church and to develop national profiles through the media: In this way, such legislation was passed in eight regions between 2006 and 2012. When Putin needed populist policies to assert his authority, he saw the value of the issue and ran with it.

This was part of a hard-right turn that Putin took during his 2011–12 election campaign, after hundreds of thousands took to the streets to protest his return to office. Prominent among them were LGBT groups under rainbow flags. Fearing a loss of his middle-class urban support base, Putin tacked toward nationalism, "traditional values," and the patronage of the Orthodox Church, and one of the first ways he demonstrated this shift was through the prosecution—on charges of blasphemy—of Pussy Riot, after the feminist punk band performed in Moscow's Cathedral of Christ the Savior advocating feminism and LGBT rights. Soon after Putin's reelection, his United Russia party announced the federal gay propaganda law that would cover the whole nation.

Inciting a moral panic against the queer people whose visibility was growing in his country provided the Russian president with an irresistible trifecta. It was a way of flexing state muscles against the civic activism and liberal individualism of the cities. It was also a populist family values plank to curry favor with the Russian electorate and solidify a relationship with the church. And it was, of course, the sharpest way of defining the imperial Russia that Putin wished to establish, against the decadence of the West.

Soviet propagandists had long ago learned the value of the "enemy from within": the benefits of stoking fear in the populace against a neighbor, a colleague, or even a relative whose pernicious counter-revolutionary influence was invisible and who needed to be rooted out of society—with the help, of course, of state force and surveillance. Homosexuals fitted this bill perfectly: even more so because they were an "enemy from within" getting their corrupting ideas from "without."

There was an ironic American precedent for this culture wars maneuver, too: Senator Joseph McCarthy's 1950 allegation that a high number of the "reds under the bed" he sought to flush out were homosexual, given that "practically every active Communist is twisted mentally or physically in some way."[22] McCarthy unleashed what has since been called a "lavender scare," which associated homosexuality with treason: thousands of federal employees were forced to resign or were dismissed between the 1940s and the 1970s. "The Cold War American hysteria over the alleged threat caused by homosexuals was unprecedented," writes the historian David K. Johnson.[23] "At a time when Americans felt threatened by an external enemy that seemed to be gaining strength and stealing its military secrets, the search for internal enemies ran rampant, and homosexuals proved an easy target." This perception of queer people as vulnerable, and thus unreliable, contributed to the archaic, post–Cold War discomforts in American governments, from Bill Clinton's Don't Ask, Don't Tell compromise in 1993 through Donald Trump's ban on transgender people in the military in 2016.

In Russia, the construction of queer people as "enemies from within" getting their ideas from "without" enabled another nifty two-step. At home, the government could define itself as a supporter of "family values" and could justify further crackdowns on civil society: LGBT organizations were among the first victims of the 2012 "foreign agents" law, which restricted the activities of organizations that did "political activity" with foreign funding. Meanwhile, it could deploy homophobia as a foreign policy instrument abroad.

This was a key component toward the establishment of what the journalist Owen Matthews dubbed a "Conservative Comintern," a Russian foreign policy centered on "traditional values."[24] Putin's diplomats used the notion as an adhesive to bond the countries of the former Soviet Union together again, in a new Eurasian sphere of Russian influence to counter the West. There were harder tactics, of course, such as threats to withhold trade and energy resources and, of course—as in Ukraine—military invasion. But the soft levers of propaganda were pulled, too: Russia's state-run federal media, which reached all over the former Soviet empire where there were large minorities of Russian speakers; and the Russian Orthodox Church, which was a powerful political player in the former Soviet countries to the west.

In the Baltic states, Russian influence created dissonance between the pro-European rights-based legal framework and the TV programming that Russian-speaking viewers watched each night. Estonia had developed a tolerant Nordic profile, but in Lithuania and Latvia, homophobic attitudes were the highest in the European Union: according to the EU's 2015 Eurobarometer survey, half of the Lithuanian population did not think that homosexuals should have the same rights as heterosexuals, and over three-quarters would be uncomfortable if their child dated a person of the same sex. Only a quarter of Lithuanians approved of same-sex marriage, as did just under a fifth of Latvians.

Lithuania had actually adopted a law banning even the discussion of homosexuality in schools in 2009. Now broader gay propaganda laws modeled on the Russian one were tabled there, and in five other countries of the former Soviet Union, from Europe across to the Asian steppes. None of these initiatives would prove successful, but the debates they kindled raised the homophobic temperature considerably in the region, in that they made the "dangers" of homosexuality a matter of public discourse. In 2017, at least eighty-three men were rounded up in Azerbaijan, tortured with electricity and forced to reveal other names, in the name of public health and safety. The same year, the Tajikistan state prosecutor unveiled a "registry" of 376 alleged homosexuals, "due to their vulnerability in society and for their safety and to prevent the transmission of sexually-transmitted diseases."[25]

And in December 2016, there was an extensive pogrom against homosexual men in the self-governing Russian territory Chechnya: over a hundred were imprisoned and tortured, and at least three killed. Masha Gessen wrote in *The New Yorker* that Chechnya was "a more extreme version of Russia: a mafia state that uses religious rhetoric to enforce control over its citizens," albeit "a crude homespun version of Islam" rather than Christianity.[26] The Russian newspaper that broke the story, *Novaya Gazeta*, suggested that the pogrom was the backlash to a call by Russian activists for Pride marches to take place in the Caucasus, but according to Gessen a more likely trigger was the revelation of gay hookup sites on the cell phone of a detainee arrested for drug use.[27]

One way or the other, a moral panic was kindled. The Russian gay propaganda legislation and the homophobia it generated sent out "a very clear signal that LGBT people are inferior," the chair of the Russian LGBT Network, Tatiana Vinnichenko, said to me; this was a signal the Chechen leader Ramzan Kadyrov was "adept at picking up and exploiting it to his own ends." The Chechnya pogrom created the next spectacle—after the global outcry around the Sochi Olympics three years earlier—along the Pink Line's Eastern European borderlands. Putin was admonished publicly by the German president Angela Merkel; there were protests outside Russian embassies in the West; Russian LGBT activists went on an American fund-raising tour and established an escape route out of Chechnya. They "evacuated" over fifty gay men and temporarily housed them elsewhere in Russia. Between April and July 2017, twenty-seven of these men were granted asylum in the West, twelve in Canada alone. Lesbian women also found themselves under new scrutiny, and some fled as well, running from the threat of an honor killing.

Such panics, writes the anthropologist Gilbert Herdt in his introduction to the 2009 book *Moral Panics, Sex Panics*, "are characteristic of states that experience times of divided public opinion, changing social, economic and political circumstances, and a clash between state mechanisms of control and the free expression and individual elaboration of sexuality."[28] The Chechnya anti-gay pogrom was, a 2017 Russian LGBT Network report noted, part of a much broader campaign by authorities against everything from alcoholism to women's rights to youth subcultures, all of which were seen as "manifestations of personal freedom" going against the rules of an idealized Chechen society.[29]

8

PASHA'S STORY

MOSCOW

Pasha Captanovska—IT consultant and former sniper, late thirties. Pronouns: she/her/hers.

Yulia Captanovska—Pasha's ex-wife, insurance executive, thirties. Pronouns: she/her/hers.

Yarik—Pasha and Yulia's son, seven. Pronouns: he/him/his.

Valentina Kuzminichna—Pasha's stepmother, retired hairdresser and factory worker, seventies. Pronouns: she/her/hers.

Alya—Pasha's girlfriend, psychotherapist, late thirties. Pronouns: she/her/hers.

Vitya—Alya's son, high school student, late teens. Pronouns: he/him/his.

Yael Demedetskaya—Co-owner of gender transition clinic, a transgender store, and a community center, mid-forties. Pronouns: she/her/hers.

Andrei Demedetskiy—Yael's husband and business partner, mid-thirties. Pronouns: he/him/his.

Varya—Bus conductor and young mother in Arkhangelsk, early twenties. Pronouns: she/her/hers.

Kate Messorosh—Tech product developer in St. Petersburg, late twenties. Pronoun: she/her/hers.

1

At the end of the first day's hearing, in Pasha Captanovska's application to gain access to her son, the two parties found themselves outside the courtroom, uncomfortably awaiting the same elevator. Pasha had given Yulia a birthday gift to hand on to Yarik—their son was about to turn eight—and now Pasha could not contain herself: "What about our shared property?" she demanded, referring to the goods taken from the apartment and even the car in which Yulia had driven off, that day she had left with Yarik, just over two years before.

"Don't you dare come near me!" Yulia screamed in response, but before Pasha could respond, Yulia's lawyer stepped between them. "Who do you think you are?" the lawyer—a woman—said to Pasha. "Just look at yourself. You're such a freak. You should never be allowed anywhere near children!"

It was August 4, 2016, and the former couple were at the Palace of Justice—as the gold lettering proclaimed above an oversize imperial arch slapped onto the facade of the new pink building—in a gritty dormitory town called Lyubertsy, southeast of Moscow. Pasha's shoulder-length strawberry-blond hair was pulled off her brow with a band, and there was the thinnest dusting of makeup over her fine features: almond eyes and high cheekbones. She was wearing unisex black trousers and a sober blouse; a discreet heart hung off a black cord around her neck and there were two rings on her fingers. Her demands were reasonable, and at first both the judge and the state-mandated social worker seemed to be encouraging. Pasha wanted to see Yarik once a week, and have a holiday with him twice a year.

But Yulia found this unacceptable, and accused Pasha of "psychological violence" against her and their son: "To imagine that he could change his gender and that the child and I would be able to live with him as if nothing happened—this could only be the work of a sick mind."[1] Yulia was tall and glamorous, with long dark hair pulled back into a taut ponytail. She told the court that Pasha used to hang around the house in women's underwear; her father added in his statement to the court that he had watched Pasha lactate into a breast pump in the presence of the boy. Pasha was incredulous, listening to these allegations: they were lies, she told me.

Pasha had "never acted in the best interests of the child, either before the divorce or after," Yulia told the court.[2] She and her father laid it on: Pasha had failed to toilet-train Yarik, did not communicate with him, and rather than taking him out to play would lie in bed until eleven in the morning "kissing and licking him, which started to look like a perversion once it turned out he was a woman," the old man sniffed censoriously. When Yarik asked where his father was, the grandfather said, "I told him that there is no more father and that his father became a woman …" Even more distressing to Pasha than hearing this was listening to how her gentle son had started taking "dogfight classes"—a form of contact fighting—and that the little boy would say, "When I grow up I will take revenge on my father."

Judge E.G. Aksenova ruled in Yulia's favor: there was to be no communication whatsoever between Pasha and her son until the latter was eighteen; until then, seeing Pasha would "cause damage" not only to the boy's physical and mental health," but to his "ethical development" and his understanding of "traditional family values."[3] In case there was any doubt as to the wisdom of her decision, the judge elevated her ruling from the lowly realms of family law to the new ideological battle that the Russian authorities were waging: "The plaintiff does not conceal her transgenderism, talking to the child about the possibility of changing sex, and thus in fact violates the Federal Law on Protection of Children from Harmful Information, which prohibits the propaganda of non-traditional sexual relationships among minors."

The judge was freely interpreting Russia's infamous law passed three years earlier: it did not, in fact, list "transgenderism" or "sex-change" alongside the "non-traditional sexual relationships" which were not to be "promoted" within earshot of minors.

Pasha had become a casualty along the Pink Line.

A YEAR BEFORE, in July 2015, I stood with Pasha in Yarik's room, the somber chapel to a lost child. When Yulia had moved out she had left behind nothing of the child, save the climbing ropes tied to his bunk bed and a sentimental portrait she had done of him with angel wings, naked with peonies, hanging on the wall. These were still in place in the otherwise empty room; the only other traces of the child were his wax-crayon drawings at child height just above the skirtings: *Angry Birds*, and the Swedish cartoon *Carlsen*.

Pasha lived in the ground-floor corner apartment of one of the Khrushchev-era blocks that marched for miles down Oktyabrsky Prospekt, Lyubertsy's main drag. The town was developed in the 1950s to house workers in the nearby factories, and in post-Soviet times it became notorious as the home of Moscow's new mafia. As I alighted from the *martrushka* taxi with Zhenya, my interpreter, it seemed as if we were stepping into a Soviet-era planned community, albeit one updated by the current politics: I counted five cars, in the short distance between the taxi rank and Pasha's block, with "Obama *shmoe* [asshole]" bumper stickers.

Transgender people sometimes move as far away as possible from their previous lives to be able to start afresh. But Pasha had been here, in the same apartment, for thirty-seven years, since she was four. It had, of course, been a communal flat in Soviet times, housing different families in three rooms around a shared kitchen, but as the other tenants moved on, Pasha's "grandmothers" moved in, so that by the time the Soviet Union collapsed it was in effect a family home. Pasha's father had been granted the title deed to the property when it was privatized, and when he died in 1995 Pasha inherited it. She renovated it in neat contemporary blues and grays, the bustle of the boulevard screened by double glazing and venetian blinds, the two bedrooms to the side overlooking a wooded strip between her apartment block and a school next door.

Pasha had changed her surname legally to the female form—Captanovska instead of Captanovsky—but had kept her first name, the gender-neutral diminutive of both the male Pavel and the female Pavla. This decision was of a piece with the one to stay in the apartment: "I want to show people I'm just the same person as I used to be." She was genderqueer, she told me: although she had assumed a female identity after having surgery and changing her documents—a laborious and unpredictable process—her style remained androgynous, as it had always been. Today she was in black unisex cutoffs and a cotton shirt; tall and athletic, she habitually hid her striking beauty behind a curtain of hair over her face, which she pulled at constantly as she sucked on a vape pen.

At the time we met she was in the midst of the custody battle for Yarik, low with the grief of losing her son and the exhaustion of trying to get him back. There were also the unexpected side effects of her vaginoplasty surgery: walking was still difficult, as a result of a problem with her epidural anesthetic. She seldom went outdoors, portioning her love of nature instead through a bird feeder she hung outside her bedroom window; she would sometimes post little videos on Facebook, taken through the venetian blinds, of the birds pecking at it. The impression these videos gave—to me, at least—was one of imprisonment, but also of hope.

Pasha was thoughtful and articulate, but very diffident. She spoke so softly it was almost a whisper. While this might have been an attempt feminize her voice, it could not be mistaken for tentativeness or a lack of self-confidence: she was convinced Yarik would be better off with her. "I was committed to my son's individuality, to him developing his own personality," she said. "Yulia felt more that a child needs to be told how to behave, what to do, what to think. She believed that I wasn't bringing him up to be a man."

Pasha framed her determination to get Yarik back as a way of saving him: "In the way they are now brainwashing him about me, I can see that he is being treated like clay that can be shaped into anything they like. That's the reason why I think I should raise him, because then he will be free to make his own choices about what he wants to be, what he thinks of others. I'm fighting to give him a few moments of safety from what's being hammered into his head right now."

Pasha's primary evidence of this "hammering" was the state-appointed psychological panel's assessment of the child, commissioned as a consequence of her custody suit. We looked at it together. "When asked about his home, [Yarik] gets tense and clenches his fists [and] gets carried away in anger, claiming, 'I don't have a father any more … He was first my good, kind dad and now he is some nutty dame.'"[4] This is a poor translation of the vulgar Russian slang he used, presumably fed to him by the adults around him. Pasha had "caused Mum and Grandma a lot of pain," the little boy told his assessors, "that's not how men should behave." He returned repeatedly to this subject: his friends were "real men," they had "balls," and together "we are learning to fight like real men in a battle." His grandfather, one of these "real men," had told him that given that "Dad is now wearing braids and earrings and hair clips," he needed "to be taught what's what." Yarik also reported that "Mum will not let me see Dad, because he could infect me with his illness."

The psychologists declined to assess the relationship between Pasha and Yarik, however, because they had not observed them together. But in a twist of logic they refused to put the two of them together for the purposes of such assessment as it might "destabilize the child."[5] They made a judgement, in the absence of proper observation, that would prove damning for Pasha: Yulia would use it to prevent Pasha from having any access at all to their son.

THE LAST TIME Pasha had seen Yarik was the previous summer, around the time of his sixth birthday, in early August 2014.[6] This was about six weeks after Yulia had left, and in the interim there had been several such playdates, always in public places, and always with Yulia and another member of her family present. This time the date was set for a nearby amusement park: Yulia brought Yarik, and hung around with a friend while the boy dragged Pasha off to a carnival stall and demanded she win him a teddy bear. The two worked as a team, taking three shots each with darts at balloons; they scored every time, and the irritated stallholder handed over a great gray bear almost bigger than the little boy himself, which Yarik immediately christened Misha. Pasha joked that they were going to be banned from the stall if they carried on this way. "What can I say, a family of snipers!" Pasha boasted on Facebook that evening: she had been one during her military service and her son seemed to have inherited her perfect aim. Pasha gave Yarik a birthday gift, a Lego Star Wars kit, and when it was time to leave "Yarik, as usual, waved goodbye to me and sent air-kisses, which I caught and sent back."

The visit was clearly a success: two days later Pasha was offered another meeting at the park. "No more bears!" she joked as she greeted her son.[7] This time Yulia's mother was the chaperone, and while they leaned against the rails of the pirate trampoline watching the boy, Pasha asked her former mother-in-law to explain why she was there. The woman did not respond, and Pasha persevered: "It's humiliating and insulting to me that I am only able to meet my child under the supervision of two people. It's not like I'm a criminal or anything."[8]

Still, the older woman refused to engage, and when Pasha prodded her as to why, she exploded: "BECAUSE I DO NOT WANT TO SPEAK TO YOU!!!! BECAUSE I WANT TO BREAK YOUR FACE!!"

"For what???"

"BECAUSE OF YOU, ALL OUR LIVES ARE DESTROYED!!!!" The capital letters are Pasha's own, recorded in a Facebook post that night, in which she described the way Yulia's mother's "pleasant female face was distorted by the grimace of unlimited anger and hatred. This woman, with whom I lived side by side for 15 years, and who called me 'my beloved son-in-law'! ... How can a person change SO quickly?" Yulia and her family countered, of course (not to me: they did not respond to repeated requests for an interview), that it was Pasha who had changed so quickly, and so inexplicably. Now, they felt, Pasha had added fuel to the fire: they were enraged that she had posted the above account on social media, airing their conflict publicly. By this point the divorce had come through and Yulia cut off all ties, despite Pasha's access rights as stipulated in the divorce settlement.

When Yarik and his minders did not show up for the next scheduled meeting, Pasha called and was told the boy was ill. Pasha went over to Yulia's parents' apartment with gifts for him, but was denied entry: Yulia's mother lobbed verbal insults at her, and Yulia's brother and some friends arrived, "all drunk, trying to drag me out into the street. I understood that they wanted to beat me up, but as an activist I have had some experience of this, so I lifted my legs so that they couldn't move me. A small crowd gathered and one old lady started screaming at them, 'What are you doing? Stop it!' And so they dropped me and walked away."

Pasha did not see Yarik again. Her only news about her son came through her stepmother, Valentina, who had a "babushka line" open to Yulia's grandmother: the woman would call from time to time with news about Yarik, clearly fishing about Pasha's legal intentions.

"PEACHES!"

Valentina Kuzminichna announced her bounty as she crossed the threshold of Pasha's flat one steamy July afternoon in 2015. "Peaches and cucumbers! I have beautiful summer peaches, and cucumbers and tomatoes, from the market for you!"

Pasha's stepmother was a retired factory worker and hairdresser. She was a short, thickset woman in a sleeveless floral frock, with no-nonsense cropped hair and that singular combination of heartiness and sentimentality that defines the babushka. "Pasha is my adopted daughter," she said to me, before even being introduced. "I've been raising her since she was seven years old."

"Actually it was eight," Pasha corrected her.

"I know better. It was seven. You were nearing your eighth birthday. I came at the end of the year."

"I was nearly eight."

"Suit yourself ! I married your father after courting for only two months. We never had a single quarrel. We were at peace, even though we had two, sometimes three, grandmothers living with us. *Quite an achievement!* The only thing we used to fight about, dear Pasha, was your refusal to eat. Your grandmother used to try to force it down you, but I always supported you."

As the old woman eased herself onto the couch next to Pasha—she had a heart condition and bad legs—she heard the latest news: Pasha had not only lost her appeal against the custody decision, but had also received a call from Yulia's lawyer, telling her that she could no longer see the child at all, given the psychologists' report that this would be "destabilizing." Valentina was outraged: "If you had ever seen Pasha and the child together you would see what a special relationship it was. I am so pained by this. I am so angry." She threw her arms around "my Pasha" and pinched her cheeks: "She has always been my child. I loved her when she was my son, and now I love her as my daughter."

Pasha had been only four years old when her own father removed her from her mother. This was after he returned from a business trip and found his child in hospital due to the mother's neglect. Pasha's only tangible memory of her mother was sitting on the floor with a toy and watching her back at the kitchen table as she drank herself into oblivion, a consequence of what Pasha now understood to be untreated postnatal depression. She saw her mother only once or twice after that, and the disappearance was a major motivation in her fight to remain in her own child's life. What compounded this, of course, was the evidence that Yulia's family was turning Yarik against her. "When I was little, a lot of harsh and dirty things were said to me about my mother. But as I have grown up, I have realized that she was not the evil person I was told about. She was a victim, who should have been helped, rather than abandoned to her fate. It kills me that Yarik's head is being filled with the idea of my being evil, just as my head was filled when I was little." As an adult Pasha had begun a search for her mother, but the leads were slender: in the Soviet Union people really did disappear.

When Pasha's father took custody of her, he moved with her to Lyubertsy because he worked nearby as an engineer at the behemoth MIL helicopter factory, and because his mother lived there. Although Pasha did not say it, her battle for the custody of Yarik must have been influenced, too, by the way her own father, atypical for a man in Russian society, raised her: "I really loved that man. He was an example to me of *humanism*."

"The grandmothers" who raised Pasha—her father's mother and aunts—were a formidable crew toughened by orphanage childhoods during the Great War: their parents had been sent to Siberia during the *kulak* purges of the 1930s. They lived with the conviction—a Russian condition—that life had to be barricaded against impending catastrophe, and they had "not a very good attitude" about the people who ruled them. From them, Pasha imbibed an early disdain for Soviet-style authoritarianism, and she stayed away from the Communist Party and the youth movements that might have advanced her, educationally and professionally.

Gender in Pasha's family was by no means conventional: certainly, her father was the primary breadwinner who taught his son to shoot, but he was also the softy who encouraged Pasha's individuality. Pasha's grandmother, on the other hand, was "the man of the house—she tolerated no dissent." From the athlete to the worker, there was, in fact, room in Soviet society for gender non-conforming women, and when Valentina Kuzminichna—a widow—joined the Captanovsky household with her ten-year-old son, she proved to be one of them: she went off to work every day, did not cook a single meal, and did no housework. She and Pasha became very close.

NOW, AS WE sat in Pasha's living room, her stepmother volunteered, without prompting, the following about her "new daughter": "Of course this is not *traditional* for our country. This is not conventional. We have our own traditions and conventions here in Russia. Not like you in the West. But you have to be *humanist*"—here it was, that word, again—"in every situation". Her take on Yulia's family was that "they're quite frightened, and I can't figure out why."

"Maybe they're frightened of what others will think?" I suggested. "Why, then, am *I* not afraid?" she shot back. She had struggled with Pasha's identity at first, but had now become her staunchest defender:

"How could I possibly turn my back on my own child, when mothers of *murderers* still go and visit their children in jail? My Pasha is not a criminal! She is my child and I must support her now that the whole world is against her." Emotion overwhelmed her: "I'm going to go over there [to Yulia's family's apartment] and beat them all up! The police will not even be able to restrain me!"

Was the whole world against Pasha?

We visited a neighbor, an elderly woman named Natalya Efseyeva. "I could see him changing, but I didn't want to pry. But then you get snatches of things on the TV, and you discover that such things happen, and that—heavens!—your neighbor, the little Pasha you have known since he was a little boy, this little Pasha is one of those!"

Mrs. Efseyeva confirmed—as did Valentina, and every other person I spoke to, including a friend of Yulia's family—that Pasha had been Yarik's primary parent until Yulia removed him. Pasha's first job, after military service, had been as a sniper in the Home Guard, but she had left after a few years: "I hated the look of fear in people's faces when they saw a man with a gun," she told me. So she retrained in information technology and worked mainly at home (her primary client was Aeroflot), while Yulia was an executive in the insurance industry who worked hard and partied hard; she was seldom around.

Pasha was "a wonderful parent," Natalya Efseyeva said, but "he was much too soft. He would never scold a child." She rolled her eyes at Pasha and addressed her with gentle sarcasm: "You always preferred to *explain* to him why something was wrong, didn't you?" Pasha's in-laws apparently agreed, and there was conflict about discipline that long predated the gender transition.

Mrs. Efseyeva's son had been Pasha's best friend at school, and while her son did not want anything to do with Pasha anymore, the older woman now counted her neighbor as a good friend—even if she could not get the pronouns right—and embraced her fondly when they met. People in the building did gossip about Pasha, but "it's not malicious. We don't know the reasons, so we just shrug. If he were immoral, we'd be more much more judging. But Pasha's such a good person. Sometimes a guy just becomes a girl, I guess. It happens. That's life."

2

Pasha usually worked at home, and when she was called to the office unexpectedly on the morning of Thursday, June 26, 2014, she had a premonition: "Yulia just seemed too keen to get me out of the house. When I came home and saw them gone, I knew immediately what had happened. I became hysterical. I tried to phone Yulia, repeatedly, but she would not pick up."

Eventually Pasha got through to Yulia, late in the night. "There's nothing to worry about," Yulia had said. "We're doing okay."

"What about me?" Pasha had responded. "Now you're free to live as you choose."

In a cruel way, Yulia was right. For years, Pasha had been deferring any thought of transition: precisely, like so many others, because of the fear she would be compelled to forfeit her wife and son. But now, she told me, "I had nothing more to lose."

A friend introduced her to a gender clinic in Moscow, and she began her transition: her submission to a board of three doctors led by a psychiatrist, a medical diagnosis of "transsexualism," vaginoplasty surgery, and then, finally, the arduous process of persuading the Russian bureaucracy to change her documents (there was no standard procedure for this, and it depended on the caprice of the local functionary).

If Pasha lost Yarik by becoming a woman, the tragic irony of her story is this: it was her son's birth that had rekindled her understanding of herself as female in the first place, a feeling she had successfully repressed since she had been about ten. Like so many transgender children, she did not understand in early childhood why she was called a boy and expected to do male things. But she was naturally athletic, and her passion was shooting: she loved the "focus" and the "tranquility" of marksmanship. She managed to suppress her femininity: "I put it deep inside, in a little box, and it was invisible to the outside," she told me. "My life was like that scene in *The Terminator*. Schwarzenegger is looking at a screen and figuring out what his options are. There are several options, and the most appropriate one is highlighted. I acted in the way that would be most appropriate, to avoid problems."

Pasha became the Terminator: "Military service: *highlighted*. So I went to the army and became a sniper. Husband: *highlighted*. So I married Yulia. Fatherhood: *highlighted*. So we had Yarik."

But when the child was born "all my female feelings rose up again. I just felt a big love for this little creature, and I wanted to protect him, feed him, take care of him. But it was considered that men should not act this way. I was rebuked for being too soft, too caring, not manly enough as a father: this shocked and confused me. Over time I came to the conclusion that a ban on manifesting these feelings was being imposed on me. Once I understood this, I realized that I had the power to reject this ban and show these feelings. Society did not have the right to manage how I felt. So I released these feelings … I freed my consciousness from everything imposed on me. That's when I accepted myself as a woman."

This was not done in a vacuum: it was, precisely, in these years that a global awareness about transgender identity was expanding dramatically, due to the digital information explosion, to increased access to drugs and surgery, and to the victories around gay rights in the West, which had opened up new frontiers and spawned a transgender rights movement. These were also the years in which a new rights movement was becoming visible in Russia, too: from

2006 onward, a group called GayRussia applied annually to hold a Moscow Pride event; every year the application was declined and the activists proceeded anyway, provoking certain assault by counter-protestors and arrest by the police. In the new LGBT alphabet that was knitting itself into the Russian lexicon (by 2012, it was pro forma even for hostile opponents to use the acronym), the *T* began asserting itself: transgender participants and signs at the annual aborted Pride events; documentaries about gender at the LGBT Film Festival in St. Petersburg; a genderqueer activist named Grey Violet who did public performances with Pussy Riot.

Pasha spent a lot of time on *transgender.ru*, which had started in 2004, and in online chat rooms. She also began a self-guided crash course in gender theory, reading in Russian and English. She watched the new activism from a distance, increasingly roused by it. In early 2012, at a time when things seemed good in the family—"We were happy, despite our difference," Pasha told me. "I'm not a masochist"—she decided to confide in Yulia about her gender identity. At first Yulia thought her husband must be gay, but when Pasha carefully explained the difference between sexual orientation and gender identity, "Yulia was so supportive, even calm. Then this whole gay propaganda thing happened in Russia, and everything changed."

For both of them.

THE TURNING POINT was Vladimir Putin's reelection campaign in 2011 and his subsequent presidency.

"Suddenly, after Putin was reelected, they started showing all these horrible programs on TV," Pasha recalled. "'It's harmful, it's an illness coming from the West aimed at the destruction of Russia from within.'" In the Captanovsky household, Yulia's views started to change. "She had been quite progressive and democratic before, but now she joined the whole gang of pseudo-patriots eventually screaming, 'Crimea belongs to Russia,'" Pasha told me. "Her views on sexual minorities fell into line, too." In discussions at home, Yulia made it clear that she supported the new anti-gay legislation, which purported to be all about protecting children.

A chasm opened up between the married couple: both were radicalized, in opposite directions.

In December 2012, Pasha read online about a kiss-in outside the State Duma, in protest of the first reading of the new federal anti-propaganda legislation, which expanded the provincial laws to include any information at all about "non-traditional sexual orientation" including—crucially—that which created "a distorted image of the social equivalence of traditional and non-traditional sexual relationships."[9] In other words, of the equality of gays and straights. Driven in part by outrage and in part by the desire for community, Pasha decided to attend. She did so quietly, as a bystander.

Two months later, on a bitterly cold January morning, she went again, when the bill was in its second reading. She had not planned to get arrested, but when she saw the force with which others were being manhandled, she sat herself down in the deep snow and refused to move. She was one of twenty activists loaded into a police van and taken off to the Tverskoy police station: "The day of kissing was successful," she posted on Facebook, alongside photographs of herself and other detainees in the van, and at the police station: "There were many participants, journalists, cops and thugs. The latter tried to attack, but did not succeed. No one was hurt."[10]

This was Pasha's public coming out, if not yet as transgender, then as an activist for LGBT rights. Yulia was predictably upset, and accused Pasha of betraying an agreement by going public. "Yulia is a perfectionist," a family friend told me. "She and her family really care about showing the world the 'right' face. Imagine if someone they knew had seen Pasha on television at one of these demonstrations! She could never have lived with the shame. She was also, correctly, worried that the child might be teased."

On June 11, 2013, Pasha went for the third time to protest: a kiss-in outside the state Duma, where the final vote was being held. The large contingent of police were much rougher than before, and less inclined to stop right-wing counter-protestors from violence: several participants were badly assaulted. It was early summer, and Pasha had impulsively bought a bunch of bright red peonies on the way. Although she was not arrested herself this time (perhaps out of deference to Yulia), she managed to hand the bunch to a protestor being dragged to the waiting police van; the image of the flowers being waved out of the bars of the van as it drove off became a vivid symbol of the day's resistance.

Inside the Duma, legislators voted almost unanimously to pass the bill: there was but one abstention. Putin signed it into law three weeks later. Then, in September, the new law found its logical consequence in a proposal to amend the Family Code, which would permit the state to remove children from homosexual parents—just as it had such powers over drug addicts, alcoholics, and others who practiced a supposedly amoral lifestyle. The measure's author, the ultra-nationalist Alexei Zhuravlev, explained that it was not enough to ban "gay propaganda" in the media and public spaces: this had to be done in "the family" too, because the harm it could do to a child's mind was "immense."[11] Even after this proposal was shelved its very existence caused panic within the LGBT community; it also played a significant role in fueling homophobic discourse. Yulia grew more anxious.

"The message is clear," said Sasha Semyonova, who ran an LGBT families network in St. Petersburg when I met her in October 2013, when Zhuravlev's bill was being mooted: "'Be quiet, or we'll take your children away from you. Maybe your nightclubs and your bars, too.'"

Semyonova conducted a survey for Coming Out St. Petersburg, where she worked, of 250 families in the city: mainly lesbian parents, but also a smattering of transgender and gay ones. Over half said they were planning to leave Russia, and another quarter were not sure; even those planning to stay spoke of how they would need to be more discreet. Semyonova was a mother herself, and she spoke of her own anguish: "These are parents who have been teaching their children to be proud of their families. Now they have to go back to their kids and tell them to be more discreet, even to hide the fact that they have two moms. Imagine that." She and her family left Russia at the end of 2013, to settle in the Czech Republic.

Semyonova's survey provides a vital clue for understanding the conditions that went into what had been happening in Russia. If queer parents were contemplating going back into the closet, it meant that they had been coming *out* of that closet in the preceding years: the very fact that there was a network of 250 queer families in St. Petersburg in the first place offers an indication of how urban Russian culture had been changing in the early twenty-first century.

There had indeed been something of a "lesbian baby boom," as Semyonova put it to me, in those years. It mirrored what had happened in many other parts of the world, too, now that the notion of queer families was being mainstreamed by the legalization of same-sex marriage in some countries, and the idea was being broadcast globally through television and social media. "It had seemed an inevitability that LGBT rights would come to Russia," Semyonova said to me. She chose her words judiciously to describe the environment during the years prior to Putin's return to the presidency in 2012: "There was, perhaps, even a spirit of some optimism." Cities had been booming, Russians were traveling, and the benefits of capitalism, only available to a thin upper crust of society during the dire 1990s, were now more widely enjoyed. The pull of the West was still strong for urban middle-class Russians, particularly when it came to the overlapping cultures of liberal personal freedoms and commodity consumption, and busy gay subcultures began to develop in the cities. By 2012, too, Russia was one of the most wired countries in the world: social media meant that isolated people across this huge country could connect and become part of a virtual community, even if they could not actually go to clubs or hook up. Activist organizations were sprouting, too, seeded in part by the funders promoting LGBT rights globally, such as George Soros's Open Society Foundations, and the Nordic and Dutch development agencies.

It was no coincidence that the first anti-gay propaganda law was passed in Ryazan in 2006, just after the first attempt at a Pride event in Moscow. There were barriers that could not be crossed: public political protest, or even visibility; any call for rights.

WOULD PASHA HAVE found the courage to go through her transition were there not an increasingly visible LGBT rights movement in Russian society in these years, and increased public contention about her rights?

Pasha herself could not be sure. But this much was certain: if Yulia was changing in one way during these difficult years—becoming increasingly what her ex-spouse would call a "pseudo-patriot"—then so, too, was Pasha: not just politically, but physically. She had begun to take estrogen (without supervision; prescription compliance is very lax in Russia) and to use a breast-enhancing cream.

Things came to a head during a family holiday in the countryside, during the spring of 2014. Yulia's aunt was a doctor, and she figured out quickly what was going on. Her diagnosis was peremptory and brutal: Pasha was mentally ill, dangerously so, she told the family.

Whatever the personal tensions in the family were over Pasha's transition, the differences between Pasha and Yulia could only have been exacerbated by the increasingly shrill public discourse over LGBT rights and homosexuality. This had risen to its highest pitch yet just a few weeks before the fateful family holiday with the opening of the Winter Olympics, hosted by Russia at Sochi: this was the moment when the country's homophobia moved from being a domestic issue into an international headline.

Over the previous decades, it had become a tradition for a Pride House to be set up at the Olympics, a hospitality tent of sorts for queer athletes and fans. In early 2012, the authorities had rejected an application by Nikolai Alekseev, Russia's most confrontational LGBT activist, for a Pride House at Sochi. This was upheld by a local court, which ruled that to promote "positive attitudes towards LGBT sportsmen" at Sochi would not only contradict "the foundations of public morality," but would also "undermine the sovereignty and the territorial integrity" of Russia, due to its advocacy of "extremism" and its promotion of "the reduction of its population."[12]

These notions were straight out of what was fast becoming the Kremlin playbook on the issue, and Alekseev and his comrades sounded the alarm bells internationally. By late 2013, there was more media on this topic, internationally, than almost anything else about Russia, and although the attention played a key role in highlighting the situation of LGBT people in Russia, the allegations of widespread pogroms were often exaggerated, the solidarity gestures in some cases misguided: a boycott of Stolichnaya vodka in gay bars and clubs, for example, when the brand was not even Russian.[13] This played perfectly into Putin's hand: the Kremlin accused the West of a smear campaign and urged Russians to defend their values against this onslaught.

At a meeting of international statesmen his proxies convened in December 2013, Putin accused the West of crossing a "Red Line" by trying to tamper with Russia's sovereignty; it was here that he described the normalization of homosexuality as "a direct path to degradation and primitivism."[14] Still, Putin insisted that homosexuals were not discriminated against in Russia, a claim to which he would frequently return in the upcoming months, usually by trundling out Tchaikovsky and Pushkin. "We aren't banning anything, we aren't rounding up anyone, we have no criminal punishment for such relations, unlike many other countries," he said to potential foreign visitors to the Sochi games.[15] He did add a postscript, once more conflating homosexuality with pedophilia, as the anti-propaganda legislation itself did: "One can feel relaxed and at ease, but please leave the kids alone."

The political analyst Alexey Mukhin put the Kremlin deal for queer people most clearly, in an interview he gave for a British documentary: "It is true that being gay in Russia can be quite difficult. But if you are not publicly active within the gay community, the vast majority of the problems simply disappear. You could say that being gay in Russia is like living in the closet; a very big and very comfortable closet."[16]

The problem, for the Russian authorities, was that an increasing number of Russians were realizing that the closet was not so comfortable after all, for the same reasons as in other parts of the globalizing world: they understood that their lives could be freer, more actualized, if they were able to stop leading double lives, that they could claim the rights that their straight compatriots had, and that queer people were winning in the West. Although Pasha's closet was one in which she hid her gender identity rather than her sexuality, the logic that drew her out was the same.

Six months after the opening of the Sochi games, and three months after that spring holiday in the countryside when Yulia's aunt pronounced on Pasha's "illness," later, Yulia left with Yarik and filed divorce proceedings.

IN THE END, the propaganda law was seldom applied, but it issued what Human Rights Watch would later call a "license to harm": online entrapments and horrendous assaults by groups such as "Occupy Pedofilia"; the hounding of gay and lesbian teachers out of jobs; a steep increase in the random assault on men who appeared to be gay, including a couple of murders; an attack on a Sunday teatime get-together at a St. Petersburg HIV center that left a young man partially blinded; the brutal assaults of LGBT activists holding public demonstrations.[17]

In October 2013, I visited the northern Russian city of Arkhangelsk. This had been the second region to pass an anti-propaganda law, two years previously, in what was a clear backlash action against an assertive local LGBT community. While I was there, a young lesbian bus conductor named Varya brought me a sticker she had found stuck to a discarded ticket on her tram that morning: "Crush faggots like a pile of shit!" it proclaimed, over the image of a fey purple-haired youth being trampled by a Nazi-style jackboot. These stickers were everywhere in Arkhangelsk; similar ones in Moscow depicted a campy rooster under the word *Petukh*: the slang meant "rooster," the derogatory word for a man who had been raped in prison. Sexual assault was part of everyday life in the Soviet carceral system, as most Russians knew. This was one of the reasons why an official policy of homophobia fell on such fertile ground.

Varya the bus conductor was a new mother; she lived with her girlfriend who also had an infant child. Varya's toddler, Serafima, was the result of a one-night stand with a guy she met in the Arkhangelsk *nieformaly* scene, the alternative Goth-inflected music world where many queer kids found space, in Russia as elsewhere. Following the announcement of a new law to remove children from homosexual parents, Serafima's father started threatening Varya with a custody suit, even though he had never met the child.

In Varya's case, it did not move beyond threats, but for others it did: in the book *Gay Propaganda: Russian Love Stories*, a Moscow woman tells the story of how she had to go to court to fight a custody battle with her own parents.[18] Unlike Pasha, she managed to keep her child by "proving" to the court that her partner was not her lover, but merely her roommate. In 2019, a gay couple found themselves under suspicion when their twelve-year-old son innocently told hospital officials, upon admission for stomach pain, that he had two fathers.[19] After an interview and an investigation, Andrey Vaganov and Evgeny Erofeyev were told that there were suspicions of "molestation" and that they might have to turn the boy over to a state rehabilitation center while the case was being investigated. The couple fled the country, and in their absence a case was opened against the adoption agency that had placed the children with them in the first place.

A St. Petersburg mother, a lesbian woman named Olga, told me how her teenage daughter had recently been exposed to vile homophobic comments and jokes from her previously tolerant father. The girl had been accompanying her mother to Coming Out St. Petersburg meetings since she was twelve; after meeting other kids she felt needed support, she attempted to start a "rainbow kids" group at the organization, but was not allowed to, since it would be a contravention of the law and could jeopardize the whole organization. After the passage of the anti-propaganda laws, none of Russia's LGBT organizations could advertise services that provided outreach or support to minors.

At the very moment that young people were coming out as never before, the services that might have helped them were abruptly withdrawn.

One audacious initiative attempted to plug the gap. And it was, indirectly, through this initiative that Pasha met her new partner, Alya, a few weeks after Yulia left her, in late 2014.

3

When I met Pasha for the first time, in June 2015, Alya was with her. It was at the cheekily named Propaganda, queer Moscow's gathering place, a steampunk-style café-restaurant in the shadows of the behemoth security police headquarters on Dzerzhinsky Square. Propaganda was famed for its Sunday-night dances; now, on a Thursday afternoon, Pasha and Alya squeezed into one of the cozy maroon booths along the side.

Pasha was dressed in mellow rock-chick style: high-tops, cropped jeans, a black T-shirt that read "WE LOVE FRIDAYS" in sparkly silver and gold. Alya looked like she might have stepped straight off a Soviet poster: she had a cascade of blond hair, a full figure, and sparkling crescent eyes the same color as her tight-fitting electric-blue dress. She and Pasha had been together for just over six months, and they acted like two women in the first flush of love. They stroked each other's cheeks, picked at each other's food, finished each other's sentences, and whenever we were outdoors during my two visits over that summer, they were always hand in hand or arm in arm, oblivious to the looks they sometimes attracted.

Alya did not live in Moscow, but had become a regular commuter on the eight-hour train ride from her Volga River hometown, where she had a husband, a teenage son, and a busy practice as a psychotherapist. A devout Christian, she had been raised in a family that had managed to retain its religious practice through the Soviet years. As a teenager, her interests in social justice and her wish for a personal relationship with God had led her into the Lutheran Church. She studied theology at university, and rose from being a youth leader in her church to the head of its Sunday School programming.

Her life, too, had changed dramatically due to the anti-propaganda laws and the hate they inspired. Suddenly, she told me, "my priest's usual sarcasm about homosexuality, his tendency to make fun of someone, became more of a righteous anger. He was giving a homophobic sermon at least once a month." At the time, Alya did not identify herself as lesbian or LGBT—"if anything, you could say that I had bisexual tendencies"—but she had some gay friends, and there was a lesbian woman in the church. Listening to the priest "refer to me as a 'sister in Christ,' then watching him ascend to the altar to spew such hate, no, I could not abide this hypocrisy." Alya left the church, and watched as "the topic became more present publicly. Russia started resembling fascist Germany, the singling out of a vulnerable group and accusing it of something. I asked myself: 'Who will be next?'"

By this point, Alya had qualified as a psychologist and was working with adolescents. She felt she had to do something, and so—given her interest in young people—she contacted Dyeti-404, "Children 404," the online initiative that ran a closed group on VKontakte for LGBT youth. Dyeti-404 was soon in the sights of the new anti-propaganda police. First, its moderator Elena Klimova was slapped with a (rare) charge of contravening the anti-propaganda law; when this was dismissed, a complaint was laid in November 2014 with the state communications regulator. Eventually, a tribunal ruled that the project's online profile "could cause children to think that to be gay means to be a person who is brave, strong, confident, persistent, who has a sense of dignity and self-respect": Klimova was fined fifty thousand rubles (about eight hundred dollars), and the site was shut down in July 2015.[20] She set up her own website, and carried on her work.

A key component of Dyeti-404 was the provision of online social services to youth, and in early 2014 Alya volunteered to help. As she listened to the testimonies of her young new clients, she became ever more convinced that Russia was heading in the direction of fascism: her politics, and her engagement, deepened. In November 2014, she traveled to Moscow to participate in Russia's first-ever "LGBT families" conference. This is where she met Pasha who had come seeking solace and solidarity, two months after Yulia had left with Yarik.

Alya had never met a transgender person and couldn't take her eyes off Pasha: "I was looking, and couldn't understand who this was. I heard her saying she was about to go through transition, that she was an activist, but still, I didn't quite get it." They did not talk, but Alya later found Pasha online, and they began chatting: "From our first conversations, I understood her as a woman. I felt she was a woman, much more of a girl than me, in fact!"

Being with Pasha, Alya told me, freed her from the gender stereotypes imposed on her: "For most of my life I tried to force myself to believe I could live as a normal female, you know, making meatballs and raising a family, but that would only last for a week or two and I'd find myself back doing some sort of social project, something a man is supposed to do. With Pasha, I don't have those internal stereotypes. I don't have to restrain myself if I feel like I am competent in certain areas. I can just be myself."

Pasha went for her transition surgery in December 2014, very soon after the LGBT Families conference: by this point the two were in the throes of an online romance. But after the surgery the line went dead and Alya panicked. She was not able to travel to Moscow, and when she found out Pasha had been admitted to a public hospital (she would be there for three hair-raising weeks), she asked a friend to check in on her. There had been complications, and Pasha was very ill. When Pasha was discharged from hospital in early January 2014, back home and unable to care for herself, Alya dropped everything and came to Moscow. She planned to be in town a few days but stayed for six weeks, until Pasha could do the most basic things by herself again. Ever since, Alya had been dividing her time between Moscow and the Volga. When she was back home, she and Pasha hung out on Skype for hours every day; when she was in Moscow, she and Pasha did the same with her sixteen-year-old son, Vitya, and her husband, too, if he was around. Alya and her husband had an "open relationship," she said, and he did not seem to mind this new interest in her life.

Vitya studied English and read it fluently, and so his mother often asked him to do translations for her. One of these was the much-circulated coming-out speech of the transgender film director Lana Wachowski; early in Alya's relationship with Pasha, when she wanted to explain her new partner to her son, she referred back to this video. He shrugged in a noncommittal adolescent way. Now, a few months later, in the summer of 2015, Alya had brought him to Moscow to be with her and Pasha during the holidays, and she was deeply anxious about how everyone would get along. "But really"—Alya laughed—"I can see that this is my concern and nobody else's. They're both introverts, but you'd never guess it when you see them together. They talk about computers, and games, and weapons, and Vitya's work as a Wiki moderator. I don't understand a word of it, but Pasha offers a lot of insight, and it thrills Vitya. It's only been a couple of days, and already they are old friends."

I met the trio in the Lyubertsy flat, the day after they had gone off to the Space Museum together. Vitya was staying in Yarik's room, and Pasha seemed pleased with this: "In many ways I look at him and see my own child. I think they even look similar. And they communicate in the same sort of way: quite shy at first, but then when they warm to you, they really shine."

Vitya was handsome and studious, with an ironic gallantry around his mother and her new girlfriend, and a dry Russian humor. He clearly adored his mother, and if he admitted to one difficulty over the previous few months, it was her absence. He was also very close to his grandparents, Alya's parents, and spent much time in their nearby village.

What would happen were Alya to bring Pasha home to meet the grandparents? I asked.

"No," he responded. "That would be very difficult."

Alya decided not to "come out" as Pasha's girlfriend precisely to prevent such difficulty for Vitya. She set up a pseudonymous Facebook profile with the name Alya Amada—"beloved" in Spanish—with a rainbow unicorn as her profile picture, and Pasha listed as her "relationship": this was Alya's LGBT profile, and she kept it separate from the other.

A couple of days later, we all wandered around Gorky Park together and ate pizza at a riverside café. Alya and Pasha had exchanged rings, and liked to fantasize about a wedding ceremony—perhaps in Denmark, a favorite destination for same-sex Russian couples. I told them same-sex marriage was legal in South Africa, and that I was married to my partner. Why not come to Cape Town?

"That is a very good idea," said Vitya, deadpan. "Get one-way tickets, please."

Everybody laughed.

4

Pasha had done her physical transition through a clinic in Moscow set up by a married couple who were both transgender themselves: Yael and Andrei Demedetskiy. Yael had been a high-flying financial analyst before her transition in 2009, and was Russia's pioneering transgender activist: she had started the Transgender Foundation with a website in 2004, and it was here that Pasha had begun her own first online explorations a few years later. Yael subsidized the foundation through an online enterprise called Transdostavka, "Trans-delivery," selling accessories and clothing, and in 2013 the couple opened a full-spectrum clinic, which they called the Reconstructive Surgery, Androgyny and Sexology (RSAS) Centre.

I went to meet them there in June 2015. It was not easy to find, deep in a warren of courtyards in a semi-industrial area, advertising its presence subtly with the words medical clinic alongside the outline of a woman's face printed onto the door. Inside, there was a reception room, a consulting room, a surgery, and a small ward. In this last room, with two beds overlooking a pleasant communal garden, Pasha had recuperated for a week before she needed to be transferred to the general hospital.

Andrei Demedetskiy, in his late thirties, was low-key and phlegmatic; Yael, a decade older, was expressive and emotional. They told me how they had found a friendly psychiatrist, and worked with her to convene an assessment panel that was granted a license by the state to give transsexualism diagnoses. They also enlisted the services of medical consultants to do the procedures, at a significantly lower cost than other private facilities (Pasha's vaginoplasty cost about three thousand dollars, two-thirds the price she would have paid anywhere else in Russia). By 2015, they were running between three and four hundred transition surgeries a year; about two-thirds of these were male-to-female, and one third female-to-male. Of the former, the vast majority of patients just had orchiectomies (their testicles removed), which were much cheaper than full vaginoplasties and would serve as enough proof of "irrevocable change" for them to change their documents officially. Of the latter, all had mastectomies or breast reductions, and a small number had phalloplasties, a very expensive procedure that was still in its early stages of development everywhere in the world.

When Pasha went for her assessment in November 2014, she had received "a good feeling" from the psychiatrist in her preliminary interview, she told me, but during the board hearing one of the other doctors asked her with some hostility: "So you realize you are never going to become a *real* woman?"

"What's your notion of a real woman?" she had challenged him, and told him that even though she understood she would never bear a child, "there are many women who can't become pregnant, and that doesn't make them any less real, as women. I already am a real woman, so it's really not a matter of becoming one."

The man wanted to argue with her, but the other two board members nipped it in the bud. I met the psychiatrist who led the team, Dr. Nadezhda Solov'yova, and she remembered Pasha's case: "We deemed her to be adaptable, communicative, capable of new skills of socialization," she told me. "She was not depressive. These are the criteria we use, in accordance with the ICD-10 [The tenth edition of the International Classification of Disease], which is what the Russian government requires." Because the ICD-10's diagnostic criteria for transsexualism were so vague and open to interpretation, she said, "the thing we concentrate most on is exclusion. For example, excluding any underlying psychopathology, such as schizophrenia, which might manifest as transgenderism." A small number of applicants to Solov'yova's board had been turned down.

Solov'yova was a brisk and affable woman in her forties. She was a specialist in treating dementia, and had not dealt with transgenderism before being recruited by the Demedetskiys. She told me that what has struck her most about her new cohort of patients was that "to go through these trials, these tests, to change your gender, you actually have to be *healthier* than most ordinary people. They have to be so balanced, level-headed, stress-resistant. It's not for the faint-hearted."

"TRANSGENDER PEOPLE HAVE a form of mental illness."[21]

This statement was put to respondents from 23 countries, conducted by Ipsos to assess attitudes toward transgender people and their rights. In Spain, 8 percent agreed; in Argentina and the United Kingdom, 13 percent; in the U.S., 32 percent. The country with the highest number of respondents who believed transgender people were mentally ill, by a long way, was Russia: 64 percent. In Russia, 59 percent of the respondents did not believe transgender people should be protected from discrimination; also the highest proportion, by far. On every measure, Spaniards and Swedes came out as the most tolerant and informed, the U.S. was somewhere in the middle, and Russia ranked last: perhaps, the pollsters surmised, "because of the anti-LGBT campaign around the passage of the so-called gay propaganda law in 2012."

Even though transgenderism was not specified in Russia's federal anti-propaganda law, transgender women were inevitably highlighted in the barrage of television programming aired on state-controlled media aired after its passage in 2013, because they stood out and appeared freakish to other Russians. In one prime-time program broadcast in 2013, a group of seemingly deranged "transgenders" are alleged to be in the service of a Ukrainian plot to destabilize Russia.[22] The message is unmistakable: the West (which had already "conquered" Ukraine) wants to give these freaks rights; keep them away from your children or they will be corrupted and cause the fall of our civilization.

Easily identifiable as the most visible manifestation of what was now widely regarded as the "perversion" of homosexuality, transgender women—always at risk in a society that disparages effeminacy in men—were now particularly vulnerable. In 2017, the lawmaker Alexei Zhuravlev tried to pass legislation that would prevent transgender people from marrying, and the St. Petersburg originator of the anti-propaganda legislation, Vitaly Milonov, was trying to ban gender transition surgery altogether. "It's beginning to feel like a witch hunt," Dr. Solov'yova said to me in 2015. "Of course, we fear we may be next."

She was referring to the way one of Russia's most illustrious psychiatrists, Dmitri Isaev, had recently been forced to resign from his state-run medical institution in St. Petersburg and disband his gender assessment board. An online smear campaign against Isaev included posts accusing him of issuing "certificates to perverts on a massive scale." When we spoke in 2017, Isaev told me that between 2006 and 2015 he had overseen about seven hundred applications for gender change, 70 percent of which had been granted, and that there had been a surge in the latter years: in St. Petersburg, in particular, there was a booming trans scene. Following his dismissal he had gone "underground" in a private clinic: although he had received certification to continue running his board, he saw people only through word-of-mouth referrals, and the fact that he was no longer in the state system meant the costs were significantly higher.

AS WELL AS their clinic, the Demedetskiys ran a community centre in the basement of a large Stalin-era apartment block, in a stately corner of the city close to the Moskva River. At the bottom of a stairwell accessed through an unmarked locked door was *Transdostavka*'s showroom, which seemed at first glance to be filled with standard cross-dressing apparel: sexy underwear, sequined frocks, crazily high heels, walls of wigs. But it had, on closer inspection, everything a transgender man or woman might need: accoutrements sober as well as wild, makeup, prosthetic breasts, binders, peckers. There was also a large meeting room and, off a seating area, a suite of treatment rooms staffed by hair-depilation therapists. In the few hours I was there one evening, someone with the body and the clothing of a middle-aged man rang the buzzer, came downstairs, disappeared into the back, reappeared made-up and dressed as a woman, hung around the seating area for a while, offered us tea, disappeared again, reappeared in men's clothing, and said goodbye. She clearly did not want to leave. She was wearing a wedding ring.

The Demedetskiys told me a little of their own lives. Like many Russian transgender men, Andrei had had an easier time of it, and was accepted by his family. There was a place for butch women in Russian society; then, if they transitioned into male identity, the testosterone kicked in very quickly, and their feminine traces disappeared beneath the facial hair and new deep voice. But as in many parts of the world, male effeminacy was deeply stigmatized in Russia, and because it was often harder, after transition, for transgender women to disguise their original sex, they were particularly vulnerable if they did not "pass." For this reason, Yael told me, "many transmen, like Andrei, can remain in contact with their families, whereas for us, transwomen, the transition means erasing your previous life and starting again."

This is what happened to Yael: "I, too, was married," she told me, as we spoke about Pasha. "I, too, had a child. I kept on postponing the transition because of the child, waiting for him to walk and talk, waiting until he goes to school, et cetera. My wife knew all about it, and when she told me we should wait until he came of age, I realized I would not be able to wait that long. I would kill myself. So I left."

The child was five. Yael carried on supporting him, but like Pasha, she was denied access, not only by her ex-wife but by her mother, too, who attempted to block her transition by trying to get her committed as mentally deranged. When her ex-wife mounted a smear campaign against her in a national tabloid ("Sex Change in a Courtroom!"), Yael tried to kill herself. She spent several days in a coma and a year in recovery, nursed back to health by Andrei. When we met in 2015 she had had no contact with her son for a decade: he was now about fifteen. As we started to talk about this she broke down, shattering a glass of water in her distress before rushing, weeping, from the room.

"I am certain the son thinks she is dead," Andrei said, after she left. He continued, after a pause: "So many of her friends have actually killed themselves."

Was this related to the anti-propaganda legislation and the hate it had engendered?

"Of course, it must be. We are talking of people who are already depressed, who have already had to leave their families. This must have an impact on self-esteem. Especially since it changes the attitudes of people around them, who think of themselves as normal and you as an abnormality."

Yael was taking the deaths of her friends very hard, Andrei said, "because she is like a mother to everyone in the transwoman community. She tells them to come to Moscow, she meets them at the railway station. She takes real care of them."

"Do you think she is making up for the loss of her own child by doing this work?" asked my interpreter Margret.

"Yes, maybe. Maybe she's spending her unspent love on them."

IN 2017 I met another woman who had also transitioned after having children, with different consequences than those experienced by

Pasha and Yael. Her name was Kate Messorosh, she was a thirty-four-year-old chemist, and the mother of two children, a nine-year-old boy and three-year-old girl. She worked in St. Petersburg's booming tech start-up sector, where her transition had been celebrated and affirmed by her Russian employer as part of its diversity profile, its connection to the very world from which Putin wished to insulate Russia. Kate's wife, Olga, a psychologist, had accepted it, and even though they were getting divorced, they were committed to raising their children together.

Preparing to come out to her nine-year-old, Lev, had been the most fraught part of the process for Kate, but as children do, the boy had distilled the matter to its utmost simplicity: "Will you always be a woman?" When Kate replied yes, he said "cool," and asked if he could go off and play. On the whole, Lev's peers accepted it, as did the school, where Kate had been forced to come out after a public campaign against her by Russia's most fervent crusader against perversion, Timur Bulatov, the activist who had gotten the psychiatrist Dmitri Isaev fired.

When Bulatov discovered that Kate was serving as a party-appointed local representative on the Russian Electoral Commission for the September 2016 elections, he distributed posters with a photograph of her: "Society and common sense demand the removal of a sick sexual pervert from control over the electoral process." If she served on the Electoral Commission, he said on a television news insert about the issue, Kate would be "working at school where there are teenagers," and thus in contravention of the anti-propaganda legislation. Worse yet: by living with her own children she was in violation of at least thirteen separate federal laws, and he vowed to lodge a complaint with the relevant authorities to get the children removed.

Bulatov announced that he would be going to Lev's school to out Kate, and so Kate and Olga rushed there first. It was the local public school in a "very typical" St. Petersburg neighborhood, "but there was no problem at all," Kate told me. Ditto with the policewoman who visited her, acting on Bulatov's complaint, annoyed that she'd been sent out for no reason: "She told me there were no grounds to take the matter further." The party that had nominated her refused to withdraw her from the commission, and the others working with her "just proceeded with the job, calmly and professionally."

Kate and Olga were highly educated professionals, and worked in a liberal bubble within Europhile St. Petersburg. Still, the way the school and the police and her party responded to her said something, to me, about the gap between the hate-mongering of the likes of Bulatov of Milanov and the decent people whose values they claimed to be defending. There were Yulias in Russia, but there also were Olgas.

Of course, Kate said, "it was a very difficult time, and I spent many hours with lawyers, trying to understand my rights." She became convinced that there was little the state could do to remove her children from her, but of course, "I always have a Plan B. This is Russia after all. I know how to get out of the country in two days, I know where to go if something happens, something like physical violence."

IN 2017, PASHA appealed Judge E.G. Aksenova's ruling denying her any rights of access to Yarik until he turned eighteen. But tragically, Pasha's absolute conviction that she was the better parent had undone her, correct though this conviction might have been. When she had launched her custody suit, her lawyers had warned her that she was making herself vulnerable by doing so, and that she should rather settle for regular access. The lawyers were right: now, as a result of the custody case that required Yarik to be observed by state-appointed psychologists, there was expert evidence that the child had issues with Pasha's new identity, even if these issues were suggested to him by his mother and her family. This was the evidence that Yulia used to deny Pasha any access at all to Yarik.

Pasha appealed, and lost. She had one last avenue open to her: the Court of Cassation, Russia's apex court of appeal. When she lost there—as she was sure to do—she would be eligible to seek relief at the European Court of Human Rights in Strasbourg, France, her lawyer Larry Vasiliev told her. Vasiliev usually worked on asylum cases, and was always game for the fight. He believed that the ruling against Pasha was a violation of Article 6 of the European Convention on Human Rights, which guarantees the right to a fair trial, and Article 8, which guarantees the "right to respect for private and family life." Since Pasha had manifestly been denied a fair trial, and since the European Convention did not view transgenderism as unhealthy or immoral, Vasiliev was confident about the outcome.

He was wrong: the European Court did not accept his arguments that it was more than a family matter, and in July 2018 it declined to hear the case—although it had ruled against Russia's anti-gay propaganda law in 2017, declaring it "inherently discriminatory" and awarding damages worth fifty thousand dollars to three litigants who had been charged under it.

IN JULY 2017, Alya's son Vitya finished high school, and he and his mother made the move to Moscow. Pasha welcomed Alya and Vitya to Moscow with a fabulous new hairstyle, a head full of braided extensions, bright red strands woven into her natural hair. Perhaps, with her new family around, her spirits would lift in the months to come. Vitya had applied to several universities in Moscow, and hoped to start studying linguistics in the fall; the plan was that he would now permanently occupy Yarik's room, making his own marks, no doubt, over the old *Angry Birds* and *Carlsen* cartoons. Alya would slowly move her practice over and see some of her existing clients on Skype; her husband would stay in the Volga. Alya and Vitya came to Moscow with only their suitcases and a geranium slip: "It is originally from the parents' home in the countryside," Alya told me, "and then I planted it at our place in the city. So now it's here, in Moscow, the child of my parents, like me."

The state had lost interest in pushing the gay issue by now—it had other ways to stoke nationalism, like the war in Ukraine—and so, too, had the national media. But all the Russian activists I checked in with insisted that life had nonetheless not improved for queer Russians: "Our statistics show that there is as much abuse and violation of individual human rights today as there was in 2012 or 2013," Svetlana Zakharova of the Russian LGBT Network told me.

Alya had her own way of assessing how things had changed: "From what I can see, coming out of the closet is by no means easier," she said. "But the LGBT community has become more aware, more active, and thus more demanding. So, for example, when I meet other psychologists at events, or when I follow the discussions on therapists' forums online, I hear all the time about this new cohort of clients seeking help. Suddenly, my colleagues want to know, 'What is a non-binary identity?' or 'Can you explain what is meant by internalized homophobia?' My colleagues are complaining to each other that they don't know what to do!"

Pasha told me that she had finally come out to her colleagues at work. She had been surprised, in particular, by the reaction of her boss, a "regular guy" who told her that his own views had changed dramatically due to her, and who had stopped making crude jokes about "faggots." He was genuinely curious rather than prurient; she liked talking to him and they became friends. A few months later, though, at the same time that she heard her case would not be heard by the European Court of Human Rights, Pasha was told that there would be no more work for her at Aeroflot either. This had nothing to do with her gender identity, but she agonized about the difficulties of finding new work as a transgender woman. In the summer of 2018, it seemed to me that she was as low as she had ever been.

This frustrated Alya, who felt that her partner needed professional help, or medication. Pasha acknowledged the stresses her state caused: "I cannot afford to show emotion anymore, because I'm so drained. And Alya gets upset about my lack of emotion in the relationship."

Certainly, the two had matured from the first flush of love I had witnessed into the complexity of a long-term relationship, each acutely aware of the roles that they played in the relationship's dynamic. Sometimes, Pasha told me, she worried that Alya's savior complex was all that held them together. Alya had been intensely supportive of Pasha's litigation to get Yarik back, making sure to be in Moscow each time there was a court appearance, but she questioned whether Pasha had made the right decision in taking the matter further: "Each time there is a court case, Pasha spends a month on the couch. She cannot get up. I don't blame her, of course…"

AT THE END of a long catch-up conversation with Pasha, after she lost the appeal in 2017, I had asked her where she got her pleasure from these days. When I had first met her, two years previously, she had spoken of the ambivalence of her transition during her long recuperation period: "The body was uncomfortable but the soul was rejoicing." Now body and soul were in harmony. She told me she no longer experienced the neuropathy in her feet, and that she was able to exercise again. She loved pushscooting, and had become a member of an informal group who pulled the Moscow pavements on a weekend: she occasionally posted photographs of these outings online.

She also listened to music, preferably heavy metal, but of the softer kind. She told me about a recording she was loving at the moment, a cover by a South African band called Seether of George Michael's torch song, "Careless Whisper."

"I'm never gonna dance again": I found it on YouTube and we listened to it together, swaying gently on Skype, between Cape Town and Moscow.

9

GENDER-THEORY PANIC

"WE WANT SEX, NOT GENDER!" the hundreds of thousands of protestors chanted, obscurely, in the Manif Pour Tous demonstrations against same-sex marriage I witnessed in Paris in 2013: they were demanding the reestablishment of God-given biological binaries over the shifting sands of social relations signified by the term *gender*.[1]

In the years to come, a battle against "gender ideology"—or sometimes "gender theory"—fueled mass mobilizations in the Catholic world, from Paris to Mexico City and São Paolo.[2] The fight against it was primarily a Catholic one, but it became the twenty-first-century ideological clearinghouse for cooperation among all conservative Christians, including Russian Orthodox ones in Eastern Europe, and evangelical ones in the Americas. It telescoped all the issues to which social conservatives hewed, from birth control through abortion and gay marriage to sexuality education, into one single pernicious theory allegedly at the heart of the Western secular "experiment": the notion that gender existed in the first place.

The Vatican first started advocating against gender in response to the feminist movement's successes in getting sexual and reproductive rights recognized at two pathbreaking United Nations conferences: the International Conference on Population and Development in Cairo in 1994 and the World Conference on Women in Beijing the year after. Even before he was elected pope a decade later, the conservative Benedict XVI was sounding the warning bells about gender, and once he was pope he spoke publicly about the dangers of "gender theories": man needed to be protected "from the destruction of himself " that would come with such ideas, he said in 2008.[3] On this score his successor Francis I agreed with him: "God created man and woman," Francis said in a 2016 speech in Poland.[4] "God created the world in a certain way ... and we are doing exactly the opposite."

Francis had developed a reputation for compassion toward homosexuals, though: "If a person is gay and seeks God and has good will, who am I to judge?" he said in 2013, and he later called on the church to apologize to gay people it had offended.[5] But he became an implacable warrior against the new enemy of gender, placing the battle—as did so many critics of LGBT rights—within the frame of geopolitical inequality: "There are genuine forms of ideological colonization taking place" in the world, he said in his Poland speech.[6]

"And one of these—I will call it clearly by its name—is 'gender.' Today children—children!—are taught in school that everyone can choose his or her sex. Why are they teaching this? Because the books are provided by the persons and institutions that give you money."

The "anti–gender theory" movement was particularly strong in France, where there had long been an ethos of "respecting" nature in reproduction: surrogacy was banned outright, as was fertility treatment for anyone other than heterosexual couples. Two years before the Manif Pour Tous in France, anti–gender theory activists scored their first major victory when they were successful in preventing the introduction of the concept of gender into high school biology textbooks. "While gay marriage only affects a minority, schooling is always a concern for the vast majority," wrote the sociologist Éric Fassin, explaining how French Catholics were shifting their tactics from the "assault on gay marriage" to "a polemic against the 'theory-of-gender.'"[7]

There was something else behind this strategic shift: lay Catholics were moving far ahead of their church when it came to accepting homosexuality, in France and elsewhere. This was part of a bigger trend: while much of the monotheistic world was becoming more devout or even theocratic in the twenty-first century, the two regions where Catholicism was dominant—Europe and Latin America—were spinning in the opposite direction. Nothing made this clearer than the battles over same-sex marriage in two Catholic countries: Argentina in 2010, and Ireland in 2015.

In Argentina, in 2010, only around 20 percent of Catholics attended weekly mass.[8] And 57.7 percent approved of same-sex marriage, according to one Americas-wide survey. This was the second-highest tally in the Americas, after Canada (63.9 percent), and notably higher than the United States (still only 47 percent). When the Argentine president Cristina Fernández led her government in championing marriage equality, some commentators believed she was using this issue instrumentally, to stake a Pink Line against a church that had been harshly critical of her and her husband, former president Néstor Kirchner, for their governments' failure to address poverty and inequality.[9]

If it was a trap, Cardinal Bergoglio—soon to be Pope Francis I—walked straight into it. He led an impassioned battle against the reform, using discourse that made little sense in the modern world: same-sex marriage was the "destructive pretension of God's plan"; "Demon's envy, by which sin entered the world, and which slyly aims to destroy God's image: man and woman, who receive the commandment of growing up, multiplying and dominating the earth."[10] President Fernandez likened the church's fervor on the issue to "the times of the Inquisition," a rhetorical flourish that fell on fertile ground in the way it highlighted Catholic hypocrisy.[11]

In Argentina, the Catholic Church had dramatically lost its moral influence because of its complicity in the "Dirty War" of the military dictatorship, between 1976 and 1983. The church had fallen from favor in a similar fashion in Ireland, primarily because of its unconscionable protection of pedophile priests. At the time of the country's same-sex marriage referendum in 2015 the author Colm Tóibín noted that moral authority had shifted from the church to its perceived victims: these would include, of course, homosexuals, along with children who had suffered abuse, and women who had been denied abortions or been forced to give up their children if unwed. In this context, as in Argentina, the church's opposition to same-sex marriage seemed only to increase the numbers of people supporting it. Sixty-two per cent of the electorate voted to legalize same-sex marriage in the referendum, the first such victory globally.

Some data from the United States suggests a second reason why so many Irish might have voted yes in the referendum, against the instructions of their church. Focus groups between 2006 and 2009 conducted by Freedom to Marry, which advocated for marriage equality in the U.S., found that while the Catholic church had "a major impact" on attitudes of Latinos about homosexuality, the impact was diminished "when direct experience and knowledge of gay people does not conform to church teachings."[12]

This might have been the clincher in the Irish referendum. Colm Tóibín put it this way: "It's an intimate society, everyone knows someone now who's gay, or whose brother is gay or whose cousin is gay … it's personal before it's political."[13] Three years later, in 2018, the Irish electorate voted by an even bigger margin to allow abortion in certain circumstances: once more, the church's fervor worked against it in the face of the experience—and personal knowledge—of women who had had to "travel," as the euphemism had it, to take care of unwanted or dangerous pregnancies in Britain.

A leading Irish campaigner, Tiernan Brady, moved to Australia to run the Australian Marriage Equality campaign after the government there agreed to a write-in "postal survey" on the issue in 2017. Brady used the Irish template, focusing on the "power of the human story," he said.[14] "People here need to see the issue through the eyes of people they can relate to." Many commentators ascribed the 61.6 percent positive vote to this strategy, in particular the saturation of personal narratives on social media, and the highly successful #RingYourRellos hashtag, urging queer Australians to get their families to participate.[15]

In the digital age, the very subjective nature of social media meant that people's stories came to dominate the news, particularly if they were about hardship or the overcoming of it. The savvy French Manif Pour Tous, which was to be the template for anti–gender theory mobilizations in other parts of the world, was wise to this: it went out of its way to condemn homophobia and violence against LGBT people, and it even had some queer people in its leadership. It was not "anti-gay," it was "anti–gay marriage"; it was against a concept, not a group of people, or your neighbor, or your son, or your "rello."

In the second decade of the twenty-first century, moral panics became abstracted. The pink folk devils were now theories, not people.

IN LATIN AMERICA, where it was used to fight other battles, the fight against "gender ideology" gained significant traction.

An early victory was in Brazil in 2011, when conservative Christians forced the vulnerable new president Dilma Rousseff to drop a curriculum package called "School without Homophobia," which became known to its detractors as the "gay kit."[16] LGBT rights had been one of her predecessor Lula da Silva's signature social reforms, and its seeming abandonment was an early salvo, across Brazil's Pink Line, by an "evangelical bloc" that would come to dominate the congress. The bloc found common cause with Catholic conservatives and militarists in a coalition bent on getting Lula's Workers' Party out of office, which they damned through allegations both of corruption and moral permissiveness.

Fighting the "gay kit" became the rallying point for a right-wing movement that had been founded a few years previously, "School without Party" (*Escola sim Partido*), dedicated to preventing children from being corrupted by the evil ideologies of both gender and communism. This movement, which sought to banish "gender ideology" from schools, was embraced by Jair Bolsonaro in his victorious 2018 election campaign. After his victory, Bolsonaro enthusiastically supported the movement's campaign to film (as his son Carlos put it in a tweet) "ideological predators who are disguised as teachers,"[17] and instructed the education ministry to prepare legislation that would "prohibit gender ideology in elementary schools."[18]

Bolsonaro explicitly fused gender and communism as the twin ideological threats of the left: grand social experiments against the natural order of things.[19] In this way, the Brazilian sociologist Gustavo Gomes da Costa Santos wrote, his election campaign forged "a homogeneous 'We,' thereby pitching good, righteous and devoted citizens in a moral struggle against the 'Them,' the communists, PT [Workers' Party]-supporters, feminazis, and queer degenerates.[20] Thus the 2018 election turned into a moral crusade against evil and Bolsonaro portrayed himself as the only one capable of saving Brazil from total collapse."

A populist battle against gender ideology was deployed similarly, two years previously, in Colombia. After the suicide of a gay teenager due to bullying, the Constitutional Court mandated the state to take remedial action. When the ministry of education complied by publishing a manual about sexuality and gender, thousands took to the streets to protest: the openly lesbian education minister Gina Parody was accused of using her office to facilitate the "gay colonization"—there was that word again—of the nation.[21] This had far-reaching—and intended—implications: the president Juan Manuel Santos had just called a referendum on his peace deal with the Revolutionary Armed Forces of Colombia (FARC), and his conservative opponent Álvaro Uribe used Santos's social liberalism to rally voters against the deal. Critics latched, for example, on to the proposed accord's use of the word *gender*, in a clause about redressing wrongs committed against women during the conflict. "If you ask me, 'Do you want peace with the FARC?' I say 'Yes!'" one of the leaders of the "no" movement says in a campaign video.[22] But if he was asked whether he wanted gender ideology "promoted as public policy … I say 'No!'"

Santos lost the referendum by a hairsbreadth; the mobilization of socially conservative voters undoubtedly tipped the balance, and two years later Uribe's protégé Iván Duque, a populist conservative, would be elected into office. The Colombian political scientist José Fernando Serrano-Amaya argues persuasively that "gender ideology" was a dog whistle the right wing used to discredit Santos's peace initiative and make its way back into power in 2018, an effective "local adaptation of the global trends of opposition to gender and sexual rights."[23]

At the same time as the Colombian demonstrations in 2016, there were even bigger marches in Mexico, against the ineluctable rollout of marriage equality across the country. When President Enrique Peña Nieto announced that he was introducing legislation to mandate same-sex marriage nationally, a National Front for the Family (NFF) was launched, modeled on the French Manif Pour Tous. As in France, the Catholic Church took a back seat in the campaign, but played a significant role in funding it and mobilizing supporters at a parish level; Pope Francis even issued a statement of support. Led by secular conservatives, the NFF was exceptionally well-choreographed and branded. The protestors were in white—many wearing T-shirts with stick figures representing a hetero family—and carried balloons, their messages carefully honed. They held protests in 125 cities, including one of over 400,000 people in Mexico City. Peña's PRI lost control of seven states in subsequent elections, and his marriage equality initiative was held partly to blame; his party defied him, and refused to take the matter any further in Congress, the first time such a rebellion had ever happened in Mexican politics.

Again as in France, the campaign went out of its way to insist that it was opposed to violence against LGBT people. Rather, it was focused on three primary messages: the sanctity of heterosexual marriage, the rights of children to a mother and a father, and the rejection of "gender ideology" in the education of children.[24] This had become the Holy Trinity of the new battle.

What was striking about all the Latin American campaigns was how they brought Catholics together with the rapidly growing

Evangelical Protestant movement, and how this new alliance significantly hardened the tone of homophobic discourse in the region, even as laws and social attitudes changed.

There had long been a strain of Latin American liberation theology—and of pastoral care—that was open to homosexual Catholics. This was best expressed in Cardinal Bergoglio's support for civil unions and anti-discrimination legislation in Argentina even as he preached fire and brimstone against same-sex marriage. But the fundamentalism of the ever-growing Evangelical churches meant a dogmatic rejection of homosexuality; using the American script, these mushrooming enterprises also used moral issues to woo congregations away from Catholic "hypocrisy," and to grow political influence, too. This was most evident in Guatemala and Honduras, where 40 percent of the population were members of Evangelical congregations by 2018, and in Brazil, where new megachurches claimed 25 percent of the population. By some measures, these countries had the highest rates of homophobic and transphobic violence in Latin America.[25]

"Gender ideology" might be a more abstracted demon, but—in the Evangelical dogma at least—it took possession of people who then had to be exorcized. And notwithstanding the campaigns' protestations that they were against violence or discrimination, the fight against gender ideology dehumanized queer people into being seen as dispensable, or provoked murderous rage against them. In the two feverish final weeks of the Mexican anti–same-sex marriage campaign in 2016, ten to fifteen transgender women were murdered—in a country that already had the highest number of such murders globally, after Brazil.

In Brazil, the Grupo Gay de Bahia, which collected hate-crime data nationally, reported that at least 445 LGBT Brazilians died as victims of homophobia—387 murders and 58 suicides—in 2017, a 30 percent increase from 2016.[26] Luiz Mott, the anthropologist who ran the organization, linked the rising violence directly to the upsurge of hate speech by Christian right-wing politicians in the country, which "equates LGBT people to animals." As speaker of the lower house of Congress, the Evangelical radio broadcaster Eduardo da Cunha led not only Dilma Rousseff 's impeachment, but also a hate-filled public offensive against LGBT people. The president-to-be, Jair Bolsonaro, was given to saying things like gay children could be beaten straight, and that if his son were gay, he would rather he died in a car accident.

ONE OF THE most bizarre battles along the global Pink Line took place at the Federal University of São Paolo in November 2017, at a lecture given by the feminist philosopher Judith Butler. When word spread she was coming, Christian groups tried to stop her visit by collecting 370,000 signatures for a petition describing her as a threat to "the natural order of gender, sexuality and the family" in Brazil.[27] Now, outside the lecture theater, a mob of about a hundred put up an effigy of her in a bright pink bra and a witch's hat, and set it alight.

A counter-demonstration secured the venue and defended Butler. Butler was best known for her 1990 book *Gender Trouble*, in which she wrote that gender was something we learn by repeatedly "performing" the scripts of masculinity or femininity; in this context, she suggested the mutability and instability of gender roles.[28] She had long been a cult figure on the academic left, and although she had critics among both transgender and feminist readers, it was to right-wing Catholics that she became a real enemy.[29] She was identified as such by none other than Cardinal Ratzinger in 2004 just before he became Pope Benedict, when he denounced her in a widely circulated letter to bishops, on "the collaboration between men and women."[30] She became viewed, erroneously, as the mother of "gender ideology" and the prime proponent of "gender studies."

In another part of the world, Hungary would effectively ban gender studies at universities in August 2018 by revoking their right to issue degrees or diplomas in the discipline. What was happening in Hungary—and in Brazil—echoed the Russian line: remember the parliamentarian Yelena Mizulina stating in 2013 that Russians were tired of grand social experiments "where the family is destroyed,"[31] and the activist Alexey Komov describing LGBT rights as "the continuation of the same radical revolutionary agenda that cost so many lives in the Soviet Union."[32]

This right-wing demonology now stretched from Russia and Eastern Europe across the Atlantic Ocean to Latin America and the United States, too, where it emerged in the determination of right-wing Christians in the Trump administration to reverse an order, arising from the Obama administration, to permit children to use facilities congruent with their gender identities. A memo leaked to *The New York Times* in October 2018 recommended that all government agencies adopt a definition of gender "on a biological basis that is clear, grounded in science, objective and administrable": one that was irrevocably tied to one's sex characteristics at birth.[33]

The man responsible for the proposed new policy was a conservative Catholic activist named Roger Severino, the new head of the Office for Civil Rights in the Department of Health and Human Services. Severino's views were well-known: he had co-written a 2016 article denouncing the initial Obama decision as "the culmination of a series of unilateral, and frequently lawless … attempts to impose a new definition of what it means to be a man or a woman on the entire nation"; one which had prompted a "massive backlash from people who … refuse to accept a federal government driven by such a radical gender ideology."[34]

And for politicians seeking to harness this supposed "backlash," from Donald Trump and Vladimir Putin through Jair Bolsonaro to Viktor Orbán, "gender ideology" did double time. It was an oppressive new ideology imposed in a way similar to communism (or, in the American case, the federal government's edict), but it was also a symptom of neoliberal globalization threatening national sovereignty (or "states' rights"). It was, as the archbishop of Krakow would put it in 2019, the new "rainbow plague" that had replaced the old "red" one.[35]

In Hungary, Viktor Orbán used an attack on gender ideology to further demonize his compatriot, the financier and philanthropist George Soros, an impassioned advocate—and funder—of the free flow of capital and ideas, including rights for LGBT people. "What we did not tolerate from the Soviet empire, we will not tolerate from the Soros Empire," Orbán said to his 2017 party congress.[36] Orbán alleged Soros and his evil empire had commandeered the European Union itself, and were determined to impose on Hungary and other nations a creature called "Homo Brusselicus," someone "wrenched out of [his] cultural, national, religious and gender identity."

The presence of *gender* in this list was carefully calibrated, as Orbán went on to exemplify the threat of this new globalized cosmopolitanism through it: Soros's "troops" wanted specifically to overturn the age-old natural environment where "there were men and women, mothers and fathers," and to "force us into a world" where "it is unclear who is a man and who is a woman, what family is, and what it means to be Hungarian and Christian. They are creating a third gender, they are ridiculing faith, and they regard families as redundant, and nations as obsolete."[37]

Orban's rhetoric linked "natural" national borders—such as those of Hungary, which had always resisted imperialism, apparently—with natural bodily borders. It drew a Pink Line around both, against a globalizing project that wanted to "eliminate nations" and "create a Europe with a mixed population" by allowing immigrants to overrun it, and by allowing people to make their own bodies and families in defiance of the natural order.

VIKTOR ORBÁN GAVE the above address on November 12, 2017, just five days after the burning of Judith Butler's effigy in São Paolo—in which likenesses of George Soros also went up in flames, as did Brazil's ex-president Fernando Henrique Cardoso, a close associate of Soros and the great liberalizer of the country's economy.

What were Soros and Cardoso doing at this bizarre auto-da-fé? Their presence highlighted the way Butler and her gender theory had come to be seen as part of the wave of neocolonial globalization threatening not only the cultural sovereignty and traditional values of nations like Brazil or Hungary or Poland, but their economic independence, too. In this, the protestors were following scripts from both Pope Francis and Viktor Orbán about gender theory as a form of "ideological colonization."

An anthropologist named Isabela Oliveira Kalil went about interviewing the protesters outside Butler's lecture about their politics, and 62 percent told her they wanted Jair Bolsonaro to be president in 2018 over other right-wing candidates.[38] The reasons became clear through another question: 45.5 percent agreed that "the solution to Brazil could come from a divine intervention"; 72.9 percent believed "a military intervention" might do the trick. Even if the survey was a petri dish of fanatics (they were burning the effigy of a philosopher, after all), it said something—as did the rallying against gender theory across the globe—about the way a Pink Line could be staked to promote a nostalgia for authoritarianism, against the perceived failures of a modernity best exemplified by these crazy new ideas.

10

ZAIRA AND MARTHA'S STORY

GUADALAJARA

Zaira de la O Gómez—salesperson and feminist activist, late twenties. Pronouns: she/her/hers.

Martha Sandoval Blanco—Zaira's wife, entrepreneur and full-time mother, mid-forties. Pronouns: she/her/hers.

Sabina—their daughter, age six. Pronouns: she/her/hers.

Alé and Max*—Zaira and Martha's neighbors, early thirties. Pronouns: she/her/hers.

Maribel Lopez and Blanca—lesbian couple with a baby, teacher and musician, early fifties and late twenties. Pronouns: she/her/hers.

Luz*—Zaira's friend, lesbian single mother, thirties. Pronouns: she/her/hers.

***Pseudonym**

1

The marriage of Zaira de la O Gómez to Martha Sandoval Blanco was scheduled for noon on December 23, 2013, at Civil Registry Number One in downtown Guadalajara, but the authorities changed it at the last minute to 8:30 a.m., to evade the anticipated protests: religious "pro-family" groups had caught wind of it, the first legal same-sex marriage in the state of Jalisco, and had been threatening all week to disrupt it. Zaira's mother had even heard a priest in church the previous Sunday telling worshippers to mobilize against her daughter, whom she heard described as the devil incarnate; on the morning of the ceremony she called Zaira at dawn begging her not to proceed, "for the sake of the child"—Zaira's toddler, Sabina.

But "it was actually *for Sabi's sake* that we needed to get married in the first place," Zaira said to me when we met at an outdoor café in downtown Guadalajara, in June 2016, under the shadow of the colonial city's magnificent cathedral. Zaira was Sabina's birth mother, and the couple had failed to get Martha registered as the other parent; now they hoped that the marriage certificate would mean Martha could have her name added to Sabina's birth certificate.

Zaira was dark and voluptuous, with an almost overripe beauty; she had just come off work at a nearby department store where she sold American beds to middle-class Mexicans. Martha was sixteen years older, fineboned and fair with long auburn hair. She had run a shop selling cleaning supplies but was now was Sabina's full-time mother. While Zaira told me their story Martha kept a watchful eye on their daughter, an ebullient four-year-old who scampered off to investigate a bandstand in the square.

Zaira opened her cell phone to show me footage of the wedding day, covered on local television. As the couple emerges from the registry into the small gathering of well-wishers and paparazzi awaiting them, emotion sweeps in waves across Zaira's open face; she is in a tight white dress, her long black hair piled magnificently high.[1] Martha is in white, too, a sleeveless dress with lace cleavage; her emotions, like her beauty, are subtler, alternating flickers of disquiet and pleasure as she holds Sabina—a bundle of fuchsia frills—close to her chest.

"*Beso! Beso! Beso!*" the crowd calls: "Kiss! Kiss! Kiss!"[2]

Martha smiles nervously and turns her face slightly away, but Zaira takes it in her hands and pulls her into an embrace. The crowd cheers.

"*Anything* can be done," Zaira says to the cameras, husky and effervescent, as if on the campaign trail. "And this is a message for anyone who has a dream as big as this one. Don't give up if you can succeed. It won't be easy."

Martha would later tell me that she struggled to enjoy the day. "I am not an activist, so it was very difficult for me, the wedding, with all the media. My family was very against it. It caused conflict."

Martha's parents were no longer alive, and none of her siblings came to the registry. But Zaira's parents were present, and the cameras caught them standing beneath a rainbow flag, stoical and elegant, her father in a wide-lapelled white suit and a matching panama tipped rakishly over his eyes, her mother draped in costume jewelry. In words that sound well-rehearsed, Señora Gómez tells a local television reporter, "Yes, there is unfortunately still lots of ignorance and intolerance, but it's their decision [to marry]. They are human beings, they have their own lives, so we have to stand by them, to prevent lots of suicides in the future, many family breakups, or losing one's kids."[3]

There had, indeed, been a straggle of protesters, but the police had closed off the street in front of the registry office, and the bridal party did not encounter them: "The people were supporting us, making a barrier," Martha later told me. "I felt like Angelina Jolie, or someone important. It was weird."

The day ended with a party in a brightly painted courtyard where the newlyweds showed off their matching rings—rainbow swooshes set in gold—and posed with all their friends, before settling down to a meal to which everyone had contributed. They cut a huge wedding cake that had been iced in rainbow colors and adorned with two silver brides.

MEXICO CITY WAS the first jurisdiction in Latin America to legalize same-sex marriage, in 2009. Argentina followed a few months later, the first country to do so in the region, the tenth in the world. In the next seven years, Latin America's attitude to marriage shifted dramatically: Brazil, Uruguay, and Colombia legalized gay marriage too, and these four countries began to play a leading role advocating for global protection mechanisms at the United Nations.

Mexico was more ambivalent. On the one hand it was the region's trailblazer: Mexico City's marriage equality was preceded by its granting of civil unions to same-sex couples in 2006, and both reforms were enabled by the country's 2001 constitution, which outlawed discrimination on the basis of "preference" (the lawmakers had been too prudish to write the word *sexual* into the country's foundation document, but this would be amended in 2011). But on the other hand, the country remained a bastion not only of conservative Catholicism but also of the kind of frontiersman *machismo* that was part of its national image. These forces would fuel the massive backlash against Enrique Peña Nieto's announcement, the year I met Zaira and Martha, that he was introducing legislation to mandate same-sex marriage nationally.

A total of eighty-one Pride events took place across Mexico in 2016, the highest number in the world after the United States and Brazil. The largest one was in Mexico City, half a million strong, and the oldest by far in Latin America, going since 1979. Mexico City had branded itself for over a decade as *La Ciudad de las Libertades*, "the City of Freedoms," with its own gay village, *La Zona Rosa,* as old as the Castro. It was a city where same-sex couples canoodled openly on the metro trains; where *la vota rosa* (the pink vote) was assiduously courted, and where gay people could marry, adopt children, and be registered as parents without fuss; where trans people could legally change their gender without having to go to court and where a public clinic offered free hormone replacement therapy. Perhaps most significantly, free abortions were available on demand in Mexico City in the first trimester of pregnancy; nowhere else in Latin America, save Cuba and Uruguay, were they even legal except in the cases of sexual assault or fetal anomaly.

Perhaps even more than its neighbor to the north, then, Mexico had its own internal Pink Line, drawn primarily around its capital city, an oasis of liberalism. It was a world in one country, with widely differing mores: a consequence of its geography and its diversity, its unwieldy federal system, and its history, too, as a devoutly Catholic country with a fiercely secular state, and a revolutionary past. Here, as in a few other countries, a broader process of legal reform was playing the leading role in changing social mores about sex and gender, alongside the Digital Revolution and a global human rights movement. As in South Africa and Colombia, a new constitution and the resulting human rights jurisprudence were the product of democratizing societies after long periods of authoritarian rule or civil war.

In the Mexican case, the constitutional reforms of the early twenty-first century came from two opposing forces in a kind of pincer-movement action against conservative Catholicism and the entrenched political elite. In the 1990s the Zapatista insurgency introduced the notion of the rights of indigenous people into the Mexican political discourse, thus opening up a national discussion about how other marginalized groups—such as disabled people, or homosexuals—might also be offered constitutional protection. Meanwhile, from the right, the modernizing agenda of President Vicente Fox embraced the liberal notion of "individual rights": Mexico had ossified under one-party rule and Fox sought to rejuvenate the country and to reintegrate it into the global economy, not only with a free-trade agenda but a human rights one, too.

But when left-wing Mexico City passed its marriage equality legislation in 2009, Fox's conservative successor Felipe Calderón immediately lodged a suit at the country's National Supreme Court of Justice: Mexico City's same-sex marriage law ran counter to the definitions of family inscribed in the constitution, the government claimed. The court ruled in Mexico City's favor: the purpose of matrimony was *not* procreation, and therefore any definition of it that was exclusively heterosexual was discriminatory. The judgment went even further: same-sex marriages conducted in Mexico City were to be recognized everywhere else in the country, too. This made Mexico's marriage equality regime very different from the one in the United States, where same-sex marriages were legal only in the American states that recognized them—until 2015, when the U.S. Supreme Court mandated compliance nationwide.

By the time Zaira and Martha got married in December 2013, there had already been 3,619 same-sex marriages in Mexico City since 2009—not a huge number—and about 10 percent of these were couples who had come from elsewhere in Mexico expressly to be wed.[4] On March 21, 2010, just days after the act became law, twenty-nine couples from across the country took part in a high-profile mass ceremony on the steps of the grand colonial city hall. "Mexico City was a social laboratory where we would see how things would unfold in the rest of the country," the veteran lesbian activist Lol Kin Castañeda told me. Castañeda organized the group marriage: "We used it to detonate the issue in the states," she said. "One of the commitments of the participating couples was that they should go home and exercise their rights—by demanding joint social security for example. This would force change across the country."

Zaira and Martha took a more radical stance, attempting to detonate the issue from within by demanding not only marriage at home, but also Martha's registration as Sabina's second parent in Guadalajara, too, even though it could be done in Mexico City.

They did not agree over the issue.

Martha made it very clear to me she would have been happy to get married in Mexico City, and to go there, too, to get certified as the other parent.

But Zaira was intractable: "It's so much easier in the capital, of course, but the easiest is not necessarily the fairest," she said to me. "Guadalajara is where we come from, where we live, where we grew up, where our daughter was born, and where she will grow up. Guadalajara is where we pay our taxes. Therefore we needed to do it here. Obviously we knew this would be longer and more complex, but we needed to think of those coming behind us. The activists who are fifty or sixty years old opened the door for us to use our rights. Now it's time for us to do the same."

GUADALAJARA IS BY no means a provincial backwater. Stately and sprawling, it is Mexico's second city. It has a pristine colonial center, a lively arts scene, a globally renowned crafts industry, the country's most developed tech industry, and a famously large gay community. Jalisco's other big city is Puerto Vallarta, a gay *gringo* holiday mecca, but the state itself is deeply conservative, a redoubt of right-wing Catholic politics. When Mexico City passed its same sex marriage legislation, Jalisco was one of two states to appeal (unsuccessfully) to the Supreme Court, in an effort to avoid having to recognize these marriages within its borders.

With its 2010 ruling on marriage equality, the court had actually opened the door, too, for Zaira and Martha to get married in Guadalajara, rather than having to go to Mexico City. Mexico's complex federal system meant that the court could not instruct states to change their laws—but it could override them, on a case-by-case basis, through an arcane mechanism called an *amparo*, literally a "protection." An *amparo* would compel the authorities to marry a same-sex couple on the grounds that the couple's constitutional rights to equality had been denied by the state, if it had refused to do so.

The first successful *amparo* for same-sex marriage came from the southern Mexican state of Oaxaca; it was granted in December 2012. In the next few years, an extraordinary grassroots network of prospective couples and activist lawyers sprouted across the country, sparking LGBT rights organizations in far-flung provincial cities, from Mexicali in the desert north to Tuxtla in the jungle south, 3,500 km away. Alex Alí Méndez Díaz, the Oaxaca lawyer who started it all and whose organization was the hub for all this activity, told me that about 200 *amparos* had been granted by 2017.

Like Zaira and Martha's, most of the marriages granted by *amparo* were conducted without incident, although sometimes the local authorities simply refused to comply.[5] This happened in Mexicali, right on the US border, where the city dragged its heels for two years on an *amparo* granted to two local hairdressers, eventually citing a formal complaint that the men were "insane." This led to a national campaign, "*#MisDerechos NoSonLocuras*" ("My rights are not madness") that caught fire across the country in January 2015, and a protest of several hundred of the couple's supporters outside Mexicali's City Hall. The mayor decided to disperse the protest by marrying the men on the spot, a rare and powerful victory for popular mobilization in the country.

Two weeks before the first same-sex marriage took place in Oaxaca in March 2013, Zaira and Martha had presented themselves at Guadalajara's civil registry. They were turned away, as they knew they would be, and they held a press conference announcing that they would be filing an *amparo* suit themselves. Their suit was one of the first in the country to be heard, and ruled on: in November 2013 they received their *amparo*.

I HAD TIMED my visit to Guadalajara to attend the annual Pride, and as we sat at the outdoor café, Zaira showed me a photograph on her Facebook page, from Pride the previous year. Sabina is leading the procession, a rainbow sash over her shoulder, attached to Zaira by a pink cord; Martha is a step behind, pushing a pram also swaddled in rainbow cloth. The women are in jeans and hiking boots and cowboy shirts, with men's rainbow ties loosely around their necks and their long hair tucked into baseball caps. A friend, marching next to them, carries a bright yellow sign: "I am SABINA and I demand a birth certificate with the names of my 2 MAMIS," a heart dotting the *i* of *mamis*.

Zaira boasted that Sabina knew the marching songs of the movement as well as she did any children's rhyme, and lifted the little girl onto her lap to prove it to me. Sabina gave a nursery lilt to "*Alerta que camina! La lucha feminista por America Latina!*,"and tense Martha relaxed into laughter, about how their daughter had woken them early on the day of the last march, brandishing her rainbow socklets (she was wearing them today, as well) and demanding they get moving.

I had expected to accompany Zaira and Martha to the march. But they were staying away, they told me. There was a dispute in the city between the NGOs and the gay businesses, which had resulted in two competing marches, on two consecutive weekends, and I had unwittingly come to town for the party, rather than the politics.

Zaira and Martha had their own domestic dispute over Pride anyway, another reason for staying away. Zaira felt there was "nothing wrong at all if people are naked, or if they express themselves wearing very little, or if they kiss, or not, as this is part of the diversity, part of who we are, as the community. But *mami*"—this was what she called Martha—"I know she feels different. Why don't you speak?"

"Well, now that we have Sabina, I don't like it that there are exhibitionists there [at Pride]," said Martha carefully. "Zaira thinks it's fine that Sabi sees protests with naked people. I don't agree. There are certain things that only come to you as you grow up. You need to earn them."

It was time to go, if I was going to catch the parade. We said goodbye, agreeing to meet at their home a little later. I mentioned that I wanted to pick up a little gift for Sabina. What would she like?

"Oh, Sabina loves *everything*," Zaira responded. "I have never met such an enthusiast. These days she wants to be Spider-Man *and* Superman, no? And then, suddenly, she's a princess." There was no gender policing in the household: "If she wants a little car, we buy it for her. If she wants a doll, we buy her a doll. She's free."

Parents look for themselves in their children. This is how Martha would later describe Sabina to me: "She is a serious little thing. She wants to talk. She wants to be herself."

2

As predicted, Sabina was delighted with the gift of an embroidered shoulder bag when my interpreter Andres and I arrived at the family's home later in the day. The little girl ran off to fill the bag with her favorite things, and she buzzed among us, pollinating our conversation with her antics as we settled into the afternoon with glasses of fresh pineapple juice. Sabina emptied and refilled the bag repeatedly, distributing knickknacks to the adults and then reclaiming them to stash away. From time to time, she would strut ostentatiously around the room, swinging the bag off her shoulder.

Their apartment was above Martha's shop in a gated *colonia* southeast of the city. In the Mexican style, the colonia's small houses ran up and down the hills in double-storied terraces, individually painted in bright colors, barbed with television antennae and security spikes, each one fronted by a parking bay that doubled as a patio when the car was out. The apartment was a long rectangular room, spare and neat, with a crimson divider separating a bedroom area to the back, and little splashes of red everywhere: the rim of the kitchen clock, the seats of the dining chairs, wooden apples on the table. There was none of the personalized religiosity—baptismal photographs in homemade frames, embellished shrines to the Virgin—one often finds in Mexican homes. Zaira was raised in an Evangelical church, and was a devout Protestant.

Martha had been the victim of two holdups in the shop—with knives and guns—but did not seem alarmed: three drug cartels were duking it out in Jalisco, but Parques Colón itself was "very safe" compared to other areas. Still, two years after I visited, Zaira's niece would be kidnapped from the house by armed intruders: she was returned safely after the De la O family paid the ransom.

Martha had bought the plot about ten years ago, with funds saved from a two-year stint in the United States, and had built her shop on it. She and Zaira hooked up a few years later, when they both needed somewhere to live after ending long-term relationships. They ended up becoming housemates in the home of a mutual friend: "Very *L Word*." We laughed. They bonded over late-night conversations about motherhood and Martha spoke of her sadness: she was infertile, following a miscarriage. They decided to have a baby together and Zaira was pregnant within six months, with the help of a sperm bank and her previous partner, a doctor. The couple decided they would build an apartment over Martha's store, and raise their child there.

But from the moment of Sabina's birth they were beset with problems due to the unofficial nature of their relationship. The baby was a month premature, and Martha was initially not allowed into the incubation room. "We became known as 'the Case,'" Zaira said. "The hospital threatened to call the police, because Martha was not allowed to be there, with our struggling baby, this little life of ours. One day she came home with a broken heart: 'They say I am not the mother.' The next day I was there, *fighting*. It took seven days, but eventually we won. And when we left, a month later, the nurses were taking photos of us. They were cheering, 'It's *the Case! The Case!*' So the next time two mothers arrive, they will not be the first ..."

Because Sabina had arrived a month early, the flat had not been ready at her birth, and in the month she was in the incubator, Martha and Zaira worked feverishly to complete it. They met the deadline, but immediately faced problems from "the self-appointed president of the *colonia*," as Zaira described a local busybody who claimed that they were violating bylaws. From day one, "this woman decided she wanted us out because we were a lesbian couple. Apparently we didn't have the moral standing of the *colonia*. But many of the other neighbors came to us and told us they had no problem with us. She bullied us repeatedly, and we had to get a restraining order. That calmed her down! And meanwhile we discovered that we had so many other friends and supporters in the *colonia*."

Among these were another lesbian couple, whom they had met on the street with their respective children. Alé popped over to tell me a bit of their story: her son Robbie's biological father was a gay friend whom he called *papa* and whose family doted on the child, but Alé and her wife, Max, were legally the parents; they had gone to Mexico City to marry, and to register Robbie. What strengthened their resolve was the attitude of Max's mother, who made it clear that she would take the child away from Alé should anything happen to her daughter.

"Nothing is more painful than for a mother to hear that, when a baby arrives!" exclaimed Zaira.

"You give all of your life," added Martha, "you give your time, you give your love ..."

THE AFTERNOON LENGTHENED INTO DUSK, and we moved from pineapple juice to beer. Saturday-evening noises floated over: the revving of cars, jousty men on corners, screeching teens. A woman called up asking if Sabina could come and play; Zaira looked across to Martha who nodded her assent, and as we chatted upstairs we heard Sabina with other kids on the street just below. She was with neighbors, old customers of Martha's who had always been friendly and welcoming. "The only problem with them is that they live in a huge family with grandparents and uncles and aunties and nephews, and Sabi often asks, 'Why it is only just the three of us?'" Martha said.

Once, Sabina had told her cousins—Martha's nephews—that she had "two *mamis*." "Your *mamis* are *tortas*," the boys responded: "sandwiches" in the Mexican vernacular, derogatory slang for lesbians, because of the way it suggests two pieces of bread pressed against each other. Martha was eavesdropping on the conversation, and was impressed by how Sabina defended her family: "She has no problem putting others right. She knows exactly how to do it."

The problem, Martha said, was her sisters: "They do not consider Sabi part of the family. The cousins are always getting little gifts, and Sabi is left out. And when Sabi calls me mom, they correct her, 'She's not your mom.'" In the beginning, they rejected Sabina, but the little girl won them over. "Still, they don't see her as a daughter."

Would it be easier once the legal recognition was granted to her?

"It will be another struggle, because they don't get it. 'Why would you want to give Sabi *our* name?' they ask. 'Why would you want to support a child that isn't even yours?'"

If Martha's mother was alive, she was certain it would be different: "She would love Sabi as one of her own, I am sure of it."

MARTHA WAS THE tenth of eleven children, raised by a single mother who sold perfumes and creams for a living; her older sisters left school to look after the younger children. Her father was an alcoholic "who effectively abandoned us, even though he lived at home," she told me.

Martha had been very close to her mother and so she was devastated when her mother threw her out after an older sister disclosed she had a girlfriend. She was twenty-two at the time, and went to live with the girlfriend, a co-worker at Guadalajara's fresh produce market. "In the end, my younger sister reconciled us. She told me my mom was crying and missing me. I have a tender heart, so I said okay." Martha never moved back home, but she and her mother became close again, and her mother ended up adoring her girlfriend: "I think she was won over by all those huge baskets of fruit."

Martha's first kiss had been with a high school sports coach, and she made most of her friends—and found her lovers—in the local women's softball league. Over time, though, she became disaffected with this world: she hated the infidelities, and the cattiness, and it was after the collapse of another relationship that she decided to go north, to try her luck in California.

It was 1995. She crossed the border at Tijuana with fake papers and made her way to Santa Barbara, where her first girlfriend had settled. "All my childhood friends were there, but still, it was lonely. Everyone was working all the time, working so hard, and for a long time I didn't have a job. Every time I talked to Mom, I'd cry." She got work as a babysitter, and eventually the job in the Mexican restaurant. Although she could see that things were much freer there than back home—a friend from high school was in the process of gender transition—she did not date anyone, and did not settle down. "I missed my homeland. And mostly I felt guilty about my mother, being so far away. It broke my heart." As Martha told me about this second separation, I had a sense of how deeply she must have been wounded by her initial banishment a few years previously.

It was a Monday morning, and I had come to speak to Martha while Zaira was at work. Martha had set Sabina up in the bedroom on her bright pink Hello Kitty tablet, and at one point, the little girl came through to tell us about the goings-on back there, with someone called Diego. Martha seemed uncomfortable, and explained Diego to me as Sabina's "ghost friend." Martha had not come from a devout family herself, but she felt strongly that Sabina needed to be baptized, to protect her from such demons: "It's not the first time. Downstairs, in the shop, Sabi said that a girl came out of the bathroom." Baptism would be "a protection, because the Bible says that, that way, the spirits won't take her soul."

But Zaira was adamantly opposed, on two scores. She was not a Catholic—and the church condemned them.

I mentioned another lesbian couple I had met in Guadalajara, who had adopted a boy at birth and had him baptized in church, with both women acknowledged as his parents. Martha knew the women—they were part of a group of lesbian mothers Zaira had established—but was astonished to hear about the baptism. I told her the story:

Maria and Soledad had been determined to have a baptism for their son Santiago in which they could participate fully. They also wanted their closest friends, an openly gay man and a single woman, to be the godparents (godparents typically had to be married parents themselves).

And so they put it to the test. First they went to their local parish, where they were turned away without even a hearing. At a second church, the priest said he would need to do some soul-searching: "*Soul-searching,*" Maria spat. "No thank you!" Finally, someone suggested an enlightened priest in another part of the city: "No problem." And so Santiago was baptized, in front of a full congregation one Sunday morning, with his lesbian mothers and his gay godfather and straight single godmother beside him at the font. "I don't believe this would have been possible even two years ago," Maria said to me. "Well, yes, it would have been possible, but in hiding. Keeping up the appearances. But now people are more willing to listen, and to change their opinions."

What had happened to cause this change?

"Politics," she replied. "Because of the changes that have taken place politically in this country, the fashion of 'no discrimination' is strong, and it is implemented. To discriminate was no big deal [in the past], but now discrimination is even punished."

ZAIRA WAS REBORN into evangelical Christianity, along with her family, at the age of thirteen. The family's conversion was part of a dramatic trend, across the whole region in the last years of the twentieth century, as U.S.-style Pentecostalism spread south on the wings of the Digital Revolution, of growing disenchantment with the Catholic Church's *doble morale* (double standards), and—in Mexico—of the terrible social upheaval that came with the war on drugs and narco-terrorism.

The passionate Zaira fell hard, and by the time she was sixteen she was a youth pastor in the Casa de Cristo, their church. This caused internal conflict: "I completed a preparation course, even though I knew I was different inside. I didn't know how to phrase it, how to find the 'Christian' word for it, but I knew I liked girls. And I knew it was wrong, given all the preaching in the church. I felt very guilty, and I remember kneeling before God and asking, 'Please take this away from me. Surely you don't want me to be bad …'"

But she *was* bad. She had started a sexual relationship with her best friend at school, and when she was eighteen, the pastor's daughter exposed them. Zaira was subjected to an arduous deliverance: forty days of fasting and a prayer-chain through the congregation "for the evil spirit to leave me, phoning each other every hour of the day. All these people, praying for me to be delivered from my lesbianism!" She was forbidden to talk to her friend and was to go straight to church after school, to pray and to fast.

At the end of the forty days, the pastor asked her how she felt. "I am really filled with the Holy Spirit," she responded. "But I still love her." She was told she was possessed by the devil and was ostracized, no longer allowed to sing in the choir and forced to sit alone at church. After three Sundays of this, the church's elders told her that she would be banished if she did not change. She left, tormenting herself with questions to God about why he had made her like this given that she had dedicated her life to serving him. To make matters worse, her girlfriend did not wait for her: "Hah! I learned she was being unfaithful to me, with half the school!"

Her turmoil was relieved by her parents'—eventual—support. When she came out to her extended family—with characteristic drama, at a New Year's Eve celebration—her father left the dinner table: "Over my dead body, to have a lesbian daughter!" And her mother blamed herself for having sent her to an all-girls' school: "I have failed you." But the elders in the family said, "We always knew. They love you. They'll come round." And they did. Her mother went to therapy and her father started asking questions, and before long they were fervently in her corner, something she ascribed to the "tolerance and respect" that was part of her upbringing.

Zaira's father, twenty-five years senior to her mother, was "a man of the world" who had lived most of his life north of the border, where he "did a little bit of everything" from working in kitchens to amateur boxing before settling into a career as the manager of a stone company. He had not joined the Casa de Cristo, telling his children that God did not reside within four walls. Now, when Zaira was expelled from the church, he reinforced this message to his daughter: "If you believe in God, he is with you."

Zaira took this seriously. Searching online, she found Other Sheep, a worldwide Christian ministry for LGBT people that took its name from John 10:16: "And I have other sheep that are not of this fold. I must bring them also." Other Sheep was very active in East Africa, too, and in fact when Michael Bashaija—another refugee from Evangelical Christianity—fled to Nairobi in 2014, one of the places he sought help was in the Kenyan chapter of the ministry.

Zaira received materials by mail from Other Sheep, and learned that "God loves me exactly as I am." She met the lesbian daughter of an Evangelical pastor while at university; the two bonded over their shared experiences and set up a prayer group. "We stopped being 'useless sheep' and now we 'worked' where God had put us, with the people who needed us (spiritually speaking)," Zaira wrote to me in a Facebook message. "Every weekend I traveled, and more and more people were waiting for us." When the other woman became ill the group stopped functioning and Zaira shifted her energy to activism.

By the time we met six years later, Zaira no longer attended any church ("They are all homophobic, here in Mexico") but her discourse was peppered with Christian invocation. "God loves us," she had said to me when telling me the story of Sabina's birth. "He loves us *more.*" There was ample proof of this: the artificial insemination had worked the very first time; Sabina's premature birth had given them the opportunity to complete the apartment in time; there had been no problems despite the premature birth; and most of all, "on top of everything else, He has granted the concession of giving us a girl."

3

One Sunday, Zaira and Martha invited me to join them at a get-together of their lesbian mothers' group. A woman named Claudia had offered her place: her mother loved to make posole, a celebratory traditional hominy soup that required much labor and inspired much love, and Zaira and Martha were very excited. We took a taxi out to a faraway suburb, stopping to buy beer along the way.

We were late; the other mothers had already eaten their posole—steaming bowls of soup with huge dried corn kernels and pork, garnished with lime, chili, and avocado—and had settled in to a game of Mexican picture bingo, the caller shouting out, "*El Azteca!*" "*El Diablo!*" or "*La Sirena!*" while their children threaded among them. The adults were drinking beer, and the children were full of sugar.

Claudia, the host, lived there with her parents. Her fourteen-year-old daughter obligingly played Pied Piper to the younger children all afternoon. Claudia had recently come out of an abusive long-term relationship with an alcoholic transgender man. She was not sure if she was a lesbian, strictly speaking, but she desperately needed community, and was too happy to host this group. There was another older couple with a teenage daughter, but the other eight families all had children under the age of five.

Was there a baby boom in lesbian Mexico, too?

The country's 2012 census offers some startling information.[6] Zaira and Martha's family were one of 229,773 households made up of same-sex couples, about 1 percent of the total. And 75 percent of these households had children. Compare this with the United States: in 2010, the U.S. Census Bureau counted around 594,000 same-sex households, also about 1 percent of the total.[7] There were as many of these families, proportionately, in the U.S. as there were in Mexico, itself an unexpected equivalence, but far fewer north of the border had children: only 115,000, or 25 percent. Perhaps this is not so surprising, as it coheres with Mexico's profile as a growing population and the United States' as a declining one, and suggests the relative value of children in Catholic Mexico compared to the United States. When Zaira and Martha chose to become parents in 2011, they were by no means exceptional among Mexican same-sex couples, as they would have been were they American.

But the demographics of the posole get-together suggested something else, too. These families were young: the children were born since 2010, when same-sex marriage became legal in Mexico City. To what extent, then, were they the direct consequence of the legal and social acceptance of gay or lesbian relationships?

The Guadalajara group, initiated by Zaira, was part of a countrywide Network of Lesbian Mothers in Mexico, known by its members simply as La Red (the Network). There were about two thousand families in La Red across the country, and according to its founder, Ana de Alejandro García, about 80 percent of the mothers had been in heterosexual relationships when they had their children, and came out later. But the number of mothers having children *as* lesbians was growing every year, she said. Alejandro García believed that this shift was not so much a consequence of a new appreciation of rights; rather, it was because of "much easier access to reproductive technology. Not just the technology itself, but the information online about it. You don't need to go to a clinic anymore and pay thousands of pesos. You can google about insemination and do it at home, with a man you know and trust. It's a big boon for lesbian mothers, this information age."

Zaira had her own take on her place in the generational shift: "Maternity is something one plans independently, whether the laws change or not. I would have become a mother no matter what. What is different is that before I might have hidden the fact that I was a lesbian, whereas now I am open about it." In a previous era, she might even have married a man to have a baby, as many of the older lesbians she knew had done.

One of the mothers at the posole get-together had done it both ways. Maribel Lopez was a feisty middle-aged woman in tight denim and cowboy boots: she had two older children, young adults now, through a shortlived heterosexual marriage she had been forced into, and she was now mother to a newborn baby with her wife, Blanca. Maribel had been born and raised in the U.S., and had owned a cleaning business back in North Carolina before moving to Guadalajara to be with Blanca: "I love all my kids," she told me in a Southern drawl, "but of course it's different now. I am raising Joushi together with my beautiful wife"—rather than alone and on the run from a heterosexual marriage. "My very own life shows the change [in society]."

Blanca was a gorgeous blond percussionist who had met Maribel while on tour in the U.S. Her mother had refused to have anything to do with her previous girlfriends but adored Maribel, and served her first at the dinner table, as one would any son-in-law. Still, Blanca said, "When I told my mother I was pregnant, she wept. 'How is the baby going to be raised without a dad?' But then my sister reminded her, 'Mom, *we* grew up without a dad. What's the problem?'" The baby was born, and Blanca's mother fell in love.

In March 2016, a few weeks after Joushi's birth, Maribel and Blanca drove with her to Mexico City, to marry and to register themselves as her mothers: "It ain't Vegas, but it sure was fun." Maribel laughed. "It made me so proud to be Mexican."

ONCE THE BINGO game had subsided into jovial chaos Zaira decided to call the party to order. "*Mami!* Please take notes!" she shouted across the room to Martha who, sitting next to me on the steps, rolled her eyes and pulled a notebook out of her handbag.

Zaira passed around a calendar that had been produced by a gay parents' group in Mexico City, and proposed the Guadalajara group do something similar: "You see, it features one family per month. We will divide up the months, we will find a photographer, and then you—the families—will decide how you want to be seen."

But a woman named Luz—a single mother with crimson hair—objected: "Believe me, I know about the dangers of visibility. When I was outed I had to quit medical school. Be very careful about this."

Maribel took her on: "It's our time," she said. "We must stand up and be seen." She told the other women that she worked at an English-language school, and that all her colleagues and students knew the score, and had even congratulated her when Blanca gave birth: "Sign us up! We're in!"

"What about the children themselves?" asked another woman. "Can we make these decisions about exposure for our children? Will it result in bullying at school, or problems with the teachers?"

"In my experience it's the children who are just fine," Maribel answered. "They know how to handle things. It's we, the adults, who carry the shame."

Night had fallen by now, and the stack of empty bottles was high. Tempers flared suddenly and then just as quickly subsided into raucous good humor. The women started playing the game of divvying up the months of the year, and when one said she really wanted to participate but was unable to show her face, another pitched in, "October! Give her October! She can wear a pumpkin on her head!" The meeting dissolved into hilarity; the women gathered up their children and their possessions and started moving slowly toward the door through a series of long embraces.

4

I had returned to Guadalajara for the posole evening from Mexico City, where I had attended the capital city's Pride. The first marches, in the late 1970s, had their roots in radical Mexican leftism and the ideas of gay liberation coming from the United States after Stonewall. Now, in 2016, the theme of the city's thirty-eighth annual Pride was *Todos Las Familias, Todos Los Derechos* (All Families, All Rights): family had become Mexico's Pink Line.[8]

The parade was led by families: Ana de Alejandro's "*lesbomaternal*" Network of Lesbian Mothers, and a "*homopaternal* " group, mainly of fathers, called Familias Diversas, founded by a celebrity gay couple who had made the first gay adoption in Mexico. Felipe Nájera, one of the dads, was an actor with Rock Hudson looks, and when the campy MC introduced him, she indulged in a little lewd banter: "I thought you would be more experienced at taking it," she said when he fumbled the microphone as she passed it to him. "Aren't you passive?"

"*Soy papa, no passivo,*" he responded irritably—"I'm a father, not passive"—before launching into an impassioned speech about extending same-sex marriage across the country. The interchange was an acute illustration of the disagreement I had witnessed between Zaira and Martha over whether Sabina should attend Pride: the culture clash between, on the one hand, the ethos of sexual dissidence that powered the gay liberation movement, and on the other, the boundary-setting that came with parenting, now that queer people were making families.

When Ana de Alejandro García took the mike, fierce and hyperfluent, there was not even an attempt at such banter. Her rapid-fire list of demands included the legalization of surrogacy (it was outlawed in all but one state) and the battle against a word she had coined: *gesto-normativity*, the legal favoring of a birth mother over the other parent. A subset of this, of course, was Zaira and Martha's issue: the right of a second mother to be recognized as a child's parent.

True to their feminist activist roots, La Red's mothers and their kids carried hand-painted signs and chanted the generations-old Latin American injunctions to struggle. The Familias Diversas group was slicker, with a brightly colored kiddies' steam train adorned with balloons in which their children sat, and even a theme song, recorded by a well-known artist. They had branded T-shirts: "Diverse Families for a better world for our children."

Back in Guadalajara, I met the author Jaime Cobián, the venerable elder of the city's gay movement. His organization had been Zaira and Martha's first port of call when they began seeking an *amparo*. Cobián was a parent himself—he was raising his sister's son—but he declined to help them: "Why?" he responded heatedly when I asked for his reasons. "There was a child involved. If you alert the authorities, they might take action you will later regret. I did not want to risk the government removing the child from them because they are lesbians." He was haunted by a previous case, when a transgender woman in the community had applied for welfare to help her raise the eight-year-old child whom she had cared for since birth; attempts by Cobián's organization to help her had resulted in the child being taken away from her.

Zaira and Martha had a different understanding of why Cobián turned them away: "They wanted to find *men* to get married, first," Martha said. "It would look better. They didn't think we were a good enough test case, because we were lesbians." Without funds of their own, the couple had finally found sponsors in the feminist organization CLADEM, the Latin American and Caribbean Committee for the Defense of Women's Rights.

But then for reasons I did not quite understand, Zaira and Martha had parted ways with CLADEM, and were now searching for someone else to help them in their quest for a second *amparo*, to get Martha registered as Sabina's other mother. Jaime Cobián rolled his eyes at their predicament: "Of course they must go to Mexico City! The child must come first."

THE COUPLE HAD first tried to get Martha registered as Sabina's second parent in early 2014, shortly after the marriage. But the authorities refused to accept their marriage certificate for the purpose: Jalisco's civil code only permitted a birth certificate to note a "mother" and a "father." Zaira and Martha appealed, twice, and failed.

As Zaira told me this story her eyes welled with rage. "It is painful for me even to think of it, that if I'm not here, if a car runs me over, my daughter is left up there in a cloud. And to think Martha has nurtured her from the time of her birth, to think she cannot keep her when really, in honesty, she has been more of a mother to Sabina than I have! Really, this is your daughter, you gave birth to her"—she was insistent that both women 'gave birth' to the child—"and *you have no rights*? It's just so unjust. I say, '*Let* them come into the house without knowing which woman actually physically bore Sabina, *let* them say which one is more the mother!'"

As I looked at Martha listening to this diatribe and registered her sadness, I felt overwhelmed by the contradictions: not only in their relationship, but also between the political meanings of the people I was meeting all over the world—their public places on the Pink

Line—and their private struggles, with one another and with their own demons.

Why was Zaira so insistent on not going to Mexico City? There was nothing in their relationship, that I had seen at least, to suggest that she did not want Martha to have rights over Sabina: she clearly accepted her wife's role as a primary parent.

I tried to make sense of her position by going back to her history, and in particular to the forty days of conversion therapy masquerading as deliverance, to which she was subjected when she was eighteen; her ostracism in church. She could not understand why she was being punished for loving a woman, when "I continue to be the same person, the same Christian, I continue to do good deeds, to minister, to pray. I said to myself: 'Nothing has changed within me, the only difference is that the Church now doesn't love me anymore.' So I got very depressed … I reproached God, asking Him: 'Why did You make me like this? I want to serve You. Please take this away from me.'"

Did Zaira mean "take the homosexuality away from me"? Or "take the depression away from me"? It began with the former but shifted to the latter, and then transformed even further, into activism, to a position of agency: she lifted the burden of the depression herself, by fighting for her rights and her dignity. I thought of these words of hers as I watched, again, the footage outside the registry on the day of her marriage, when she described—elatedly—"the satisfaction and the triumph" of winning the fight, and getting a higher power—in this instance, the state—to recognize her for who she was. It seemed to me that her stubbornness about doing it all in Guadalajara, rather than going to Mexico, was rooted deeply in the trauma of her conversion therapy, and the way she overcame it.

Her wife, Martha, it seemed to me, had her own demons and anxieties: the beloved mother who had thrown her out when she discovered her daughter was in a lesbian relationship; her infertility; the insecurity of being the much older partner of a labile, beautiful woman. Who could blame her for wanting to go to Mexico City?

But who could blame Zaira, either, for insisting on fighting for dignity, for seeking to overcome depression by taking on the fight?

5

"We have been a bit afraid," Martha told my researcher Julieta, when they spoke on the phone some weeks after my visit to Guadalajara, in August 2016. The National Front for the Family was gathering steam in its mission to stop President Peña's initiative to make same-sex marriage legal nationally; all the priests were talking about it from their pulpits, and there were signs mobilizing protesters all over the city. She and Zaira had taken Sabina along to a counter-march organized by the LGBT community, and had been startled at the hostility of protesters toward them. Even left-wing activists who had marched in solidarity with LGBT causes before had joined the National Front, perhaps convinced by its "anti-homophobic" messaging, and she wondered whether this was one of the reasons why human rights organizations were declining to help her and Zaira with their suit.

Why had Peña announced the reform in the first place? The prominent Mexican political journalist Jenaro Villamil told me he believed the president was using the issue "like a small-town guy who wants to appear as if he is a *capitalino*." He sought to gain membership in the club of enlightened global leaders—epitomized by the U.S. president Barack Obama, whom he emulated—by embracing same-sex marriage as a badge of modernity and sophistication. Villamil and other critics accused Peña of attempting to "pinkwash" his abysmal human rights record—the word was used in the Mexican media, borrowed from the debate about Israel and

LGBT rights—with "soft" issues (his other quixotic crusade was the legalization of marijuana).

But the fact that the president and his counselors perceived LGBT rights as "soft" in the first place demonstrates just how far Mexican society had moved in the six years since Mexico City legalized same-sex marriage. While a 2010 poll found that 20 percent of Mexicans supported same-sex marriage,[9] a May 2016 one, taken after the Peña announcement, put the figure at 65 percent.[10] Even with margins of error, the shift was astonishing.

Still, the issue was deeply divisive, as was evidenced by the backlash it fomented.

One conservative opposition candidate elected two weeks later called the Peña initiative "a gift from heaven" at the polls; the Christian right wing now had its Pink Line.[11] And what had seemed to be an ineluctable state-by-state rolling-out of marriage equality in Mexico was slowed down: *amparo* suits continued to be filed and won, on a case-by-case basis, but several states planning to legalize same-sex marriage put these initiatives on ice.

In 2018, the radical populist Andrés Manuel López Obrador (or AMLO, as he was universally known) was elected, the first left-wing president in decades. AMLO's party, MORENA, had a strong LGBT platform, but its leader maintained his huge popularity among ordinary people by staying well away from the Pink Line: a devout Christian, he never said anything about either abortion or same-sex marriage. In his victory speech, though, he included "beings of all currents of thought and all sexual preferences" among the long list of people his government would serve.[12]

"SABINA IS DOING REALLY WELL," Martha said in the same conversation with Julieta. "She's at school and very happy. She even wants to go on weekends!" Zaira and Martha had leveled with the school about their situation and Sabina had been accepted without a birth certificate, for the time being.

I tried to remain in touch, but the line went dead. I called, I wrote, I contacted others, but no one knew how to reach them. Finally, in May 2017, Zaira responded to a Facebook message. She and Martha were taking strain over the registration issue, and this was affecting their relationship negatively. Meanwhile, the school was turning up the heat: The family had until the end of the school year—two months—to get a birth certificate in, one way or the other. If they did not find a way to write Martha into it, it would have to be submitted without her name. Zaira said, "I would appear alone as her only mother, and legally Sabi will be the daughter of a single mom, me. Which implies Martha would lose her chance to also be her legal mom."

Zaira told me that she felt abandoned, even by the mothers' group I had met at the posole evening: "They take the easy way, they have money and go to Mexico City, they never seek to achieve a change at home, a change for all the generations to come." Obviously, she continued, "everything that I'm telling you creates stress and discussions between Martha and myself … sadness, hopelessness, frustration … It all invaded us …" She signed off: "Oh, Mark, I guess this is why I haven't answered you. I didn't know how to tell you, what we are living [through] hurts me deeply. Let me go and smoke a cigarette, for I am crying again."

ZAIRA AND MARTHA separated during the course of 2018, but they did not let up in their quest for an *amparo* to get Sabina's birth certificate changed, so that Martha could be recognized as the other parent. By the end of the year, they had been refused an *amparo* four times. They could not get any more extensions from Sabina's school. And so Zaira gave up, she wrote to me in early 2019: they would go to Mexico City after all. The plan was to do it in March, but the kidnapping of Zaira's niece had thrown the family into "economic turmoil."

Two months later, I woke up one morning to the following message from Zaira: "Greeting you with bad news. I have cancer"—a form of leukemia. The infection was detected too late for chemotherapy, and she was about to start treatment in a naturopathic clinic. "I have to be strong, because, as if it were decreed, and with my bad luck, I haven't registered my daughter and I'm a step from dying. I've done everything I can to pressure the state to demand a birth certificate for two moms. My wife, my daughter and I, we deserve it. It has been six years and we are fighting to present yet another *amparo*. Even if it's from a hospital or my deathbed, I will demand a certificate for Sabina."

Zaira had run out of funds for her treatment, and was posting adverts for a fund-raiser event at a local club, sponsored by Guadalajara's Pride organization. A lawyer from an LGBT organization was helping her with a fifth attempt to get Martha registered as Sabina's parent: "Now with more urgency than ever, I need Martha to be recognized as Sabina's mother with an official birth certificate. I can't even die in peace. That's what I said six years ago, and now look at me, living that precise situation. That's the story, Mark."

I steeled myself against the grief by scrolling back through Zaira's exuberant Facebook posts, usually selfies, often with Sabina: at amusement parks, winning medals in tae kwon do, slurping sodas, swimming. Martha had pretty much gone offline, but just under a year before Zaira's letter to me, she had posted a rare status update with photographs of Sabina at kindergarten graduation: "Proud of my daughter 100 percent, watching her conclude her first level in school, and the start of a new one. As difficult as it seemed, we did it Zaira. Let's go for more, De La O Sandoval family."

“I’m so happy for her, because it’s a step further,” Zaira had responded, addressing Martha directly. “Proud of you for your effort and your will. We are doing alright, my dearest. Nobody said it would be easy, but our baby girl advances with solid steps. Thank you! Love you.”

Whatever the status of Zaira and Martha’s relationship, whatever the law said, and whatever Zaira’s medical prognosis, one thing was clear: Sabina had two mothers.

11

PINK DOLLARS, GLOBAL GAY

ON MARCH 17, 2012, the cruise ship *Celebrity Summit* left Puerto Rico with two thousand gay men on board for an eight-day Caribbean cruise. In what was becoming a booming industry, the ship had been chartered by Atlantis Events, an American company that specialized in "all-gay" cruises, "a carefree experience based around friendship, camaraderie, relaxation, indulgence, adventure and pure uninhibited fun."[1] Gay cruises had become so popular because they offered clients a hedonistic "all gay" world, where they could be themselves in the anywhereland of the high seas, without the usual strictures of the heteronormative world: the law, the family, the workplace, the street. You spent your days sunbathing in skimpy bathing suits and your evenings dressed up, or undressed, at themed parties; sex and drugs were very much part of the scene. But when you were in the territorial waters of the country the ship was visiting, you were subject to its laws. And so when dockworkers in Dominica saw two naked men having sex on their balcony as Celebrity Summit docked, they called the police.

The island of Dominica had been a British colony; here, as in all the Anglophone Caribbean, "buggery" was illegal and carried a sentence of up to fourteen years. Police officers boarded the ship and arrested the two men on suspicion of these charges and of indecent exposure, and removed them from the ship to a local jail. After a night in the cells the men agreed to a plea bargain: the buggery charges were dropped and they pleaded guilty to indecent exposure. They were fined nine hundred U.S. dollars and deported at their own expense. The ship sailed on without them.

The Dominican police released mugshots of the culprits to the media: tanned and muscled in blue tank tops, their names were Dennis Mayer—a retired police officer age fifty-three—and his forty-one-year-old partner, John Hart. They had been together for seventeen years, and when they returned to Palm Springs, California, they told American media how they were held for nineteen hours in a dark, bug-infested cell with no light or water or toilet: "We were taunted all night long. They paraded us around like we were some oddity."[2] The police threatened rectal examinations; people were "chanting and protesting in the street" as they entered the court, where the judge called them "rogues" and "vagabonds." What he had learned from the experience, Mayer said, was that "hatred and bigotry" still existed in the world; he was particularly angry with the tour operator for having led "2,000 gay people to a port where we are hated."[3] A photograph of the men taken from the quay, clearly having sex, found its way onto the website Queerty, but "the real question is not what we were doing on our balcony," Mayer responded, "but why is one of the largest promoters of gay cruises and events taking folks from the LGBT community to these countries with laws against homosexuals on their books?"[4] Were Mayer and Hart thumbing a nose at Dominica's laws and mores, or had they been so unmoored by their fantasy holiday that they had forgotten they were no longer in a floating twenty-four-hour gay nightclub? Whichever: they could not be compared to Tiwonge Chimbalanga, humiliated and jailed for just being herself in Malawi, or Caleb Orozco just across the water, fighting to overturn the same buggery laws in Belize. They framed themselves as victims, but some Dominicans—and some online commentators back home—saw them as arrogant or ignorant American tourists, oblivious to or contemptuous of the mores of the place they were visiting and even the struggles of LGBT Dominicans.

Mayer and Hart had crossed a Pink Line. Their arrests exposed the way worlds could clash in the twenty-first century as ideas about sexuality and sexual freedom—and the people who embodied them, of course—crossed borders. The fact that these ships disgorged hundreds of (overwhelmingly) white men only substantiated local perceptions that homosexuality was an American phenomenon, which islanders needed to bear if they wanted the income, but against which they felt they needed to fight if they wished to protect their values. A few weeks later the Dominican education minister appointed an investigation into "the root causes of deviance and the increasing incidents of homosexuality" in schools.[5] The investigation proved the situation to be far worse than he had imagined, he reported back, and so he appointed a special committee "to mitigate the spreading of crime, violence, homosexuality and deviant behaviors in schools."

When I made contact with Dominica's LGBT leader Daryl Phillip in 2018, he described the *Celebrity Summit* incident as a collision between ideologies from different parts of the world that "caused us to rethink our rights in the society. It will not be tolerated anywhere in the world for someone to have sex in the full viewing of the public, but at the same time it raised the issue of buggery being illegal in a country, something which provides fuel for open homophobia." The arrests might have provoked the education minister's investigation—an initiative which came to nothing, Phillip told me—but it also forced people in the tourism industry into statements of support for gay cruises, and made space for "public discussion for the repeal of the anti-buggery laws on the island."

Farther north in the Caribbean, Jamaica had long been known for extreme homophobic violence, emanating more from music-hall culture and the lyrics of singers such as Buju Banton than from the pulpit. But Jamaica was not exceptional: a 2018 Human Rights Watch investigation demonstrated that this was a phenomenon across all Anglophone Caribbean nations.[6] An activist named Bennet, from Saint Lucia, told HRW that "people called a radio station saying they're going to shoot me in the head, cut my throat."[7] Bennet recalled that when the first gay cruise ship came to the island, cabbies refused to take the fares, but that when it became known that gay tourists were big spenders, the drivers changed their minds: "People were thinking we were bringing a foreign concept, that the youth would become 'more gay.' But then people realized that, at the end of the day, people were coming to enjoy a vacation."

Could the cruise ships, then, be an agent of change in a part of the world where the anti-sodomy laws still on the books made the

Anglophone Caribbean islands outliers in a region where there was much progress elsewhere?

In 2018, Bermuda—a self-governing British territory—became the first state in the world to reverse marriage equality, when its governor-general nullified a Supreme Court decision to allow two men to marry, after pressure from a Christian lobby, and replaced it with a domestic partnership bill. Kevin Dallas, the openly gay executive of the Bermuda Tourism Authority wrote to parliament that this posed "an unnecessary threat to the success of our tourism industry … [and could] cause us serious reputational damage."[8] He noted that $165 billion was spent in LGBT travel worldwide.

Ellen DeGeneres called for a tourism boycott of the country, and the huge Carnival cruise line company announced it would support the local LGBT organization's legal appeal. Carnival Cruise regularly scored 100 percent on the Human Rights Campaign's Corporate Equality Index, a tool developed by the organization to rate American businesses on their treatment of LGBT employees, consumers, and investors. The company issued a statement: "While we always abide by the laws of the countries we sail to and from, we believe travel and tourism brings people and cultures together in powerful ways. As a result, we believe it is important to stand by the LGBTQ community in Bermuda and its many allies to oppose any actions that restrict travel and tourism."[9] The threat was clear.

In November 2018, the Bermuda Court of Appeal instructed the state to resume granting same-sex marriages, and the following year the territory held its first ever Pride parade, enthusiastically supported by the Bermuda Tourism Authority. "People travel not just for these events, but to places where they know they are welcomed," said Kevin Dallas.[10] "In the past couple of years, Bermuda has moved an extremely long way … There is a lot more positive reaction to the island on social media than we had last year."

Earlier in 2019, Brunei, a Muslim country in southeast Asia, introduced a new penal code that made homosexual sex punishable by death—together with adultery, and insulting the Prophet Muhammad. The actor George Clooney and the rock star Elton John headlined a global boycott of the Sultan of Brunei's properties, which include the Beverly Hills Hotel in Los Angeles and the Dorchester in London. Organizations ranging from the Police Federation of England and Wales to Deutsche Bank and JPMorgan took their substantial business away from the hotels, Virgin Australia canceled its agreement with Royal Brunei Airlines, the British government took down tourism advertisements for the country, and tour operators threatened to stop sending clients there.

After just a month, the Sultan of Brunei put a moratorium on the death penalty provisions of the new code, with respect to homosexuality and adultery. "You can't shame the 'bad guys,' but you can shame the people who do business with them," said Clooney to Ellen DeGeneres on her TV talk show, warning neighboring Indonesia and Malaysia—also looking to strengthen their anti-homosexuality laws—to view the successful campaign as a "warning shot."[11] Such pressure, of course, is exactly what the Malaysian premier Mahathir Mohamad was railing against in 2003, when he said the West's promotion of "free sex including sodomy" was a threat to Asian values.[12]

Speaking on that Russian TV program *Play Actors* in 2013, the Kremlin-aligned political analyst Alexey Mukhin had claimed that "the LGBT industry is a global industry and it needs new markets": the basis of the West's support of an LGBT rights movement in Russia was "the desire for money and power."[13] In the rhetoric of global political homophobia, this line was played repeatedly: if the recruitment canard provided one way that LGBT rights were perceived to be about "money and power" (people were "paid" to be homosexual, by funders or sex tourists or older men), consumerism was the other.

The Brazilian president Jair Bolsonaro also took aim at the pink dollar—a significant contributor to his country's tourism economy—when he told journalists in April 2019 that while he welcomed straight sex tourists to his country: "We can't let this place become known as a gay tourism paradise. Brazil can't be a country of the gay world, of gay tourism. We have families."[14] Framed from this side of the Pink Line, the battle was between local traditional values and global commodity culture.

Seen from the other side—from Daryl Phillip's perspective in Dominica, for example, or by Bermuda's Kevin Dallas trying to boost his country's economy—consumerism and tourism opened the insular world of an island to fresh ideas and capital and people, and to new ideas about freedom. Still, reports from Brunei at the time of the international campaign suggested that the sultan's moratorium did not offer much hope for an easier life: "It's living hell here either way," a gay man told *The Telegraph*.[15]

AFTER THE U.S. Supreme Court ruling mandating marriage equality across the United States on June 26, 2015, President Barack Obama gave the instruction that the White House be bathed in the colors of the rainbow flag, and spoke of how, through "the countless small acts of courage of millions of people across decades … an entire country" had come to "realize that love is love."[16]

Love was also money.

Visa put out an ad with the tag "Love. Accepted Everywhere," and Jell-O ran the slogan "JELL-O-V-E is for everyone" beneath wobbly cubes the colors of the rainbow.[17] And while high-end liquor brands like Absolut had long courted a gay market, even the more downmarket beer brands started draping themselves in the rainbow flag: Budweiser introduced a special-edition bottle with the Statue of Liberty imposed over the rainbow flag. At least fifty major American corporations dipped their brands into rainbow colors.[18] These included Coca-Cola, AT&T, YouTube, Levi's, Mastercard, MTV, Gap, and American Airlines.

The previous year, to protest Russia's anti-homosexual laws, Google had done a rainbow doodle on the day the Winter Olympics opened at Sochi. Nike, Adidas, and Converse competed with special rainbow editions of their sneakers. In 2012, Target, an American retailer that had drawn criticism for funding conservative anti-gay politicians, joined the marriage equality campaign with a new ad for its wedding registry, in which two smiling men held hands above the words, "Be yourself, together."[19]

That year's June World Pride in London was dominated by corporate phalanxes competing with one another for the cleverest gay-themed corporate branding, and some even used the opportunity to do direct marketing: British Airways handed out a "Pride Special" offer of a 20 percent discount on your next flight. A few months later, in India, I watched employees from three American multinational corporations with hubs in the city—Google, Hewlett Packard, and Goldman Sachs—join the *hijras* and the queer activists at Bangalore Pride. Google's "Gayglers," the company's in-house LGBT affinity group, stole the show with their cute same-sex android couples holding hands and waving rainbow flags.

Two decades before, in the 1990s, some scholars and activists had begun predicting what Bob Cant called "McPink" : "a global pink economy which promotes a series of ever-changing lifestyle options," rather than a battle for rights and freedom.[20] Was consumerism the new battleground in the rights battle, or had it overwhelmed the struggle and turned it into a brand? The art historian Frank Smigiel imagined a time not too far off when sexual utopia would mean "not a place of liberated bodies and pleasures where 'love knows no boundaries,' but a time when the Mall of America wraps itself in rainbow flags as if to say 'Welcome Gay Shoppers.'[21] Repackaged, homosexuality would occur in consumer society like any other corporate logo or brand name."

In an influential and prescient 1996 essay called "On Global Queering," the Australian sociologist Dennis Altman tracked the way the expansion of the free market had opened the world to American gay branding and thus to the—primarily American—"idea that (homo)sexuality is the basis for a social, political and commercial identity."[22] Gay people the world over were wearing the same clothes and aping the same styles, dancing to the same music, watching the same porn, aspiring toward a lifestyle made for American consumers. The Pride parades mushrooming across the globe celebrated an American liberation mythology, too. Even in Germany, the birthplace of a homosexual rights movement, the Pride parade is Christopher Street Day to commemorate the riots at the Stonewall Inn in New York's Greenwich Village a century later.

It is certainly true that American ideas of what "gay" meant went global toward the end of the twentieth century. Gay subculture moved out of the ghetto and into the mainstream, setting trends through the rapidly globalizing entertainment, design, and fashion industries: look, for example, at how Madonna elevated gay Harlem voguing to an international style phenomenon in the early 1990s. In these same years, the terms *pink pound* and *pink dollar* came to be used to express the purchasing power of "DINK" (Double Income, No Kids) homosexuals.

As in the case of Carnival cruise lines and Bermuda or the boycotts of the sultan of Brunei's luxury hotels, the ever-growing pink market was one motivation for many multinational corporations to embrace

LGBT rights as one of their core "values." The other was the changing legal position of their own workforces. North American and European companies were incorporated in countries where labor legislation now expressly forbade discrimination on the basis of sexual orientation and gender identity, and this influenced corporate policy, particularly when it came to partner rights. Some corporations went further, setting out specifically to make LGBT-friendly work environments so as to attract queer staff. As the Goldman Sachs branding at Bangalore Pride in 2012 declared: "Inclusion Shapes Our Culture."

While in Bangalore, I met a Google account strategist named Yash Godbole, who told me how, after he had signed on anonymously to the company's global Gayglers listserv, a human resources manager "joined the dots" and contacted him to ask him if he would like to set up an India chapter. To help him make up his mind, his employers sent him to Sydney Mardi Gras so that "I could see what happens elsewhere, and how people around the world behave around these issues." With the encouragement of his bosses, Godbole first came out to his colleagues, and then to his family: the fact that he was accepted at work made "all the difference" at home, he told me.

But if "diversity and inclusivity" was a labor recruitment strategy, it was also a mode of corporate branding, suggesting the kind of trendsetting forward motion—the essence of modernity—that these particular brands sought to project. As a Heineken campaign launched as early as 2011 put it: "Open your world."[23]

OPEN BOTTLES, OPEN SOCIETIES, open closets. From Heineken to Google to George Soros to the ideological descendants of Harvey Milk ("Gay brothers and sisters, you must come out!"), the people who sent these messages out spoke to a particular way—a primarily American way—of being gay or LGBT in the world. In almost every country I visited doing this research, I met some young person who called him or herself Beyoncé. And I saw rainbow flags and stickers in rural Indian villages and slick Mexico City apartments, in Soviet-era tower blocks in provincial Russian cities and in refugee doss-houses on the outskirts of Nairobi.

By 2017, Grindr, the gay geolocation hookup app, had twenty-seven million users in 192 countries. I heard, from users in repressive Egypt or Nigeria or the Palestinian West Bank, how the app had been not only a safer way to help them find people in the same district or even on the same street, but had also spun them out into a broader, boundaryless world where their nationalities were just one way of defining themselves: they could also identify themselves by signing on to one or more of Grindr's twelve "tribes": Bear, Clean-cut, Daddy, Discreet, Geek, Jock, Leather, Otter, Poz (HIV-positive), Rugged, Trans, and Twink.

But by 2018, Grindr—founded by an American Israeli in New York—was fully owned by a Chinese gaming company based in Beijing, although it was not yet available in most Chinese cities: here Blued prevailed, with its forty million users. The American-inflected "global gay" language was thus no longer only funded by Western capital flows, but it had profoundly different meanings, depending on where it was spoken. The global language of "gay" was appropriated, and indigenized, too.

In India, the hookup site PlanetRomeo—originally German, now run out of Amsterdam—was the primary online mode of communication for homosexual and bisexual men in the country, used not only to hook up, but also to promote gay products and parties, and to find other queer people nearby. In his 2011 doctoral study of the app in India, Akhil Katyal describes the way it "sets the stage for the idiom of a worldwide 'genuine gay community' that the [Planet Romeo] team constantly uses in its publicity material, and for the heavily globalized references that frame most of its user profiles. It is not surprising to find photographs of Brad Pitt, Backstreet Boys or Daniel Radcliffe used as profile pictures by people in Raipur or Meerut in India, references to the San Francisco 'bondage scene' or the Chilean Pokémon subcultures among Kolkata users, or citations from Ghalib and Robert Frost and Timberlake or Sultanpuri jostling with each other in the same profile."[24]

There might, thus, have been a surface continuity to the images one saw of Pride parades from Manila to Montevideo, or a similar beat to music in gay discos, or even a shared coded language on hookup sites when it came to specifying sexual preference. But in the end these were all surface wrappers, like the rainbow flag itself, furled as it was around various agendas and subjectivities and brands.

Where there was continuity, of course, was in the reason why people wore these wrappers in the first place: a common experience of marginalization, or repression, and the role that the wrapper played as some kind of talisman, as a portent of liberation. There *was* something in common structurally about the lives of all the Beyoncés I met, in Nigeria and Egypt and Uganda and the Philippines and India, not least in the violence they had experienced because they were effeminate. Perhaps this is why they had taken on the name of a glorious, resilient Amazon. But they shared almost nothing culturally, because of their different family structures and religious faiths, their different classes and national or ethnic cultures.

As with the Beyoncés at one end of the social scale, so, too, with the Gayglers at the other. On the surface the Google staffers I saw marching at Bangalore Pride in 2012 looked just the same as those at World Pride London or the Sydney Mardi Gras, dressed as they all were in their cute gay android T-shirts. But the Indian Gayglers were different in one dramatic way: except for Yash Godbole himself, not one of them was openly gay. The rest—about 150 in total—were "allies," associating with the group because it was hip and a sign of modernity. As Dennis Altman observed in 2000, "the claiming of lesbian/gay identities can be as much about being Western as about sexuality."[25] This, he said, was why southeast Asians imported the word *gay* into their vernacular rather than using long-established local terms, and why the words *modern* and *internacionale* were used to describe "gayness" in Peru and Mexico respectively.

Back in Bangalore, the non-gay Gayglers were "giving cover to those people who cannot yet risk being seen on the streets," Yash Godbole told me. Google might have a global diversity and inclusivity policy, but "of course it gets diluted in countries where it's still against the law, and where there's still a lot of taboo in society."

OF ALL THE PLACES I VISITED, Lagos seemed to be the place where this dissonance was most intense. The Nigerian megacity was the West African hub to dozens of multinational corporations, in a country where the mere implication of homosexuality was punishable by fourteen years in jail. A Pride parade was unimaginable.

One evening in October 2014, I went to the stylish Lagos offices of a man I will call Teddy, who had started a gay Facebook group. Teddy was in his late thirties, worldly and well-traveled, with the kind of gym body and knowing look you would find in Chelsea or Soho but also, increasingly, in the shopping malls and fancy clubs of Lagos' Victoria Island. Sitting around his boardroom table over pizza and red wine with me were about fifteen members of the Facebook group, men and women: lawyers, entrepreneurs, actuaries, senior managers. Many of them had the resources to enable them to slip easily into and out of double lives. Some were married with kids in Nigeria, but had long-term same-sex lovers abroad: "Wheels up, hair down!" was the way one described the plane ride between Lagos and London.

Several of the group worked for multinational corporations that trumpeted their LGBT diversity policies, and yet not one of them was out of the closet, at work or at home. Lagos was the wealthiest place on the African continent, with a huge middle-class population that was literate, worldly, and wired. Why, I asked my fellow diners, did they think that Lagos was not following the globalizing, urbanizing trend when it came to sexual mores?

One of the women present—I will call her Ife—worked for a multinational corporation with a strong diversity profile. Had she come out at work? She snorted in derision: "Are you *crazy*? My *boss* is in my church!" Without exception, every person at the pizza evening went to church, mainly to one or another of the Pentecostal congregations mushrooming across Africa. "It's not just about religion," Ife said. "It's about society, and culture, and about networking. You have to go to church to belong—and to move up in the world. I just shut my ears when I need to—and work hard to save for my next trip abroad."

IN JULY 2018, corporations in Israel engaged themselves directly in a battle along that country's Pink Line.

Even under the right-wing government of Binyamin Netanyahu, Israel was a staunch promoter of LGBT rights, at home and internationally. Although same-sex marriages could not be granted in the country (only religious marriages were legal), a Supreme Court judgment had compelled the state to register same-sex marriages from elsewhere in 2006. But as had happened in gender ideology battles elsewhere, the Jewish religious right wing drew the line at families: adoption by anyone other than a married heterosexual couple was almost impossible, and while obtaining a surrogate had been legal for heterosexual couples since 1996, it was only legalized for single women in 2018, through a law that continued to exclude single men.

This effectively barred gay men from seeking surrogacy within Israel (they could still do it abroad).

Netanyahu had initially pledged that gay men would be included in amended legislation, but had been forced to backtrack by his religious coalition partners in government. Enraged, the country's LGBT movement called for a nationwide strike, and on Sunday, July 22, an estimated hundred thousand people protested, blocking traffic and filling Tel Aviv's Rabin Square. It was one of the largest public demonstrations Israel had ever seen, in large part because of the way corporations—multinational and local, private and public—became involved, with at least forty giving their workers the day off to participate.

Israel's huge tech industry set the trend, with a statement from IBM: "No one should be denied the basic human right—the right to have a family—because of the decision to be faithful to themselves and their identity."[26] Facebook, Microsoft, Apple, and many others followed, as did public entities such as El Al and the national transport authority. Microsoft, Mellanox, and iStore even offered financial incentives to any employees seeking surrogacy.

Three sentiments powered this unexpected surge in corporate-sponsored LGBT activism. The first was Israel's strong pro-natalist culture: fertility treatment is free, and unlike European countries, Israel has a growing population. In this context, the global shift toward marriage and parenting in gay culture and rights struggles had a particularly strong impact here: bringing children into the world was something "close to their national duty," Lee Walzer wrote in his 2000 gay travelogue of Israel.[27] This imperative stemmed from Judaism's emphasis on family life and the memory of the Holocaust in which one million Jewish children perished, Walzer said, but also from "the perceived need to produce more Israelis to counter Arab demographic trends."

The second sentiment was outrage at the Israeli government's hypocrisy. As an article in *Haaretz* put it: "Wait, didn't Israel have a massive Gay Pride Month? Is [the government] LGBT-friendly or not?"[28] The Israeli state had been investing heavily in Tel Aviv as an international gay tourism destination since 2010, when it first announced an eighty-eight-million-dollar campaign to this end. Tel Aviv's Pride Week was funded and organized by the promotions department of the city. This was both good business—in 2013, it brought twenty thousand international tourists to the country—and good propaganda: through its support of LGBT rights the country promoted itself as an oasis of liberal freedom, the only democracy in a tough neighborhood.

In this context, Netanyahu's retreat was seen by secular Israelis as yet another harbinger of encroaching theocracy. This was the third—and main—reason why so many Israelis turned out to protest, and why the country's corporate sector objected so strenuously. "One of Israel's greatest gifts is the creativity, diversity and talent of all of its people," read Apple's statement.[29] "Unfortunately, recent legislation … undermines those values. Apple will always maintain its values of fairness, dignity, and mutual respect, and we stand with all of our employees seeking equality under the law." Although Palestinians might see the hypocrisy in such a statement, the Israel that Apple sought to identify with—and that so many Israelis took to the streets to defend—was enlightened, global, and open.

12

FADI AND NADAV'S STORY

I'BILLIN—TELAVIV—JAFFA (ANDRAMALLAH)

Fadi Daeem—nurse, resident of Jaffa, late twenties. Pronouns: he/him/his.

Nadav Kain—Fadi's boyfriend, party organizer and fashion industry worker, late twenties. Pronouns: he/him/his.

Khader Abu-Seif—Fadi's best friend, journalist and copywriter, late twenties. Pronouns: he/him/his.

Nabil*—university student, Ramallah, mid-twenties. Pronouns: he/him/his.

Dan*—Nabil's husband, software engineer, Tel Aviv, late twenties. Pronouns: he/him/his.

Zeinab*—human rights activist, Ramallah, late twenties. Pronouns: she/her/hers.

***Pseudonyms**

1

When Fadi Daeem took his boyfriend Nadav Kain to his sister's wedding in his home village of I'Billin in northern Israel in July 2016, the two sported matching hairstyles—shaven into a bowl on top of the head, almost like yarmulkes—and hipsterish whiskers. Fadi wore a black suit with a bow tie–shaped metal brooch pinned over the top button of his white shirt, and had all his facial jewelry in place: nose ring, silver barbell through an eyebrow, diamanté studs. Nadav had scaled his usually lurid nails down to "something more relaxed, nude with rhinestones," he said: "I didn't want to be the extremist boyfriend at the family wedding."

Fadi was not particularly anxious about taking Nadav to the village for the wedding, he said. The three of us were sitting at their regular sidewalk table at the Casino San Remo, a café around the corner from their home in the trendy Noga district of the old Arab port city of Jaffa, now incorporated into Tel Aviv. With their coiffed Maltese dog, Sushi, at our feet, we drank Levantine lemonades out of Mason jars and then cosmopolitans into the afternoon as they laughed about the previous time Nadav had been to visit the Daeems in I'Billin, with his parents:

"My mother!" said Fadi, turning his palms to the heavens in mock exasperation. "Typical control-freak Arab mother! She needs to know everything about my life." Fadi had told her he went most weekends to the Kains' for Shabbat dinner, "and so she wanted to know, 'who are these people who cook for my son on Friday nights?'"

"'You think you can cook for my son?'" Nadav chipped in, doing his mother-in-law-as-diva impersonation. "'I'll show you! I can do it better.' And she did! I've never seen so much food. All these incredible little plates covering the table, each with something different. Crazy! I love her food."

"And my mom in her pajamas ..." In her *pajamas*?

"Yes," Fadi explained. "She does this whole routine, 'Oh, I'm *so* sorry!

I've been cooking since dawn. I didn't have a *moment* to change ...'" "And yet her face is beautifully made up and her hair perfectly coiffed ... It was the first time my folks had been in an Arabic home.

They didn't know how to behave, all these aunts and uncles walking in and out…"

Nadav's parents were the secular children of religious Ashkenazi Jews; his father had just retired as a senior civilian official in the military. One of his grandmothers was an Auschwitz survivor, her number tattooed on her arm; she was thirteen when liberated, having lost all her family. The new Jewish homeland provided her with sanctuary and meaning.

Fadi's parents were from a Christian Arab family; they had been communist activists in their youth, and had raised their son on the story of the Palestinian people and their dispossession during the 1948 Nakba. One of Fadi's grandmothers still had the keys to the home she had fled in Haifa; the other told horror stories of the Jewish capture of I'Billin. When Fadi was a child his mother banned Israeli television from the home because she could not stand the sound of Hebrew.

What, I wondered, did the Daeems and the Kains talk about, over their meal in I'billin?

"Food," the two men sang together.

"My mom said she had bought everything for the meal for cheap in Ramallah," said Fadi.

"So *my* mom asks, 'How is it, in Ramallah, these days?'" added Nadav. "'It's great! I love it there. I'm going next week.'"

"Basic talk, nothing spicy."

Ramallah is the de facto capital of Palestine, of course, in the Occupied Territories of the West Bank; a symbol of Palestinian self-determination. As an Israeli citizen, Fadi's mother was permitted to go there, and did so often, to visit a close friend. But since the Second Intifada in the first years of the twenty-first century and the subsequent clampdown, her friend—like all Palestinians resident in the West Bank and Gaza—was no longer allowed into Israel without a special permit. In this context, Fadi and Nadav agreed that a chat between Arabs and Jews about Ramallah was never just about the price of vegetables. And yet, stepping out of themselves for a moment and looking down at the lines *they* had crossed with their relationship, they marveled at both the absurdity and the banality of the coming together of their families, their mothers talking about shopping across the Green Line that separates Israel from the Occupied Territories.

FADI WAS TWENTY-EIGHT years old when I first met him in 2016, a nurse in the internal medicine department at the Wolfson Medical Center south of Tel Aviv. He was shy and thoughtful, his large eyes looking intently out of a long, handsome face framed by a low brow and a dense beard. Nursing was one of the more viable vocations for upwardly mobile Arabs in Israel, and he was very focused on his career: he worked long hours and was training to be an instructor. He also volunteered for Al-Qaws (The Rainbow), the Palestinian LGBT organization, staffing the hotline one night a week: he was struck by the growing number of transgender Palestinians calling in from both sides of the Green Line.

Fadi spoke a careful, fluent English and his movements were economical. But then his long limbs would uncoil unexpectedly into a gesture of camp to accompany his wry humor, or snap into purpose if he needed to be emphatic. He seemed always to be rolling both a cigarette and his eyes; he held passionately to his principles but was forgiving of human foibles, even if not always of himself. He had been a hard-core Goth as a teenager—his gang of "funny, freaky" misfits at his elite Arab school called themselves "the United Bitches"—and before he met Nadav, who worked in the fashion industry, his look had been that of a slacker. But now his beard was more styled and his wardrobe more adventurous: he wore patterned shirts beneath overalls, long black tunics buttoned to the neck and aviator shades. Over six feet tall and with a long gait, he turned heads in laid-back Tel Aviv.

Fadi told his mother he was gay when he was twenty, during a collapse following his first breakup. There were tears and he was taken off to a psychologist—an Arab one, in I'Billin—who gave him antidepressants and support, and spoke at length to his mother, too. Fadi's mother was a secretary at the local council; his father cared for the elderly in the village. Both parents adored their only son (Fadi had two sisters), and kept his childhood room intact, a shrine to his adolescence: the Palestinian flag over the door, the swirling graffiti on the wall in Palestinian national colors ("freedom"), the slogans painted directly onto the wall in black and white.

The most meaningful of these, for Fadi, was Khalil Gibran's verse: "Your children are not your children. / They are the sons and daughters of Life's longing for itself." As he grew into adulthood, Fadi told me, "it was important for me to tell my parents—to tell *myself*—that while they brought me into life, I have my own desires and dreams." It seemed to work: "I didn't raise and educate my son in order to keep him close," his mother liked to say, and both parents were proud of the life he had made in Tel Aviv, given the constraints on Arabs in Israel.[1]

Still, there was inevitable conflict: "My mother will phone me out of the blue to tell me to remove my relationship status from Facebook because she heard something bad in the village. I will refuse: 'If you don't want to accept this, it's your problem.' And she will phone back in two days and apologize: 'I didn't mean it. Of course I accept you.'"

If this was the case, I wondered, as we sat talking in the Casino San Remo a few weeks before Fadi's sister's wedding, how would his mother cope with Nadav's presence there?

Nadav imagined that no-one would pay him much notice: "I'll just be this weird friend from Tel Aviv. They'll be so busy, they won't even notice me."

His prediction could not have been more wrong: a stream of Daeems would line up to greet him. "It seems that my extended family knows *exactly* who you are," Fadi reported back to him, a little later. "My mother must have told them."

Fadi was moved by the way his broader family—religious, conservative, village people—were "opening up to the idea of me being with a man."

FOLLOWING THE WEDDING, Fadi's mother and his fourteen-year-old sister friended Nadav on Facebook, where Nadav posted outrageous videos under the pretext of doing promotions for a monthly Tel Aviv "Homo-TechnoParty" called Kok-Schok. The videos usually starred himself in impossible heels and wigs, the kind of outré demi-drag that has its roots in the East Village or Berlin, but that he used to take aim at the hypocrisies and banalities of Israeli society. The Daeem women had taken to "liking" these videos in particular—which meant, Nadav said, that "all *their* friends are going to see Fadi's man dancing and in heels. We list each other as each other's partners. So our relationship is not a secret, in I'Billin, at Fadi's mom's work, at his sister's school, because of this. I guess that's the power of social media: you can let people know, while keeping some kind of distance from letting them know that you want them to know..."

Nadav was two years younger than Fadi and worked for one of Israel's preeminent fashion designers. He was a slender redhead, animated and amiable; he offset his painted nails with a mustache and broad sideburns that approached his chin, and he often wore heels, even on a weekday. He had lived in Europe for several years before he met Fadi and was—like so many young Israelis—keen to move on again, "away from the hate and the tension."

But Fadi was committed to staying: not just because of his career and his friends and particularly his family, but because, "I want to be here when Palestine wins the war. I don't want to miss it. I want to be part of the revolution, if it happens. And I believe it will."

Still, even if his dream was to be part of a free Palestine, he readily admitted that he had trouble imagining what this would look like. In *Oriented*, a 2015 documentary film about him and two friends—gay Palestinians like himself—he says that he envies his grandmother with the keys to her house in Haifa, "because she lived in the Palestine of the past.[2] She knows what she longs for, she knows what she wants. Unlike myself, I don't know. If there will ever be a Palestinian state, or a state for everyone, I don't know if I feel like I'll belong."

He is talking, at least in part, about his sexuality—and the strange place he finds himself in, as a Palestinian gay man in Israel, particularly one dating a Jew. Given the different mores and laws on either side of it, the Green Line had become something of a Pink Line, too, and LGBT Rights had been instrumentalized, on both sides, as a dividing line between Jews and Arabs, Israelis and Palestinians.

WHEN FADI WAS FOURTEEN, he told his mother he wanted to be an Israeli (as in a Jew, rather than Arab).

"What? What the fuck???" was her response, as he remembered it. "*Why?*"

"I think maybe I belong more there. It's more accepting and open."

She was firm: "You're just a little kid, you don't understand anything. You'll get over it."

What had led Fadi to the conclusion that he would be better off in Jewish society, I asked him?

"The Internet," he responded without hesitation. When he was fourteen, he started a physical relationship with a boy in his class. Even though they had known to hide it, there had been no particular shame to it, and no name for it either. The name had been provided by others, on the playground: a group of boys had taunted his friend—more effeminate than Fadi—with the word *homo*. "Yes I *am* homo," the friend had responded. "What of it?"

The encounter had sent Fadi to investigate online, and he had found articles he shared with his friend "about homosexuality and whether we can be cured. We realized we were not alone." The articles were in English or Hebrew, and Fadi soon found himself in a gay Israeli chat room: "My Hebrew wasn't that good, so I would sit there with a dictionary." He developed an online friendship with a man in Haifa: "I found out about the gay scene, and I realized there was a whole world out there, full of gays, this place called Tel Aviv and how great it was, how accepting the Jewish community was to gays ..."

Later in life Fadi would meet Palestinians who came to Tel Aviv expecting "a gay heaven. They think they are going to be happy and satisfied, only to realize that they have to hide another identity, their Arab one. They can be openly gay in Tel Aviv, but they have to change their names, or accents, in order to fit in. They have left one closet, they find themselves in another."

These men were not just trying to pass in Israeli society, but also trying to disappear from Palestinian society: "This is a small world, and all the Arab families know each other," Fadi said. "If you become 'Jewish' and only sleep with Jewish guys, no one from the village is going to find out about you. You're safe."

Another gay Palestinian man, Marwan, said something similar to me. He came from a devout Muslim home in East Jerusalem, and when he started acting on his homosexual desires "it felt easier for me to do this 'sin' in Hebrew, a foreign language; not to have it in your own house, your own language." For gay Arab kids like Fadi and Marwan, Hebrew was the language not just of sin (and oppression), but also—confusingly—of possibility, even liberation.

Still, in the end, Fadi's flirtation with Israeli identity lasted no more than a few months. Soon after, he moved to Haifa to board at the Christian Orthodox School: it was one of the training-grounds of the Palestinian elite, and ensured that its students learned "the real story" alongside the Israeli curriculum. Fadi's understanding of his Palestinian identity deepened, in tandem with his gay one. He began searching online in Arabic, and he came across Al-Qaws, which had been founded in Jerusalem in 2006. Al-Qaws had a weekly Wednesday-evening meeting group in Haifa and when Fadi nervously showed up "a nice girl approached me: 'Come in! don't be afraid!' She was also a high school student. Also queer and Arab. Also a Goth! Wow."

Then Fadi was invited to one of Al-Qaws' fabled parties, held at a Jaffa club: "Arab music, Arab people dancing, Arabic drag show!" A 2008 report in *Haaretz* sets the scene Fadi would have encountered: "A black drag queen with a dark blond wig, wearing a tunic sewn from a keffiyeh, gets onstage.[3] 'I don't care what they say,' she sings to her beloved. 'Every day I'll be what I want to be.' Later on a performance artist appears as the character called Arus Falasteen, the Bride of Palestine, to the strains of songs of struggle." One partygoer describes it as "a place where you don't apologize for anything about your identity. In the nightclubs and at other parties we are asked to leave the Palestinian aspect outside the club before we enter. Here it's a place that doesn't ask for that. On the contrary, it nurtures our identity."

In Al-Qaws, at its meetings and parties, Fadi found himself "talking about gay politics and Palestinian identity. And it was nice to have these conversations in *Arabic* for the first time, rather than Hebrew. It felt good. It felt that it was where I belonged."

Fadi's boyfriend stayed in the village "and became a straight boy, in order to survive."

But Fadi discovered that he could be queer, and Arab. He didn't have to choose.

2

Fadi and Nadav went to Tel Aviv Pride for the first time, coincidentally, in the same year: 2004. Fadi was sixteen, Nadav fourteen. It was at the height of the Second Intifada. The fighting was particularly severe in Gaza, and Prime Minister Ariel Sharon had just announced his controversial plan to withdraw settlers from the territory. There were also frequent suicide bombing attacks, and Israelis were more unsettled than ever.

Nadav's mother drove him into Tel Aviv for Pride, from Rosh Ha'ayin, his nearby hometown. Although Nadav was already downloading gay pornography online, he did not think of himself as gay, and he recalled that he had "no clue" that Pride was even a gay event, or what that might even mean: "I wanted to go to Pride because some of my favorite groups were playing, that's all. But once I was there, there was all this craziness going on. Men in underwear, nudity, the different lifestyle, it definitely opened things up for me, gave me a sense of what was possible in my life."

Fadi's response to the very same event could not have been more different. He was in his second year at boarding school, and he and his best friend decided to go together, although neither was yet out to his family. "We didn't know how to prepare, so we asked some Jewish friends what we should wear, and we went shopping for new clothes. Skinny jeans and tank tops." The boys took a *sherut*—an Israeli communal taxi—from Haifa and got hopelessly lost, but eventually found their way to the festivities.

"It was big and colorful," Fadi recalled, "and we both felt we didn't belong there, I'm not sure why. Maybe it was too open. You know, guys kissing, naked people dancing." He liked the drag queens and he remembered the heat of the day "and the hot guys, of course." But "we felt, like, 'we're nothing.' Everyone was happy, celebrating their freedom. I remember, I asked myself, 'Will I ever get back to Tel Aviv and live here?' And I asked myself, 'How will I be?'"

The boys could not stay for the beach party as they were expected home for dinner: on the way back they agreed that Pride was not for them.

Did Fadi feel he was "nothing" because he was an Arab in this Jewish city, at this Jewish Pride?

"I didn't feel like I belonged," he repeated. "I didn't celebrate my freedom, like they were all doing, because I had an identity that was not free at all. I might be able to live in areas of Tel Aviv and be gay and proud, but in other parts of Israel or Palestine, I don't feel proud, acceptable, close to who I am. And I'm not even talking about my *Palestinian* identity here!"

I noted how Fadi had slipped from the past to the present tense, and I was struck by the way he used the expression "close to who I am" rather than, more simply, "myself." Was it possible for the queer grandchild of dispossessed Palestinians, living in Israel, to be anything, ever, more than just "close" to his true self? Or was the gift of his dislocated identity that it made manifest a deeper truth in all of us: that there is no such thing as a "true" self, and we are all constructed by where we live and the things that happen around us, by the lines drawn around us and the way we submit to them or try to breach or expand them?

BEING IN ISRAEL inflamed such questions in me.

Unlike Fadi, I *was* supposed to "belong" here, and there were ways in which I did: not just as a Jew but—very uncomfortably—as a white South African who recognized in this country so much of the structural racism of the apartheid in which I had been reared. Israel was a fun-house mirror: it warped my sense of self-perception.

I had timed my first research visit to Israel, in June 2013, to coincide with Tel Aviv's fabled Pride Week. Tel Aviv was frequently described as "the gayest city on earth," and indeed, the entire metropole had been festooned with rainbow bunting. Half the city seemed to have turned out: around 150,000 people. At the opening rally, members of every mainstream political party—including Binyamin Netanyahu's Likud—gave messages of support to a crowd where the numbers of marchers with kids was almost equal to those with exposed six-packs. You do not see many Stars and Stripes at New York Pride, or *tricolores* at Paris Pride, but the procession that moved down Ben Yehuda Street was awash with Israeli flags, sometimes in rainbow colors. To participate in Pride, it seemed to me, was an act of patriotism as well as of affirmation.

After a few hours of the popping muscles and the pulsing music, I decided to peel off from the beach party and attend instead a queer *havdalah* service in Independence Park. The *havdalah* is a beautiful ritual at the end of the Jewish Sabbath and I found about fifty people sitting in a circle under the trees. A gay rabbi began the service with tambourines and incense, lifting us above the disco bass line from the beach below. He reminded us that we were sitting in one of Tel Aviv's most famous cruising spots, and told us that we were channeling not only our Jewish ancestors but the spirits of other cultures, too: this was the very site of a Muslim cemetery. I had not known this, and I was horrified, perhaps naively; this is the story of modern Israel, after all.

I thought of a recent film made by the porn tycoon Michael Lucas, an ardent propagandist for Israel. *Men of Israel* featured magnificent Israeli men, sculpted by compulsory military service, having sex in various alluring places, including the ruins of a village outside Jerusalem. Lucas described the village as having been "deserted centuries ago," but it was, of course, abandoned far more recently, during the Nakba.[4] He also said that he was making the film as an act of patriotism (he had recently become Israeli), to boost its pink-dollar tourism industry in the way the Belami porn studio had for the Czech Republic. A critic had described *Men of Israel* as "desecration porn," and while the *havdalah* service was by no means its equivalent, I was nonetheless discomfited by its own form of desecration: the way the spirits of dispossessed Palestinians were being summoned to provide multicultural color to the ritual, rather than honored through reparation, or assuaged with contrition.[5]

Much of my family lives in Israel, where our roots go back to the early-nineteenth century, when my mother's father's family, rabbis from Lithuania, settled in Jerusalem. More recently, some of my family—Holocaust survivors—moved here once the Soviet Union permitted them to leave in the 1970s; others exercised their "right of return" from South Africa at around the same time. Some of the latter were both vocal opponents of apartheid and passionate Zionists: this was not a contradiction in the mid-twentieth century, in the Holocaust's shadow, when Zionism was socialist and Israel appeared to be a beacon of multiculturalism.

I met a group of friendly Americans at the *havdalah* service and they invited me to accompany them to a glamorous party in a penthouse that was part of the ancient walls of Arab Jaffa. I had some interesting conversations there, until a man probed about my Israeli family.

Why had I not contacted any of them, he wanted to know? I responded, perhaps too glibly, that my trip was intense enough without having to have dinner-table arguments about Israeli apartheid. He looked at me, shook his head slowly, and walked away.

I left without saying good-bye to anyone. My queer self was in the Holy Land, not my Jewish-family one. I don't think I have ever felt more alienated in my travels along the Pink Line.

ALTHOUGH FADI WAS reared on the story of the Nakba and had slept beneath a Palestinian flag since childhood, it was only when he moved to Jerusalem after graduating from high school in 2007 that he realized "what it meant to be an Arab in Israel," he told me.

Fadi's first job was as a nurse's aide at Hadassah hospital, and he found lodgings in Arab East Jerusalem. On the long daily bus commute to the Jewish west he experienced "being an enemy in your own country. People look at you differently, treat you differently." Once, in winter, "I was very cold in the early morning. I was wearing my keffiyeh because it was the only warm scarf I had. My *God*! I went in the bus, people were looking at me like I was about to kill them." A security guard on the bus asked for his papers; he didn't have them with him, and he was told to get off. He tried to reason, in his now-impeccable Hebrew, but the man "grabbed me and physically threw me off." He never wore his keffiyeh in West Jerusalem again.

At Hadassah many of his patients were ultra-Orthodox, and he was stunned that they refused to let him touch them: "They would say, 'I don't want an Arab to take care of me.' And it's acceptable! My boss told me, 'It's their belief. They're not allowed to be touched by non-Jews.'" Fadi was radicalized by his three years in Jerusalem: "I didn't want to delete my identity to get along. I became aware that I would have to fight for my existence as a Palestinian."

Moving to Tel Aviv to study nursing was "a big relief." He befriended other Arab students, some of them gay, and he became friendly with Jewish guys, too. But he never went back to Pride: "I have other ways of celebrating my sexuality apart from participating in a party that is designed to show the world that Israel is 'the gay heaven.' And of course, Pride excludes Palestinians. Gay guys from all over the world can come and celebrate their freedom here in Tel Aviv, but Palestinian gay guys have a *wall* preventing them from even *thinking* about coming to Tel Aviv. It's absurd!" In the year we met, 2016, Fadi was faced with a dilemma. *Oriented*, the film about him and his friends, was headlining the LGBT film festival in a glitzy event launching Pride Week.[6] Would he go? After turning it over for a while, he made up his mind, and wrote a statement that he asked the director Jake Witzenfeld to read at the event. He also posted it online: "Screening the film during TLV Fest, a festival sponsored by the Israeli government, is a direct act of Pinkwashing and represents the opposite of what I tried to accomplish with the film. An occupying country cannot celebrate freedom while denying it from a whole nation. A racist country cannot celebrate diversity. I will not take part in these screenings and celebrations. I hope you won't either."

The term "pinkwashing" was being increasingly used to describe what some activists saw to be Israel's use of its liberal gay rights record to launder its violations against Palestinians. The term had originally been coined in the United States in 1985 to describe the way pharmaceutical companies claimed to support women with breast cancer while profiting by their illness.[7] Now it was appropriated by the Palestinian solidarity movement and introduced into the American mainstream by the writer Sarah Schulman, who in 2011 described it in *The New York Times* as "a deliberate strategy to conceal the continuing violations of Palestinians' human rights behind an image of modernity signified by Israeli gay life."[8]

The assertion that Israel promoted LGBT rights as a fig leaf covering its other human rights violations drew much fire, given that Israeli gay people indisputably had it easier than they did in any other Middle Eastern country, and that their victories were primarily a result of their own struggles. But the Israeli government did instrumentalize the issue, using it to draw a Pink Line between the country and its neighbors, in a campaign heavily supported by the broader Zionist movement, too: "Where in the Middle East Can Gay Officers Serve Their Country?" asked a fundraising poster put out by an American Zionist organization in 2008: "Only in Israel ... Support Democracy. Support Israel."[9] The comparison even entered Israeli jurisprudence: in a landmark 2010 case over the legal status of the Jerusalem Open House (an LGBT center), the judge ruled that "the treatment of the gay community is one of the measures of Israel as a liberal-democratic state, in contrast to the situation in the overwhelming majority of Middle-Eastern states."[10]

When I met Fadi and Nadav in 2016, the state had just announced it was spending three million dollars on a tourism campaign that would include an international competition, the winners of which would be flown to Tel Aviv in a rainbow-colored El Al jet. The budget for this promotion was ten times that of the government's entire social services program to the LGBT community, and Israel's major LGBT organizations threatened to pull out of Pride. The government quickly agreed to increase its spending on the latter.

Nadav, who rarely posted anything political online, took to Facebook to express his outrage. The government's campaign was not "just to bring rich tourists" to Israel, "but to create a more innocent picture of the state ... and to distract from the terrible way it treats its minorities," including gay people, the trans community, and

"Palestinians in the occupied territory."[11] Nadav also made a video for a Kok-Schok after-Pride party, which he branded "FUCK PRIDE."[12] In the video he plays a street hustler in fishnet stockings and suspenders who gets lured into a big black German car by the soothing tones of Prime Minister Binyamin Netanyahu's 2016 Pride message—"We are all created in the image of God. We are all Israelis"—before realizing it is a trap, tumbling out of the car, spewing pink vomit, and rushing off to a laundromat to get cleaned up.

Since 2013, the Israeli Ministry of Foreign Affairs had published a "Gay Israel" page on its website which described the country as "one of the most inclusive societies in the world for the LGBT community. Israel adamantly protects the rights of its gay citizens, and the LGBT community is represented in the highest echelons and in all facets of Israeli society."[13]

What did he think of this, I asked Nadav?

He dismissed it briskly as "public relations bullshit," and said he used his nails as the litmus test. They were a deep metallic purple that day, and he flashed them at me: "Sure, Tel Aviv might be the gayest city on the planet, and I can walk around as I please here. But Tel Aviv is a bubble. Beyond its borders? I keep my hands in my pockets."

EVEN SO, NADAV conceded that he was the generational beneficiary of a revolution in sexual mores in Israel, of which an embrace of gay people was part. Nadav had even found acceptance in his extended religious Orthodox family: he had taken his previous boyfriend, a Swiss gentile, to the family Passover Seder without incident.

Like Fadi, Nadav had been a teenage Goth. His group of friends was called Kadisha, after the Chevra Kadisha, the Jewish burial society, "because we always wore black," and most had turned out queer. Kadisha's driving force was a boy who started presenting as female very early on, and had now fully transitioned with the support of her family.

Also like Fadi, Nadav had been a beneficiary of the Digital Revolution—Israelis were early adopters. Nadav honed his identity and expanded his community through Myspace, "a kind of free zone, perfect for someone pushing boundaries like me." It was here, poring over "the open books of private people," that he first got the idea of wearing heels, and began to develop a look for himself. More important was the affirmation: "I was able to dress up in the privacy of my room and upload images of myself, and get such praise for it. Something that would *never* have happened if I walked down the street in Rosh Ha'ayin in a corset and heels. I would have had rocks thrown at me."

Scrolling through Myspace profiles led him to his first boyfriend, an older guy with his own place, and Nadav came out to his parents when he started staying over, "Mainly because I didn't want to lie to them." He was sixteen. After an initial upset, his parents embraced him and his gender play: his mother would do up his corset before ferrying him and his friends to Goth parties and then to gay ones in Tel Aviv.

Like all Israeli kids, Nadav did three years of military service after school. He went under duress, miserable that he had to cut off his pink dreadlock extensions and shave his head. Nadav gave a chipper rendition of his service: he was an army intelligence photographer, and given that "everyone always wanted to go to the field because the men with guns were so *hot*, I always managed to get what I wanted, which was to keep well away from the violence, and to do as little as possible, documenting that film screening for the elderly in Tel Aviv, or staying in the offices and printing." But Fadi told me, separately, that Nadav's military service was the one thing he could not talk about, and he believed his boyfriend had been "deeply traumatized" by the experience.

Nadav did not recall his homosexuality ever being a problem in the army. The Israel Defense Forces had signed off on an anti-discrimination policy protecting gay and lesbian conscripts as early as 1993. If Nadav had wished to, he could have attended Pride in his military uniform; the year after he finished his service, in 2012, the IDF posted a photograph of two soldiers in uniform holding hands at the parade, with the caption: "It's Pride Month. Did you know that the IDF treats all its soldiers equally?"[14] (That year, research by the respected state-funded Israeli Gay Youth organization found that the army was "not always so tolerant" in practice: in a survey of LGBT conscripts it conducted, 40 percent of the LGBT soldiers said they had been verbally abused, 20 percent physically abused, and 4 percent sexually abused.)[15]

It was not so surprising to Nadav that Israel seemingly welcomed gay soldiers so many years before Barack Obama would repeal the Don't Ask, Don't Tell policy in the United States: "Israelis *need* the army, unlike Americans. We're at war, so every single body is necessary. Everyone has to go. If that's the case, you might as well take the gays, too."

Haneen Maikey of Al-Qaws, the Palestinian LGBT organization, has given her perspective on this equality within the Israel Defense Forces, from the other side: "It doesn't matter what the sexual orientation of the soldier at a checkpoint is, whether he can serve openly or not. What matters is that he's there at all."[16]

BY 2016, OVER THREE QUARTERS of Jewish Israelis supported same-sex marriage, according to one poll.[17] This included, even, small majorities of those who identified as "mainstream religious" and "right wing." The dramatic exception was among the ultra-Orthodox, where 84 percent opposed it. Since it began in 2002, the Jerusalem Pride event—only seventy kilometers away from Tel Aviv—had frequently been marred by protests, and even violence, from this conservative community. In 2005, after the city's ultra-Orthodox mayor called for the event to be banned, one Yishai Schlissel broke through the security cordon to stab three people. "I came to murder on behalf of God," he said during his interrogation.[18] "We can't have such abomination in the country." He spent ten years in jail, and three weeks after his release in 2015, he went on the rampage again, this time stabbing six people at Jerusalem Pride, one of whom—a sixteen-year-old—died from her wounds.

In an era when many liberal Israelis were becoming increasingly uncomfortable with the growing influence and aggression of their religious compatriots, LGBT rights became an emblem of the outward-looking modern state, as opposed to a theocratic shtetl. As one prominent lesbian activist put it as early as 1994, after a trailblazing anti-discrimination judgment brought by an air steward: "We were in the Middle Ages in 1988 [when Israel finally repealed its anti-sodomy laws].[19] Now we're at the same level as about any other country in Europe." The El Al judgment mandated partner benefits for gay and lesbian state employees. Eight years later, the Israeli Supreme Court ruled that same-sex marriages performed abroad must be recognized in the country.

The issue gained mainstream support not just because gay rights became an emblem of modernity: a shot across the bows of the theocrats and, later, a pinkwashing propaganda initiative. It was also because of the way LGBT Israelis presented themselves as patriotic: by wanting to be "soldiers and mothers," as one of the country's pioneering lesbian mothers, Ruti Kadish, has written; by signing up not only to defend their vulnerable homeland, but also to make families and produce Jewish children.[20] By 2018, these were the sentiments that would power the almost national consensus—outside of religious conservative Jews—that gay men should have access to surrogacy services, and the outrage that led a hundred thousand people to protest that year at Rabin Square.

Both Fadi and Nadav were among the protesters—although both felt some discomfort about being there, they would later tell me.

NINE YEARS PREVIOUSLY, in August 2009, a seventeen-year-old Nadav accompanied his mother to Israel's first major protest on gay issues, also at Rabin Square.[21]

An armed intruder had interrupted a meeting at Tel Aviv's LGBT youth center and shot indiscriminately, killing a fifteen-year-old girl and a twenty-six-year-old man and wounding several others. "It was shocking, personally," Nadav recalled. "The feeling that it could have been me, here, in this city that is so open, in the same part of town I was headed for, that very night. Suddenly you remember you're gay, and that people want to kill you for being gay."

In a society finely attuned to terror, the attack resonated deeply, not least because the prime suspect was a Jewish man, allegedly avenging the honor of a relative: it triggered an outpouring of support for LGBT people across Israeli society's usual left-right divides. The suspect was released and the case remains unsolved, but the episode's legacy is that it brought LGBT issues into the political mainstream as never before.

Nadav and his mother joined about twenty thousand in the square, waving Israeli flags and listening to speakers from across the social and political spectrum. The keynote address was by the Israeli president, the venerable Shimon Peres, who reminded the country that "we are a nation of 'Thou shalt not kill.'"[22] But as the legal scholar and activist Aeyal Gross wrote, while having Peres "was a historical moment of sorts, it was difficult to hear him proclaim [this] without wondering if the same applies to killing of Palestinians by Israelis, particularly given recent hostilities in Gaza."[23]

Only one Palestinian, an LGBT activist, spoke at the rally. An Arab parliamentarian on the program was not permitted to take the mike because he refused to submit his speech for advance review: "Our event was dedicated to the memory of two young people whose death was brought about due to sexual preferences, and this has nothing to do with [things like] the occupation," one organizer was cited as saying.[24]

The killings might have brought Israeli political leaders "out of the closet" on LGBT issues, the scholar Gil Hochberg wrote, but most of these leaders "chose to isolate the event, presenting it as an exception to the otherwise peaceful, tolerant, and liberal nature of Israeli society."[25] Certainly, this was the approach of Binyamin Netanyahu: "We are a tolerant, democratic country," he said in response to the attack, "governed by the rule of law and we must respect each and every person."[26]

Six years later, in 2015, Netanyahu issued another statement after another attack on a gay venue, the Pulse nightclub in Orlando, Florida: here, the "terrorist" had murdered fifty people "because he was driven by a fanatical hatred" against "the LGBT community."[27] And he "wasn't alone": there was ISIS, which "throws people from rooftops," and Iran, "which hangs gays from cranes." The intolerance of such "regimes and terrorist organizations" was ranged against all "infidels," indiscriminately: "This week it was gays in Orlando, a few days before that it was Jews in Tel Aviv."

This was as close as Netanyahu got to accusing his Arab enemies of murderous gay hatred. But others—usually from the American Zionist movement—did so more explicitly. "While the Palestinian government officials and families destroy the lives of gay Palestinians,

Israel is a sanctuary to the LGBT community," read a 2011 booklet on the subject by the Zionist organization StandWithUs.[28] In the same year, the gay American Jewish commentator James Kirchik accused anti-pinkwashing activists of doing their own "whitewashing" of the "plight of Palestinian gays" and "the horrible repression of homosexuals in the West Bank and Gaza Strip."[29]

Was he right?

3

In 2013 I spent time in the West Bank, mainly around Ramallah, a cosmopolitan outpost in the Occupied Territories with foreign diplomats and aid workers, some international hotels, and many cafés and restaurants.[30] Ramallah had a discreet gay scene too, in a couple of the cafés and in private homes, particularly of expatriates and diplomats; it was a place you could travel to, to study at Bir Zeit University, or to work in government, and so be away from your family. "It's not Tel Aviv or Beirut," a student from Nablus told me, "but at least I can breathe."

The queer people I met in Ramallah requested anonymity; this in itself underscored the very different way of life for queer people across the Green Line. But "just because we are under cover it does not follow that we are repressed," one woman—I will call her Zeinab—told me. "Rather, it is about priorities. We are an occupied people, fighting for our freedom."

Zeinab, who wore a hijab, was in her twenties and worked for the Palestinian Authority. She was out at her job, and she spoke of the difficulties this entailed; in the end, though, she was valued because of the work she did. The fact that there was an organization called Palestinian Queers for BDS had made a significant difference to her life: "BDS" stood for "Boycott, Divestment and Sanctions," and was the Palestinian civil society initiative to isolate Israel internationally, along the lines of the anti-apartheid boycott. The Palestinian Queers component was set up by Haneen Maikey of Al-Qaws, whom I also met in Ramallah. Maikey told me that the involvement of LGBT people in the civil society movement was beginning to introduce Palestinians to the notion that queer people were among them and not only in Israel; that they were patriotic, too.

"Did you know," Zeinab asked me, "that homosexual acts were made legal here *forty years* before Israel?" This was true: Jordan decriminalized sodomy in 1951, a year after it annexed the West Bank. But sodomy was still a crime in Gaza because the British penal code had never been reviewed there. And in both parts of "independent" Palestine, the public expression of homosexuality was taboo, as was the call for rights on the basis of it. These taboos had religious and social roots, as in the rest of the Islamic world. But they had also been inflamed by the very specific politics of the Palestine-Israel conflict. In the tradition of twentieth-century liberation movements worldwide, mainstream Palestinian politics saw any kind of special claim as a distraction from the primary freedom struggle. On top of this, homosexuality carried a very particular—and deadly—stigma here: of Israeli contamination, and of collaboration with the oppressor.

This thinking had its roots in an Israeli intelligence policy that began in the First Intifada of 1987, when Israeli agents began blackmailing Palestinians guilty of indiscretions—such as extramarital affairs, or homosexuality—into becoming informers. So corrosive was this policy, Haneen Maikey said at a solidarity meeting in Paris I attended in 2012, that twenty-five years later "my best friend from Ramallah does not like being out in public with me because his parents think I am a collaborator with the Israeli government."

The existence of such a policy was verified in 2014, when forty-three veterans and reservists in the country's elite intelligence unit signed a public letter refusing to continue serving in the Occupied

Territories, in part because they were instructed to use sexual orientation to blackmail Palestinians into becoming informers. "If you're homosexual and know someone who knows a wanted person—and we need to know about it—Israel will make your life miserable," one signatory testified.[31] "Any such case, in which you 'fish out' an innocent person from whom information might be squeezed, or who could be recruited as a collaborator, was like striking gold for us and for Israel's entire intelligence community."

In this way, a Pink Line was superimposed onto the Green Line. On one side of it, some Israelis described Palestinian homophobia as yet another example of how Arabs were savage and backward, even as they blackmailed gay Palestinians into becoming informers. On the other side, some Palestinians cited Israel's acceptance of homosexuality as yet another instance of the decadence of Western settlers on Arab land, and a weapon that was used against them.

There were, of course, conservative Islamists who repeated the same canards that "traditional values" warriors everywhere used against the liberal West. As the Hamas leader Mahmoud al-Zahar said in a 2003 interview with Reuters: "You [in the West] have no religion. You are secular. You do not live like human beings. You do not [even] live like animals. You accept homosexuality. And now you criticize us?"[32]

That was said before there was any public sign of LGBT organization among Palestinians in the Occupied Territories. Sixteen years later, after Al-Qaws had become a visible part of Palestinian civil society, particularly in the BDS movement, the Palestinian Authority took action with a 2019 ban on the organization's activities, following an event in Nablus. Such events infringed "upon the higher principles and values of Palestinian society," a police spokesman said, and set out to "sow discord" and undermine Palestinian "peace."[33]

Here was a secular Palestinian official staking a Pink Line, according to the global culture wars script. What made it specific to the Israel-Palestine conflict was the way it delineated a besieged native culture not just from the broadly defined liberal capitalist West but from an occupier that seemed to be *using* homosexuality in its war against the people it had subjugated—and even blackmailing the people it purported to save.

This became clear to me as I sat on a Ramallah rooftop one evening in June 2013, listening to the story of Nabil, and his husband Dan.

NABIL WAS FROM conservative Jenin in the West Bank; he was twenty-four and a business student at Bir Zeit. Dan was five years older, an Israeli Jew of Canadian origin who worked as a coder in Ra'anana, Israel's Silicon Valley. The couple lived together in Ramallah, and Dan commuted the scant forty minutes across the Green Line daily; if stopped, Dan would vaguely suggest he was visiting relatives in a settlement. They shared their flat with two foreign aid workers, and their social world, such as it was, revolved around the expat scene. Nabil lived in terror of exposure, and it manifested in an overwhelming anxiety that he struggled to conceal beneath his hospitable charm as he kept my glass filled with mint tea.

Nabil had begun exploring his sexuality by looking for men on Manjam, a hookup site popular in the Arab world: "The guys I found were usually older, and married. They were full of guilt." He came from a devout family, and he staved off his own self-hate by turning adamantly against the Islam he heard preached, with its proscriptions against homosexuality and the Western life he found increasingly attractive. His atheist identity was even stronger than his gay one, and he railed frequently online against the hypocrisy of all religions.

Nabil was raised in the Gulf and spoke no Hebrew at all, but like Fadi, he came to understand that homosexuality was easier across the Green Line. And so—again like Fadi—he found a Hebrew-Arabic dictionary and put himself onto Atraf, the Israeli hookup app. Here is where he met Dan, a self-described "outsider and misfit" who was already part of the small mixed gay scene in Tel Aviv that included Fadi and his friends.

Nabil was living with relatives in Amman at the time. There was actually a thriving gay scene in the Jordanian capital centered around Books@Café, the bookshop-café owned by an older gay Palestinian man, but Nabil kept well away from it. He was—as he put it to me—"more comfortable to show my face and chat about life [with someone like Dan], because he is behind the border. I didn't feel much comfortable to do so with Palestinians due to the sensitivity of the issue."

In late 2011, Dan came to Amman to meet Nabil, and they began a relationship. The following year Nabil moved to Ramallah to study. He became desperate to see Tel Aviv's gay paradise and its shore, so close and yet so inaccessible. Palestinian residents of the Occupied Territories were given passes into Israel for specific reasons, such as seeking medical attention, and in May 2012 Nabil obtained a one-day permit for cardiology tests. Dan met him at the checkpoint, and they drove into Jerusalem: they would take a walk around the Old City, which Nabil had not seen since childhood, before moving on to the seaside.

But the romantic day trip went horribly awry. Not twenty minutes after parking they were stopped by police in what seemed to be a routine check: because Nabil's papers stipulated that he was to go only to the hospital, they were detained at a nearby police station. In several rough hours of separate interrogation, Nabil admitted that he and Dan were lovers. At one point a phone was brought to him and a man introduced himself, in Arabic, as an officer from the Shin Bet—the Israeli security agency—responsible for Ramallah: "You are free to go," the man told him, "but only if you come and see me in three days' time at my office at the Qalandiyah checkpoint. We have something to talk about."

Nabil understood immediately that he was going to be blackmailed. But he was terrified that if he did not go to the appointment his relationship with Dan would be publicly exposed. He had been to one or two Al-Qaws get-togethers in Ramallah and he contacted a leader, who was dismissive of him: "She said, 'You gay boys who just want to go and see the good life in Tel Aviv and then come crying to us when you get into trouble!'"

Feeling he had no choice, Nabil went to meet the Shin Bet officer, who asked detailed personal questions before suggesting that Nabil become an informer of activities on the Bir Zeit campus. When Nabil asked for a lawyer, the Shin Bet officer turned nasty, and threatened him with jail. But if Nabil did the "very small favors" requested of him he could visit Israel as often as he wished. Exposure was not specifically mentioned, but clearly implied.

Nabil declined, but left anxious that he was now vulnerable to being shamed and even physically attacked. The Shin Bet officer did not contact him again, or expose him as had been threatened, but he lived in fear now, and felt, desperately, that he needed leave Palestine. He and Dan had only been together for several months at this point, but given that Dan held dual nationality they decided that Nabil's best option was to marry him, and for him to seek residency on that basis in Canada. Like many West Bankers, Nabil held a Jordanian passport: South Africa was the only country that performed same-sex marriages to which Jordanians could travel without a visa, and so Dan bought them tickets to Cape Town in October 2012. Here they were hosted by a gay guesthouse that provided the full marriage experience to visiting couples—including a licensed celebrant and a glamorous photo shoot—and they passed an idyllic week.

Nabil briefly considered applying for asylum in South Africa, but went back to Ramallah with the intention of applying for the Canadian visa. This had to be done through Egypt, and because of the turmoil in Cairo following the revolution, his application foundered. By the time I met him a year after the Old City arrest, he was still stuck in Ramallah, prone to terrible panic attacks. Dan had moved in, in part to help look after him, but his presence only made Nabil even more vulnerable: their housemates had recently been cross-questioned by Palestinian friends about the "Canadian guy" living with them. In the weeks after I met them the questioning increased, and Dan felt it was no longer safe for him to be in Ramallah. He returned to Tel Aviv and Nabil fled to Istanbul, where the couple had some contacts, to await his visa.

I had been introduced to Nabil and Dan by Amira Hass, the Israeli journalist who lived in Ramallah and reported for *Haaretz*. In her 2012 article on the case, Hass published confirmation by the Jerusalem police that they had detained Nabil and passed on his information to the West Bank's "Civil Administration liaison unit." But, concluded Hass drily, "the police did not reply to *Haaretz*'s question as to whether it informs the Shin Bet of details of every illegal sojourner that it detains."[34]

BEFORE 2003, SOMEONE like Nabil could have visited Tel Aviv—and even decided to stay there—with relative ease. At the turn of the millennium there was much coverage of gay Palestinian runaways who had fled persecution and found their way to the city. A *New Republic* report from 2002 cited a man from Gaza who had been brutally tortured, apparently by his own people, left to hang with his head covered in feces and raped with a Coke bottle for refusing to "become an undercover sex agent"; others alleged they were held and tortured, accused of being "collaborators."[35] A credible 2008 report called *Nowhere to Run*, published by the Public Interest Law Program at Tel Aviv University, documented testimonies by Palestinians now in Israel who alleged they had been persecuted by militias and organs of the Palestinian state.[36]

In 2012, Fadi saw a much-feted Israeli documentary called *The Invisible Men*, about three gay Palestinians who had fled to Tel Aviv from what they described as horrific circumstances, and had been assisted to gain resettlement elsewhere.[37] "I felt, 'Good for them!'" Fadi told me. "It's impossible to leave the Occupied Territories, to get a visa to go anywhere, and here they were, actually using Israel, the occupier, to help them fly away." Still, Fadi wondered about the veracity of their claims: "I come from Arab culture. I know that the Arab culture does not tolerate homosexuality easily, and that we queers have to fight for our acceptance. But in my experience families don't abuse you like that, try to murder you, for being gay."

Fadi was emphatic that his own experience of acceptance was not as a result of his family's exposure to Israeli media and mores: "My family live in Israel, but before that, they live in the village. Their life is in Arabic and their world is Arabic. They don't watch Israeli TV, they don't read Hebrew newspapers. When I told them I was gay, it was the first time they heard the word. I had to take them step by step, explaining everything. I'm quite unique in my family in that I had to learn about Israeli society and immerse myself in it, in order to survive. So I don't believe my family is that different to a family living on the West Bank."

Of course, he acknowledged, the lives of gay people in the West Bank "are so much harder than mine. They can't travel, for example. And I have the privilege to live in Tel Aviv, go to parties, gay clubs, live as I choose. It's not the same way in Ramallah." But still, he felt, the stories he heard from the West Bankers he met when he went on the annual Al-Qaws retreats there were "not nearly as tough" as the ones about them he saw, or read, in the Israeli media. The people I met in Ramallah agreed, although after the 2019 Palestinian Authority ban on Al-Qaws activities, the organization acknowledged that there had been an increase in threats against its members on social media.

Whatever the veracity of the claims of these Palestinians who had fled to Israel around the turn of the millennium, their stories were nonetheless deployed ideologically, spun into a rescue narrative: Palestinian homosexuals were fleeing their brutal homeland to find sanctuary in welcoming Israel. "I support Israel because I support gay rights," Alan Dershowitz said in 2004, claiming he had worked with the Israeli authorities to grant asylum to forty gay Palestinian refugees.[38] Actually, Israeli law prohibited asylum for *any* Palestinians, and when this was pointed out to the celebrity law professor he retracted, claiming he had been misinformed: the forty had in fact been granted a form of house arrest—a far cry indeed from asylum—which enabled them to stay, temporarily, within the borders of Israel.

No one knows how many runaways came to Israel between 1995 and 2003. Fadi told me he met "a lot" of them. Shaul Ganon, the Israeli activist who was most involved in helping them, offered estimates ranging from three hundred to nine hundred, but there is only evidence that three—the three in *The Invisible Men*—actually went through the resettlement process to be relocated elsewhere. The rest, whatever their number, slipped into the cracks of Tel Aviv, it seemed, often living on the street, many subsisting as sex workers. These runaways were "caught in the middle of the Israeli-Palestinian conflict," concluded the *Nowhere to Run* report.[39] Persecuted back home, but "hunted inside Israel by police who seek to return them to the territories from which they have escaped, usually forcing them to live in hiding and eventually run away again."

4

"Welcome to Palestine!"

Fadi's best friend Khader Abu-Seif greeted me with these words and a mischievous glint in his eye when we first met in Tel Aviv in June 2013, surrounded as we were by trendy Israelis in a garden café around the corner from his apartment. He was quite deliberately performing, for an outsider, the confidence that his generation had found in their Palestinian identity, beneficiaries in their own way of the Arab Spring.

Khader, whom I met before I did Fadi, was a charismatic man-about-town. He possessed a rakish charm and an irrepressible energy, and he seemed to have become the public voice of the gay Arab world in Tel Aviv: he was often quoted in the media, and had a column in the Israeli *Time Out*. Unlike Fadi, he was a city boy: he came from a notorious Jaffa underworld family, was schooled with Jewish kids, was more comfortable writing in Hebrew than in Arabic, and had been a denizen of the city's gay clubs from his early teenage years. When I met him, he was the head of Arab affairs at the Aguda, Israel's umbrella LGBT organization; he was thus reviled as a collaborator by Fadi's comrades in Al-Qaws, which adopted the BDS movement's line about no "normalization" of relationships with Israeli institutions.

Khader made no bones about the fact that he lived among Jews—they were his friends and his lovers—but was clear that he was not for saving, or submission. We see him in the film *Oriented* telling a Jewish audience how irritated he gets when journalists expect to find in him a "suffering" Palestinian, when in fact he is accepted by his family: "It feels that Israel and the West have monopolized the concept of liberalism and being out of the closet," he says.[40]

When Khader and Fadi met online as teenagers they seemed incompatible: "I was Gothic," Fadi told me, "and Khader was … *jumpy*." But although their politics were very different, they became close when Fadi moved to Tel Aviv to study nursing. Khader introduced Fadi to gay Tel Aviv, and Fadi took on the responsibility for his friend's political education, noting wryly that while Khader "had a column writing about gay Palestinians, he didn't actually *know* any."

A lively group of friends and collaborators developed, gay men—and straight women also straining against social convention—around a collective they called Qambuta (the word means "cauliflower"), hatched over cooking the vegetable one night in Fadi's kitchen. Fadi and his friend Na'eem—also a nurse—lived in a charming and somewhat derelict Ottoman-era house they had found in a very mixed part of Jaffa, between an Arab grocery store and the city's most famous hummus eatery, Abu Hassan.

***ORIENTED* OPENS WITH** Fadi and Khader and Na'eem bopping around the Jaffa house, swilling vodka cocktails and preparing for a Qambuta party. They are speaking their usual polyglot of Arabic, English, and Hebrew, as they discuss who will be there. Khader's boyfriend, an Israeli DJ who specializes in Arabic music, will be spinning the turntables.

"How many friends is he bringing?" asks Na'eem.[41]

"He's only bringing one," Khader replies, "but more will come."

"I just want to know how many Jews will be there. A quarter? Half the crowd?"

"There will be Jews, obviously."

Na'eem presses him: "What percentage? Seventy-five? Fifty percent?" "What's wrong with that?" Khader snaps.

"*Everything's* wrong with that," Fadi chimes in.

"Why? They're lefties. If it's cool that they go to Anna Loulou [a Jaffa club], then why not to our party?"

"Because it's *our* party …" says Fadi.

"But still, they love partying, and they support us. They're not coming to bum [sic] us down and say, 'Viva la Occupation!'"

"They're coming to save us," says Fadi drily.

Khader rolls his eyes and does hijab-camp with a scarf: "Our saviors, yes."

LATER WE SEE FADI IN BED, talking on the phone to his best girlfriend. The suggestion is that this is the morning after the Qambuta party.

"My head is going to explode," Fadi says. "Oh my God … I sinned."[42] "What did you do?"

"I went home with someone … He was hot. Very hot." "What's his name?"

"Binyamin."

"*Binyamin?* Binyamin as in *Binyamin*?" "A Jew. A Jew."

"No!"

IN FACT, FADI AND BINYAMIN—"Ben"—did not meet at the Qambuta party, but at Anna Loulou, the little club burrowed into the fortress walls that was the epicenter of Jaffa's queer scene and a home away from home for Fadi and friends; a place almost unique in how mixed it was, Arab and Jew, gay and straight.

Ben was American, blond and well-built, and there was an immediate fire between the two. Fadi took him home: "We had sex, and then he saw all the Palestinian flags in my bedroom and was like, 'You need to add me to Facebook before I leave.'" Fadi did not understand his insistence but complied, and as soon as he saw the profile he figured out this was Ben's way of telling his date that he was a soldier, a committed Zionist who had made *aliya* to join the Israel Defense Forces.

The two fell madly in love—and fought, "like crazy people," Fadi said. "Once it was so bad we even got kicked out of Anna Loulou. One minute you see us having drinks in the bar, everything nice and fun, and then the subject comes up. He said he had no problem with me being Palestinian but of course it was a lie. He felt I was trying to push him away from his Zionism."

In *Oriented*, the camera finds Fadi with his girlfriend in a quiet corner at a wedding a few weeks after he met Ben, discussing his predicament: "I feel weak," he says.[43] "I'm falling for a Zionist … I'm in love with the enemy." He doesn't have a problem with Ben being Jewish but "I have a problem that he doesn't think that there's an Israeli occupation here … that my people underwent a catastrophe … How can you love someone like that?" After six months Fadi called it quits; the breakup was acrimonious. When the 2014 war broke out some months later Ben sent Fadi a message: "very sorry about the things happening to Gaza." Fadi was amazed to see that his profile picture showed the Israeli flag joined with the Palestinian one, a meme among Israeli lefties at the time. "What's happened to you?" Fadi wrote.

"I just thought about it," Ben responded.

FADI MET NADAV at a party in early 2014, six months after he split up with Ben. The *Oriented* camera was still following Fadi at the time, and it captures a chat between him and Khader about the new guy in his life. "It's quite visible that there is no battle of identity between you two," Khader says to his friend.[44] "There's no Jew and Arab. Just Fadi and Nadav."

"Like two lost girls finding each other," says Fadi, typically deadpan. "With Ben it was a game of who felt more inferior, [but] my relationship with Nadav is where I go to relax, to breathe."

As always seemed to happen with Fadi, he fell hard for Nadav, and fast. Nadav had been living abroad for several years: "I was so clueless," he said to me. "I didn't even know Fadi was an Arab name. The fact that he was Arab, it didn't cross my mind. I had zero political ideas about anything." When Fadi revealed his ethnicity and politics Nadav shrugged and carried on.

One could imagine this incensing Fadi, but it did not. After the doctrines of Al-Qaws and the conflict with Ben, he found it immensely refreshing. "Politics is just not an issue for Nadav," Fadi told me. "Of course, he defines himself as an Israeli, and he knows Palestinian history. He doesn't deny it, like Ben did. But we don't talk about politics. That's one of the things I love about him, that he's apolitical. About sexual identity, gender identity, he loves that, he lives for it, he breathes it. But about Israel and Palestine? He's not into it."

After dating for about a year, Fadi and Nadav decided to live together. They found a neat corner unit in an upmarket new stone-clad condo development, built on the site of the old Jaffa Fresh Market, a block away from the Noga cafés they frequented. For the first time in his life, Fadi did not hang his Palestinian flag above his bed: "I didn't feel I needed to prove to Nadav that I was Palestinian. I still have it, of course, but I don't use it." Still, when Fadi brought home a final cut of *Oriented*, Nadav was bothered: "It was difficult for me to see it," Nadav told me. "It was 'Jews, Jews, Jews,' I mean why are you talking about 'Jews' all the time like that?"

Fadi explained to him that when Palestinians said "Jews," they meant "Zionists," but Nadav found it racist: "I'm a Jew, and I'm with you on every level. I love you. And yet you see me as 'one of the Jews ...'" Fadi took the point, and in the end the production agreed to replace the subtitle *Jews* with *Israeli Jews*—even though this is not the verbatim translation.

Fadi told Nadav all about Ben, "and I tried to explain to him how different to Ben he was. I also told him that, just as I seemed to have changed Ben's attitudes about Palestinians, Ben changed me, too. Before Ben, I was totally against the idea of even *trying* to fall for a Jewish guy, I'm sorry, I mean an *Israeli* Jewish guy!" The three of us laughed. "And then when it happened with Ben, I realized, you can't control your feelings. It was so extreme. I realized that love respects no religion, no difference of political views, no nationalities …"

Fadi stopped himself before saying "no borders"—he was wise to how corny this might sound—but still, he meant it. He was wise, too, he said, to the power dynamics in his relationship with Nadav, and the way it reflected their respective places in Israeli society. As politics became more polarized following the Gaza war of 2014, he felt suspicious eyes on him as never before, and he stopped expressing any political opinion at all at work. He was also bothered by the way it had to be Nadav who went looking for a new apartment to rent, even though he was the one with a dependable public service job.

And then there was language. Hebrew was the tongue of their relationship, and Nadav showed no inclination to learn Arabic. "In the beginning I felt, I can't be with a guy who doesn't understand my culture and my music, and it is still hard sometimes," Fadi said. The language issue raised a bigger sense of alienation for Fadi: he was not allowed to speak Arabic at work, even to Arab colleagues—this was a national rule, he told me, allegedly to prevent divisiveness in the workplace—"and there are *days* that go by when I do not speak my own language."

I told Fadi how struck I had been by his use of the expression, in describing himself to me, as "close to who I am." He laughed: "I've come to realize that I will *never* be fully myself, wherever I go. It's a relief to come to that realization. I don't cry about it. I accept it, and I even play with it. When I need my home, my parents, my language, I go to the village. When I need Nadav, I come to Nadav." People looked at the couple "from the outside, and they think we're weird. We like different stuff to other people. We have a different language that no one else understands. We know we're different, but we feel comfortable with each other, more comfortable than either of us have been, anywhere else."

Fadi felt the words he used in *Oriented* to describe his relationship with Nadav were spot-on. "'Two little girls, lost in the world.' I like that."

THE QAMBUTA COLLECTIVE MADE TWO VIDEOS, directed by Khader, who posted them on YouTube.[45] In the first, a tribute video to a torch song by the Lebanese singer Yasmine Hamdan, Fadi and friends play young Arabs struggling with their destiny: queer men and women forced into heterosexual marriage. "But we felt we were maybe being too judgmental of the Arab community," Fadi said, "and so for our next video, we wanted to show people, 'We also have the same thoughts as you. We are also Palestinians.'"

They chose to make a video on the theme of the right to return, set to another torch song (these are gay men, after all), this time by the Lebanese boy band Adonis, a plaint to lost love called "Sawt el Madini: The Sounds of the City."[46] The idea for this video came from the fact that all the group's grandparents had kept the keys to the homes from which they were evicted in 1948. In nightmarish sequences, Fadi and friends rush around ruins, the dreamscapes of their elders' dispossession; the keys to their grandparents' homes seem to be, in the end, a key to their own identities as Palestinian millennials living in Israel. In the final sequence they run free.

I detected another meaning in their choice of "Sawt el Madini," suggested by the first line of the song: "The voice of the city calls me." There is a clue to it in Khader's own thinking about his urban identity, to which he frequently referred, as in one interview where he contrasted himself with "the gay Arabs of Haifa": they were "village boys and we're city boys," and this meant "they are way more political than us.[47] They will only speak in Arabic or in English, never in Hebrew. For us in Tel Aviv, we fool around with other cultures."

Fadi—actually a village boy himself—also held to the idea that the city was a place beyond politics: "In every country," he told me, "the 'big city' is a place where politics is not a big deal. The freedom you find, personally, it makes you feel that there's other things to life than politics. When you first come to the big city, you want to have fun, party, sleep with everyone! That's what Tel Aviv makes you feel. I forget about politics. Then when I need to remember where I come from, I go to the village."

In a country like Israel, politics is a byword for sectarianism, and there was a hunger in these men—in Fadi and Nadav, in Khader, in Nabil over in Ramallah perhaps more than anyone—for an urban meld where ethnicity, nationality, or religion were not one's defining, or even primary, characteristic, even if they were acknowledged and celebrated. And because their national identities were so overdetermined by the conflict, these men were particularly attracted to some kind of cosmopolitan identity that transcended bloody lines in the sand.

While I was in Israel and Palestine, I also hung out with several of the women who had founded Aswat, the pioneering Palestinian lesbian organization in Haifa. Like Fadi and his friends, they were all Israeli citizens, and they, too, walked the line between a growing Palestinian nationalism and the feminist Israeli Jewish world of their comrades and lovers. I met one of them when she visited Paris in

2014: "People," she exhaled as she observed Parisians walking by from our perch on a sidewalk café in our ethnically mixed *quartier*. "Are they Arabs? Are they Jews? Who knows? Who cares?"

"THE VOICE OF the city calls me."[48]

In early 2017, Fadi and Nadav moved to a bigger apartment on Ahad Ha'am, a gritty street just off Rothschild Boulevard in the very center of Tel Aviv. You could not get more urban in Israel.

When I checked in with them a year later I was sorry to hear they had just split up after four years together; amicably, they both insisted. "There's still Sushi, after all," Nadav said. They had joint custody of the dog.

Fadi did not want to talk about the separation. Nadav explained, "We weren't pushing each other forward in the direction we individually wanted to go." Nadav was more involved than ever in his nightlife entrepreneurship and Fadi was studying to become an emergency-unit nurse. "We realized that neither of us was willing to sacrifice for the relationship, and so we needed to let each other go."

Nadav moved out, and Khader and Na'eem moved in: the Qambuta household was reconstituted, this time not in Arab Jaffa but in the very heart of the Jewish city. "I love it here," Fadi told me, "in the middle of everything." Jaffa had become "very touristic. All the rich and white people have moved there, because it's 'oriental.'" Anyway, Tel Aviv was more Arab than one might imagine: "You hear Arabic all the time, the street is very mixed, even our neighbors in the building are Arab." Nadav was still turning over the issue of living abroad, but things were clearer than ever for Fadi: this was home. "If I'm in a long-term relationship with anyone it's Tel Aviv."

Nadav and Fadi went, separately, to the huge demonstration in Rabin Square on July 22, 2018, protesting the government's exclusion of gay men from its new surrogacy laws. Fadi felt he "didn't belong" in Rabin Square. It seemed "a white man issue, demanding surrogacy for gays in Israel, while in Palestine you cannot even talk about being gay." I was struck by the way he was now using the word *white*, rather than *Jewish* or *Zionist*. These were the new radical politics of Israel, integrating newly globalized notions of "settler colonialism" and Black Lives Matter race politics into an analysis of the country. There was a new freedom to the way Fadi spoke, too, no longer treading on eggshells about the reality of life for Palestinian queer people, for fear of being branded an Israeli propagandist.

Fadi attended an event he found far more meaningful the following week. It was a Pride event in Lod, the ancient Arab city just outside Tel Aviv, next to Ben Gurion Airport. His friend Khader was one of the speakers. As Fadi remembered it, Khader said: "We're making a better future for all children, together. One where it's okay to be Arab, Palestinian, Jewish, gay, transgender, whatever the hell you like ..." This was the increasingly compelling vision of his generation: a single secular democratic state where all were equal.

Fadi was particularly "emotional," he told me, listening to "Arab people talking about how similar homophobia is to hating someone for being Arab ... Making the point that discrimination against Arabs is so much like discrimination against gays." There were only fifty participants in the march, but it was "a start." Fadi found himself flooded with "hope" that Sunday morning in the ancient medina of dusty Lod. Given that Lod was the site of one of the most brutal expulsions of Palestinian people during the Nakba, it actually felt like a homecoming of sorts: "If a gay parade can even go to Lod, a city that is Arabic in its core, what else might be possible?"

Nadav told me he found the surrogacy issue "problematic" but went to Rabin Square anyway: "The entire day was emotional as it brought nationwide attention to gay issues, not just surrogacy." He was far more moved, personally, by a demonstration he had attended earlier in the day, protesting violence against transgender people: "That's the *real* issue. Gay men wanting to pay someone to have their babies for them, versus people who risk their lives every time they leave the house? No contest."

13

THE TRANSGENDER CULTURE WARS

SOMETHING PROFOUND WAS HAPPENING to LGBT politics in the West in the first two decades of the twenty-first century, as the dial of public attention shifted across from the *L* and the G toward the *T*.

Openly gay people could join the army, get married, have kids, host TV talk shows, run large corporations, win elections, even govern countries (albeit small ones: Ireland, Iceland, Belgium, Luxembourg).

In the twentieth century, the gay agenda had been radical and transgressive: from the 1969 Stonewall riots through the free-sex era of the 1970s and the angry response to the AIDS epidemic. Now, in the twenty-first century, the movement claimed its victories and came inside. It buttoned up and moved to the suburbs, into school carpools and military uniforms. It was, as the TV sitcom would have it, *The New Normal*: "I support same-sex marriage *because* I'm a conservative," the British prime minister David Cameron could say at his Conservative Party's 2011 conference.[1]

Eight years later, an openly gay man was running a credible campaign for the Democratic presidential nomination in the United States, his husband by his side: "First Family," declared a *Time* cover in May 2019, over a portrait of Pete and Chasten Buttigieg, clean-shaven in buttoned-collar shirts and navy chinos outside their all-American clapboard home in South Bend, Indiana.[2] Barely four years after the Supreme Court ruled that same-sex marriage was legal across the country, an April 2019 poll found that 70 percent of U.S. voters were "open to electing a gay president"—although only 36 percent thought the country was actually ready for one.[3]

When Peter Buttigieg came out publicly in 2015 while the mayor of South Bend, he wrote in his hometown newspaper that "if different sides steer clear of name-calling and fear-mongering, we can navigate these issues based on what is best about Indiana: values like respect, decency, and support for families—all families."[4] He was referring to divisive Indiana legislation that would have permitted businesses to discriminate against LGBT people in the name of "religious liberty." Buttigieg's politics were progressive—he was an ardent advocate for electoral reform—but the fact that he was a married churchgoer and a military veteran hailing from the Red State heartland meant that he could claim "family values," long the terrain of the right, for himself.

If this was now its agenda, the historian Martin Duberman asked in his 2018 book of the same name, "has the gay movement failed?"[5] Duberman articulated a left perspective: such establishment status had betrayed—or exiled—the radical nature of the gay struggle, from its challenges to the nuclear family to the way it unfurled sexual freedom. This critique was the foundational premise of the increasing number of people who now called themselves "queer": they rejected "homonormativity," or they challenged it.

But this dismissal was sometimes too easy. The gay movement had opened up new frontiers deep in the heart of society: the classroom, the school board, the military base, the workplace, the legislature. My gay friends who were parents, attending school meetings and medical clinics and kiddies' birthday parties, were more on the frontline than I was, even if their lives appeared to be more conventional. And their presence exposed more people than ever to the notion that love was not only between heterosexual couples, that families could be made in different ways.

It would be a mistake, too, to assume that just because gay people had become celebrated as "the new normal"—able to marry, raise kids, and defend their countries—their struggles were over. A 2017 survey of LGBTQ youth across the United States found that 70.1 percent of its respondents experienced verbal harassment and 28.9 percent physical harassment because of their sexual orientation;[6] in 2018, one in four respondents to the U.K. government's National LGBT Survey reported that they had been subject to harassment, insults, or negative comments in the previous year because of their sexual orientation or gender identity.[7] Nearly half of LGBTQ American employees were closeted at work, according to a 2018 survey;[8] one in five British employees experienced bullying on the job because of sexual orientation, according to a 2013 one.[9]

Still, inevitably, as the culture wars over homosexuality began to fade in some parts of the world, other battlegrounds came to be staked, not just over "gender ideology," as in France and Latin America, but over "gender identity" specifically. In the United States and the United Kingdom in particular, transgender rights were seen increasingly, by some, to be the new civil rights frontier, and by others as the reductio ad absurdum of identity politics, the special pleasing of an entitled minority that threatened to encroach on the well-being of the majority.

IN JUNE 2014 *Time* famously declared a "Transgender Tipping Point" in the United States, with Laverne Cox—the glamorous star of *Orange Is the New Black*—on the cover.[10] The magazine framed this, explicitly, in relation to the victories of the gay movement. "Almost one year after the Supreme Court ruled that Americans were free to marry the person they loved, no matter their sex, another civil rights movement is poised to challenge long-held cultural norms and beliefs," wrote the author Katy Steinmetz.[11]

"Gay brothers and sisters, you must come out!" The Harvey Milk maxim that was the foundational premise of the gay movement was now to be taken up by transgender people as well; they, too, were "emerging from the margins to fight for an equal place in society," wrote Steinmetz in *Time*.[12] This "new transparency" was "improving the lives of a long-misunderstood minority and beginning to yield new policies, as trans activists and their supporters pushed for changes in schools, hospitals, workplaces, prisons, and the military."

The transgender narrative became a major feature in the American media. In a time of contraction and of the reevaluation of the "American dream," from Black Lives Matter on one side and Rust Belt Trumpers on the other, the chrysalis nature of a successful gender transition came to signal a particularly American form of redemption: a person who succeeds, against all odds, by being true to themselves. "More of us are living visibly and pursuing our dreams visibly," Laverne Cox said in *Time*.[13] "And so people can say, 'Oh yeah, I know someone who is trans.' When people have points of reference that are humanizing, that demystifies difference." The number of people in the United States who knew someone transgender doubled from 8 percent in 2008 to 16 percent in 2015, according to a survey.[14]

The summer of 2015 was the high-water mark of trans visibility in the United States, a trend that was disseminated globally, of course, given the reach of American soft power: the TLC network launched *I Am Jazz*, a reality TV show about a transgender teen; *The New York Times* inaugurated its "Transgender Today" series; the TV celebrity Bruce Jenner—a former Olympic athletics champion—came out as Caitlyn on the cover of *Vanity Fair* and across television. Perhaps more important in terms of youth culture, Miley Cyrus came out as gender-fluid.

But visibility was double edged. As the Michigan trans activist Charlotte Cleo Wolf put it to me: "There had been a slow trend of cultural adjustment, and then with Caitlyn, suddenly things got sensationalist." The fact that gay marriage was normalized at exactly the same time, Wolf felt, meant that "trans folks have become the new untouchable caste," a position previously occupied by gay people.

Like many transfeminine activists, Wolf was convinced that "things are more scary and dangerous" than they had been before, precisely "because of [being in] the public view. It's not that the degree to which people hate us has increased. It's that people both hate us and now know we are real. Before, if someone noticed us, they might get violent. Now people are *looking* for us."

The data seemed to bear Wolf 's perception out: there were nine documented murders of transgender people in the United States in

2014, twenty-two in 2015, and thirty in 2016.[15] But this could have been "transvisibility" working in either or both of two ways: making transgender people more vulnerable, or counting them—in life and in death—as never before.

IN 2014, A Bay Area child psychiatrist named Herb Schreier told me about a seven-year-old patient who had been struggling, for years, with gender identity. The kid went off to a trans summer camp and came back with an announcement: "Mommy, at last I think I know what I am. I'm a 'they.'" Shreier, a man in his seventies, remarked on how quickly social attitudes had already changed around homosexuality: "Who would have imagined a generation ago that two men or two women could marry and make a family? In the generation to come, we're going to look back at gender and say, 'Oh, that gender binary stuff of male and female, we're over it, thank God!'"

It is hard to imagine something as entrenched in human culture as the gender binary disappearing, ever. Still, something unprecedented was happening in the U.S. in particular, in the unexpected two-step of the transgender phenomenon—which was about crossing the gender line—and its corollary, the non-binary movement, which was about doing away with it altogether.

In 2002, not a single Fortune 500 company in the U.S. provided insurance that offered transition-related health care to its employees and their families; by 2017 one-third did.[16] By 2018, seventeen American states provided such care to state employees, and eighteen provided it through their Medicaid state health-care programs. The first gender identity clinic for children in the United States was established at Boston Children's Hospital in 2007; only a decade later there were over forty such facilities.[17] Between 2010 and 2017 the number of referrals to the Center for Transyouth Health and Development at the

Children's Hospital of Los Angeles (CHLA)—the largest such facility in the country—increased tenfold from twenty-five to two hundred fifty-five per annum.[18] By that year, the center was helping over a thousand young people undergo gender transition.

Something similar was happening in other parts of the world, too. The Royal Children's Hospital in Melbourne, Australia, recorded eighteen referrals of youths seeking transition in 2012; in 2017 the number was over two hundred fifty.[19] The British Gender Identity Development Service (GIDS) registered a *twentyfold* increase in annual referrals of people under eighteen to its gender clinic, from under a hundred in 2010 to over two thousand in 2017.[20] Still, the actual numbers were tiny: incommensurate with the amount of attention the issue was now getting, publicly and politically.

There had, of course, been a transgender rights movement reaching back to Magnus Hirschfeld's pioneering work in Berlin at the turn of the twentieth century, even if not under that name. The notion hit the mainstream Anglophone media in 1952 when the American ex-GI Christine Jorgensen came out as a "blonde bombshell," as the press put it, after a sex-change operation in Denmark.[21] While middle-class white trans women went indoors and formed organizations such as the Hose and Heels Club, poor trans women of color took to the streets to fight discrimination in diners and bars, culminating in the Stonewall riots of 1968. But there was a new component to this movement in the twenty-first century, one that made it more contentious, but also far bigger than it had ever been: it was a youth movement.

Five decades before, Alfred Kinsey had shown how sexual orientation was not set into the immutable binary of "heterosexual" and "homosexual" but existed along a spectrum. Now, in the twenty-first century, people were demanding that gender be understood this way, too, rather than as being at one or the other fixed pole of masculinity or femininity. The big difference was that this was being driven not by men in white coats but by youth challenging the gender conventions of their elders. Through "gender" they demanded to be heard, and through "gender" they critiqued the system in which they had been raised. This might have been about human behavior and biology, but it was also about politics, and generational change.

The medical anthropologist Eric A, from the pioneering Trans Studies initiative at the University of Arizona, told me that when he worked at a drop-in center for queer homeless youth in Portland, there was a whiteboard on which clients were to write their names and pronouns. These could change every day, and the pronouns were not limited to *he*, *she*, and *they* either: other options included *ze*, *hir*, and *em*, and kids were also taking to nouns, particularly animals, like *wolf* or *bird*, to be used in place of pronouns.

"No matter what was on the board," Plemons told me, "the expectation was that the adults in that space would be responsive to and respectful of it." Plemons—transgender himself, and in his forties when we spoke—was both exasperated by and envious of "the way that these kids could make demands on adults that people like me never could, in my generation." He understood it not so much as a form of bratty entitlement, as some adults did, but rather as a "powerful position for those youth to have: 'You must listen to me.' It's an appeal to adults for a kind of recognition that kids don't traditionally have in society."

This mirrored a fundamental shift, alongside the medical and information revolutions, in how children were raised, in the Anglophone world in particular. Joel Baum, who ran an advocacy and education organization called Gender Spectrum, put it to me this way: "The idea that 'children should be seen and not heard' doesn't hold anymore. So when we start asking children, 'Who are you?' they tell us. It is our responsibility to listen to them."

This would became one of the most contentious tenets of the new transgender advocacy movement: whether parents should "listen" to children who asserted a transgender identity, or push back against it if they suspected it was just a "phase," a form of rebellion, or even—as some parents believed—a "social contagion" that was the result of intense peer pressure, online and off.

"Identity is a process," the sexologist Kenneth Zucker said in a 2017 BBC documentary.[22] "It's complicated. It takes a long time to know who a child really is. A four-year-old might say he's a dog. Do you go out and buy dog food?" Zucker had been the pioneer in gender care for children in North America, but because he believed that transition was a last resort and that there were less permanent ways of treating juvenile gender dysphoria, his methods were seen increasingly by trans people and their allies to be a form of conversion therapy. After an external review, he was fired as head of the Family Gender Identity Clinic at Toronto's CAMH (the Centre for Addiction and Mental Health) in 2015.

Many among the trans community and their allies celebrated a victory. But five hundred clinicians and researchers signed a petition in Zucker's defense; after an in-depth investigation for *The Cut*, the journalist Jesse Singal provocatively labelled Zucker's dismissal "a show trial."[23] Zucker sued CAMH for unfair dismissal and in 2018 the hospital settled and apologized to him for having erroneously represented his behavior. Although CAMH declined to reappoint him or to reopen his clinic, Zucker felt "vindicated," he said: he maintained that his approach by no means approximated conversion therapy, an "incredibly inflammatory" term, and felt that the field of gender dysphoria had become "poisoned by politics" in a way that stifled legitimate scientific inquiry.[24]

One of the most prominent critics of the Zucker approach was the psychologist Diane Ehrensaft, of the Child and Adolescent Gender

Center in San Francisco, the author of several books on children and gender identity. "When we say, 'Listen to the children,' the pushback we get is, 'Children can't know who they are," she said to me. But good parenting is about careful listening: "Demanding a later bedtime is something very different to a young person trying to tell us something core about themselves."

The Zucker approach called itself "watchful waiting," but its critics said it advocated correcting cross-gender expression and looked for underlying psychological causes to resolve rather than affirming its young patients; clinicians such as Ehrensaft alleged this could do great harm to children. Some also made the point that adolescents would find information about hormones online and the actual drugs on the street; since they were exploring gender anyway, best it were done safely, and under supervision. This "gender-affirming" approach increasingly came to represent the mainstream in North American medicine, but as the transgender movement grew over the course of the decade, so too did its critics, and the Zucker approach—styled "regulatory" by its opponents—was supported by an increasing number of concerned parents: what if a child was affirmed in a transgender identity at an early age but then came to regret it?

In the United Kingdom, the Gender Identity Development Service tried to steer a middle course by practising an approach its director, Polly Carmichael, described as "affirming without confirming": "We try to be affirmative and supportive without advancing our own (*or others'*) agendas," she said in a 2017 presentation, adding that "a curious stance can be useful towards ideas and value systems."[25]

But in North America, Eric Plemons told me, the two camps increasingly held "divergent but passionately held positions," locked in intractable conflict. Plemons felt that both sides "cherry-picked evidence," and said that there was no consensus yet, clinical or otherwise. He was concerned, though: "You don't change diabetes treatments because of one or two small studies, but it's happening here, in transgender health, because it's not just about health. It's about morality and politics. There's a right side and a wrong side."

Gender transition was a new Pink Line.

THIS WAS BECAUSE the transgender rights struggle was not just about access to health care, or even about freedom from discrimination and violence. It was also, emphatically, about the right to be acknowledged or affirmed for who you were, and the right to decide this for yourself. As a result, it put a controversial new spin on the fundamental human right to self-determination. People began challenging not only the way they had been "assigned" a gender at birth, but also the way they were then pathologized with "gender identity disorder" or "gender dysphoria." Just as homosexuality had become understood to be a natural variance of human behavior, so, too, was gender variance now to be viewed. It was an identity, not an illness.

In 2013, the DSM-5, the American psychiatric diagnostic manual, replaced the diagnosis of "Gender Identity Disorder" with "Gender Dysphoria": a "state of unease" with one's body.[26] Later in the decade, health professionals lobbied to expunge gender dysphoria entirely from the DSM's list of pathologies, as had been done with homosexuality in 1973.

The trend, now, was to use a scale of "gender congruence" to measure "the degree to which transgender individuals feel genuine, authentic, and comfortable with their gender identity and external appearance"—as the originators of the concept phrased it in their 2012 study.[27] Transgender people would now be measured according to a positive value rather than the negative one of unease or disorder.

This mirrored a broader cultural revolution in understandings of the body, from "illness" to "wellness," a catchphrase of the era. From diet and exercise to anti-aging regimes and cosmetic surgery, there was "an increasing understanding of health as being about optimization and self-actualization rather than cure," Eric Plemons said to me. Plemons spoke of how the discourse previously owned by transgender people—"I'm a female trapped in a male body"—had "become the lingua franca of everyone: 'I'm a thin person trapped in a fat body,' 'I'm a beautiful person trapped in an ugly person's body' … It used to be that transsexualism was a pathology that you treated. Now it's just one more in a number of American discourses about self-optimization: 'I want to be the real me.'"

And, of course, *you* were the only person who could know who the real "you" was. In 2012, Argentina became the world's first country to pass legislation enabling people to change their gender legally solely on the basis of "self-identification."[28] This meant you could alter your gender marker legally without any external certification, psychiatric diagnosis, or medical intervention. By 2018, this was now the law in nine other countries, too: Denmark, Ireland, Norway, Malta, Belgium, Colombia, Portugal, Brazil, and Pakistan. Medically, the World Professional Association for Transgender Health (WPATH) began advocating an "informed consent" model, recommending that patients have the right to decide unilaterally if they wanted to transition medically—except when it came to surgery, where a psychologist's referral should still be required.[29]

But as so often happened in human rights discourse around "minority rights," some voices began to argue that the rights of the majority ran the risk of being compromised. In the U.S., this would become a new battleground of the culture wars.

And in the U.K., it ignited the most contested debate on sexual orientation and gender identity the country had experienced since

Margaret Thatcher banned the "promotion" of homosexuality in schools, in her notorious Section 28 amendment to the Local Government Act in 1988. It set off "a savage culture war," the *Guardian* columnist Hadley Freeman would later write, "in which the losers were women, trans or not, all of whom felt unfairly attacked ... Biological women felt like they were being told to engage in magical thinking, deny their lived experience and accept the irrelevancy of biology, while trans women felt like they were being asked to defend their identity."[30]

In 2004 the U.K. had become the world's first country to permit a legal change in gender identity without the precondition of surgery, after a judgment against the government in the European Court of Human Rights. But a psychiatric diagnosis was still necessary, as was the obligation to live in your felt gender for two years. Transgender people found the process "overly bureaucratic and invasive," Prime Minister Theresa May said in 2018, after her government conducted an unprecedented national LGBT survey.[31] May pledged a process "more streamlined and de-medicalized—because being trans should never be treated as an illness," and she opened public consultation on changing the law.

Perhaps, in the heat of the corrosive Brexit debate at the time, May's government hoped to score a feel-good victory, but the public consultations brought serious objections into the public domain.

In a strong editorial, *The Economist* alleged that "self-identification" would compromise the welfare of children by tempting them with irrevocable treatment, and that "predatory males will claim to be trans in order to commit crimes more easily," by using female identity to access women's-only spaces, from bathrooms to prisons to homeless shelters.[32] A senior editor at the *Economist*, Helen Joyce, described elsewhere how she believed gender identity had become a "political platform": "The fight for same-sex marriage was over, and the groups that had campaigned for it, by now large, rich and politically powerful, were not averse to turning their attention to a fresh cause ... [in order] to survive.[33] Many on the left were naturally inclined to believe in a new axis of oppression. Some on the right, including many British Conservatives, regretted having been slow to support same-sex marriage."

From Joyce's perspective, institutions and ideologues were redrawing the Pink Line to meet their own needs for forward motion on civil rights, even if ill-advised, now that the previous one over same-sex marriage had faded.

But the major substantive argument made by *The Economist* and others against self-identification—that it would open women and children up to predatory abuse—was easily countered. The 2010 Equality Act *already* gave transgender women the right to enter most female-only spaces, and although there had been very occasional abuse, the government claimed these were adequately dealt with by existing criminal laws. There was, furthermore, no evidence from pioneering countries such as Argentina or Denmark to suggest gender-identity fraud, or an increase in gender-based violence as a result of self-identification.[34]

Why, then, did this become the issue now? In an *Economist* forum on the topic, the journalist Nick Duffy identified a moment when "the switch flipped": on November 3, 2015, when voters in Houston, Texas, voted down an Equal Rights Ordinance.[35] Duffy describes, accurately, the way the campaign against this proposed law, led by American Christian conservatives, "hammered one constant message: if you vote for [it], you are voting to allow transgender women into the women's bathroom. Women are not safe; girls are not safe; your family members are not safe. It was repeated in every interview, every release, every advert"—including one that depicted an implied rape of a little girl in a bathroom.

Here was Duffy's point: the conservative Evangelical movement, having been "on a losing streak across America" with its "tired hymn sheet on the perils of homosexuality failing hard against the 'love is love' mantra" of the marriage equality movement, had found a new way of fighting the culture wars: against transgender rights.[36] And now, in a "surreal" transfer, some British feminists were importing from across the water an argument hatched by right-wing American fundamentalists. British feminists skeptical about transgender identity retorted that they were freer than their American sisters to voice their concerns, because of the absence of the Christian right wing as in the United States: they did not need to fear being allied with homophobes and anti-abortion crusaders.[37]

Both sides in these new culture wars, then, saw the other side as staking a new Pink Line over gender identity.

In Britain, this Pink Line was formed over a debate about self-identification. In the United States, it ran right through public restrooms, and became known as "the bathroom debate."

FROM 2015 ONWARD, I followed the school bathrooms issue in two rural school districts near Ann Arbor in Michigan, in the American Midwest. Both districts had been compelled to revise their policies about bathroom use because of the presence of transgender children.

It so happened that in one of these districts, Dexter, there was a transgender parent too, a man named Will Sherry, who ran the LGBTI student center at the University of Michigan in Ann Arbor. Sherry and his wife had three kids in the Dexter school system and, once the issue was raised, he ran sensitization workshops. He believed, he told me, that the new trans visibility was "as much a consequence of these grassroots initiatives, when someone comes out in a community, as it is of the Caitlyn Jenner moments in mass media."

There were no problems in Dexter, but in Grass Lake, at more of a distance from liberal Ann Arbor, a fierce battle erupted in the fall of 2017, when a ten-year-old named Cruz Neely was given permission to use the boys' bathroom after he came out at the school as a boy. The Neely family had been seeing a gender therapist for over a year already, to help them make sense of their child's insistence that he was a boy, and to address his dark almost suicidal moods—exacerbated by going to school, where he refused to use the bathroom. Together with the therapist, the family decided he would enter the third grade as a boy, with his new name: they notified the school, and initially received no pushback. "The difference in Cruz was astonishing," Terri Neely told me. "When people say, 'Oh it's just a bathroom, you're raising a snowflake,' they don't understand. No: it's a symbol of acceptance. It's adults saying to a child, 'We believe you are who you say you are.' It tells the other kids too that you're a boy rather than some freak who has to use the staff bathroom."

Still, the Neely family agreed that Cruz could continue using a staff bathroom until stalls were built around the boys' urinals: these already existed, as in most school bathrooms, around the toilets. But the compromise was unacceptable to some in the community, who took up the issue in school board meetings and over the town's Facebook community page. The complaints fell into two categories: that Cruz's presence in the boys' bathroom violated the religious freedom of other children, and that it put the "real" boys at risk, because it opened them to accusations of sexual impropriety given that Cruz was actually a girl.[38]

Terri Neely showed me some of the Facebook hate posts. They were sneering and vulgar, and explicitly articulated the rebellion against elite liberalism that had just brought Donald Trump to power: "They need to move their progressive selves to Ann Arbor ... They are not enlightening our sleepy little town with music [the Neelys had just opened a music school], but pushing transgender bs [bullshit] on our kids … GO AWAY!!!!!!"[39]

Grass Lake was in a county that gave nearly 60 percent of its vote to Donald Trump in 2016. Terri Neely, who described herself as a moderate Democrat, had no doubt that her antagonists "were emboldened by Trump. It was as if discrimination was allowed again. They think 'political correctness' is a bunch of crap and makes you a sissy.'" After the Republican Party in Kansas voted to "oppose all efforts to validate transgender identity" in early 2018, the Neelys' primary antagonist posted a link: "Smart! Sensible! Sane!"[40] The woman also set up a hashtag to make her political alignment explicit: "#buildthewallnotthestall"—the "wall," of course, being Trump's signature anti-migrant barrier across the Mexican border.[41]

The school board eventually agreed to accommodate Cruz in the boys' toilets, and Neely told me she believed a silent majority supported the move: they were "decent people" who had just "never previously had the opportunity to think about transgender people, but were now doing their best to make sense of it." In fact, she thought that what pushed them in supporting her family was the virulence of the other side: "People saw how extreme things were getting all around, from white supremacist rallies in Charlottesville to calls on Facebook for the police to *march into the bathroom and arrest my ten-year-old here in Grass Lake!!* I do think we became a flashpoint issue, and motivated people who wouldn't speak up otherwise." Still, a group of Grass Lake citizens planned to take the matter to court, alleging that the "mixing of the sexes" in school bathrooms was impinging upon their children's "bodily privacy and freedom of speech." They were supported by the Alliance Defending Freedom, a conservative Christian organization that advocated for "religious freedom," and was leading such litigation across the country. They stood little chance of success: Even as Trump tried to dial back the reforms of the Obama administration, jurisprudence in several cases was slowly but surely enshrining the rights of transgender students. This, Terri Neely believed, was ultimately behind the school board's accommodation of her son: legal advice that it had no choice.

IN MAY 2016, at the same time that the Neelys were figuring things out with the gender therapist, Barack Obama's government had made the decision to send out what is called a "Dear Colleague Letter" to all school districts, stipulating that Title IX—the law prohibiting sex discrimination in educational institutions that receive federal funding—covered gender identity, too.[42] This meant, in essence, that schools were compelled to permit transgender children use the facilities "consistent with their gender identities."

The Obama administration had taken the transgender rights issue on because of the way the LGBT rights movement itself had begun shifting its emphasis from marriage equality toward a new frontier. In 2012, vice president Joe Biden had deftly called transgender rights "the civil rights issue of our times"; in 2010, the State Department under Hillary Clinton changed its regulations to allow transgender people to change the gender markers on their passports without evidence of surgery.[43] Obama made some high-level transgender hires and included trans kids in the annual White House Easter Egg Roll; more substantively, he rescinded the ban on transgender people serving in the military in 2016, and his government expressly guaranteed transgender people equal access to health care in the Affordable Care Act.

But it was his government's stance on Title IX that rallied the conservative Christian lobby, already wise to the potential of this new crusade following the 2015 defeat of the Houston Equal Rights Ordinance. After the "Dear Colleague Letter," the state legislature of

North Carolina passed a law expressly prohibiting transgender people from using public facilities according to their gender identities. The attorney general Loretta Lynch responded with a suit alleging violations of the Civil Rights Act, and a number of cities and states, California among them, passed resolutions *prohibiting* their state employees to travel to North Carolina or conduct any business there. Private corporations joined the condemnation, too, withdrawing their business; several big sports events were canceled or shifted elsewhere.

The state rescinded the legislation because of the financial cost rather than any moral or legal consideration. But eleven other states decided to sue the Obama administration over federal protections for transgender students. Led by Texas and mainly from the South, these states accused the federal government of wanting to turn "educational settings across the country into laboratories for a massive social experiment, flouting the democratic process, and running roughshod over common-sense policies protecting children and basic privacy rights."[44] By early 2017, the states could withdraw their suit: Donald Trump was in power. He reversed Obama's interpretation of Title IX two months after he came into office.

In many liberal parts of the country, the culture had already shifted anyway. Massachusetts and New York City had policies in place mandating schools to permit children to use facilities consistent with their gender identities; an Oakland psychologist working with transgender children told me that, in the Bay Area, "questioning one's gender has become the norm in the schoolyard." But in more conservative regions, the bathrooms issue became a Pink Line in the Christian right's three great battles: defending "the family," protecting "religious freedom," and fighting federal interference in local issues.

Across the country, several cases were taken up by the Alliance Defending Freedom, which had made its name fighting same-sex marriage and abortion in the name of religious freedom. The

ADF and its allies defined the fight as being against the Obama administration's "obsession with the transgender agenda," the Family Research Council's Tony Perkins wrote, and its placing of "sexual extremism above the well-being of area kids" by threatening to cut funding.[45] In this way, the American right wing's criticism of LGBT rights was similar to that in other parts of the world: the wishes of fringe individuals were being privileged over the well-being of the majority.

Here, in the struggling American heartland, the fight was now also—to use Pope Francis's words—against the "ideological colonization" of "theory-of-gender," Washington, D.C., being the colonizer in this instance.[46] As the FRC's Perkins put it in a 2016 newsletter: "Clearly, the Obama administration will stop at nothing to advance this agenda, which they're willing to risk an entire generation of children to accomplish. We tip our hats to groups like ADF who are standing in the gap for families and school districts who refuse to sacrifice their children on this altar of gender anarchy."[47]

In May 2018, an Appeals Court judge ruled that Title IX did indeed apply to "gender identity" as well as "sex," thereby contradicting the Trump administration. There had been similar rulings in other courts, but conservative organizations seemed determined to continue litigating, for reasons of political mobilization if not because of prospects of success.

From the very beginning of his tenure in 2017, Donald Trump had drawn a line against the liberal excesses of the Obama era by attempting to roll back transgender rights: his announced intention to prevent transgender people from entering the military, and his reversal of Title IX. By 2018 his diplomats were trying to replace the word *gender* with *woman* in human rights documents at the United Nations,[48] and a Department of Justice official told the U.S. Supreme Court he did not believe transgender workers were protected from discrimination under federal law.[49] Then, in late 2018, a draft memo from his Department of Health and Human Services was leaked to *The New York Times*, showing that the administration was seeking to define sex as "immutable," thereby rendering any legal sex change or transgender identity impossible.[50] All this sprang from Trump's efforts to consolidate his conservative Evangelical base, for whom "gender ideology" had become the new evil; the latest bulwark against assaults on "the family" now that same-sex marriage was legal and supported by a majority of Americans.

As in the battles against "gender theory" elsewhere in the world, this was a logical extension of the prior backlash to gay rights, too, where moral panics were about the need to protect children and families from corrupting influences and predatory adults.

THE MOST HIGH PROFILE of the bathroom cases of these years demonstrated the unique nature of these culture wars.

When Gavin Grimm was a teenager, he sued the Gloucester County school board in Virginia after he, having transitioned to masculinity, was prohibited from using the boys' toilets in 2015. As in Grass Lake, permission had been rescinded following complaints. Grimm lost the case but then won on appeal; the school board petitioned the Supreme Court, which initially agreed to hear the matter but later sent it back to the circuit court now that Trump was in office and the federal government's attitude to Title IX had changed.

Even though the Supreme Court declined to hear the Grimm case, the way litigants lined up on both sides offered a cross section of just how much bathrooms had become a new national culture wars battleground. Gavin Grimm was represented—as he had been from the start—by the American Civil Liberties Union, and supported by a phalanx of human rights organizations. On the side of Gloucester County was a roll call of conservative organizations, including the ADF, with one telling exception: the Women's Liberation Front (WoLF), a feminist organization that partnered with the right-wing Family Policy Alliance to file a brief insisting that transgender girls and women were in fact "men" trying to steal opportunities from women "merely by 'identifying' as a woman."[51]

On its website, WoLF itemized its objections to the Obama interpretation of Title IX: It had not only eliminated "the ability to legally distinguish between males and females in federally funded schools," but "girls' rights to personal privacy and freedom from male sexual harassment, forced exposure to male nudity, and voyeurism."[52] It thus stripped "women and girls of their legal protections." In 2019, WoLF would join forces with the right wing Heritage Foundation to lobby against the 1964 Civil Rights Act being extended to protect people on the basis of gender identity: this, the group said, was out of "concern" for "the safety and bodily integrity of the women and children whose lives would be placed at risk or ruined" if gender identity was enshrined into law.[53]

WoLF's arguments about transgender women being imposters and sexual predators—arguments that the Houston campaign had mobilized, and that opponents to self-identification in Britain would espouse—echoed the earliest feminist critiques of transgender identity. In 1972, lesbian feminists (and gay men) refused to allow transgender women to participate in San Francisco Pride and in 1973 the transsexual singer Beth Elliott was ejected from a feminist conference after being decried by the keynote speaker, Robin Morgan, as "an opportunist, an infiltrator, and a destroyer—with the mentality of a rapist."[54]

From Janice Raymond's 1979 book *The Transsexual Empire*, in which she compared transsexual medicine to Nazi eugenics,[55] to Germaine Greer's snide dismissal of transgender women as "pantomime dames," this was a constant thread in one line of feminist thought.[56] Now, in the 2010s, the critique was reignited, not least because of the number of transgender men coming out. Not all of it was ideological: there was particular concern among some mothers and professionals about the number of adolescent girls transitioning: were they finding their true selves, or were they victims of a gender bias, evacuating womanhood in a misogynistic society?

In the United Kingdom, a group of ten women commandeered London Pride in July 2018, with banners proclaiming "Transactivism erases lesbians" and "Lesbian = Female."[57] They were members of a group called Get the L Out, as in 'get the 'L' out of LGBT Pride.'" One of the protestors told a reporter: "A man cannot be a lesbian, a person with a penis cannot be a lesbian."

Most mainstream British LGBT leaders decried the "Get the L Out" protest as "transphobic."[58] But despite the small number of women involved, it was not a marginal position in the country. In October 2018, a petition lead by thirty-three prominent gay and lesbian figures gathered over seven thousand signatures to decry the way the country's leading LGBT organization, Stonewall, had taken on transgender advocacy, because of the way it threatened lesbian identity and culture.[59]

IF THE BATHROOM was one battleground of the twenty-first century's gender culture wars, the sports field became another. The WoLF feminists spoke of the "cruel irony" of the Obama administration's decision to describe "gender identity" as a form of "sex discrimination": "Title IX, which was enacted in part to champion female sports, would now be used to dismantle them, as male athletes use 'gender identity' to demand access to female teams, occupying places which would have otherwise gone to females and dominating the competition."[60]

The issue became a matter of global debate in 2018: around Caster Semenya, the record-breaking South African Olympic middle-distance champion. Even though Semenya was raised as a woman and had always thought herself to be one, medical testing revealed her to have "differences in sexual development," with high testosterone levels. When Semenya was told by the International Association of Athletics Federations in 2018 that she must lower her testosterone levels medically if she wished to continue to compete as a woman, she took the matter on appeal. The international Court of Arbitration for Sport (CAS) ruled against her in April 2019: while the IAAF decision was indeed discriminatory to the athlete, such discrimination was "necessary" to preserve "the integrity of female athletics."[61]

In 2015, the Indian athlete Dutee Chand had been banned from competition for similar reasons. Sex testing of female athletes began in the 1950s, and in previous eras, the few women who were found to have "differences in sexual development" (which usually meant having XY rather than XX chromosomes, or ambiguous genitalia) were simply ejected from the competition, as had happened to the sprinter Ewa Klobukowska in 1967. The Polish athlete actually had her 1964 Olympics medals rescinded: at twenty-one, her career was over.

But in fifty years times had changed. Semenya would not go quietly: she was an out lesbian, married to another woman, with the moral weight of the South African constitution *and* the financial weight of a Nike sponsorship behind her. Her butchness and valor were celebrated rather than denigrated: she became an international human rights icon. Both the clamor against her and her determination to fight it were the consequence of the gender culture wars. For those who opposed her, she became a symbol of the way new notions of gender-fluidity might jeopardize hard-won female space. For those who supported her, she was the victim not only of a violation against her dignity and bodily integrity, but also of an increasingly untenable insistence on a line in the sand between men and women at a time when both science and culture were understanding gender to be more of a spectrum.

One of those to voice concern was the great Martina Navratilova, an ardent champion of both women's and gay rights. Navratilova wrote an opinion piece in *The Times* in early 2019, not specifically about Semenya, but about her more general fears for female sports in an era that affirmed transgender identity: "A man can decide to be female, take hormones if required by whatever sporting organization is concerned, win everything in sight and perhaps earn a small fortune, and then reverse his decision and go back to making babies if he so desires," she wrote.[62] "It's insane and it's cheating. I am happy to address a transgender woman in whatever form she prefers, but I would not be happy to compete against her. It would not be fair."

Navratilova was talking in the abstract, voicing anxiety about what might happen in the future. With the exception of a much-cited Connecticut track event won by two transgender girls in 2018 there were few actual examples of transwomen's victories on the sports field, let alone abuse. Given this—and, of course, the obstacles that those transgender teens in Connecticut must have had to overcome just to be on the track in the first place—the trans activist Julia Serano suggested that such scaremongering was part of the larger culture wars around gender identity: "The targeting of transgender and intersex athletes and gender non-conforming athletes seems very similar to what is happening with policing of bathrooms and just generally the anti-trans hysteria that's been going on," she said at the time of the Semenya ruling.[63] "People want to believe that there's some essential difference between women and men that makes them completely distinct and explicit categories. That essence doesn't exist in real life."

Semenya herself had no doubts as to her gender—and her prowess: "I am a woman and I am fast," she said when she launched her appeal.[64] Her case became something of a litmus test for a defining question in the age of identity politics: What was the relationship between how you felt inside, and how the world saw and defined you?

IN THE UNITED STATES, in particular, the gender culture wars threw spaces and institutions beyond bathrooms and sports fields into crisis: from the iconic Michigan Womyn's Music Festival, which controversially insisted on a "womyn born womyn" door policy to, more seriously, women's colleges now being compelled to revise their admissions criteria—and their very reason for existence.[65] After a transgender woman was twice denied admission to Smith College, protest pressured the college to change its policies in 2015, joining several others—Mills, Bryn Mawr, Barnard, and Wellesley—that now admitted transgender women, even before they changed their status legally, so long as they lived as women. By 2018, about half of the U.S.'s thirty-four women's colleges accepted transgender women.

These institutions were also forced to grapple with the situation of transgender men: applicants who identified as women but then transitioned to masculinity while on campus. Could you have a *man* in a women-only space? Some, like Wellesley, would not consider the applications of transgender men, but allowed those who transitioned while enrolled to remain. There were twenty-four such students at Wellesley in 2014, and the dean of students was quoted as saying the school had "not yet worked out how to be a women's college at a time when gender is no longer considered binary."[66]

This brought a significant new dimension to the nature of the culture wars as they shifted from gay rights to transgender rights in the twenty-first century, in the Western world, and particularly in the United States. The wars were being fought on two fronts: religious conservatism to the right, and a particular strain of feminism to the left. What made it even more complicated was the way these ideologies fused with anxieties over children and young adults undergoing transition.

If a new Pink Line was opening up around transgender rights in countries like the U.S. and the U.K., it became confused with a youth rebellion over gender, with generational battles over children's rights and roles in society, and with the responsibilities of the adults who took care of them.

14

THE RIOT YOUTH STORIES

ANN ARBOR AND BEYOND

LIAM

Liam Kai*—Riot Youth member, high school senior, then University of Michigan undergraduate, late teens. Pronouns: he/him/his.

Beth*—Liam's mother, social worker, fifties. Pronouns: she/her/hers.

Susan*—Liam's estranged second mother, late fifties. Pronouns: she/her/hers.

Andrea*—Beth's wife, social worker, fifties. Pronouns: she/her/hers.

***Pseudonyms**

Waking up with a headache—kinda sucks.[1]
Waking up with a flat chest—priceless.

LIAM KAI, eighteen years old and just graduated from high school in a town near Ann Arbor, Michigan, tweeted these words on June 18, 2014. It was nine days after his top surgery and the day after the dressings and drains were removed. On the same day he also posted a video on Instagram. As the doctor unwraps his bandages Liam looks down over his newly boyish chest and whoops, "*Dude!*" In a few weeks' time he would begin injecting the testosterone that would—finally—vault him out of what he saw as the purgatory of an androgynous childhood into the manhood of body hair and a deep voice.

Liam was assigned female at birth, adopted from China at six months. He had in fact been living as a boy since the age of thirteen, binding his growing breasts daily in constricting nylon vests. "I'm thanking whatever force out there that this is my last week having to bind," he tweeted before his surgery.[2] "It's painful, embarrassing, frustrating, and tiring."

Until his eighteenth birthday, though, Liam could do nothing medically to assist his gender transition process. This was because his legal parents, a lesbian couple who had split when he was six, disagreed over the issue. After a somewhat rocky beginning his mother Beth, with whom he lived, accepted Liam's transgender identity: "I see the procedure as the plastic surgery my son needs to have rather than the double mastectomy my daughter needs to have," she told me just before Liam's surgery. But the other parent, Susan, with whom Liam had broken entirely, was fiercely opposed to it. Both mothers were committed feminists, but while Beth rooted her acceptance of Liam in a feminism that taught her about gender as a construct, Susan felt that Liam would be much healthier and happier if he just accepted himself as girl. Using court orders, she effectively withheld consent for any medical treatment while he was a minor.

I met Liam and his family in their home outside Ann Arbor in April 2014, just before his eighteenth birthday, as he was preparing for the surgery. Beth had been with her wife Andrea for over twelve years. The women had raised Liam together; he addressed them collectively as "Moms" (often with mock-exasperation: *Mo-oms!?!*) and on Twitter he liked to call himself "a mommas' boy (get the plural?)." There was something redemptive, even victorious, for all of them in the moment of the surgery, not just in the way they believed it would make Liam's life better, but in the physical, irrevocable marking of what they all knew to be true: he was a man.

I had come to the U.S. looking, specifically, for a family like this. I wanted to understand the relationship between my generation of pioneers—women like Beth who pushed the boundaries of the definition of family by raising their own children outside the institution of heterosexual marriage—and this new generation of pioneers, exemplified by transgender children such as Liam. I found a few such families in the Bay Area, or around New York City and Washington, D.C. (most trans kids had straight parents, of course). But here was one in a most unexpected place, in a modest but comfortable home along a row of identical face-brick bungalows, just off one of those endless commercial strips that define American suburbia.

What helped the family was, undoubtedly, its proximity to Ann Arbor, home of the University of Michigan, a liberal oasis on the Midwestern prairie. There was an after-school program here called Riot Youth, for LGBTQQA (Lesbian, Gay, Bisexual, Transgender, Queer, Questioning, and Allies) teens, hosted by a local youth center. While I was in Ann Arbor I met other Riot Youth kids, too. I would follow them over the next five years as they became adults, transforming not only their identities and—in some cases—their bodies, but also the way their society and culture thought about gender in the second decade of the twenty-first century.

BETH WENT ALL the way to China to get a daughter, she told me.

It was partly a response to baby girls being abandoned. She was approaching forty and wanted to be a parent; Susan was willing to go along with it. Disguising herself as a "single mother," Beth submitted her application to the Chinese authorities, and in November 1996, she joined a group going over to collect their children. The conditions at the orphanage were appalling: the little girl handed over was malnourished and very ill, but, like the other infants, had been ghoulishly made up with rouge and painted eyebrows, prettified for their new parents.

Beth was heavyset and grey-haired when we met in 2014, with an unkempt charm and a deadpan delivery that skated a thin line between Midwestern earnestness and irony. Andrea was her foil, a wisecracking Jewish woman from the East Coast, every story a routine. As we sat around their kitchen with Liam one Saturday evening over a pot of vegetable soup and a bottomless jug of iced tea, they showed me the photographs of their recent "elopement" to Niagara Falls. At that point same-sex marriage was not yet legal in Michigan, but Andrea, a federal employee, wanted benefits for her family. And so as soon as the U.S. Supreme Court struck down the Defense of Marriage Act in June 2013 they made the trip to New York, a state that would marry them. Liam was their best man. There was a lot of laughter and good-natured ribbing around the table as they told me this and other stories; Liam was—literally—the straight guy of the trio.

Liam had a handsome broad face and an easy smile; he carried himself with the studied elegance of someone who had spent much of his life looking at others to try to figure out how to comport himself. He was fastidiously neat and impeccably groomed, with a preppy wardrobe: this evening he was in a crisp pink-and-blue button-down shirt over neat navy shorts. "I've *studied* the way guys speak," he said to me when we went for a burger one night, "I've trained my voice to hit the floor, but I can go no further until I get the T [testosterone]." Still, many guys don't hit the floor anyway, and when we were just shooting the breeze, I was only reminded that he had been assigned female at birth when he laughed unselfconsciously or when I paid attention to his smooth skin.

As we sat around the dinner table in the family home, Andrea had a way of addressing Liam directly: "Girls have to confine themselves, not take up too much space, but you didn't have that. You *sprawled*. And you'd chug like in the beer commercials, and give a frat boy belch at the end! Being an old-fashioned lesbian myself, I thought that that's what we had on our hands."

"I don't think I ever thought Liam was transgender," Beth added. "I'd buy him a lot of girl-power stuff. '*Girls Rule!*' I wanted my daughter to be a strong, confident girl."

Inevitably, we spent much time talking about clothes, those primary gender markers, and frequently the first site of resistance for gender non-conforming kids. Liam was oblivious to clothes as a girl, Beth said: "He would just wear whatever. Pick it out of a pile on the floor. But you should see his wardrobe now. Everything is *very* organized. He cares very much exactly what every article of clothing is."

"I was okay *being* a girl," Liam chipped in. "I just hated *looking* like a girl." Until puberty, that is, when his breasts started growing, and his unease developed into depression. Mandated by court to attend therapy as part of his parents' custody battle in 2009, Liam mentioned his distress over Susan's rigidity about gender, and told the therapist that he sometimes had to remind himself he was a girl. The therapist called Beth into the consulting room, and told both of them, quick-fire, that Liam was transgender. "Liam was so excited," his mother remembered. "He wanted it all. Now. But all I knew about transgender was what I saw on talk shows. I was terrified. I kept thinking, 'This isn't what I want for my child.' He had always been so healthy. I could not think of hormones and surgery. I wish I'd been prepared."

In shock, Beth complied. All of Liam's girl stuff was given away. Binders were ordered to compress Liam's growing breasts, letters written to the school. But then Beth panicked, and insisted that Liam return to girlhood—at least until there was more clarity. He had to send back the binders and return to clothing that was at least gender-neutral. Perhaps the crash was inevitable, and it came a few months later: when Liam was watching *Twilight: The New Moon*, in which boys become werewolves at a certain age. With that came a new physique, Liam explained to me: "Taylor Lautner goes from scrawny to muscular and cuts off his long hair. It's a huge transformation of identity into a kind of supernatural being with a big, sculpted body. It was a teen phenomenon, and I was very excited about seeing it." He paused, and his eyes welled up. "It was painful, to see that this guy had muscles instead of breasts. Muscles that everyone was attracted to, and that I would never have."

Liam began planning to overdose on painkillers. He did not do anything, but for the first time "I had a *plan*." At his next therapy session, he collapsed, weeping: he could no longer live as a girl. This was a different therapist from the first one, a more careful one, or perhaps a better-informed one in this rapidly evolving field: she referred the family to a gender specialist, and Liam and his parents began planning his social transition more carefully. For Beth, this was the turning point: "I became a momma bear, 100 percent behind Liam's transition."

The three decided on his name the way they made all major decisions: "On the back of a napkin at our favorite diner." Liam chose a name to reflect, in part, his Chinese heritage: a thirteen-year-old girl left her eighth-grade class one day, and a thirteen-year-old boy named Liam Kai came back the next.

So quickly did Liam transform from a depressed, introverted, and untidy little girl into a confident, talkative, and shipshape little boy, that when the school year ended four months later, he received the annual boys' prize for "Leadership, Scholarship and Service." "I was the *dude*!" he kept on saying to his moms after winning it. "They have one for girls and one for boys, and I was the *dude*!"

The school—a regular public school in Middle America—was willing to put Liam's male name on a trophy before it had even been changed legally. The glory of the "Dude Award," as the family called it, offset some of the difficulties that followed. Liam stopped hanging out with the girls he'd been friends with since the beginning of school, which saddened him: there was a new barrier between them that he did not quite understand. And he never quite made friends with the boys, perhaps because he did not go through male puberty along with them. Some of them gallantly lent him a hand, by showing him the guy way to wear a hat or to sag one's jeans, but if he tried to talk about girls or dating, "things would get shady. That would mean this was real."

Because of the breast-binding, Liam stopped swimming, his passion. His life took place outside the rituals of a suburban American life, like summer camp and sports meets; he spent most of his time at home. He became very involved at Riot Youth but his weekends were lonely and isolated. He found company in television dramas, and a creative outlet through his own writing: he was an obsessive drafter of fan fiction, which he posted online.

Liam told me, too, that he had been unlucky with dating. The girls he met at Riot Youth were too often involved in adolescent self-harming such as cutting; the girls he courted at high school would back off because he was transgender. Still, when he ran through his history, it was clear that he had dated. There was something quite typical in his account of his love life: like his peers, he had experienced the adolescent intensity of longing and loss.

Liam started high school the year after he transitioned. He made the decision not to "go stealth"—the trans lingo for just living in your felt gender, without coming out and acknowledging that you had transitioned—because "I hate secrets," and because there would be some kids at his new school who would have known him from before. Before he found a way to come out, though, the issue was precipitated when he overheard a male classmate say, referring to him, "I don't know what to call *it*." He was very upset. Together with his parents and his peers at Riot Youth, he decided to confront the issue. He approached his homeroom adviser and asked to lead a class discussion.

The atmosphere had been somewhat tense beforehand, recalled Carol, one of Liam's teachers: "Talk was spreading, not necessarily malicious, but gossipy. But things pretty much changed immediately when he said, 'This is who I am.' A ninth grader! *Insane*, right? This shift happened. After everyone knew, it was just like, 'Okay, then.' Sure there were students who were still uncomfortable. But the behind-the-back talk stopped, because Liam said, 'If you have questions, ask me.'"

Carol had actually first known Liam as a girl in middle school. When Liam had mentioned transition back then, Carol wanted to be supportive, "but in the back of my mind, I couldn't stop the questions: 'This is such a huge decision at such a young age. How does she really know?'" But when Carol encountered Liam again in high school, "I could not get over the transformation. This very depressed, even verge-of-suicidal, girl had turned into a self-confident leader, educating others, one of the school's tour guides, the initiator of the annual talent show." Liam's gender transition was "a no-brainer. He is who he is supposed to be."

All the adults I spoke to about Liam were filled with similar awe. I understood it as something beyond the sometimes-knee-jerk affirmation that is an identity politics boilerplate. It seemed to me that they, the best kind of prairie liberals, reveled in the story about a kid who is transformed—who succeeds—against the odds, by being true to himself. Even if they were writing a Hollywood movie in their heads, they were expanding their consciousness about who people were, and what rights they deserved.

BY THE TIME Liam told his moms he was a boy at age thirteen in 2009, a new medical protocol had been approved in the Netherlands and was beginning to be used in the United States. Puberty could be delayed in children who knew or believed they might be transgender with drugs that blocked the production of hormones. The data bore Liam's personal experience out: adolescence was the time when gender-dysphoric children became seriously at risk of self-harm because of the way their bodies were changing. Suddenly your voice dropped and you grew facial hair, or your breasts sprouted and you began menstruating. But with puberty-blockers you could delay this process, and then begin taking cross-sex hormones a little later to transition into adulthood in your felt gender—without, in the case of transgender men, having to submit to a mastectomy, because your breasts would not have grown in the first place.

The "Dutch protocols" stipulated that minors only be allowed to start cross-sex hormones later in adolescence. This would buy time, until children were able to make more mature decisions. Most Western European countries—including the United Kingdom—did not permit medical gender transition before sixteen, using national health plans to regulate it. Toward the end of the decade, though, endocrine research was showing that long-term use of puberty-blockers could be dangerous, and in 2017 the American Pediatric Endocrine Society recommended the use of cross-sex hormones earlier than sixteen for gender-dysphoric children. The feeling in the U.S. was increasingly: Why wait? Liam's moms Beth and Andrea concurred: why not let him have his male adolescence along with everyone else, rather than keeping him back, thereby adding to his already considerable social problems? The only thing that constrained them was the refusal of Susan, his other parent, to give consent, even for the use of puberty-blockers.

While hormones were cheap, puberty-blockers cost over $1,200 a month (in 2018), and were very seldom covered by insurance: this option was thus way out of reach for poorer kids, or those without parental support. But given that health care in the United States is consumer-driven and that there is also a culture of interventionist parenting, you could now make things happen for your child if you had the resources and the will.

There were diagnostic criteria, of course, which gender-care professionals paraphrase as "Persistence, Consistency, Insistence": persistent cross-gender identification, insistence on presenting as the other sex, and a constant wish to be that sex. But the child psychologist Diane Ehrensaft often advised parents to live with ambiguity for a while, she told me, until things became clearer. She made a careful distinction between two types of children: those who articulated their sense they were the opposite gender from the moment they could talk, and those who were "gender-creative."

The latter might grow up to be gay or lesbian—or, increasingly, as the concept took hold in American culture, to assume a "genderqueer" or "non-binary" identity. "But for our youngest transgender children, we usually can tell quite early, although not always in one moment in time," Ehrensaft said. "When we do know, we should let them fly."

THE NOTION THAT Liam was transgender first came to him when he watched *The L Word*, the American TV series. He heard Max, the trans character, talk about binders, punched the word into Google, and he was off. He became obsessed with YouTube vlogs of transitioning men, showing week by week how they were changing through grooming, hormone therapy, gym workouts, tattoos, and even surgery. And once he knew he was going to transition he researched his surgery options by poring over graphic videos posted online by doctors marketing their products.

As an eighteenth birthday present Beth and Andrea agreed to pay for Liam's first tattoo. Like muscles, tattoos are fetishes of masculinity—and had become very much part of transmasculine culture; a way of authoring one's own body, as the trans author Jay Prosser put it in his path-breaking 1998 memoir, *Second Skins*.[3] Liam had been craving one for years. He had been particularly close to Beth's father, a farmer, who after a brief struggle with the fact that his granddaughter was now a grandson had said simply to Beth: "You have a very good son. He's just good." Grandpa Bob had died shortly after Liam's transition, and Liam now chose these words for his tattoo: "He's just good" would be inked on the inside of his right upper arm.

"Guys work out, they get those tattoos, they get those biceps," Liam said to me. "They have to work their *asses* off for those surgeries and hormones. They create the person that they always knew they were, and take pride in it." There was a phrase for this that Liam had found on the Internet, and that he liked: "self-made man."

The term had become something of a meme, from T-shirts (Liam had one) to tattoos. It was used by the sociologist Henry Rubin to describe the transgender men he was studying, and he meant it to hold a double entendre: that gender transition was an act of personal will and creativity, but also the conforming of your outer shell to your inner "true self."[4] If you are "self-made" you are made by your true "self" rather than by your external characteristics. In most people, internal and external cohered, but in some they did not, and for such people, transition brought them together, made them whole. "Authenticity" had become the holy grail of contemporary Western psychology, and there was a move away from a reparative approach—"we are going to cure you"—to one more in tune with the zeitgeist of the early twenty-first century: "We are going to affirm you. We are going to help you be your best self, your truest self."

When Henry Rubin published *Self-Made Men* in 2003 he acknowledged that "the idea of an essential self is not currently a popular one," but felt that "we must ask ourselves what it means that individuals feel like they have a true self ", even if we accepted that gender identities were fictionalized constructs of our collective imagination."[5] But something dramatic had happened to identity discourse since Rubin wrote these words, and the transgender movement had much to do with it. The sociologist Tey Meadow put her finger on it in her 2018 book *Trans Kids*: gender was now understood to be "a fundamental, immutable part of the psychic self " rather than a social construct (as the early feminists had it) or performed and learned (as the later ones, such as Judith Butler, did).[6] In just fifteen years, it was now social constructionism—the idea that identity is contextual or fungible—that was out of vogue.

Researchers began looking for a biological basis to transgender identity. The leading endocrinologist in the field, Stephen Rosenthal, published a review of the research in 2014, in which he described gender identity as "a complex interplay of biologic, environmental, and cultural factors."[7] The strongest contenders for the first were a mother's hormonal imbalances during pregnancy.

The urge to conduct research into a gendered brain, Tey Meadow writes, was not dissimilar to the explosion of "gay gene" studies in the late-twentieth century: "If there is a biological basis for homo or transsexuality, then gay and transgender people can't be other than what they are, and the majority has a social and legal responsibility to protect them"—in a liberal democracy, at least.[8] But what was attractive about this potential diagnostic tool, to some, was also the cause for skepticism or even fear for others: while it might provide information to enable families to make decisions about children's transitions, it could also be used to provide prospective parents with information that caused them to abort unattractive fetuses, or to bar those who did not test "positive" from transitioning.

Thus was the eternal nature-versus-nurture debate refracted, in twenty-first-century America, through a discussion of transgender identity. Were we destined to live according to the consequences of our genes and our upbringing, or could we overcome these legacies? Gender transition seemed to lay open the dance that is identity-development: between the notion that it is constructed by our relationship to others (what we think of them, and what they think of us) and the notion that we generate it ourselves, or that it is passed on to us in our genes. What agency do we have over our bodies, and our destinies? Were we self-made or other-made?

The United States is the ideal petri dish for such investigations, given the consumer-driven nature of health care: in the twenty-first century, patients were increasingly taking control of their own health care if they could afford to. There was a particular tradition to this in the gay community, given the way patients and activists had held medics and the drug industry to account in the AIDS epidemic. If the AIDS activism of the late-twentieth century nudged American medicine into patient-driven care, then the Digital Revolution of the early twenty-first century gave it a decisive shove in the way it enabled people to do their own research, via online networks and information. "The parents and the kids themselves are driving this," the child psychiatrist Herb Schreier said to me: "They're way ahead of the medical profession. *They're* challenging *us*."

LIAM SCHEDULED HIS top surgery for as soon as possible after his eighteenth birthday. After poring, for months, over websites and reviews and YouTube vlogs, he chose a specialist in Cleveland. Beth drove him the three hours for the preliminary appointment: he was advised to have "periareolar mastectomy with purse-string closure and chest liposuction" rather than a full double-incision mastectomy, due to his slender build and small breasts.[9] Liam was happy with this advice: the double incision might be more effective in removing all breast tissue, but it would leave unsightly scars beneath the nipples. Liam's doctor posted a video on YouTube demonstrating the surgery, and Liam viewed this with some discomfort. I, too, forced myself to watch it: a circular incision is made around the nipple and areola, which is removed and held hanging by a "purse-string" thread, while the breast tissue is sucked out of the cavity, before the skin is pulled back around the nipple. It is like watching a red rosebud unfurl where the nipple should be.

Liam was terrified by the surgery and struggled with the convalescence. But he saw it as pain that had to be taken, so that he could be his true self. Culturally, he came from a different world from mine; a *Nip/Tuck* world where cosmetic surgery was increasingly common, a *Twilight* world where digitally enhanced bodies were perpetually in flux. Body ink and piercing defined hipster culture in these days in much the way that long hair had defined hippie culture forty years previously, and it was not such a big step from such superficial body modification to the more profound alterations of hormone therapy and surgery.

"Bottom surgery," as genital surgery is known, had been available for over seventy years for transgender women; even longer, if one includes the castration of eunuchs in the Middle East and South Asia.

But for transgender men, it was still in its early stages, and many chose to live without it. There were two options: metoidioplasty, which enlarges the clitoris with hormones and then releases it so it stands away from the body as a small phallus; or phalloplasty, which creates a penis out of skin tissue grafted from the arm or thigh. In either case, the urethra can be rerouted through the phallus to allow urination, and the labia majora can be sewn together to form a scrotum, into which prosthetic testicles can be inserted.

Liam told me he was in no hurry to do any of this—and hoped that, by the time he was ready for it, the procedures would be more advanced.

SHORTLY AFTER I spent time with Liam in the spring of 2014 he entered adulthood with an extraordinary velocity. He turned eighteen. He attended his high school prom: he wore a silver tux, and his best girlfriends were in extravagant organza. He graduated from high school, second in his class. He had his top surgery and moved out of home to a summer school program at the University of Michigan, where he would start, as a freshman, in September 2014. He began dating again, and started his testosterone injections through the student health facility at the university, which now offered gender transition as part of its services.

He celebrated the Fourth of July by posting his first shirtless portrait on Twitter. "Happy Independence Day!" he wrote, relishing his own.[10] "They say never to post something that you might regret, but honestly, I'd regret NOT uploading this: the first time I've felt the sun on my chest. Three weeks, four days post-op and two days on testosterone. It's all still so hard to believe! … Thanks moms for everything you've done; I wouldn't be here without you."

In the photograph, taken by Beth in the park near their house, Liam is wearing cargo shorts, sagged, of course, to show the band of his American Eagle underwear. His chest is boyish but his hips are still round—the testosterone will soon change that—and he has the serious self-conscious look of any teenage boy figuring out what to do with his new adolescent body.

"I'm happy," he wrote in his post, eighteen and shirtless, next to the image he has posted on Twitter.[11] "Even when I'm upset, I'm happy."

SEAN AND CHARLOTTE

Sean—Riot Youth member, high school senior, then undergraduate in Massachusetts, late teens. Pronouns: they/them/theirs.

Charlotte—Riot Youth alum, Sean's partner, activist and part-time student, early twenties. Pronouns: she/her/hers.

Augustine—Sean's subsequent partner, food worker, early twenties. Pronouns: they/them/theirs.

Elizabeth—Sean's mother, university professor, early fifties. Pronouns: she/her/hers.

Every year, Riot Youth held a Queer Prom, and I timed my spring 2014 visit to Michigan to coincide with this. The theme, this year, was "80s versus 90s," and a meeting hall in downtown Ann Arbor was done up as a disco. At around 5:00 p.m., the kids started to trickle in—some seemed barely through puberty—beneath a sign that set the house rules: "Queer Prom is for LGBTQQA youth because regular school proms are not always safe and welcoming." No drugs, no nudity, no touching without permission, "no staring, no pointing and no gawking at others"—and, of course: "Respect people's preferred names and pronouns. If you don't know, just *ask*."

The '80s seemed to be remembered as fluorescent Gothic and the '90s as flannel grunge: the former was perfect for the gay boys and the emos, and the latter great for the queer kids. But there was little to distinguish this from any other teen party, save for the fact that some girls had shaved heads with rattails and were kissing other girls.

Liam was there, wearing chinos and plaid. He told me he was doing *Boy Meets World*, an iconic '90s sitcom, but he looked just like himself. He did not dance, and he slipped out early. He had become increasingly uncomfortable with the term *queer*, he said, which seemed to have "taken over the space at Riot Youth. When they spoke about 'straight' people, it was usually to talk about *other* people, who were either homophobic enemies, or 'allies.' I thought, 'Hey! What about me? I'm sitting here. *I'm* straight!'"

AT THAT QUEER PROM the most popular song by far was the theme from Disney's *Frozen*. When it played the kids gathered in ecstatic circles, throwing their arms in the air and singing along: "*Let it go! Let it* GOOOOOOOOO*!*" In one of the most frenzied of these circles was a couple very much at the center of the Riot Youth community: Sean and Charlotte.

Sean, just turned eighteen, was petite and curvy and had a *manga* look: hiking boots and short-short denim cutoffs; oversized bookish glasses under similarly exaggerated bangs, cartoonish wisps of which seemed to live in their owner's mouth. Charlotte, two years older, wore long dyed auburn hair in two Valkyrie plaits that fell out from under her trademark vintage fedora hat.

Charlotte towered over Sean and, sometime toward the end of the evening, scooped her partner up into an extended French kiss; the kids in their circle erupted into a whooping American cheer. A bit later, when we were talking about this moment, Sean gave a theatrical eye-roll behind those big glasses: "Straight allies! They can piss me off. Sometimes I feel we need our own space as queer people."

Earlier in the day, as we hung out together at the Neutral Zone—the youth center that was Riot Youth's home—Sean had schooled me in the sexual and gender taxonomies of the day: "I am pansexual but homoromantic. This means I have no problem having sex with any gender, but in a relationship I would only date women or genderqueer people. I am genderqueer myself, which means I use 'they' and 'their' pronouns."

Sean had a sweet and somewhat tentative manner, and an almost courtly politeness that belied their role as Riot Youth's chief ideologue. Their mother, Elizabeth, was a feminist philosopher who had raised her daughter on the precept that gender was a social construct of the patriarchy, designed with its prescribed roles to keep women subjugated. But if the project of Elizabeth's generation was to overturn this "caste system" by empowering women, Sean subscribed to a revolutionary new project: "to wipe the slate clean entirely," as Sean put it to me. "If the gender binary is 'man' and 'woman' we break out of that. We don't pay attention to gender as a social contract at all. I actually think it's kinda stupid, very violent. Why would I want any part of it?'"

The Riot Youth meeting room was strewn with colorful beanbags and covered in artworks; downstairs, there were communal tables, a bank of computer terminals, a recording studio, and the cavernous space where the party would take place. As we talked, Sean kept an eye on the decorating team: the "80s versus 90s" theme seemed to call for bucketloads of glitter. When I asked what the genders of the other kids were, Sean responded with exaggerated patience: "Everyone has their own gender. There are as many genders in the world as there are people on the planet, which means about seven billion, as no two people experience masculinity and femininity the same way. We are all our own selves." And yet there were subcultural markers, which Sean outlined to me: "The way people walk or carry themselves; the way we stick out our tongues at each other in a friendly way; the way you shave parts of your hair or have rattails; the way you hold yourself and smile and talk."

And there was politics, too, of course: Sean had chosen to be queer "because it's a very angry term. It's radical." In an era when gay people were interested in getting married and having kids, "I feel we're *not* like everyone else. I don't *want* to be assimilated into straight culture."

I wondered if the "queer" assignation wasn't—at least in part—just a lexical change: *queer* was not widely used as a slur in the United States the way it was still in Britain, and even in liberal Ann Arbor, "you're so gay" remained the schoolyard insult of choice, applicable to anyone doing something you didn't like. For Sean's generation, *queer* was actually less burdened with negative connotation.

Sean's friend Indigo was sitting with us that afternoon, over the glitter glue and construction paper. She explained queerness through a comparison with her mother's generation. Ever since she was a little girl, she had been taken by her mother—a bisexual feminist—to the Michigan Womyn's Music Festival. Indigo went every year, although she struggled with the festival's increasingly controversial door policy: transgender women were excluded. "There's a huge divide between the generations," Indigo told me, and this was not only because the older women at the festival liked "body painting and acoustic guitars" while the younger ones did "mosh pits and candle circles": "We are more fluid. Less bothered by categories. That's what makes us queer."

Queer youth culture oscillated between the two seemingly contradictory positions articulated by Indigo and Sean: on the one hand an embrace of fluidity and on the other an ever-proliferating string of named identities. As I spent time with these kids, I realized that the impulse to categorize and the assertion of fluidity were not as contradictory as they might at first seem: it was their attempt to expand the gender binary they had inherited into a spectrum, using the categories to notch themselves in along the way, in a manner they believed best fitted how they felt. And the very decision to release themselves from the prescribed masculinity or femininity of their birth (along with their presumed heterosexuality) gave them common cause. As Sean put it to me, explaining the difference between *queer* and *gay*: "*Queer* is our culture. It's who we are. *Gay* simply describes the kind of sex we have. What we do."

In my generation *homosexuality* was what we did and *gay* was who we were. It seemed to me that, for Sean's genderqueer generation, *they* was the new *gay*. For me, coming out as gay in the 1980s was not just about acknowledging my sexuality and being true to myself: it was also about identifying with a subculture—political and social—and setting myself apart, with some defiance, from the mainstream. Perhaps Sean was doing the same, with the male name and the grammar-warping pronouns?

"When I came out as a lesbian at age fifteen, my parents were completely chill," Sean told me. "But when I came out as genderqueer the next year, they said, 'No way can we do that.'"

Sean was Ann Arbor blue blood, the child of an illustrious professor and a medical doctor. Upon receiving a letter from their daughter informing them of the name and gender change, Sean's parents called a meeting: "They said to me, 'You're Jewish, and Sean is an Irish name! You're feminine and Sean is a male name! Impossible!'" Now, a year later, "They still keep calling me by my legal name, and use *she*. In their minds, it's just too difficult to change. I'm, like, 'If you try for two months it'll be difficult, and then you'll get it, okay?'"

"I WAS A NERD AND A DORK, obsessed with good grades," Sean told me, "very isolated socially when I started freshman year at Community"—Ann Arbor's magnet public high school. This was until a cool kid in

Sean's homeroom started paying attention. The kid was known as Max and everyone used *he* pronouns for him, the teachers included: he was a rock musician who dressed and groomed in a completely male way although he had not yet started taking hormones.

"You're a sasquatch!" Max said to Sean, and adopted them.

The sasquatch was a half-human beast from Native American mythology, otherwise known as Bigfoot. It had the resonance of something unformed and was Max's term "for a queer person who wasn't yet out," Sean told me later, with a laugh: "Max said I had the potential," and invited his new friend to the school's Queer Straight Alliance. Community High, like other progressive schools, had changed the name of its LGBT affinity club from Gay Straight Alliance (or GSA), to Queer Straight Alliance. GSAs had been around since the 1980s, overseen by faculty advisers, to combat homophobic bullying; by 2018 there were thousands of these in schools across the country.[12] They provided space for queer students and a way for kids to come out, too: you could go in, quite safely, as a "straight ally."

At the very first QSA party Sean attended, a sleepover in the basement of an older girl's house, the kids were playing "ten fingers", one of those teenage games that forces you into thrilling and uncomfortable confession. When the question was "Have you ever had sex before?" Sean lifted a finger without even realizing it, "and everyone looked at me, like, 'Whoo, the sasquatch!'" Sean recounted an incident with a girl when they were much younger, and said they were bi.

"Oh come on," one of the older girls said. "We've seen that all before, lesbians who say they are bi because they're too embarrassed to admit it." The others agreed, and "that pissed me off," Sean said, "because I knew I was attracted to men." What followed was "a hot minute of confusion"—actually, a good six months—when Sean agonized over whether they were really bi at all, or just saying so to gain social currency in this new group of cool people who seemed to want to befriend them. "In the end I did a cost-benefit analysis of coming out as a straight ally, as bi, or as a lesbian, and I thought, You know what, I'm just queer. So that's what I said I was. And that's what I became."

Then Sean started dating Charlotte, who had just come out as trans. "Charlotte was the first person you saw and heard," Sean recalled. "*Booming* voice. *Towering* over everyone—she was her full six feet already—with long dark hair. You couldn't miss her. She said whatever came into mind. I couldn't believe some of the things that came out of her mouth. 'Use your edit button!' This continued to be a tension in our relationship." But it is what compelled Sean, too: "She was so radical."

One day, hanging out at Max's house, Sean and Charlotte got irritated with the way "Max was just playing the same five notes on the piano, over and over again. We started cuddling, almost out of boredom." Within a week, Sean was hanging out at Charlotte's place and they began dating. It was Sean's first relationship.

CHARLOTTE WAS ASSIGNED MALE AT BIRTH. The first time she heard the word *transsexual* was on National Public Radio, she told me, when she was about ten: "These people are terrible," her mother had said, but Charlotte thought: "Wow! I'm not alone!" This was around 2005, and Charlotte was already online. She found Laura's Playground, a "transgender resources" website, and through its chat function, befriended a girl in Australia. Then, on an MMO (massively multiplayer online) game called *Guild Wars*, Charlotte decided on a whim to take on a female avatar: a fire-breathing sorceress. She teamed up with a warrior queen: they protected each other in the game, and became close in a private room, where they chatted for hours. The warrior queen turned out to be a German woman going blind—and Charlotte confided in her that she was assigned male at birth but felt herself to be a girl. This was the first time she had told anyone. By the time she was sixteen—in the fall of 2010—she had decided to come out. She came to school in female clothing and gave her teachers her new name and pronouns.

"That was that," Charlotte told me, when we met earlier in the day of the Queer Prom, drinking tea out of oversize mugs in an Ann Arbor café. The *Frozen* song really was the season's teen anthem: "Coming out was, oh my God, just … *letting go*," Charlotte said. "I was dealing with so much other stuff in my life, my messed-up family—sorting out my little brother's life." Charlotte had heard enough other stories about how hard it was to come out, but for her, "It took stuff off my plate and, honestly, that made life easier for me."

Like Sean, Charlotte was Jewish, but came from a different background. Her parents had split when she was very young; her father was largely absent, and she and her brother lived with a difficult mother and stepfather. Charlotte left home at sixteen and moved in with a relative; on her father's insurance, she managed to get cover for hormone treatment by saying she had an endocrine disorder. Three years later she still had an Adam's apple and facial hair but she now had curves ("my hips hurt so bad, the bones are growing way later in life than they should be") and breasts. "It's not like, 'My boobs! I love my boobs!' It's more, like, hormones make me just feel more normal."

Still, the gap remained between how Charlotte felt and how she looked. She described the dysphoria of puberty—when her body began sprouting hair and her voice started dropping—with the fluency of someone who has long used words to bridge this gap: to explain herself to professionals or family members or the world at large. "As a kid, I knew *exactly* who I was," she told me. "But I was scared to come out. So it was like I had a different person living inside my head. My thought process and my doing process separated into different people. My physical body didn't follow what my brain wanted." As her body mutated from the androgyny of childhood into masculinity, "it was like you're in a space ship hitting the controls trying to do stuff, but it [the space ship, the body] won't obey. That person in my brain aged, had a personality, while that person in my body developed upon a totally different route. It was emotionally traumatizing just being in my own body, because it couldn't look like the person in my head."

IF CHARLOTTE USED Laura's Playground and *Guild Wars* to understand her gender identity, then Sean's online coach was Tumblr, the favored blogging platform for alternative kids, and a touchstone of queer youth culture: on Tumblr, kids could try on different styles and identities with text and image that were easy to curate online, before putting these out into the world, as Nadav had done growing up in Israel.

Sean's new name came to them "suddenly one night, and it felt just right." They told Charlotte, who "switched immediately. I was so impressed." Sean then started using the name and trying out both *he* and *they* pronouns, online and at Riot Youth for a good few months, before writing that letter to their parents.

"I hated my body," Sean told me. "I really *hated* it. And now I had a word for what I was feeling: *dysphoria*." Sean dealt with this feeling by binding "with Ace bandages, something that was incredibly uncomfortable, dangerous, too." The dysphoric feelings fluctuated, and on days when the feelings were not there Sean let their breasts hang free, as they were when I met them, on the day of the Queer Prom.

When we spoke several years later, Sean linked their dysphoria and binding directly to depression, and a feeling of "powerlessness" around being female during adolescence. This was connected, they told me, to repeated experiences of sexual harassment on the streets of Ann Arbor: they had attracted an undue amount of lecherous attention from older men as a result of their looks. Sean wanted to make sure that I understood that this had been their own personal experience, and that "patriarchy" was by no means the cause of most transgender people's dysphoria.

In high school, Sean came to think of themselves as "trans non-binary": they were dating Charlotte and becoming part of a subculture that valorized both the authenticity and struggles of transgender people. But although they did not feel comfortable as a woman, they also did not feel strongly enough about being a man to undergo medical transition. If the go-around at the beginning of each Riot Youth meeting introduced Sean to the *they/them/theirs* pronoun possibility, then Tumblr gave them the category of genderqueer, and an identity.[13]

With this new identity, Sean emerged from the shy-girl shell. They joined GayRilla, Riot Youth's theater program that went into schools to do consciousness-raising and advocacy, and they became involved in the group's most ambitious project: a "climate survey" of schools in southeast Michigan.

THE MONDAY AFTER QUEER PROM, I accompanied Sean to a climate survey meeting with the Gay Straight Alliance at the Detroit School of Arts. Detroit was only forty miles away, but these kids came from a very different place to their white college-town guests. The Detroit kids, almost all African American, used a different language—they rejected the word *queer,* which they saw as a suburban indulgence—and they were only just beginning to talk about their sexual orientations and gender identities. One girl came out dramatically during the meeting, and for a while the proceedings veered into affirming her and helping her figure out how to deal with teachers and parents. Sean handled it with aplomb.

I stayed on in Detroit after the meeting, to visit the Ruth Ellis Center, a social services agency and shelter for LGBT youth. Like the Neutral Zone, Riot Youth's home in Ann Arbor, the center was also housed in a repurposed industrial space. But its context could not have been more different, in the postapocalyptic wasteland of Highland Park, next to the derelict Ford plant. It was close to Palmer Park, Detroit's prime cruising area and hangout for black gay and trans folk. At least nine trans or gender non-conforming people had been murdered in Detroit between 2011 and 2018; all were last seen in Palmer Park, where many of the young people who accessed the Ruth Ellis services earned their livings—and paid for the hormones they bought on the street—through sex work. Statistics are hard to verify, but studies estimate that anywhere between 20 percent and 40 percent of the U.S.'s homeless youth were LGBT in the 2010s[14], and in an extensive 2015 survey of transgender people, a third reported having experienced homelessness at some point in their lives, and 39 percent said they had attempted suicide.[15] These dire outcomes were connected, of course, to another statistic: 50 percent had experienced some form of family rejection.

Mondays were Drop-In Night at Ruth Ellis, and while most of those dropping in were letting it go in a voguing session in the big communal space to the back, I sat in on a trans youth discussion group in the meeting room. After I introduced myself and spoke a little about my research in Ann Arbor, the six people gathered there looked at me as if I were visiting from another planet. "That's a different country," the irrepressible group leader, a twenty-one-year-old autodidact named Emani Love said. "Did you bring your passport?" Everybody laughed.

Jay was the only white kid (and the only transguy) in the room, a runaway from foster care in North Carolina. He had, quite unusually, found himself in a well-managed hormone replacement program thanks to a disability grant the center had helped him secure. But he could not easily take the next step into gainful employment: a legal name and gendermarker change alone—the prerequisite for new documents—cost four hundred dollars. He lived off his disability grant and occasional sex work, which he advertised online.

"If a person like me wants surgery, I'm just not going to get it," said Emani Love. This had led her to a certain level of self-acceptance: "My body is as it is."

A kid who identified as trans but was dressed—for the street—in male attire, agreed. "We work with what we got. *But we know who we are.*" This last point was key. Even if they did not have the support of their families the way Liam did, or access to medicine the way Charlotte did, or he freedom to explore the way Sean did, they had a very clear understanding of what gender meant: they could slot themselves into the gender and sexuality matrix as well as any of the kids over in Ann Arbor, even if they sometimes used different words.

Like many of the Riot Youth kids, Emani had known about herself since childhood. Like Liam and Charlotte and Sean, she also initially struggled with a parent—a single mother, an amputee on a disability grant—who eventually came around to accepting her. But unlike the Ann Arbor kids, she had no support when she plunged into crisis during the gender dysphoria that was activated by puberty: in her case, the dropping of her voice, which meant that she could no longer sing with the girls in the church choir.

She left school and had "four lost years," until she found the Ruth Ellis Center.

EVEN BEFORE SEAN wrote that trans coming-out letter, family life was fraught. Sean's father and younger brother were in constant conflict—"There was so much shouting in the house," Sean told me, "and I fought with my father, too, over wanting more autonomy. And also over politics. He just thought capitalism was the best system on earth, and nothing else could deliver."

After the name and gender change, family relations deteriorated even further. Just after Sean's eighteenth birthday, there was a row about coming home late. Sean stormed out of the house and moved in with Charlotte, who had just found a place with a friend in an apartment complex on the edge of town, a bus-ride away from Community, where Sean was still in final year.

The couple was living here when I first met them a few months later, the weekend of Queer Prom. Sean had just won a full scholarship to a liberal arts college in Massachusetts, and their parents were pushing them to take it up, in no small part because they did not like Charlotte's influence and wanted Sean to be exposed to a bigger world. But Sean was determined to stay in Ann Arbor and study photography at the local community college.

Sean had been "very depressed" in the period prior to taking on the new name and identity, they told me: "There were months on end when I did not sleep at all." Becoming Sean and shedding the female gender was a "huge relief": "All these expectations that were embodied in my female name just disappeared, about femininity, about being a superachiever. I was my own person, at last. I could make myself."

"WE HAD BEEN hugely impressed by the way Sean seemed to open up socially after coming out as gay and joining Riot Youth," Sean's mother, Elizabeth told me, when we met one afternoon in her office on the University of Michigan campus. "It went so far as chopping her hair off and dying it a bright color, almost as a way of forcing herself to be extroverted." Elizabeth also appreciated the way Sean became a Riot Youth leader. "But what shocked us was her coming out as trans" a year or so later. "It was a bolt from the blue. It made no sense to us."

Elizabeth was a renowned feminist scholar, and looked the part: nononsense bangs and granny glasses; a simple sweater and unfashionably pleated slacks. She wanted to make it clear that she was by no means critical of transgender identity: "It's reactionary to oppose trans identity on principle. People have to find themselves." But she was "deeply confused" by her own child: "In so far as Sean's identity amounts to a repudiation of gender norms and the identification with a community that similarly rejects that whole system of categorization, I can grasp that. But I think what Sean means by being 'trans' or 'queer' goes beyond that and I just don't know how to understand it."

Elizabeth remembered that Sean's first coming out—as a lesbian—was appropriately lighthearted: "She literally hid behind the closet in our bedroom, and burst out! It was funny, because it was not as if she needed to be closeted with us. 'Fine! Okay! Good to know!'" It was actually "something of a relief " given the perils of teen heterosexuality: "If you think about it, a lesbian identity is way safer. No pregnancy. No getting drunk at parties and then some creepozoid date-rapes you. Ugh! Gross! I was relieved she wouldn't be exposed to that and—even more important, this comes from my feminism—I think a big danger of heterosexual adolescent girls is that they feel their identity has to be attached to some guy. I didn't want Sean to have any of those self-esteem problems."

But when Sean came out as trans it was in an entirely different way: "that long letter, laying down the law: the name-change, the pronouns." In our conversation nearly three years later Elizabeth had mastered the name but was still struggling with the pronouns. This signaled a disquiet about Sean's new identity beyond grammatical awkwardness, in that Elizabeth still could not understand it. "Sean always liked girly-girl things when she was little. She revels in her female body—I love that about her—and she had never expressed any interest in masculinity before this." I said to Elizabeth that her recollection of Sean's relationship to their female body was starkly at odds with Sean's own account of dysphoria: Did she remember any of the experiences Sean had told me about, around inappropriate sexual attention?

It turned out that Elizabeth did, vividly: when Sean served ice cream behind a glass storefront downtown "men would approach, doing creepy things, like taking a sticky note and putting a number on it on the window. To a fourteen-year-old! One guy came to the window and started licking it when she was making a waffle cone." Sean was indeed subject to "an unusually large number of predatory men at a young age ... Not every woman has the same experience of female embodiment, at such a young age, as Sean did." Still, if this was the problem, Elizabeth was not sure if evacuating womanhood was the answer.

Elizabeth understood the politics of Sean's identity, but she worried it was just that: an enactment, a political or social gesture, or a form of covering up, rather than something deeply felt. Sean's retort was the "Born This Way" argument, Lady Gaga's 2011 refrain that had become something of an anthem for queer American youth. I said to Elizabeth that I understood this as a kid warning parents to back off: "Don't try and change me." I had used the same gambit with my parents when I came out as gay at age eighteen, although I had by no means been sure of my argument. But to Elizabeth, who understood gender as a construct, this made no sense at all. It seemed to her that, if anything, her child's acquisition of a genderqueer identity was precisely the opposite: "Sean found a community of people where she fit in, and that drove an identity transformation. In my view, that's perfectly legitimate. *Why not?*"

IN NOVEMBER 2014, six months after I had first met Sean and Charlotte, I took them to dinner at their favorite Chinese restaurant on South Main in Ann Arbor, and while we were talking about activism they had a fight, one which I sensed was familiar.

"You get to a point where you stop saying 'screw you' to the world," Charlotte said. "I can either go around and be radical and queer, or I can just be any other girl and fit into the culture. I'm questioning which is the true self-direction."

"My core identity is being queer," Sean said quietly but firmly.

"There are a lot of people in the trans community who aren't really transsexual," Charlotte responded, using the third person but taking a clear swipe at her partner, "and for them, it's like, 'Let's be angry, hit the streets, cause an uproar.' But for others"—the true transsexuals such as herself—"it's a safety thing. They don't necessarily want to bring things majorly into the light. They just want to survive. I'm realizing I'm kind of in that old culture rather than the new."

"I'm the opposite," Sean said.

"That's because you are not a transsexual," Charlotte snapped, and then turned to me: "Sean is a big 'Go out and change the world person.' A lot of older transsexuals are rather putting their energy into taking care of people in their community."

Charlotte was making a point about the difference between herself and Sean. Charlotte called herself a transsexual because she had modified her body permanently with hormones—although not, yet, with any surgery. Sean, on the other hand, had not undergone any form of medical intervention and Charlotte was saying this gave her partner a lot more choice in the world.

The couple had a nifty and somewhat derisive word for people attracted to the subculture because it was cool or rebellious: *trans-trenders*. In my own days at an American college, three decades previously, the trans-trender equivalents were the LUGs—lesbians until graduation. They caught flak from the hard-core dykes, but when I looked at them now, my friends, some married to men and with kids, it seemed to me that, rather than having abandoned their undergraduate experimentation they had transported these experiences into their professional lives, their relationships, and their child-rearing. Following the same logic, I wondered: If kids like Sean did turn out to be trans-trenders, was it such a bad thing?

After leaving Ann Arbor, I went west to find out.

ROSE

Rose*—Riot Youth alum, chemist, Oakland, mid-twenties. Pronouns: she/her/hers.

Janie*—Rose's partner, law student, mid-twenties. Pronouns: she/ her/ hers.

Fiona*—Rose's subsequent partner and wife, editor in publishing industry, mid-twenties. Pronouns: she/her/hers.

***Pseudonyms**

Rose was a Riot Youth alum a few years older than Sean and Liam. When I first met her, in November 2014, she was living in the Bay Area, in a cute bungalow in Oakland with her partner, Janie. They had met as undergraduates at Reed College in Oregon; Rose now worked in the petrochemical industry, and Janie was a law student. Rose had a dry and gallant charm; she was slim, boyish, and dark, and liked to "strut and play tough like any butch," she told me. For a few years she had lived as a man named Fynn, and she still had a deep male voice and some facial hair, a consequence of her seven months on testosterone when she was nineteen, in her freshman year at Reed.

Always a tomboy, Rose came out early as gay, at age twelve. Her adolescence was not easy: not only was she boyish, but she was poor and biracial in white Ann Arbor; her mother is an Asian immigrant. She was bullied at Huron, a large public school, usually by other girls: she was once beaten up and pushed down the stairs. "I didn't feel comfortable reporting it," she told me. "Then everyone would know I was gay." Unlike at the more progressive Community, where Sean and Charlotte went, the teachers were of no help: "There were these two older women who were not out, even though they had pictures of the same damn children on their screen savers! But they would not greet each other in the hallways, and they avoided the gay kids like the plague. *Tragic*."

Rose found a notice for Riot Youth "in a forgotten little corner" in seventh grade. "I was terrified," she said, "but I went. I don't think anyone noticed me for weeks." The group was life-changing, primarily "because I was exposed to older people with degrees, money, connections all over the world. I said, 'I want that!' If it wasn't for Riot Youth, I don't think I'd have gone to college."

Rose was only four years ahead of Sean, but the notions of genderqueer and the non-binary pronouns were still newly hatched when she joined the group in 2008. And so she always felt a little scrambled in the pronoun-go-around: "I'd say 'I use masculine *she* pronouns,' or 'I use feminine *he* pronouns,' and everyone laughed at me, because it made no sense."

Rose evoked Liam, whom she knew I had been interviewing, to make a point: "Liam's a *dude*! God, he's *such* a dude. He's a teenage boy, that's what he is. I was different. I never had a strong conviction that it was just 'man' or just 'woman' going for me." Eventually she made a decision "which seemed the easiest one available at the time":

she changed her name to Fynn and her pronoun to "the good old understandable masculine *he*."

Looking back, Rose felt she was pushed into the change by a forceful older trans guy at Riot Youth whom she was dating, and who had derided her indecision. She did not go unwillingly, though; she wanted to rise above her family's social station, and she sensed masculinity would help. "Being a man in our culture is having agency, being aggressive and strong rather than bitchy and scheming. I'm not saying transmen don't exist—of course they exist, and for some people transition is obviously right—but for many young women like myself, young women in adolescence at a time of great vulnerability, it's attractive to become a guy." Particularly if you were a tomboy teenager, and the other option was to become "a big fat predatory leather-jacketed dyke-on-a-bike, that's how we saw them. Who wants to be *that*?" When she became Fynn she noticed the difference immediately: "The way people looked me in the eye, a level of respect and politeness that was never present when people thought I was a woman, or saw me as a tomboy."

The affirmation only increased when she arrived at the famously progressive Reed. "I was wanting some sort of validation for who I was. I wasn't getting it from my family," she said. "I wasn't getting it as a working-class masculine woman of color. I wasn't getting that support. Then I saw this community of people who were *very* supported, and I thought, 'I want that! I want to be celebrated. I want people to like me.'"

And they did: transguys were the hottest ticket on campus. "There were girls all *over* me! Oh my God, the sexual capital! I could have had sex with a different girl every night of the week. It went to my head. After being a young woman who was invalidated, unappreciated, suddenly I was the big man on campus. When you're nineteen that's pretty much all that matters."

Rose met Janie during freshman orientation, and they started dating soon after. They came up with a name for all the other trans-groupies buzzing around Rose: "the Annas," because more than one of them bore that name. "I wasn't threatening, because I wasn't a real man," is how Rose described her appeal to the Annas. "But still, I was man enough to be sexually attractive."

Janie had started off as an Anna, too, and she understood it retrospectively as a portal into accepting herself as gay, she told me. She had agonized over her sexual orientation in high school and now, when she started dating "Flynn," "I was thinking, 'Oh, this is great! Because this is a *dude*! I'm with a dude! My sexuality is safe."

The couple was "very hetero for a while," Janie said.

"But gay!" Rose chipped in.

"Well, we had sex that was culturally gay. And we dated in a way that was culturally gay. She slept on my floor for three weeks before we slept together, and then she slept in my bed without sex for another week and a half."

Where exactly was the hetero part, then? "In how others saw us," Rose said.

"And in how *I* saw us, too. I was very insistent on, 'I'm a straight woman, she's a man.'"

"It was funny for us," Rose said. "'Giggle giggle. We're straight.'" "'Giggle giggle. We pass.'"

Rose found the name of a prominent transgender counselor in Portland. After two sessions, the counselor gave her the referral that enabled her to start a hormone replacement regime through Reed's student health services. But every time she shot up she plummeted into anxiety. On injection days she had fainting fits and would cry all morning. "I was saying, 'I don't think this is right for me,'" she recalled.

Janie could laugh now about how Rose changed on testosterone: "She wanted sex *all the time*. I was used to telling straight men to back off, but it was different here. Rose was someone I really wanted to be with." As we sat together in their yard, Rose's pit bull Puck snuffling around us, Janie turned to her partner: "I still wanted sex with you, *just not seven times a day*!"

"You said I was different," Rose responded.

"You smelled different. Your temper was different. The hair-trigger was very intense. I had an abusive stepfather, and it felt really scary, but I felt I couldn't say anything about it. I'm not saying T makes people abusive, of course it doesn't, but it makes them irritable, and hungry, and our culture doesn't talk about any of this. There are a lot of women, young women, vulnerable queer women, who are entering these relationships with people who are hormonally transitioning, and no one is talking about it."

Things came to a head over a women's group that Janie decided to set up on campus, where the door policy was that you had to identify as a woman.

"I want to come," Rose had said.

Janie told Rose she could not have her cake and eat it: "This is women's space. This door is closed. I experience patriarchy in this relationship, and I need a space to talk about it."

"You're not acknowledging my female experience!" Rose would cry. "You're a *man*!" Janie would yell back. "I'm fine with that. But you don't get to come into a women's space. If you're a man, *be* a man."

This was the turning point for Rose: "I needed those women's communities and spaces. I wanted to be part of them. I had to make a choice." Still, it was not easy. She stopped the testosterone for a few months, started it again, and stopped it, finally, seven months later. At this point she chose a new female name, different from her legal one:

"I wasn't the girl that my parents had raised. I was someone different now, and I needed to acknowledge it."

To help Rose understand herself, Janie gave her *Stone Butch Blues*, Leslie Feinberg's iconic 1993 autobiographical novel.[16] Reading Feinberg, Rose told me, "helped me realize that all those things I loved about being a man—including loving *women*—could be part of stone-butch lesbian culture."

But now, four years later, Rose found herself somewhat at sea as a young stone butch in the Bay Area. In her own age group, there were "almost no other butch lesbians, since everyone is now either trans or genderqueer," and among these peers she was uncomfortable sharing her own story of transition for fear of being labeled transphobic: so worried was she about this reaction that she asked me to use pseudonyms when writing about her.

In her first weeks in the Bay Area, Rose came across a notice for a butch lesbian personal support group and went along, "but I really struggled with it. I was the youngest person in the room by twenty years. And when I said something about our trans sisters, they just didn't get it at all. They looked surprised, a little hostile. 'How can you call yourself a lesbian if you have a penis?' I really respect my elders, but I can't get with some of their rhetoric. It's just so wrong."

Rose did worry that girls starting testosterone or having surgery in adolescence "don't necessarily have the mental capacity to understand the misogyny in our culture that might be informing their decisions. *I* certainly didn't." But in the retelling of her story there was only one person toward whom she expressed anger: that gender counselor who referred her for hormone treatment after only two consultations. "I was hugely excited, but when I look back at it now, I think it was *nuts*! I was only nineteen years old! Only two sessions, before sending me on this irrevocable path?"

Still, Rose rejected point-blank the word *regretter*, increasingly used to describe people like her, who had moved one way and then back across the gender border. She actually loved her deep voice and the prickles of hair on her upper lip and chin: although she was happy being a woman, this made her appearance more congruent with how she felt inside. "I had to go through being a man to understand that I am a woman," she said to me. "You know, if I'd been born male, it would have been the same: I'd have had to spend some time as a woman. That's just how it is with me: I don't fit into the boxes."

The fact that Rose chose a new female name rather than going back to her birth name was an indication of how she was constructing femininity to her own specifications rather than accepting it as preordained. Here she was, a young person of the twenty-first century, fashioning a gender for herself in a way that felt right to her, with the tools available to her—now testosterone, now feminism—at different points in life. Her gender changed in high school because of what she learned through Riot Youth, and then changed again at college because she fell in love with Janie and discovered feminism.

In this way, it seemed to me, she was like most of us, in that she was molded in her youth by the shape of her context. If she had grown up in rural Appalachia, where her father came from, she might not have found the transgender category; if she had fallen in love with someone else on campus and found a different kind of feminism, she might have carried on with the testosterone. This might be a measure of the fluidity of the United States in the second decade of the twenty-first century—the proliferation of options facing young Americans—but it was also a function of human development: we are all formed by the paths we chose to take or ignore, driven by the callow passions of youth, or inertia, before we know better.

UNLIKE ROSE'S NARRATIVE, the "regretter" stories making it into the public domain toward the end of the decade were usually desolate or angry. On a 2017 BBC program a white British woman named Lou recounts how she was told: "'If you don't transition you will self-harm and kill yourself.' I became convinced my options were transition or die."[17] Lou's female body had seemed grotesque to her, when it was actually a normal girl's body: "Now, having transitioned, I will always have a female body that is freakish. I will always have a flat chest and a beard and there's nothing I can do about that."

As the decade progressed, media coverage of transgender youth moved from being celebratory to cautionary, as in a 2018 *Atlantic* cover story: "When Children Say They're Trans … The choices are fraught—and there are no easy answers."[18] A prominent transgender therapist, Erica Anderson, told *The Washington Post* the same year that she worried "a fair number of kids are getting into it because it's trendy … [and] in our haste to be supportive, we're missing that element. Kids are all about being accepted by their peers. It's trendy for professionals, too."[19] Anderson told me that she was "deeply concerned" about "a future generation, some of which are going to say it was necessary, but others who will be angry, and critical of health professionals who didn't properly vet these decisions."

But others felt that the figure of the de-transitioner was being used to discredit the entire notion of transgender identity, and to put the brakes on a cultural and medical shift that was preventing terrible distress and saving lives. The "regretter discourse" serves "as proxy, in some cases, for arguments against early transition," writes Tey Meadow in *Trans Kids*, although the data showed that "only a tiny percentage of individuals who make full social and medical transitions regret those decisions."[20]

At the core of this debate was evidence suggesting that most gender non-conforming children "desist" in their desire to be the other gender and grow up instead to be gay or lesbian.[21] Critics of early transition argued forcefully that intervention would foreclose this natural development and that stopping it was even a form of homophobia, in that it preferred to turn "sissy boys" into girls rather than let them flourish as gender non-conforming gay boys. But others argued that most gender non-conforming children simply matured into gender non-conforming adults: only the "persistent, insistent, consistent" ones actually sought out transition. Data from the United Kingdom seemed to back this up.[22]

One trend was causing particular concern: the dramatic increase of teenage girls, like Rose, seeking transition.[23] From 2010 and 2017 the U.K. recorded an increase of such referrals from 40 to *1,400* per annum. In the same period, referrals of boys seeking to transition to femininity increased from 56 to 616 per annum. There was a similar disproportion at the U.S.'s largest gender-care program for youth, at the Children's Hospital of Los Angeles.[24]

The program's director, Johanna Olson-Kennedy, told me she understood this at least in part as a consequence of the politics of the era: "There's a political movement about the gender binary and it's hardly surprising that it is being led by people assigned female at birth. They're reacting to misogyny, patriarchy, privilege. Their attitude is, 'Look, this binary you old people got used to, it's not useful to us.'" These were the high-water years, too, of course, of the #MeToo movement: young Americans assigned female at birth—whether or not they identified as male—were conscious as never before of the gender bias in their society.

But a more plausible reason for the disproportion, Olson-Kennedy believed, was that society was so much more accepting of tomboys than of girly boys: "The trans girls are out there. We're just seeing less of them come forward, because it's so taboo." The Riot Youth kids agreed. One—an effeminate boy himself—put it bluntly: "When girls are lesbians or become trans, they're taking a step up to a guy, but when guys are femme-y, it's almost like they're taking a step down to a girl, in the social marking."

An increasing number of parents—particularly mothers, who were the beneficiaries of the women's movement themselves—also understood the phenomenon as a reaction to social gender bias. But some, perhaps like Sean's mother, Elizabeth, saw their daughters' desire to transition as a false solution, in that it came from a wish to opt out of fragile femininity.

I was introduced, through mutual friends, to another mother, who had taken a much stronger stand over her transitioning child than Elizabeth had over Sean. She was a high-powered lawyer I will call Dee: "Imagine just starting out sexually as a girl today," she said to me. "Take one look at porn, and what it does to women, and wouldn't you want to get the hell out of there? It's hard to be a young woman today—I'd be tempted to opt out of it myself if I were my daughter's age. I hoped that by being a successful professional, I'd modeled the fact that women can in fact succeed. But I can't fight the culture all by myself."

As early transition became an increasing possibility through the second decade of the twenty-first century, the transgender movement itself became, in no small part, a movement of parents advocating for their children. It was parents who sought solutions: taking their kids to gender clinics, battling with schools, fiercely advocating for their kids' happiness, safety, and rights. I met many mama-bears like Liam's mother Beth: they were more at the barricades than their children; the kids themselves often preferred to go "stealth" and just get on with life in their newly affirmed genders. But as the decade progressed, a counter-movement grew, of mothers like Dee, who worried deeply about the "transtrender" possibility, and who were convinced their children were making decisions they would later regret.

Dee's nineteen-year-old, who now called himself Todd, had announced "out of the blue" that he was transgender, and that he was on hormones prescribed by Planned Parenthood dispensed after only one consultation, Dee said. Todd struggled with depression, and Dee was convinced that he had been seduced online by the redemptive narratives of transgender men. She saw Todd as a player in "a reverse *Handmaid's Tale*," a dystopian science-fiction plot come real, in which a whole generation of young women were being duped into unsexing themselves and "boxing themselves in, by this hideous uniform." She thought it was a terrible mistake and was determined to fight it.

Dee blamed the health industry, which she believed had "caved in" to this latest "political fad" and was profiteering off it. She introduced me to a website called 4thWaveNow (after trans-skeptical "fourth-wave" feminism), set up in early 2015. Here she had found dozens of other mothers across the political spectrum with uncannily similar stories about their daughters and who were in similar despair. The mothers of 4thWaveNow felt their daughters were guinea pigs in an unethical social experiment, and the victims of online "social contagion" to which such girls were particularly susceptible: a latter-day anorexia, or hysteria.[25] There was even, now, a diagnosis for such a condition, coined by the Brown University psychologist Lisa Littman in a controversial 2017 paper: "Rapid Onset Gender Dysphoria."[26]

Littman's research suggested—as did Finnish research referred to on 4thWaveNow—that a large proportion of those girls who transitioned were seeking relief from other mental health problems.[27] The psychoanalyst Lisa Marchiano claimed in 2017 she had consulted "hundreds" of families with such daughters.[28] Marchiano was concerned, she wrote, that an "affirming" identity-based model of therapeutic care had replaced a "mental health model which asked questions about underlying causes."[29] She echoed a more tempered voice, the child psychologist Avgi Saketopoulou, who asked, in a prescient 2011 essay: "How are we to know when gender acts as proxy for psychopathology?"[30] Saketopoulou identified a gap in the current culture between the old way—which pathologized transgender identities—and the new wave of political transgender activism, which "fails to inquire about gender's psychic meanings."

Parents like Dee were anxious that their children ran the risk of falling into that gap. One mother, interviewed for *The New Yorker* in 2012, spoke of "tides of history that wash in, and when they wash out they leave some people stranded. The drug culture of the sixties was like that, and the sexual culture of the eighties, with AIDS. I think [the transgender explosion] could be the next wave like that, and I don't want my daughter to be a casualty."[31]

In the American gender culture of these years, the image of the stranded child became a lightning rod for so many of society's anxieties about the new phenomenon of early transition: for feminists who believed it compromised womanhood or represented a capitulation to patriarchy; for the increasing number of Christians who felt that "gender ideology" was messing with God's plan; for clinicians, understandably daunted by the task of having to make irrevocable recommendations about a child's gender identity; for parents, deeply concerned about their children's mental and physical health.

And, of course, for young people themselves, trying to plot a path into adulthood in a world filled with new possibilities, but fraught with so many dangers, too.

DESPITE—OR MAY BE EVEN because of—her own experiences, Rose told me as we ate pomegranate seeds in the afternoon sun of her Oakland garden, she believed in "encouraging experimentation, as long as it's not blind." She lived her adult life on the Pacific Rim, after all, that edge of American experimentation—from psychedelic drugs to gay liberation to the Internet; in a generational ecosystem, too, of the trans and queer people with whom she had come of age. Still, she understood her gender as elective: "I choose to be a woman. I could choose to be a man tomorrow and no one would be surprised. It's my choice."

In the "self-making" ethos of the current moment, Rose toyed with going on testosterone for a while and was even seriously considering having top surgery, as many stone butches had already done, without becoming men. "I just love taking my shirt off. And there's not a lot of places I can do that, with breasts." She snorted, with playful irony: "In what book is it written that you need to have breasts to be a woman?"

I thought of these comments when watching a video, later, of a presentation by Johanna Olson-Kennedy at a conference on transgender health. Olson-Kennedy spoke about how some of her young clients wanted "no menses" *and* "no mustache": "'I really don't want facial hair, [but] I'm super dysphoric about bleeding.'"[32] The doctor professed to be "so excited" about the possibilities of what was becoming known as "partial transition."

This enraged an anonymous commentator on 4thWaveNow: "It's 2017, and designer endocrine systems are all the rage. Human beings should tinker and tamper with their delicate hormonal balance, because it's what they want right here, right now. Mix and match–why not?"[33]

Was this just bratty consumerism? Or was it an entirely new mode of self-definition, in line with the cultural phenomenon not just of body modification and self-improvement, but also of the opening of a gender binary out into a spectrum, too? The gender therapist Diane Ehrensaft told me in 2018 that the single major shift in her practice was the emergence of young people claiming non-binary identity. There were definitely de-transitioners on the books at San Francisco's Child and Adolescent Gender Center, but she understood these young people to be "strategists" rather than "regretters": "They come and tell us what they think we want to hear, in order to get treatment. Then, when they have the dosage they want, they stop: their voice is just deep enough, their breasts just big enough. They never wanted to cross the binary altogether in the first place; rather, they are finding their place in the new gender mosaic."

As early as 2011, the World Professional Association for Transgender Health (WPATH) had amended its standards of care to include "gender non-conforming people."[34] The law lagged behind, and almost everywhere in the world still required you to be either male or female. In 2018, the only countries that allowed for a third gender legally were Nepal, Bangladesh, and India; Australia and New Zealand; and Denmark. The first American jurisdiction to do so, following a court judgment, was Oregon, in 2016, which started permitting the third-gender option on drivers' licenses. In 2018, New York City changed its laws to allow for an *X* rather than *M* or *F* on birth certificates.

In many ways, the non-binary identity was a retort to the binarism of transgender identity itself. In fact, one of the more compelling critiques of the transgender movement was that—as *The Economist* put it in 2018—"outdated gender stereotypes have come roaring back," now that people were claiming the right to determine their own genders: once you relied on "introspection" rather than "anatomy" to help children determine their genders, you inevitably "fall back on stereotypes: if you're a leader and planner you're a boy; if you're nurturing and a gossip, you're a girl."[35] The magazine offered several examples: Australian teachers were to get children to "explore gender" by listing behavior typical of boys and girls; a U.K. transgender youth organization had a presentation about the gender spectrum with

Barbie on one side and G.I. Joe on the other.[36] Even "The Genderbread Person," a nifty explanatory graphic beloved of gender activists, plotted a "gender expression" axis from "masculine" to "feminine": How was one to define either, without resorting to stereotypes?

If this was a fault, though, surely it lay with society's division of humanity into masculinity and femininity rather than the transgender movement itself. And in this context, the efforts of gender non-conforming people to define themselves outside of it, or to muddle through it, were bracing. An early experimenter, the Spanish writer Paul B. Preciado, described himself as a "gender-hacker" rather than a "gender-dysphoric."[37] And when he came out online in 2012, Stephen Beatty—the oldest child of Warren Beatty and Annette Bening—wittily listed his intersections: "I identify as a transman, a faggy queen, a homosexual, a queer, a nerdfighter, a writer, an artist, and a guy who needs a haircut."[38] He was taking testosterone while "presenting in a femme way": "It's nice to finally be able to have my identity be legible to people."

The assumption of the "self-made man" is that you know—or can find, with a little bit of help—your truest interior self and structure your exterior accordingly. But who really knows their truest self? And what if your truest self is—as it was for Sean and Rose through much of their adolescence—something quite hard to pin down? Gender-fluid identities opened up these possibilities, with their shifting sands, and provided interesting solutions, too.

In Ann Arbor I met an undergraduate named Jay. While Stephen Beatty might have loved being "legible at last," being non-binary gave Jay the very opposite: an *illegibility* that suited them just fine: "I like it that people don't know whether I am male or female, or have to ask me. Because, honestly, I myself don't know what my gender is, and so when people are unsure how to place me, that reflects how I feel inside."

If the journey of transition expressed by traditional transgender identity was teleological, in that you crossed the bridge to a final destination of the other gender, then this new non-binary movement—increasing called "gender-fluid"—was developing the somewhat destabilizing, but perhaps liberating, notion of perpetual transition. The psychoanalyst Virginia Goldner characterized the body-consciousness of this generation as follows: "My body is no longer my destiny. It is now my canvas."[39] In a 2011 essay, Goldner called for an understanding of gender in this context as "a process rather than a thing in itself, a gerund, rather than a noun or adjective, a permanent state of becoming, rather than a finished product."

By the end of the decade an increasing number of transgender theorists were suggesting this definition of transition. In the 2018 edition of her landmark *Transgender History* (originally published in 2008), Susan Stryker defined "the concept of transgender" as "the movement across a socially imposed boundary away from an unchosen starting place, rather than any particular destination or mode of transition."[40]

The self-making person (rather than the self-made man) was an ineluctable feature of human development, and transgender or gendervariant people seemed, increasingly, to be the most visible manifestation of this. "The project of constantly managing, curating, arranging, strategizing, producing legible and desirable gender is one that all humans share," Eric Plemons said to me. What, really, was the difference between the body-enhancing work that cisgender women did, from makeup to gym and dieting to Botox and plastic surgery, and the hormone and surgery regimes that transgender women underwent?

Some took this further, riffing on the startling speculative feminism of Donna Haraway's 1985 "Cyborg Manifesto," which imagined a future consciousness beyond the "antagonistic dualisms" that define us: human-animal, human-machine, black-white, male-female.[41] In the age of cybernetics, of prosthetics and virtual reality, trans folk could be "the first to evolve toward the post-human," speculated Laura Jacobs, a leading transgender psychotherapist.[42] "Our identities will be unlike anything currently conceivable. Gender itself may become infinite."

BY 2019, THE CENTER FOR Transyouth Health and Development at the Children's Hospital of Los Angeles was helping over a thousand youths to transition.[43] But as we looked over the data, the center's director, Johanna Olson-Kennedy, made the point to me that, despite the steep rise in referrals her clinic was getting, the numbers were "still tiny, way smaller than the estimates we have of the number of trans youth in the general population"—over twenty thousand in Los Angeles alone, using the best available estimates. "Even if all our clients came from LA, which they don't, this would mean we're still only seeing one in twenty-six trans kids. What's happening to the other twenty-five?"

Her point was this: The vast majority of transgender youth were not getting care and thus remained at risk. Seen this way, those young people undergoing transition through surgery and hormones were not "guinea pigs" in some grand and unethical social experiment, as claimed by Dee and the anxious mothers on 4thWaveNow. Rather, they were a small band of "pioneers" in a new era of children's rights, in transgender rights, and in health care.

Like all pioneers, they faced high risks. Olson-Kennedy was worried that not enough research was being done to predict how children who transitioned before puberty would deal with intimacy and sexuality as adults. Erica Anderson, the transgender therapist, told me she was deeply concerned that young people were transitioning without having had sexual experience in their born bodies. Other clinicians wrestled with the dilemmas of the infertility that came with early transition: were twelve-year-olds really able to make such decisions about their futures? Medical research suggested a host of side effects to long-term hormone replacement therapy, not least a shortened life span. How did one weigh this against the data suggesting self-harm and suicidal tendencies in people with gender dysphoria, and with a 2015 study that found testosterone "significantly increased trans men's quality of life"?[44]

Call them "guinea pigs" or call them "pioneers": the other young people I met through Riot Youth and elsewhere in the second decade of the twenty-first century were moving themselves, and the culture, into uncharted territory. They were the first generation to undergo early transition: How could there be guarantees of what would happen to them later in life, psychologically and physiologically? The science was fresh and its beneficiaries still young, the oldest only in their late twenties.

What would happen to their bones, and their relationships, as they aged? Would their life expectancy be shorter, and—if this was the cost of living what Liam called his "true self "—would it matter?

GROWING UP

As Liam attended college and then graduate school at the University of Michigan, he assiduously used social media to document his transition; an effort, he said, to increase transvisibility, and to provide vital information to other kids considering the process. He posted YouTube videos of himself injecting testosterone, describing his bodily changes and how was feeling. He was featured on news sites, and in 2015, he became part of a high-profile online campaign advocating for transgender youth. When I wrote to him to congratulate him on his involvement in this campaign he responded that he had found the experience "immensely empowering": he felt as if he was "finally in control" of his life and his story and that, for this reason, he needed "to withdraw as a subject from your current and future publications."

In early 2014, I had published an essay about Liam in *Granta*, with his full approval, and that of his family; he knew, of course, that I was preparing this book. Everyone has the right to tell his own story and, disappointed though I was, I recognized that Liam's decision to withdraw was a consequence of his growing up, his coming into himself. I had met him when he was a tentative teenager, on the cusp of adulthood and physical transition, and he was now a self-assured activist and leader. I also understood his decision as a consequence of his coming into political consciousness, not just as a transgender man but as a person of color—this was a key part of his identity—in the era of Black Lives Matter. A primary tenet of this new generation of activism—for trans people, as well as for people of color—was that it was time for people to tell their own stories, rather than to endure what was often called the "violence" of misrepresentation or appropriation. Although Liam made it clear that he had not felt violated in any way by my *Granta* piece, he would rather his story "come directly from me, from my own voice."

We agreed that for this book I would use the material already published in the *Granta* piece, but nothing else except for this postscript, and that I would continue to use pseudonyms for him and his family. And so even though I followed him online, I lost touch with him.

SEAN BROKE UP with Charlotte in February 2015, four months after I watched that fight in the Chinese restaurant. Things had become "unbearably turbulent," Sean told me. It was the nadir of troubled teen years for both of them, one from which they seemed to have recovered when I spent time together with them—separately, online—two years later.

"We're very good friends now, although we argue like crazy," Sean told me. "We have very divergent views on politics. But now I have a voice, and I can say, 'It's different to yours, get over it!' Charlotte gets infuriated! We have a Jewish sense of argument. She can't say whatever she wants anymore, I'm going to disagree with her."

Charlotte now lived with her new partner, a transgender woman, in Detroit; she had graduated from community college with honors and was applying to social work graduate programs. Sean, too, had finally gone to college and when we connected on Skype in 2017 they were in junior year at a small progressive school outside Boston, majoring in philosophy and sociology, and doing volunteer teaching in a nearby prison.

Sean now wore big round glasses and had hair down to the waist; from their Facebook portfolio I saw that they liked to glam it up a bit, too, with vampy makeup. They had come to agree with their mother, Elizabeth, that "gender *is* a kind of caste system, and within that system I've been designated a woman. There's nothing I can do to escape that, if I'm not going to change my body medically. And so if the world is going to see me as a woman, I'm not going to fight it." But however others might see them, Sean remained very clear: "I am trans, or a-gender. That describes who I am inside. I'm still Sean. I still use *they* and *them*."

From the vantage point of a twenty-two-year-old now doing well at college, Sean could look back with some hindsight. Their experience at Riot Youth was "very important, in terms of giving me a sense of empowerment, community, the ability to change my surroundings. But I'm so glad I'm no longer restricted by the assumption there that the more oppressed identities you have, the closer you are to the truth. I think that led me to assume a trans identity that I might otherwise not have."

Sean now understood their gender dysphoria to be connected to both "mental health issues" and "the misogyny of society": "I didn't like that people gendered me as a woman—I felt a sense of inferiority and powerlessness. Was my dysphoria the result of misogyny, or from something internal? I've struggled for so long to find the answer, and I don't know. Does it matter? However I got here, I'm here."

Perhaps it might have been different had hormones or surgery been involved, but rather than being left "stranded" by the tide, Sean was taken to a new place by it, one they cherished and that defined them.

And one that brought them to Augustine.

AUGUSTINE FIRST SAW Sean on a bus in Ann Arbor, around Christmas 2015. "I was attracted to the red leather jacket," Augustine told me two years later. "Anyone can put on a red leather jacket, but it's typically only the queer people, in this region at least, who would choose to …"

On that bus, Augustine noticed that Sean had Tumblr open on their phone: "I reached out and complimented them on their style, and asked for their Tumblr address." Augustine's hunch was confirmed: both used the *they* pronouns. The two chatted online, and it took several months before they started dating.

Two and a half years later, in the summer of 2018, they were living together in Augustine's ramshackle rental on the west side of town. Augustine worked nights at a bakery and Sean was taking courses at the community college for the summer, so they barely saw each other, but they were happy together. Sean was now "for compassion and empathy," and against the "callout culture" that seemed increasingly to dominate social justice movements. Things had settled with their parents, too, who were thrilled that Sean was doing well at college and who seemed to like Augustine.

Augustine seemed impossible to dislike, I thought, as we hung out through video chat. They were tawny and lanky—six foot four—and calm and gentle in manner, with facial piercings and hair growing out into an Afro. Like Sean, they had left home at eighteen before finishing high school, due to family conflict. They had run away to Ann Arbor and had been supporting themselves ever since; they had been a math whiz at school and were saving up to study engineering.

If Sean found it hard to articulate a relationship with gender, Augustine dissected their own with cool dispassion: "Long before I had appropriate words to talk about it, I had a general, pervasive sense of discomfort when anyone spoke of me as male. I felt sort of embarrassed, as if I were catching them in a lie."

This came from two places. The first was Augustine's mother's "oppressive" idea of what men were for: "To be a good father. To spend your life, give it up in fact, so that the house can keep running. Work, sleep, eat." The second was "this other thing, out there in the culture, which seemed to involve a lot of sex and violence." This dichotomy—the self-sacrificing father, the badass thug—seemed particularly strong in African American culture, Augustine felt, where "hypermasculinity" was a defense against the violence of racism. And so "when Mom or people out there said I was a 'man' I really didn't know what they were talking about. It wasn't me."

Augustine discovered the notion of gender-fluidity through Tumblr and began secretly wearing frilly feminine underwear sent to them by trans friends they met online "to remind myself that I was not male." Then, after leaving home, "I started wearing skirts."

But it was through hair that Augustine came to understand gender, and its intersection with race: "When I do my hair in cornrows, people see me as more masculine and are generally more afraid of me.

I'm black, and six foot four. If someone comes upon me, they'll get surprised and alarmed, or clutch their purse. But when I wear more feminine hairstyles, like yarn braids or extensions, people don't see me as much as a threat. The racism is more subtle."

The very first thing Augustine had told me about childhood was how they were raised with a sense that "people would target me, because here in America, being black and a boy is reason enough to be targeted." They did not consciously evacuate masculinity for this reason, they said. But they did remember, from childhood, "Some public figure saying that young black men were superpredators" (the comment had, in fact, been made by Hillary Clinton in 1996). "I was always unusually tall for my age, towering over everyone, and my emotional response was disgust: 'No, I'm not going to be like that. I'm going to distance myself from that [pervasive image of black masculinity].'"

While Augustine was telling me this, I thought back to their account of their first meeting with Sean, and the red leather jacket as a signifier of its bearer's queerness. "It was therefore safer to talk to them," Augustine had said. "I didn't risk as much by reaching out to them."

Risk what, exactly, I had asked?

"Risk being seen as male, and creating the same fear that I sometimes did when I spoke to people who expected me to be a man."

IN SEAN'S TELLING of the encounter on the bus, they were tapped on the shoulder and—quite sweetly, it seems—hit upon: "I was done with men, by now, after an experience with a crazy guy who had become so abusive, and I didn't want to risk anything by giving my phone number. But I thought, let's see what happens on Tumblr. At least they'll know who I am."

I was struck by the way both Sean and Augustine used the word *risk*. It made me think of something I had just been told by Will Sherry, the director of Spectrum, the LGBTQA student support center at the University of Michigan. "The key word now is *safety*," he said when I asked him what had changed in his work over the past few years. "It has become of primary concern to our clients, and much of our programming revolves around it."

This was the zeitgeist in which Sean and Augustine met, and grew their relationship: the increase of shootings on school and college campuses; a consciousness about the safety of people of color and particularly black men, through the Black Lives Matter movement; a consciousness, about the safety of women through campus harassment cases and later the #MeToo movement. The Riot Youth kids were of a generation that came of age in an era of fear, too: the fear of a rampant white heterosexual masculinity represented by Donald Trump, one that separated migrant children from their parents, that stood in the way of letting transgender children use the bathrooms congruent with their gender identities, that sneered at people who were different or weak, that seemed to care less about the destruction of the planet and what would be left for their children to inherit.

There were elders who felt that young adults like Sean and Augustine were of a "snowflake" generation, and that the coddling culture of identity politics was ill-preparing them for adulthood. They had both, clearly, been at risk during their turbulent adolescences, but both of them seemed to have made it through (as had Liam, Rose, and Charlotte): perhaps, indeed, they had been strengthened by needing to fight, so forcefully, to be themselves. In a previous generation, without the collective carapace of a queer or non-binary subculture (or without the access, in Liam and Charlotte's cases, to medical solutions), they might have shipped out—self-destructed, so many adolescents do—or they might have shaped up: buttoned it all up and become the women and men society wanted them to be.

Would this have helped them, or bound them? Rendered them violated, or violent? Who knows? But the way Sean and Augustine talked when they were living together in the summer of 2018, two and a half years after they met on that bus, gave me a sense of the safety they felt with each other; some shelter in the storm.

I felt happy for them.

IN 2016, ROSE split up with Janie and started a relationship with another of the "Annas" she had first met at Reed: Fiona, who worked in publishing.

The couple returned to Portland, where Rose took a demanding job in the construction industry and spent much of her life on the road: "I'm a man in the field and a woman at home," she laughed. "When I'm in a town in the middle of Idaho, it just seems easier to be this small Asian man than some weird butch dyke with a man's voice." Her colleagues knew the score, and she always warned them to look out for her when she needed to use a restroom, "in case something sketchy happens in there."

But with Fiona and her circle of friends in Portland, "I am a woman, no question."

In early 2017, the two wed, as women—it was legal by now—on the top of Mount Tabor, with twenty-dollar rings from a pawnshop, and many of their friends present; Rose wore a tux, of course. The wedding seemed to have brought her closer to her parents back in Ann Arbor, from whom she had been estranged for several years: "My mom was thrilled. She loves Fiona."

Breast surgery was still something very much on Rose's agenda when we spoke again the following year: she was consulting a specialist, and "doing the finances" on it. Still, she admitted that she often hoped she would "age in womanlike ways," perhaps "become less ambiguous": "It's nice always to be able to change, like a chameleon, blending into this situation or that, but at the same time I do have this desire for consistency between the internal sphere and public sphere. It would be nice if people saw me the way I see myself. I'm hoping I can grow into that as I age."

We were hanging out on Skype, Rose and Fiona in their cozy Portland apartment, me in my Cape Town study. Rose was sprawled out on her chair, in jeans and a collared shirt, while Fiona—slight and studious, with long reddish hair—was curled around a mug of tea.

Rose sighed. "I guess I could dress differently, more femme-y, grow my hair. But that wouldn't be me either. So here I am."

"Yes, here you are," said Fiona. We laughed.

15

THE WORLD'S NEW PINK LINE

"IF I HAD STAYED IN THE PHILIPPINES, I don't think I would have transitioned, because there's space in the culture for gender non-conforming people. But when I came to the U.S. to study in the 1990s, I found only a binary. And because I didn't fit into the male, I chose the female." These words were spoken to me by the writer Meredith Talusan in late 2018. Even in the unflappable Brooklyn café where we met, Talusan turned heads. With Asian features, freckles, and blond hair in a boyish side-parting, she confounded both racial and gender categories; she was an albino, too.

We were discussing how ideas about gender identity were shifting across the world in the globalized twenty-first century, in particular between her native Philippines and the United States, where she had lived all her adult life. Back home, she might have found a way to express her femininity *without* becoming a woman. But when she arrived as an eighteen-year-old freshman at Harvard in 1993, she had made landfall in a society where there were only two genders, male and female, and also where there was a particular faith in medical "solutions" and in a rights-based approach to identity. These factors—the cultural, the medical, the political-legal—played their role in Talusan's own transition in 2006.

A decade later, she was a leading voice in a second wave of trans thinkers, disrupting earlier ideas about the inherent and immutable binary nature of gender identity. "I'm not the type of woman who believes that there is something unchanging about me that makes me a woman," she told an interviewer, shortly after she was appointed executive editor of *them*, Condé Nast's new online LGBT magazine, in 2017.[1] "Mainly, I'm a woman because there are huge parts of me that have come to be coded in this culture as feminine, and that this culture makes so difficult to express unless I identify as a woman."

I asked Talusan if she would have made different choices had she been a generation younger and arrived in the United States today, in 2018, now that there was a non-binary option in American culture.

"I'm not sure if I could have resisted the pull of being attractive," she replied. "If you are gender non-conforming, you are not attractive to anyone. You sacrifice your desirability. You might have political capital, but you have no sexual capital."

Talusan's perspective was provocative: not only because it insisted on the binary nature of sexual desire, but also because of how it explored the role of context, and of desire itself, in the formulation of gender identity. This view had been roundly rejected by earlier trans activists because it suggested psychopathology, and thus the possibility of remedial therapy. But now Talusan and others were reclaiming—as another second-wave writer, Andrea Long Chu, put it—an understanding of "transness as a matter not of who one *is*, but what one *wants*."[2] The point of these writers was that even if gender identities were mutable, or object-related, they were no less valid for that.

When we met in Brooklyn in 2018, Talusan said that she felt increasingly free to play with androgyny. The tentlike overalls she was wearing were a case in point: she had picked them up in a thrift store; who knew if they were made for a man or a woman. They seemed to acquire a gender all of their own on their current wearer's body. This, too, was a feature of the second wave: an increasing drift into fluidity from people of Talusan's generation, who had initially crossed the gender binary from male to female, or vice versa.

We chatted about the way non-binary people in the U.S. were referencing the gender-fluid gender categories of precolonial societies to understand themselves, from "two-spirited" Native Americans to the *bakla* of her native Philippines: the word is an abbreviation of "man-woman" in Tagalog, and *bakla* Filipinos have their roots in the precolonial *babaylan*, shamans who presented as female but could be either male or female-bodied.

In the West, the effect of the transgender movement as it progressed through the decade was to blur the boundaries between male and female that Talusan had found to be so rigid two decades previously. Activists, journalists, doctors, therapists, and social scientists spoke of a "gender spectrum" rather than a "gender divide," and young people like the Riot Youth kids found their places somewhere along it, sometimes with and sometimes without medical help.

But back in the Philippines—as in many other societies where there had always been third-gender identities—the effect of the global transgender revolution could be exactly the opposite. The increased access to information about transgender rights and medical options meant a *sharpening* of more fluid cultural conceptions of gender and sexuality into the binary of male or female. In places all over the world, digital and medical technology now enabled broader access to a whole new set of social and biological possibilities. At the same time, the new global LGBT rights movement came into contact with societies that had age-old ways of accommodating people who did not fit neatly into one gender or the other.

In these societies there were new debates, and new politics: about who was male and who female and whether one could be neither or both; about the rights to self-determination of people to select their own genders, and whether—and how—the state had a duty to respect this and the health system to facilitate it. In the early twenty-first century this conversation became a new global human rights frontier, sometimes running alongside the Pink Line staked over homosexuality and sometimes traced directly over it, in societies where gender identity and sexual orientation were not separated out, the way they increasingly were in the West. You might have previously been *bakla*, but now there was the possibility of being either transgender or gay; but not both.

In the Philippines, the advent of a globalized LGBT movement—and specifically a transgender movement—heralded the beginnings of a change in the *bakla* subculture, and in the place of *bakla* in society. In this way, it may have worked to limit the gender non-conformity that was so much part of *bakla* identity, and to assert a more rigid gender binary.

IN MAY 2013, five years before I met Meredith Talusan, I had been to the Philippines myself, to follow a remarkable election campaign: a transgender woman named Bemz Benedito was running for Congress, heading the list of what was hailed as "the first LGBT party in the world." The party was called Ang Ladlad and had been registered as a special interest party in the country's arcane party list system. If the party garnered three hundred thousand votes nationwide Benedito would be elected to Congress specifically to represent LGBT Filipinos, and would become the fourth elected transgender official in the world: after a Polish parliamentarian, a Venezuelan congresswoman, and a Peruvian councilor.

The Philippines was famously "gay friendly": 73 percent of those polled in 2013 agreed that "homosexuality should be accepted by society," the highest score by far in Asia, according to the Pew Global Attitudes & Trends survey.[3] And yet anti-discrimination legislation had been languishing in Congress for over twelve years due to opposition from the church in this fervently Catholic country. Ang Ladlad had constituted itself around this single issue: it had tried to register to fight the previous election, in 2010, but was initially barred after the election commission ruled that it promoted "immorality." The party went to the Supreme Court and won the right to contest; thanks to sympathetic media coverage and some outrage at the commission's homophobia, the party won 120,000 votes despite barely campaigning.

Now, three years later, Bemz Benedito headed the Ang Ladlad list. In her mid-thirties, she had a telegenic beauty, but also a master's degree from the country's top university and a decade of work as a congressional aide behind her: she projected diligence and sobriety on the campaign trail, rather than the exaggerated hyperfemininity people usually associated with *bakla*. Still, Ang Ladlad had a novel get-out-the-vote strategy: to hit every beauty parlor in the vast archipelago.

The Philippines' *bakla* run the country's ubiquitous hairdressing salons and the annual Miss Gay Pageants that take place in almost every neighborhood. "The *parloristas* are our backbone," Benedito explained to me as we entered yet another of these kitschy jewel boxes, in the city of Baguio, staffed by a bustling claque of beauticians at various points along the gender spectrum.[4] "These are the nerve centers of the community, and also the place where *bakla* come into contact, as professionals, with the broader community. Every Filipina woman has a *bakla* hairdresser!"

But one of Benedito's explicit missions was to make sure that *bakla* were no longer limited to working in the beauty industry, or as entertainers. And this is what made her campaign—and the Philippines' transgender movement—so interesting: it staked a Pink Line, as elsewhere in the world, between the established but limited place in society occupied by traditional third-gender people, and the possibilities of a new, Westernstyle transgender identity, such as Benedito's own.

Benedito was a leading member of STRAP, the very assertive Society of Transsexual Women of the Philippines. Another STRAP leader, Mikee Nuñez-Inton, recounted to me her experience when she first joined the organization: "The first thing they told me was, 'You're not a *bakla*, you're a woman!" Initially, she understood this as a wish for transgender women to distance themselves from a word often used pejoratively, but later she came to see it as a matter of class, and aspiration.

Nuñez-Inton was lecturing in gender studies at De La Salle University in Manila when we spoke in 2018: "While our *Babaylan* ancestors were treated with respect and performed essential ritualistic functions in pre-colonial societies," she has written, "the contemporary *bakla* has become relegated to the relatively lower class beauty industries"; "Now the word conjures up tragic-comic images of the parlorista."[5]

And so, Nuñez-Inton said to me, "really, it is economics that separates the *bakla* from the transgender": you needed resources—and the English language—to access the Internet and globalized notions of transgender identity, not to mention surgery, which would require a trip to Hong Kong or Bangkok.

The word *bakla* is capacious, and encompasses anyone who is assigned male at birth but presents in a feminine way: a campy guy is bakla; so, too, is someone who has gone to Bangkok for breasts. Some *bakla* use male pronouns, some female, some switch according to context. But now, in the twenty-first century, transgender activists were urging *bakla* to claim their rights, and their bodies, as *women*: If they did so, they would be able to compete in society for all the things that women did. They could break free from the constraints of their muddy identities, and the walls of their beauty parlors. They could cross the gender divide rather than languishing within it. They could even run for Congress! (Benedito lost her bid to become the country's first transgender congresswoman, but three years later, another succeeded, when Geraldine Roman inherited her father's constituency.)

In the Philippines, *bakla* spoke of having *pusong babae*, "a woman's heart."[6] In South India, similarly, *kothis*—who wore men's clothing but felt themselves to be women—described themselves in Tamil as *pen manaam konda aan*: "a woman's heart in a man's body." For indigenous Asian trans people, Mikee Nuñez-Inton told me, "The seat of identity is not in the mind, as in the West. It's in the heart, the spirit, the interior self." The significance was that, "In the West, where it's seen to be in the mind, it's treated as a pathology and something that can be cured, with therapy or psychiatry or by changing your body. Whereas if it's in the heart, *it's just who you are*. There is no pathologizing function."

I was struck by the similarity of these self-definitions to Karl Heinrich Ulrichs's pre-Freudian description of the *urning* as a female soul within a male body,[7] or Edward Carpenter's third-sex uranian, whom he described in 1908 as having the emotions of one sex in the body of the other.[8] Being defined through the heart or the soul rather than the mind had another effect, Mikee Nuñez-Inton said: "Because there's no diagnosis of body dysmorphia, and the expectation that healing can come with the body being manipulated and changed, gender identity is not about the body. It's more about expression and behavior as an outward manifestation of the interior rather than an alignment of the body with the mind."

BEMZ BENEDITO AND the STRAP activists might have been trying to help *bakla* see the liberation that came with being a woman, but Meredith Talusan gave me a different take on the *bakla*-trans hierarchy: "In the Philippines, transwomen are more stigmatized than *bakla*, because it's considered deceitful to 'pass' as a woman if you are not biologically one. If you're gender non-conforming, it's better to be open about it."

In the United States, Meredith Talusan was legally a woman. But back in the Philippines, Mikee Nuñez-Inton had no option but to remain a man legally. There was simply no provision in Philippines law to change one's gender and this, of course, provoked the allegation of deceit every time you had to show an identity document.

This was the case in most of the world. According to *National Geographic* in 2016, you could change your gender markers legally in only fifty of the world's one hundred ninety-five sovereign states.

In another twenty-seven countries gender change was legal but extremely difficult. In sixty-seven countries it was not legally possible, while in the remaining fifty-four, "data addressing legal gender change has yet to be collected, and discussion of the issue is a new frontier."[9]

Even in countries where it was possible to transition legally or medically, the process could be arduous in the extreme, notwithstanding the way transgender people were sometimes celebrated. One country where this bifurcation was most pronounced was China. From the art of the Ming Dynasty to the Beijing Opera, female transvestism had been valued in Chinese art and performance, and this was reflected in the twenty-first-century popular culture through the figure of Liu Ting. Liu had won an award—as a man—as "national role model of virtue" after she carried her mother on her back to and from the hospital.[10] When she publicly announced her gender transition in 2015, she became a media superstar, as glamorous as Caitlyn Jenner but with far more virtue. Another glamorous transgender woman, Jin Xing, hosted China's most-watched variety show, with an estimated one hundred million online viewers a week.

But the actual process of legal transition in China was nigh impossible. You could not qualify for surgery without the written consent of your family members and having been under a doctor's care for transsexualism for more than five years. You also needed to prove that psychotherapy had been ineffective—and to have a psychologist's verification that you would be heterosexual after the surgery. As in many countries, you could only change your gender legally after surgery, and even then your problems were by no means over: your education certificates could not be changed—and since they contradicted the way you now looked and identified yourself, they were seldom accepted. A 2017 survey of trans teens by the Beijing LGBT Center confirmed how this reflected social norms: one in five reported that they had been forced into conversion therapy, and among those respondents who reported that their parents knew their gender identity, 93 percent reported abuse or neglect.[11]

In my native South Africa, legislation from 2003 allowed for those who had undergone any medical treatment to apply for a legal gender change, but most government officials refused—incorrectly—to accept hormone treatment as grounds enough. And while Cape Town's Groote Schuur Hospital had a world-class state-run gender clinic that offered free transition treatment to South Africans, it only allocated four days a year to genital surgery, which meant that in 2018 the waiting list was twenty-five years long. There were private services, but these were out of reach for most people.

In neighboring Botswana, a transgender activist named Ricki Kgositau won a landmark case in 2017 when a court ordered the government to issue her a new female identity card. (A similar battle was won in Puerto Rico in June 2018, using U.S. law, on behalf of three transgender teens.) Kgositau had gone—like so many people who could afford it, from all over the world—to Thailand for surgery. The Thai medical tourism industry attracted over two million people a year in the 2010s, and gender-affirming surgery had become an important niche within it. Tens of thousands of people, the vast majority of them foreign, are believed to have used the services in the three decades they have been available, at a fraction of the cost in the West—and with much-lauded outcomes.

Those who can afford it have always traveled for surgery, from "the Danish Girl" to Berlin in the 1930s, through Christine Jorgensen to Denmark in 1952, and Jan Morris to Casablanca in 1972. By 2018, the description of a journey for gender surgery qualified as mainstream travel writing: Meredith Talusan published a piece in *Condé Nast Traveler* about her experience in Thailand, which gave her, she wrote, "the space to make that process [of healing] easier, and allowed me to find solace and comfort in myself without the world's expectations of gender.[12] Alone in that Pattaya hotel room on the other side of the ocean, I not only began to recover from the procedure, but from the world's overwhelming impositions. It was in that room where I began to figure out how to simply be."

The irony was that while Thailand might be renowned globally both for its medical gender services and its tolerance, the law did not allow Thai *kathoey*—"ladyboys"—to change their names or genders legally. This was a significant bar to their ability to work and travel outside of the sex industry. In 2013, Bangkok circumvented this problem by replacing identity cards with fingerprint identification but still, transgender Thais there and elsewhere could not get passports or driver's licenses after they transitioned. You found yourself in a twilight zone if you had undergone your surgery or were living as a woman, unable to travel or apply for jobs, and unable to change your documentation.

EVEN AS TRANSGENDER people were legalized and depathologized in countries from Argentina to Pakistan by 2018, they were still criminalized and prosecuted in various ways in at least fifty-seven countries.[13] Several continued to enforce laws that prohibited "posing," or cross-dressing in public; these were often part of anti-vagrancy (or "vagabond") codes inherited from the colonial era, initially used to control both homosexuality and prostitution in Britain, and then later the free passage of emancipated slaves in the Americas.

A precedent-setting judgment was made against Guyana in the Caribbean Court of Justice in November 2018, when it found the country's anti-vagrancy law to be unconstitutional. Four transgender women had been randomly arrested and found guilty of wearing "female attire" for "improper purpose" in 2009; the court now ruled that "difference is as natural as breathing" and that "no one should have his or her dignity trampled upon, or human rights denied, merely on account of a difference, especially one that poses no threat to public safety or public order."[14] The Guyanese government accepted the judgment and stated that more had to be done to integrate the LGBT community into society.

But the law took the opposite direction in some other former British colonies. As Wahhabi Islam extended its influence alongside a growing LGBT rights movement, new laws were promulgated to target transgender people, using—ironically—the British colonial definitions of *vagabond*. This had an impact, specifically, on transgender communities at the geographical extremes of the Muslim world: Nigeria in West Africa, and Malaysia in Southeast Asia.

As with *babaylan* in the Philippines, the third-gender 'yan daudu of northern Nigeria had precolonial roots, and histories as healers among the Hausa peoples. By the late-twentieth century, *'yan daudu* were associated with female trades, such as cooking and selling food in markets, and also with sex work. They had remained very much part of Hausa society, even under Islam: particularly in smaller communities, social life often revolved around their celebrations. This changed after 2000, though, when Sharia, was adopted in Nigeria's twelve northern Muslim states. Among the new laws was the death penalty for homosexuality in some states, and lesser punishments for being a "vagabond"—defined, in most states, as "any male person who dresses or is attired in the fashion of a woman in a public place or who practices sodomy as a means of livelihood or as a profession."[15]

Morality police called *hisba* were recruited to enforce the new laws; the result, wrote the Nigerian journalist Elnathan John in 2016, was that *'yan daudu* were now "visible" to the law for the first time: they could "no longer hold open parties or send out open invitations to their celebrations. Their 'female' occupations were under threat, and many of them felt uncomfortable doing work that easily identified them."[16] Such "visibility" meant they had to become invisible.

Something comparable was happening in Malaysia at the same time where, as in neighboring Thailand and Indonesia, there had always been gender-variant people. Between 1985 and 2013, each of Malaysia's thirteen states passed Sharia laws criminalizing "men posing as women." When Malaysia's prime minister Mahathir Mohamed had railed against the West's attempts to impose its values on the world in 2003, it was "the practice of free sex including sodomy" that was the threat to Asian values.[17] In 2012, his successor, Najib Razak, told a meeting of eleven thousand imams and religious leaders that "LGBTs, pluralism, liberalism—all these 'isms' are against Islam and it is compulsory for us to fight these."[18] In the interceding nine years, something had happened to the global discourse of the Pink Line: the gay enemy, with its crime of "sodomy," had mutated into "LGBT": this meant that transgender people were in the line of fire too.

Of course, in the years of these new global culture wars, any anti-gay moral panic often hit gender non-conforming people the hardest. Religious and political leaders staked a Pink Line in favor of "cultural sovereignty" and against the degrading influences of the West by lashing back against the perversion represented by same-sex marriage, rather than specifically against transgender people or gender variance. But because of their visibility and seeming "freakishness," transgender women in particular became the most visible manifestations of this new threat. And in countries such as Nigeria and Malaysia, third-gender people now found their place in society threatened by the new global politics—and awareness—of LGBT rights.

We saw the effects of this in the way Indonesia's third-gender *waria* became a kind of pink folk-devil in the moral panic that took hold in that country from 2016 onward. Kyle Knight, the author of a Human Rights Watch report on the subject, told me of his meeting with an older *waria* in Sulawesi in March 2016. The previous six weeks had been the first time in her life she had been bothered by her community, she said: "Some kids rode by me and started pointing at me, shouting 'LGBT! LGBT!' I had no idea what they meant. They had obviously picked it up in the media, received a strong message from government: I was someone they were now allowed to hate."

Like Tiwonge Chimbalanga in Malawi seven years previously, she first encountered the term *LGBT* as an insult: a concept that had set out to empower her was being used against her.

STILL, WARIAS REMAINED very much part of life in Indonesia even after the crisis that began in 2016, as did transgender people in Malaysia. What happened in some parts of West Africa was more severe. As gay people became visible and counted, and as religious fundamentalists defined themselves in large part against this "abomination," gender non-conforming men or transgender women went on the down-low in direct proportion to the intensity of the moral panic unleashed.

In Ghana, where there was a sustained anti-LGBT campaign driven by Christian Evangelists between 2006 and 2011, gender non-conforming folk retreated from public when the term *kodjo-besia* ("man-woman" in Twi) shifted from being a rather neutral descriptor of gender identity to a homosexual slur.

What happened in Senegal was more extreme. *Goor-jigeens* ("men-women" in Wolof) had long been part of society in Senegal's cities: often attached to wealthy houses, they were responsible for organizing ceremonies, for providing entertainment, and for dressing and grooming the women. All through the twentieth century, they were a visible thread in Dakar's diverse urban tapestry, but by the early twenty-first century there were no longer any to be found: at least not in this form. As with *kodjo-besia* in Ghana, the word *goor-*

jigeen was now "used to insult individuals who are thought to be gay, or who are perceived as effeminate, as a result of sexual preferences," write the scholars Christophe Broqua and Karine Geoffrion.[19] And so they disappeared.

When I visited Dakar in December 2012, I met the veteran Senegalese LGBT activist Djiadji Diouf. He had been one of those arrested and sentenced to five years in jail in 2008, during the anti-gay moral panic that swept through the country that year. He explained to me what had happened to *goor-jigeens*: "The Senegalese didn't know that two men could have sexual relations. They saw *goor-jigeens*, and they thought it was just effeminacy. They didn't mind that. It was something you could laugh at. But now, with technology and the Internet, they came to know something: *men look for men*! It's when they realized that two men actually can have sexual relations. And then the resistance began."

Diouf told me that whatever gay scene might have been germinating before his arrest and trial was now deeply underground, returned to covert and furtive encounters now enabled—for those with access—by online dating hookup apps such as Grindr. The situation was no better six years later, a younger activist named Ababacar Sadikh Ndoye told me, when we spoke in 2018. Eleven people had recently been arrested at a house party after complaints from neighbors, and assaulted and abused while in custody; such raids were regular.

Ndoye gave me his explanation for the disappearance of *goor-jigeens*: "In the past, they were accepted as entertainers who danced in ceremonies to make the crowds laugh. But with the arrests of 2008 [of Djiadji Diouf and others], Senegalese came to see *goor-jigeens* differently, thanks to the media. They came to think that these people were no longer just clowns but, rather, organized groups financed by

Western funders to pervert the young, and to destroy Senegalese culture, religion, and values."

There were still two occasions in the year when you could see a flicker of Dakar's *goor-jigeen* spirit: during Mardi Gras and, more so, at Tajabone, a Muslim Halloween, where the tradition of trick-or-treating in disguise had traditionally given queer folk sanction to cross-dress publicly. A more severe Islam had seen off this custom, too, but Tajabone remained "a night when the LGBTQI community can dress up and go to clubs or parties without being hassled," Ndoye told me.

For the rest of the year, the *goor-jiggeens* (in the original sense of the word) now put away their feminine apparel. Many had wives and children and did not even have sex with men, but they became the most visible face of this new threat, a debauchery now named and identified, coming from the West.

Something dramatic had happened along the Pink Line: an accepted gender identity had become an unacceptable sexual behavior in the wake of a global LGBT rights movement.

GOOR-JIGGEEN, 'YAN DAUDA, and *kodjo-besia* in Africa. *Bakla, waria,* and *kathoey* in Southeast Asia. In so many societies, in South Asia, the Pacific Islands, and the Americas, too, there has been space for people who did not fit neatly into the male-female binary.

These are all words describing effeminate male-bodied people, and there are far fewer examples of the other way around. One is from Southern Africa, where butch women can be "called" to be *sangomas*, or traditional healers, because their masculine appearance is seen to be a sign of their possession by a male ancestor, and therefore their proximity to the ancestral world.[20] Two others are *burrneshas* in Albania, and *bacha posh* in Afghanistan. In both, gender switching was originally for material reasons. *Burrneshas* swore a vow of chastity and lived as men perhaps originally to allow for property to remain in a bloodline if there were no male heirs. *Bacha posh* were girls selected to "dress as a boy" (which is what it means, in Farsi) if there were no sons in the family, so as to obtain male privileges such as access to schooling and the ability to earn. In both instances, some gender non-conforming people found space within these categories to be themselves. The *burrneshas* seemed to be a dying breed in the twenty-first century—perhaps, one of them told *The Guardian*, because women were now more empowered in the Balkans.[21] But *bacha posh* were very much part of life in modern Afghanistan.[22]

For *burrneshas* and *bacha posh*, taking on masculinity meant a rise in social status. But when male-bodied people lived or behaved as women, it usually accompanied a loss of social status. In precolonial society, this might have not been the case. Indian *hijras* were originally exalted: being unsexed brought them closer to the divine, and they had the power to convey fertility. Now, in India, you paid *hijras* to prevent them from cursing you, or to have sex with you, rather than to bless you with children.

There is similar evidence of two-spirited healers in Native American cultures. But sometimes these precolonial identities have been "romanticized," the trans American historian Genny Beemyn notes, as an alternative to the severely binarist settler culture which criminalized cross-dressing.[23] The reality was more complex. Citing the anthropologist Sabine Lang, Beemyn writes that the way gender-fluid people were treated in a Native American society usually mirrored the way women themselves were treated: "If women predominated in particular occupations, such as being healers, shamans, and handcrafters, then male-assigned individuals who took on female roles engaged in the same professions."

There is, of course, much to differentiate these very different people scattered all over the globe, but they have two things in common. The first is that they are understood to be a third gender, rather than male or female. The second is that they have an assigned role to play in society, often because their fusion of genders is perceived as a gift or a power, even if it is one that can be used negatively. In some societies the role is more practical, in others it is more spiritual. But in almost all cases—and this is the important point—the role of a gender-variant person is circumscribed: a *bakla* cannot aspire to do more than hairdressing; an Indian *hijra* more than sex work and begging. You are acknowledged, and you have your space in society, but it is a limited space. You must stay within it.

The global transgender movement, as embodied by Bemz Benedito in the Philippines, sought to change that, in one direction: become a woman.

Meanwhile, the middle-class "global gay" subculture, with its emphasis on conventional masculinity, tried to move it in the other direction: become a man.

Would third-gender people like the *bakla* get squeezed out of the middle by "gay" and "transgender," these two powerful global identities?

Or would the rights that came with these new identities provide them with new freedoms, and more expanded space?

Would new hybrids develop, localizing the "global" in new ways?

NOWHERE WERE THESE questions sharper than on the Indian subcontinent, where there had been significant populations of third-gender people for millennia: *hijras* in India and Bangladesh, *metis* in Nepal, *khwaja sara* in Pakistan. Transgender or third-gender activists across the region were energized by the global LGBT rights movement of the twenty-first century, and used their countries' constitutions and courts to gain victories for the legal recognition.

The first such judgment had been won in Nepal, through a lawsuit filed by the country's pioneering Blue Diamond Society. It would take the state several years to implement the ruling comprehensively, but by 2015 Nepalese passports could be issued in the third gender, and that year's constitution made it a right to be recognized as third gender on citizenship documents. In Pakistan, a 2009 Supreme Court judgment called for reporting on the rights and welfare of third-gender people, and then in 2017, the chief justice directed authorities to register transgender people as third gender in that year's census. Bangladesh, too, made a decision in 2013 to recognize *hijras* as a third gender.

And in 2014 the Indian Supreme Court confirmed, in a landmark judgment, "the right of every person to choose their gender."[24] The judgment was in response to a suit brought by the state's own National Legal Services Authority (NALSA) and mandated the inclusion of transgender people in state welfare programs, much as the *dalits*—or untouchable castes—were. By 2019, this ruling had barely been implemented, and was challenged or watered down in various ways by government policy and new legislation. Still, in the years since the NALSA judgment, the way gender-variant people were thinking of themselves and their rights began to change dramatically in India.

Increasingly, people who used to call themselves *hijras* were reformatting themselves as *transgenders* or *TGs*. This was partly because of the publicity around the NALSA judgment and also the public health industry's new interest in transgender populations, particularly in the fight against AIDS. It was also—of course—due to the Information Revolution, which carried the Western "transgender explosion" over to Asia and the rest of the world.

In the United States, I had met homeless transgender sex workers in Detroit's Palmer Park and also transgender Riot Youth alumni from nearby Ann Arbor who were at Ivy League law schools. In India, too, I met *hijras* who, cast out from their poor families, lived in parallel societies, feudal and violent, subsisting through sex work and begging. But I also met urban and educated young people who were increasingly developing their gender identities online rather than through the *hijra* society, and finding space in the globalized upper reaches of the Indian economy. There was Anita, for example, who worked for Amazon as a principal engineer, one of only six in the country, and who was fully "out" at work in Hyderabad, connected via a listserv to sixty other trans Amazon employees throughout the world. And there was Sameera Jahagirdar, the specialist anesthetist who had set up India's first full-spectrum gendercare clinic at a teaching hospital in Pondicherry.

But such cases were exceptional. More common, among educated young people, were those who had identified themselves as transgender online or through new LGBT groups, but could not imagine coming out to their families or in their workplaces, or undergoing any form of permanent transition, if they remained in India. Or, among poorer people, those who were trying to balance their gender identities with their family or communal obligations.

In a Tamil fishing village named Devanampattinam, a twenty-year-old named Lakshaya explained her dilemma to me. Assigned male at birth, she was indistinguishable from any of the boys in the village when I first met her in 2012, but for her languid sashay, her plucked eyebrows, and her diamanté ear studs. Had she been born in a Filipino fishing village, she might have found her place as a *bakla* beautician, but here in India, such gender-fluidity was not socially acceptable. Had she been born a generation earlier, she might have pretended to be a "real man," hiding her true female self, marrying a bride chosen for her by her family. Or she might have fled marriage and become an outcast, inducted into a *hijra* community she feared and despised, wearing saris full time, growing her hair, and submitting to castration.

But Lakshaya and her friends in the village—they called themselves *kothis*—had attained a level of personal autonomy and political consciousness through India's fight against AIDS, and also through the Internet. Neither of the above options was acceptable: "We want to stay in our village and stay as we are," she told me forcefully.

This book ends with their story, and their struggle to be themselves.

16

THE KOTHI STORIES

DEVANAMPATTINAM—CUDDALORE—PONDICHERRY

Sivagami—kothi priestess, thirties, Devanampattinam. Pronouns: she/her/hers.

Lakshaya—village kothi, AIDS worker, early twenties, Devanampattinam. Pronouns: she/her/hers.

Mohana—Lakshaya's best friend, fisherman and temple performer, Devanampattinam, mid-twenties. Pronouns: she/her/hers.

Dinisha—Lakshaya's school classmate and colleague at the AIDS organization, early twenties, Devanampattinam. Pronouns: she/her/hers.

Gomati—Lakshaya's mother, construction worker, late forties, Devanampattinam. Pronouns: she/her/hers.

Sheetal—Lakshaya's boss in the AIDS organization, the local hijra leader, a hospital manager, late thirties. Pronouns: she/her/hers.

Sameera Jahagirdar—Sheetal's colleague at the hospital, doctor and founder of the gender clinic at the nearby hospital, late thirties, Pondicherry. Pronouns: she/her/hers.

SIVAGAMI

The priestess Sivagami was waiting for us at the entrance to her temple, a small rectangular box covered with zinc roofing along a litter-strewn backwater. Just beyond was a huge new sewage plant, and across the water was Cuddalore, the old colonial port. Behind us, the fishing village of Devanampattinam spilled out beneath coconut palms onto one of Tamil Nadu's endless beaches, two hundred kilometers south of Chennai.

Sivagami was in her late thirties, brisk and statuesque, with a studied dignity and a dazzling smile that hinted at charisma. Her long hair was oiled and gathered in a low bun and she had floral studs in her ears, but she was otherwise dressed in the standard uniform of South Indian men: a Madras-check shirt over the *lungi* tied around her waist. As she led us into the temple she explained that it was dedicated to Angalamman, a particularly fierce iteration of the goddess Kali. The space was spare and makeshift: a few modest shrines were ranged along pale pink walls; light bulbs and fans hung from beams across the exposed zinc roof; a collection of saris were draped along a washing line.

Why so many saris, I asked.

Sivagami laughed. She knew it was a leading question. "Angalamman is a very convenient goddess for us," she said in Tamil, stretching an arm out to take in the dozen or so people squatting on the mats laid out on the tiled floor or lolling about outside. "When we are praying to her we must dress as women. Even when we go into the village to raise funds for her, the goddess requires it. No one will make fun of us."

In 2011, when the census counters arrived in Devanampattinam with a new category on their forms, Sivagami could have chosen to get herself counted as "transgender"—one of 487,803 Indians nationwide to do so. The vast majority of these would have identified themselves as *hijras*, as transgender or third-gender Indians had called themselves for centuries. But Sivagami was something else, she insisted: a *kothi*, because although she felt like a woman inside and had long hair and wore jewelry, she usually wore male clothing and had not undergone the "cut"—the emasculation ritual that defines *hijra* identity.

The word *kothi* was *hijra* slang—it had its derivation in a word for "monkey"—and its meaning was roughly equivalent to the western "bottom": the passive partner in homosexual sex. But in the first decades of the twenty-first century, "*kothi*" had become an identity category all of its own in India, distinct from *hijra*. This was exactly at the same time that the notions of "gay" and "LGBT" were spreading globally, partly on the wings of the fight against AIDS. Suddenly *kothi* communities exploded across the subcontinent—particularly among poor and rural people—in a way that rivaled the boom of a middle-class gay scene in the cities. The story of how this had happened—and what it meant—was one I hoped to understand through the visits I made to India and Devanampattinam from 2012 onward.

The village was one of the first places I visited as I explored the world's Pink Lines, and despite the distance and the absolute lack of a common language, I came to know the *kothis* of the village well over the next five years, and to develop a strong affection and respect for them. This book began with the story of Tiwonge Chimbalanga, who headed out into the world from her home, an isolated village on the Thyolo escarpment in Malawi. It seems fitting to end it another village, this one on the shores of the Indian Ocean, so as to try to understand how the "world," with all its globalized notions of sexual orientation and gender identity, entered the village during the early twenty-first century, and transformed it—or not. Such symmetries aside, I bring our journey to a close here for a more substantive reason: if gender identity really was a new global frontier of the twenty-first century that brought contemporary notions of transgender rights into play with age-old traditions, the *kothis* of Devanampattinam really were on the frontline.

AFTER MY TIME with Sivagami inside the temple that first visit, I went out to sit with the other *kothis* on the scrubby grass outside. There were about ten of them, from late teens to early forties, lying in each other's laps, daydreaming, gossiping, ribbing one another, singing snatches of Tamil film songs. Some, like Ramu the milkman, were married with children and looked and behaved like any other man from the village. As I sat down, Ramu was being teased for this very fact by the fisherman Mohan ("Mohana"). Using bawdy *hijra* slang, Mohana was working up a routine questioning how Ramu had managed to impregnate his wife, twice at least, before she left him. Ramu feigned outrage and humiliation, but seemed to be enjoying the attention and the raucous laughter at his expense.

Mohana was clearly the linchpin of the community. Only twenty-three, she had the muscular physique of a fisherman and a mesmerizing beauty. She was nicknamed All-India Pass, after the railway season ticket: she went everywhere, knew everyone. Although she was uneducated and illiterate, she kept the temple's books: she was excellent with numbers, and in my visits to the village, I always found her busy with one scheme or another, arranging financial loans or marriages.

Mohana had a tendency to break into the falsetto torch song of a Bollywood-style playback singer. When performing she was haughty and, when not, somewhat diffident. Her best friend, Lakshaya, was the brainy chatterbox of the group: twenty years old, she was studying by correspondence for a BSc, and was an outreach worker at an AIDS organization across the backwaters in Cuddalore (it was through this organization that I had been introduced to the temple in the first place). Mohana mistrusted my arrival in the village but Lakshaya embraced it. She was bursting with ideas and questions about the wider world—which entered the village through the tattered Tamil-English dictionary always at her side, and her Samsung smartphone, the only one I saw in the village.

It was at this first meeting that Lakshaya had told me how, as *kothis*, she and the other temple workers wished to "stay in the village and stay as we are." In the years to come I would watch their determination grow, even as society—family and economics—conspired to limit their horizons and force them back into the gender binary: get married and have children, or run away and join the *hijras*. In another place or another time, they might have found their space, some perhaps as gay men and others as transgender women. But these options were not available to them when they were coming of age in the village in the first years of the twenty-first century.

Indeed, in 2012, when I first met them, they had never even heard the word *gay*. When I visited them three years later they knew the word, thanks both to the Indian film industry, which had found the gay character, and their growing exposure to the LGBT rights movement. Lakshaya explained the difference between gays and *kothis* to me: "Gays wear nice clothes and have parties and sex. A *kothi* is someone who lives in the village and does women's work."

By this point, attitudes toward sexual orientation and gender identity had changed dramatically in India, reflecting the global spread of LGBT rights. In July 2009, the Delhi High Court had decriminalized homosexual sex, after an eight-year effort to strike down the Indian penal code's Section 377, which outlawed "carnal intercourse against the order of nature."[1] Even though the Indian Supreme Court would decide to uphold Section 377 in 2013, the Voices Against 377 campaign had significantly shifted public opinion about homosexuality, particularly among India's huge middle class: when I first visited India in 2012, the Delhi High Court judgment was widely celebrated as a mark of the country's modernity.

Then, in April 2014, the Indian Supreme Court gave its NALSA ruling that transgender people were entitled to full equal rights, and to self-determination. The world had begun seeping into Devanampattinam, through the cracked screen of Lakshaya's smartphone and through her work at the AIDS organization, and when I visited in 2015, Lakshaya and her friends were fully aware of these advances, which would substantially change the way they thought about themselves and their place in this world.

But when I first met them in 2012, they had not even heard of Section 377, let alone the effort to repeal it. When I told them about it, Mohana offered one of her haughtiest dismissals: "We know how to deal with the law. If policemen bother us we either fuck them or we bribe them. It is our families that we struggle with! *That's* where we need a campaign!"

During the years I knew them and visited them, from 2012 onward, the *kothis* of Devanampattinam became beneficiaries of a new rights-based culture—national and global—that allowed them to imagine a life free of the constraints of previous generations. But they were trying to apply it in a village that still followed the old ways. They found themselves in a borderland along the stark frontiers of the Pink Line, bodily and territorial. What made their struggle so interesting to me was the way they were trying to use the old ways—traditional Hindu devotional practice—to achieve their aims: their temple on the edge of the village where Sivagami now led them, and the village, in shared devotion to the goddess Angalamman.

The goddess was beloved of poor folk and outcasts, of fishermen and *hijras* and *kothis*. Because she patrols the perimeters to protect villagers from evil, small shrines to her are usually to be found on the outskirts, as here at Devanampattinam, where a girl had once seen a palm tree weeping milk, a sign of her presence. Once the priestess Sivagami had discovered a personal connection to the deity, she had begun leading *poojas* (communal prayers) at the shrine, and the fisherman Mohana was an early devotee. Mohana began the fund-raising drive among her fellow fisherfolk, and supervised the building of the temple on the site; she also drew in some of the elders of the village to serve as temple trustees. Thus, through the shared worship of Angalamman with the villagers, the *kothis* hoped to knit themselves into their home community, rather than having to flee it to a *hijra* destiny as the priestess Sivagami herself had once done.

SIVAGAMI HAD ALWAYS been interested in female things as a child. She hung around her mother's sari folds, she told me, possible in her family because her father had died young. When at fifteen she began a relationship with an older boy she decided this meant she was a *hijra*, and she ran away to Bombay. She hoped to find her older sibling, who had gone to the city a decade previously for the same reason. The myth, perpetuated by British colonial law, is that *hijras* kidnap children to groom and castrate them, but the truth is that the *hijra* communities in the cities actually provide refuge to runaways often fleeing arranged marriages or the prospect of them; misfits who could not find space in their home communities because they were not typically male.

In precolonial times, *hijras* were exalted: being unsexed brought them closer to the divine, and they had the power to convey fertility. The space they occupied between male and female also gave them a role managing harems in Muslim courts. But their status had declined through the twentieth century, in part because they were outlawed by the British as a "criminal tribe."[2] Then, as urban India modernized, their social space contracted further: by the time Sivagami found herself in Bombay in the mid-1990s, *hijras* earned their livings through begging and sex work. In these two roles, they became fixtures of modern urban life: as beggars, they extorted shopkeepers by threatening to curse them through lifting their saris; as sex workers, their release from traditional gender roles made them available to men outside of marriage in ways not permitted to biological women. Ironically, given their original status, they carried the scent of sex—its allure, but also its stigma and its violence—as no one else did in Indian society.

When Sivagami arrived in Bombay she became the *chela*—the word means "disciple" but sometimes has the meaning of "daughter," too—of an older "guru." Sivagami's guru inducted the young runaway into her "house" and tutored her in feminine grooming before pimping her out so that she could earn her keep. The guru gave Sivagami a female name, and after about two years, began preparing her for the ritual emasculation that would enable her to take on her own disciples and work her way up the *hijra* hierarchy.

At the time I first came to Devanampattinam in 2012 and met Sivagami, the global transgender rights movement was beginning to gain some traction in India, too, and several *hijras* had broken their society's taboos to tell their stories, often of abject violence and sex slavery.[3] Had Sivagami's *hijra* life been in any way like that?

"No, Mark," she insisted. "They were good to me. They gave me a home. And they would never force me to do sex. But this meant I had to do a lot of begging, day and night, and sometimes if I have not made enough from begging then yes, of course I must do *dhanda*, " which means "business" in Hindi but is also *hijra* slang for "sex work."

How did she feel about this?

"I did not like it."

Neither did she like the prospect of emasculation. Technically illegal in India, it was traditionally done by a *hijra* herself, but more frequently these days by an extortionate backroom doctor who often made a hash of things. Sivagami thought she had no choice: "How else would I survive, and advance?"

Her older sibling found her and hauled her back to Devanampattinam before the cutting took place. Home in the village, Sivagami fell in with a priest who trained her—in exchange for sexual favors. "I didn't mind," she told me. "When people like us walk on the street, rowdies pull us aside and force us to have sex with them. The priest was better than that. At least I learned something. And now people come to me to help solve their problems, rather than for me to suck their dicks."

Sivagami quickly drew renown as a healer. Supplicants made a donation, in cash or kind, in return for a prayer. Her mother, Vijaya, acted as her manager, touting for clients and preparing supplicants for their consultation. Vijaya was a bustling sort, only too happy to talk to me. "Once when we were offering prayer at home, he became possessed by the goddess Angalamman," she said of her child. "That was when we knew he had God's grace. You see, he has Angalamman inside him. That is why he is the way he is."

IF THE PRIESTESS Sivagami and her *kothis* strove to find a place for themselves in their home community through their devotion to the goddess Angalamman, then their primary weapon was a ten-day festival called Mayana Kollai, a Tamil Halloween (the phrase translates as "Graveyard Raid") that they turned into the focal point of the village's calendar. I went in March 2013.

I arrived in the middle of one of the daytime *poojas* at the beginning of the festival, together with the photographer Candace Feit and our interpreter, Lavanya Keshavraj. We watched Sivagami slaughter a goat in the sandy forecourt of the temple. In a trance, she had removed her shirt and shaken her ponytail loose into snakelike coils: the way they fell over her hairy torso rendered her appropriately otherworldly and fierce beyond the gender categories that this world imposed, as she channeled the goddess Angalamman into the village. While she was possessed, there was always an assistant around to keep her safe or reel her in; once she had collapsed and been revived, she emerged from the temple clothed and poised, to assume control of the gathering crowd. Wielding a big stick, she led a raucous percussive procession of the temple's deities up into the village.

Lakshaya became our guide and protector: she did not participate in Mayana Kollai for reasons I would later discover. As she walked with us, she pointed out a large sand sculpture. It was in the form of a supine Angalamman, about a meter high and at least ten long, the sand dyed in different colors, and crowned with a face of the goddess rendered in turmeric and kohl. This was to be the stage on which the *kothis* and other devotees would enact the story of Mayana Kollai.

The midday procession culminated at the village's main temple. Here, surrounded by a crush of chanting women in yellow saris, Sivagami led devotees into a trance, pushing metal skewers through their tongues. Then the crowd dispersed, and we spent the rest of the day in one or another of the *kothis*' homes, or in the small palm-reed hut that was to serve as a dressing room, watching them prepare for the evening's ritual. Mohana, the All-India Pass, was to play "blue Kali," the fiercest deity, and we watched her being painted head to toe in the color. "We are in a trance, so we don't really know what happens to us," she said when I asked her what to expect. "We would normally be nervous about the men who tease us, but when we are here before God we get the power and we lose all fear and inhibition."

By dusk the *kothi* goddesses were ready, as were a supporting cast of other villagers. A generator roared into life and a ring of colored lights flickered on. Several spotlights illuminated the ritual space, around which villagers began to gather. Standing out among them were small groups of *kothis* and *hijras* from neighboring towns. There were musician and dancers, and vendors of religious paraphernalia and of food. Some of these had been arranged by the temple *kothis* but many had just shown up. Lakshaya was delighted: the temple's repute was spreading! She fixed herself to us like glue as the atmosphere grew raucous and edgy, the men reeking of palm toddy and the drums beating up a frenzy.

Finally, the performers went into trances and assumed their deity roles, telling the story of how the goddess Angalamman saved the world by dancing with her consort Shiva. Each performer was controlled by a handler, like a puppet about to break her strings: the villagers appeared genuinely fearful of these dancing deities, especially the three *kothi* goddesses: red, yellow, and blue. The priestess Sivagami's role was to marshal both the crowds and the performers, and she encircled the sand mound pounding her big stick.

Later, under a full moon, Sivagami led the entire congregation to the village graveyard, where seemingly spontaneous performances erupted on tombs as actual graves seemed to be dug up. Reflected off the ocean just beyond the graveyard walls, the moon held the enactment in its ghostly light, and although I could not keep track of all the *kothi* goddesses, Sivagami seemed to be everywhere, wielding her big stick. She kept things on a knife's edge: a balance between performance and reality, this world and the other, order and the threat of chaos. There was something carnivalesque about the *kothis*' performances, in the way they wielded their power almost vengefully, to offset the humiliations they suffered for the rest of the year: the slights at their femininity, the pressure to conform and marry, the compulsion to do sex work; the constant innuendoes that surrounded them; the violence against them, both sexual and physical.

Later, I read an article in *The Times of India* suggesting that the recent revival of the Mayana Kollai tradition might be fueled by the increased visibility and empowerment of transgender people. The author wrote that the festival symbolized "one of the main cultural scripts of Tamil life," which was that "feminine energy is capable of rejuvenating, recovering, and revitalising human life beyond death and destruction."[4] Its high point was when a "woman dressed as Kali or Angalamman skins a fowl, drinks its blood, hangs it by the mouth and gets into a trance while drummers play."

In Devanampattinam, this role was played by the beautiful Mohana, resplendent in a blue-and-gold sari, with fierce warrior-like face markings and a wig that cascaded down below her waist. When she appeared, quite convincingly, to bite the head off a chicken and drink its blood (Lakshaya bellowed to me over the din that there was sleight of hand involved) the crowd roared with awe and revulsion, and seemed barely held in check by Sivagami. These were not pantomime shrieks: there was genuine panic, and the threat of a stampede. An anxious Lakshaya whisked us away into the little palm-reed dressing hut, where Mohana and the other *kothis* later joined us.

I expected Mohana to be exhilarated, but she was distraught: tears ran rivers through her blue makeup. Despite her devotional role, a group of drunk village boys had cornered her as she had made her way to the performance, fully dressed as Kali. They felt her up and wanted to fuck her, she told us, and she was enraged: "Even when I am as Kali, even when I am doing the work of the temple, the work of God, I am treated like a whore!"

None of the Devanampattinam *kothis* sold sex regularly, but most would admit that they did it from time to time, because of the relatively easy income it provided—and because, apart from the temple, it was the one place they could publicly perform and experience a form of womanhood. Now, in the dressing room, Sivagami tried to soothe her blue Kali. "It takes time," she said. "You can't expect the villagers to see you as a goddess all at once, when for the rest of the year you are someone they meet behind the casuarinas."

A feisty young woman was with us; her name was Soorya, she was Mohana's best girlfriend. How, I asked her, would the crowds have behaved had she played the part of Kali?

"It would have been worse." Soorya snorted. "You would have had to call the police to close it down." She referred to what had happened just three months before, the gang-rape and murder of a young woman on a Delhi bus, sparking outrage and public protest throughout India. "That's how men treat women in this society," Soorya said to me. "If I were Kali tonight, I too would probably have been raped by now."

LAKSHAYA

When I returned to Devanampattinam two years later, Soorya was nowhere to be seen. Lakshaya told me that their friend had been forced to give up her dreams of becoming a bookkeeper and had been married off to a boy in another village: she had a baby now. I asked if we could visit, and we made the hour-long drive to her new home. "I wish I was back in Devanampattinam," Soorya scowled, sotto voce, as she greeted us. "I'm not allowed to go anywhere. And I'm not allowed to work."

Soorya served us vegetable biryani in a modest but comfortable little house, and looked grim as Mohana and Lakshaya chatted sweetly with her husband, a handsome lad in a pressed white shirt. The boy seemed anxious to please his wife—around these guests, at least—and told us he planned to be present as a father, unlike his own, who had abandoned the family. Whenever he left the room, Soorya mugged disdain, or even revulsion.

"You should have been born a *kothi*," Lakshaya said to her, with not a little irony, while Mohana longingly dandled the baby. "Then you'd be free."

LAKSHAYA FIRST HEARD the word *kothi* when she was fourteen, newly arrived in Cuddalore, where her mother—an itinerant construction worker—had come to find work. The two had been on the road for several years, after her mother had fled a financially comfortable but abusive marriage. Lakshaya enrolled in a local school and became friends with a boy named Dinesh, who commuted to school from Devanampattinam across the backwater. The two were attracted to each other, Lakshaya told me, because they were both "girlish," although Lakshaya did not yet have a name for it. Dinesh provided one: they were *kothis*—"women's hearts in men's bodies." In fact, Dinesh's preferred name was Dinisha and *he* was a *she*.

Dinisha had learned about *kothis* through her after-school job: she was an outreach worker for the local AIDS organization where Lakshaya herself would later find employment. Its remit, like similar organizations all over India, was to identify high-risk individuals and entice them into its Drop-In Centre, the officially designated name for such places. Here, they would receive safe-sex counseling, HIV testing, and referrals for treatment if needed. Dinisha's job as an outreach worker was to go to "hot spots"—such as bus terminals, or dense undergrowth along the beach—and search for "contacts." She was to strike up a conversation with them and attempt to bring them in to the Drop-In Centre. For this she was paid five thousand rupees (about seventy-five dollars) a month, provided by the Indian government, and to earn it she was required to bring in a minimum number of contacts: these were to be enumerated as *kothis* (passive or effeminate homosexuals), *panthis* (active bisexual men), or "doubledeckers," those who were what Americans would call "versatile"—all words borrowed from *hijra* slang.

And so Lakshaya was not only a new friend for Dinisha but a "contact," too—albeit a diffident one. Although Lakshaya readily accepted a female name she did not seem interested in the Drop-In Centre; the way Dinisha lured her in was by suggesting that they go there to find clothes for an upcoming dress-up party. In Cuddalore, as all over India, the Drop-In Centre had become the local meeting place for the *kothi* community. It was housed in a crumbling mansion built in the traditional Tamil way around a covered central courtyard, and when the two school friends arrived there and Lakshaya saw the scene, she fled. "I was still scared of those people back then," she said. "And my school was so close by. What if they found out?"

Dinisha had better success taking her new friend home to Devanampattinam, where she introduced Lakshaya to Mohana the fisherman. The two quickly bonded and, with typical energy, Mohana set about finding Lakshaya and her mother a place to live in the village. It was two years after the 2004 tsunami had ravaged the village, destroying much of it and killing over sixty people; many of the villagers had been moved into new state housing on higher ground. Lakshaya and her mother moved into an abandoned mud-and-palm-leaf hut; they were still living there when I first came to Devanampattinam, six years later.

Dinisha and Mohana introduced their new friend to the other *kothis* of the village—although not, yet, Sivagami. Lakshaya would meet the priestess a little later, in a most fortuitous way. It took Lakshaya a while for her to settle into the notion of herself as "a woman's heart in a man's body," but she soon started accompanying Dinisha to the Drop-In Centre, and experimenting with feminine presentation: she pierced her ears and began painting her nails.

Because of her precarious family situation, Lakshaya knew she would not be able to continue her schooling if she did not earn some kind of living—and so a couple of years after arriving in town she signed up to become an AIDS outreach worker herself. She, too, began to spend her evenings rounding up *kothis* and bringing them in to the Drop-In Centre to be counted and counseled.

"BEFORE THE AIDS EPIDEMIC, only upper-class gay men or *hijras* had the space [among gender or sexual minority groups in India] to be themselves. Now, with this official support for *kothis*, there was space for poor people, rural people, to be themselves, too. It was a big shift."

These words were said to me by a man named Sunil Menon, the person who had first proposed the use of the terms *kothi* and *panthi* in the fight against AIDS, over two decades before I met Lakshaya and her friends. Menon was one of the first openly gay men in Tamil Nadu. A Chennai-based anthropologist and a fashion "choreographer," he was the founder of the first community-based AIDS organization in South India. He was particularly keen to find a way of getting the people he labeled *kothis* out from under the folds of *hijra* society, where they were subject to rigid and arcane hierarchies, and thus much harder to reach through public-health campaigns. When I visited Sahodaran, his organization in Chennai, two decades after it had been founded, I was struck by its mission, which was to convince *kothis* they did not need to undergo surgery or become women in order to be true to themselves, and to find a place in the world.

Sunil Menon's research caught the attention of the public-health world and he was invited to present a paper at the International AIDS Conference in 1993, in the early days of the Indian epidemic. The *kothi* idea caught fire, not least because epidemiologists and activists working in India saw the value of adopting indigenous words to describe homosexual behavior, rather than the clinical and Western MSM—men who have sex with men.

Epidemiologists were particularly interested in *kothis* because, as passive recipients of anal sex, they were seen to be at the highest risk of HIV infection—and the ones most likely to spread the virus, because so many of them were sex workers with multiple sexual partners. The person most responsible for popularizing this notion was another flamboyant social entrepreneur, a British-born man of South Asian descent called Shivananda Khan, the founder of Naz Foundation International, which would become the largest AIDS NGO on the subcontinent.[5]

The *kothi* strategy became a textbook-case success, and was one of the reasons why India was lauded for its management of the epidemic. It had a profound effect at the grassroots level, too: as funding flowed toward them, *kothi* communities blossomed all over India, clustering around Drop-In Centres in the slums of the cities and in provincial towns like Cuddalore. Given that outreach workers were paid to find *kothis*, it is little wonder that they found so many of them: it was a monetized identity. "*Kothis* were always there," Manohar Elavarthi—a leading activist from the city of Bangalore—told me, "but previously under the wing of the *hijra* community. Through the AIDS epidemic they came out. Their position was formalized. They became empowered."

THIS CERTAINLY SEEMED true for Lakshaya. Her work at SCOHD—the Sahodaran Community Oriented Health Development—in Cuddalore expanded her social network substantially, and she grew in self-confidence. Before long she caught the eye of SCOHD's founder, an imposing older *hijra* named Sheetal, and when Lakshaya finished school, at the age of twenty, she was given the responsibility of running a program at the Drop-In Centre. She learned how to use the center's wheezing desktop computer and, through it, she began exploring the world online. A colleague told her about Facebook, and she entered the blogosphere on December 12, 2011, under the image of a glamorous, androgynous birdwoman. According to the profile, "Lakshaya Johnny" was male. When I friended her a year later, she had 103 Facebook friends: her gender was "other" and her profile picture was that of a famous Tamil film star, "Because I'm tired of people asking me if I'm man or woman." By 2017 she felt confident enough to put her own face online, in a studied portrait that represented her as I knew her: with a smiling plump face framed by diamond-studded ears and short hair in bangs; in "pant-shirt," as Indians describe male attire, but with sari-cloth draped over one shoulder to signal her gender identity.

Lakshaya's original reason to go online was to search for *panthis*, she told me, "but then I became political about it." In the years after we first met, I watched her network grow to about three hundred people, and her political consciousness develop, too. She followed prominent transgender activists, and she often issued broadsides about the lot of "transgenders," a word she was using increasingly. "We have place as 'third gender' in the government book [the census], but not in peoples' hearts," she wrote in a 2014 post.[6] She wrote poetry, and posted some compelling verse, too: "We *kothis* are carved as statues, but people see us only as rock."

When I picked up an important new Indian book in 2017—Akshay Khanna's *Sexualness*—I felt I was reading about Lakshaya and her friends. Khanna wrote that official sponsorship of *kothi*-driven, community-based organizations meant "regular employment in NGOs, the creation of networks of support and services, and the inauguration of a realm of respectability for hitherto despised folk."[7]

But it was not just about the money: in fact, you earned much more by begging or sex work than by rounding up *kothis* and herding them into a Drop-In Centre. Far more important, Khanna said, was "a social mobility, a political mobility, the option of the cloak of respectability, of the acceptance of one's choices and sense of self as legitimate."[8] There was a downside, though: the construction of what Khanna terms "the epidemiological *Kothi*," an identity category created by the AIDS industry around the act of being penetrated, or being effeminate.[9] And this, he and others maintained, had serious consequences.

In one of my visits to India, I made a detour to the North Indian city of Lucknow, to see the historian Saleem Kidwai, a historian and the father of queer Indian scholarship: he had coedited the landmark *Same-Sex Love in India*, published in 2000.[10] When I described my time with the *kothis* of Devinampattinam, he disputed the notion that there was a *kothi* gender tradition in India: "I have found no references to it before the twentieth century in my historical research."

I told Kidwai what Lakshaya had said to me about the difference between gays and *kothis*: that the former were from the city and lived glamorous lives while the latter were from the village and "did women's' work." This confirmed his analysis: "The AIDS industry has glorified *kothis* as stereotypes of battered women, sex workers and 'second wives.'" How could this be "empowering," he wondered. And if this marginalized group *became* empowered, might the funding dry up?

Certainly, in my visits to Devanampattinam, I witnessed the way the village *kothis* took on subordinate female roles. Dinisha's love life was a case in point. In high school, a *panthi* had teased her for being effeminate. He pushed her off a swing and forced himself on her, and she had been with him ever since. He only came to her when drunk, though—and he had, of course, a girlfriend. He still often forced himself on her, but she did not mind this, she said, as it confirmed her femininity.

The fisherman Mohana seemed different. She had been with her *panthi* for over five years: they were cousins and in business together, with shares in the same fishing boat. They had a secret meeting spot in a casuarina grove beyond the village, and were reportedly madly in love. But when I met Mohana again in 2015, her heart was sore. Her *panthi* needed to marry, she told me, to counter the gossip beginning to spread about their relationship. Mohana was preoccupied with seeking out the right spouse for the *panthi*, someone not too pretty, not too well-off. "It is for the better" she told me, dabbing her eyes. "If he does not marry, his younger brother will not be able to marry, too. The world will talk! This way, he will have his wife and children, and we will still meet in our special place."

The priestess Sivagami was dubious. She summed up *panthis* for me: "They will stay with you only for as long as you have money to support them. When you fall, they will not be there to lift you up. So I tell my *kothis*, 'In our life, we can only depend on each other.'" Sivagami's own most lasting relationship had also been with a cousin—this was often the case with village *kothis*—but she had ended it. "He would get drunk and abuse me." Celibacy was a far preferable option, and she had embraced it as part of her divine calling.

Human rights activism was Lakshaya's calling, and it seemed to offer her a similar escape route from gender oppression. She offered strong online pronouncements on the rights of women, particularly after the 2012 Delhi gang-rape and murder. "If Prabhu and I make house together," she told me in 2015, fantasizing about her latest *panthi* crush, "I tell you, Mark, I will not be cooking for one whole year. I am not going to be one of those *kothis* who are just there to cook and pay for their man."

But Lakshaya was always mooning over this or that *panthi*, and having her heart broken by them: she wanted love, they wanted sex. As she put it in a poem: "I am one heart with two lives. I act as a man, and suffer as a woman."[11]

LAKSHAYA'S MOTHER, WHOSE NAME WAS GOMATI, certainly saw no value in her child's increasing embrace of femininity. When Gomati heard others in the village calling her child Laskhaya she chastised her: "You were born male. Why would you want to lower yourself?"

Since childhood, Lakshaya told me, Gomati had restrained her from dressing like a girl, and the tension only increased once they moved to Devanampattinam and Lakshaya entered the world of *kothis*. And so when the Drop-In Centre organized a workshop for families, Lakshaya decided to bring Gomati along. A stunned mother heard that her son was actually her daughter, and although she swallowed hard and said she would accept it, she marched Lakshaya straight off to a local priest to try to sort things out. The priest gave her no comfort: Lakshaya had been born this way and nothing could be done about it. It was Lakshaya's immense good fortune that this priest was Sivagami—at that point still officiating as a man. Still, Gomati railed against Lakshaya and redoubled her efforts to find a daughter-in-law. There were years of bitter conflict. But they had been alone in the world together since Lakshaya's early childhood, and neither could bear the thought of separating. Lakshaya had internalized some of the precepts of the broader rights movement, through her work at the Drop-In Centre and her online exposure. "If I can't get you to accept me, how can I get society to accept me?" she said to her mother in what both told me was their worst fight ever.

When we met in 2014, Gomati was in her early forties, a petite woman whose fine beauty was callused by years of hard labor. Although she told me the story of how she came to accept Lakshaya as if it were a well-rehearsed script I did not doubt her sincerity, given the strong affection I witnessed between them. "Finally I understood what they had told me [in the Drop-In Centre's family workshop],"

Gomati told me. "I understood that it's God's mistake, not Mathi's mistake [she still used Lakshaya's male name], not our mistake. We should not treat them different. We should accept them."

But there was a condition to this acceptance: Lakshaya was not to wear saris, even in the temple. It was for this reason that Lakshaya did not participate in the Mayana Kollai festival. Lakshaya did not see this as an unacceptable compromise. Rather, she understood it as the glue that would keep her family together.

Fiercely intelligent, Lakshaya rose rapidly through the ranks at SCOHD, earning herself the nickname Indira Gandhi among her coworkers. With her increased salary and the help (of course) of Mohana in finding informal credit she finally procured a proper home for herself and Gomati: when I visited in 2015, they lived in a bungalow under the palms right on the beach, with two beloved white dogs chained to a broad balcony overlooking piles of litter and the palm-framed sea beyond. As often in India, the spotlessly clean interior contrasted dramatically with the filth outside: two bright clean rooms, washed vibrant with indigo.

Although Gomati could not shake calling Lakshaya by her male name, she had begun referring to "my daughter" and using feminine pronouns, and the home had become something of a gathering place for the village *kothis*. Gomati's own outsider status—a single woman, a migrant—made it easier, perhaps, for her to accept her daughter. So, too, did economic interdependency, and Lakshaya's own increasing status in the world: for the first time in two decades Gomati had her own home, the direct consequence of Lakshaya's *kothi* identity.

Gomati made us a delicious meal of *dosa*—the South Indian fermented-rice pancake—with vegetable curry and coconut chutney. Mohana was with us, and after the meal the girls opened up the Godrej cabinet, a fixture in almost all Indian households no matter how modest, and pulled out saris. We had brought Mohana a wig as a gift and Gomati participated enthusiastically in a dress-up session that culminated in wrapping me in six yards of silk.

"LOOK AT THIS! Is this me?"

Lakshaya slapped an identity card down on the table as she and Mohana met us for lunch at the vegetarian restaurant that had become our Cuddalore hangout. It was February 2015, nearly two years after I had last seen them. The card had a mug shot of a pretty girl in a sari and makeup bearing a passing resemblance to the indignant young person sitting opposite me.

The previous week, Lakshaya said, she had applied for what is known as an "Aravani Identity Card." "Aravani" is the official Tamil designation for *hijra* and was chosen by a police official in 2008 as a non-derogatory term for people to whom the government had now decided to accord the status of "most backward class"—like, for example, the *dalits* (or "untouchables"). Bearers of Aravani cards were entitled to a range of social and welfare services, including access to a pension at forty (the rationale being that at that age you will no longer be able to earn as a sex worker); to housing; and even—on paper at least—to free sexual reassignment surgery. In practice, the state offered a more sanitary and professional version of the ritual castration that *hijras* underwent, but there was only one hospital in the state—with a long waiting list—that offered it free. Still, after 2008, Tamil Nadu became the most progressive state in India on transgender rights, and the model for a proposed new national policy after the Supreme Court's NALSA decision in 2014.

Lakshaya had decided to go for the card not so much for the benefits as for the official recognition she believed was her due as a TG, the term she was now using interchangeably with *kothi*. No one I met in Devanampattinam or Cuddalore had used it when I first visited, two years ago, but in the interim the notion had taken root, with its implications of rights and of biomedical transition.

To get the Aravani card, you had to undergo an interview at a District Screening Committee, comprised of five people, including a medical doctor, a psychologist, and a local *hijra* leader. Lakshaya had set out for her interview in her habitual pant-shirt, bending gender with no more than an earring and plucked eyebrows. She was turned away before she even got a hearing by *hijras* sitting outside: they chastised her and told her that by presenting herself that way she was jeopardizing the whole process.

And so she returned, the following day, in a rage and a sari, to have the (successful) interview and the photograph she now showed me on her newly minted card. She was still furious: "I have nothing against those who wear saris, but I am not one of them. And I have my arrangement with my mother. This is disrespectful to her and humiliating to me. And it is wrong, *wrong*! We must fight it."

We spoke about the research I had seen, about how assessment criteria varied wildly from district to district in Tamil Nadu, depending largely on the opinion of the "transgender community member" on the screening committee: some insisted that to qualify you needed to present as a woman, or even show proof of surgery. Lakshaya was adamant that she should not be compelled to wear a sari to qualify as transgender: "It is how I feel inside, not how I look. That's what the Supreme Court says!"

She was referring to the 2014 NALSA judgment, whose key finding was that it was a constitutional right for Indians to choose for themselves whether they were male, female, or third gender. But the government itself was bent on contesting the judgment: a Ministry of Social Justice and Empowerment experts' report insisted that there would need to be the kind of "psycho social assessment" already in place in Tamil Nadu; so, too, did a parliamentary bill introduced to forge national legislation out of the judgment.[12]

These positions were buttressed by the lobbying of some of the powerful *hijras* who led India's transgender community, and who insisted on some kind of gatekeeping. As Sudha, a *hijra* leader from Chennai, put it to me: "Only someone who is always in feminine attire can be called transgender. If someone calls themselves trans and is wearing pant-shirt, I cannot agree to it. If you wear a mustache and say you feel female inside, I'm sorry, you don't face our problems!"

Like the *hijras* who turned Lakshaya away, Sudha believed that if anyone could walk in and claim entitlements on the basis of a felt identity the system would be abused, and "authentic" transgender women discredited. She and other *hijra* leaders also believed that, given the historical discrimination against them, only transgender women should qualify for entitlements. Lakshaya found herself in the opposing camp: a new queer coalition that included non-binary people and transgender men from the cities, and that insisted on holding the state to the NALSA decision, with its confirmation of the right to self-identification.

When the Transgender Persons (Protection of Rights) Bill was finally approved by parliament in August 2019, it stipulated that you did, still, have to submit to a certification process if you wished to change your legal gender marker: no longer a screening committee but a district magistrate and a government doctor. Activists were enraged, and some labeled the day it was passed "Gender Justice Murder Day."[13] There were other objections. The bill had initially banned begging by transgenders (the word was a noun in India), and stipulated that it was illegal for anyone other than a court to remove transgender children from their families; if families were unable or unwilling to take care of transgender children themselves, the children would be placed in "rehabilitation" facilities.[14] This was a throwback to the colonial myth that *hijras* kidnapped children.

Through intense lobbying, activists succeeded in getting the begging ban dropped, but the effective ban on taking in minors remained. Particularly given the abuse (along with the shelter) that young *chelas* found in the *hijra* society, this might have been a well-intentioned attempt to bring trans minors into the ambit of India's other child-protection laws. Still, the very word *rehabilitation* suggested criminality or conversion rather than care—and threatened the very fundaments of age-old *hijra* society: its intergenerational family structure. The state might have been setting out to modernize and regularize India's millions of transgender people, but it was doing so in a way that would demolish the social and economic structure on which *hijras* depended.

SHEETAL

Identities are contextual, of course, and are determined by many things, including access to information and to material resources. Suddenly, in a country where transgender identity held out the possibility of social and economic benefit and even political power, *kothis* like Lakshaya found themselves at the center of a new and heated debate. But what made life complicated for them was that even if they now called themselves TGs—with all the allure of self-determination this promised—they were still bound to the old ways: this is what was made manifest in the debates over the Transgender Act of 2019. Nowhere was this contraction clearer to me than in the role of Sheetal, Lakshaya's boss at SCOHD, in the lives of the Devanampattinam *kothis*.

I first met Sheetal in Devanampattinam, where she presided over the Mayana Kollai festival as something of a mother figure. Over six feet tall and with a commanding gait, she generally wore the female *salwaar kameez* and had long wavy hair with a slight henna tint, but she sat like a man, her legs open, and drew on a cigarette like one, too. She lived in nearby Pondicherry with her *panthi*, a younger man always in leather boots and jacket. He was devoted to her, it seemed, and was her driver, too: she got around on the back of his motorbike. She had the typical husky voice—and bluntness—of a *hijra* but she spoke passable English: she was from a middle-class family and had an engineering degree, in shipbuilding technology of all things.

To what did she owe her status at the Mayana Kollai festival, I asked her. Was it because she was the director of SCOHD, where Lakshaya worked?

No, she responded. It was because of her status in the *hijra* society: she was the *nayak*, or leader, and so "all these girls are part of my family." This was a surprise to me: I had assumed that by eschewing the *hijra* identity, the village *kothis* were not part of the elaborate *hijra* society either. But it turned out they were Sheetal's "daughters." Sheetal had sixty-two daughters across two districts, she told me, and many of these, like the priestess Sivagami, had their own daughters, too. "It's a very big job. Big family! People are attracted to me because I'm very free. I'm not the kind of *nayak* who says, 'Hey, come press my legs!' I'm very jovial. I suffered when I used to go to a guru's house, sitting all the way over there, [the guru] refusing to greet me. I didn't want that for my daughters."

And so Sheetal was the "mother" of Sivagami and the "grandmother" of the village's younger *kothis*, including Lakhshaya and Mohana, many of them from when they were in their early teens. This was not just sentiment, the assertion of a chosen family in the way queer folk did the world over: it was highly regulated, through centuries-old code, with obligations on both sides.

Sheetal's primary ritual role was to lead her daughters through the process of becoming *nirvan*, or emasculated. She also "looked after" them when they were in need, and she resolved disputes among them—although her control was not as tight as in the big cities, where a "house" was often actually a physical space in which *hijras* lived and worked, such as the priestess Sivagami had experienced in Bombay.

Without this direct physical or labor-broking connection, it was not entirely clear what the village *kothis*' reciprocal obligations to Sheetal were. This was in part because it was taboo to talk about internal *hijra* matters, and in part because they feared and even resented her, too, " jovial" though she might be. Even though none of her Devanampattinam daughters were jobbing regularly as sex workers or beggars, Sheetal tithed them relentlessly. This seemed to reach into her management of SCOHD, too, although none of her employees felt comfortable confirming this to me. Still, Lakshaya chafed against it: "As long as there is a guru chela system we are going to lead an oppressed life," she wrote on her Facebook timeline in 2015.[15]

But Lakshaya was trapped. Sheetal was not just her grandmother in the *hijra* society. She was her boss in the AIDS world, too.

SHEETAL LOOKED ON the choices her young protégé Lakshaya had made, and the familial reconciliation it enabled, with not a little envy. "My parents threw me out," she told me. "Engineering degree and all, I had no choice but to run to Bombay. I had no family support. If I had the family support, I would never have had to go for *dhanda* [sex work], and to do this."

She sliced her hand through the air, sharply downward towards her groin.

Sheetal had initially come out as gay when studying in Goa in the 1990s: there was already a gay scene there, largely due to expats and holidaymakers from Bombay and Delhi. After her graduation her parents had wanted to send her to Dubai to join her brother, "but I knew that I would not survive there, with my walk that is not manly," and so she settled in Chennai instead, where she became involved with Sunil Menon's AIDS work. Having learned about community-based organization there, she returned to Pondicherry to set up a branch—and that's where the family problems really began for her, she said. Her parents left town, returning to their native Kerala, and cut all ties.

"Perhaps that gives you a certain kind of freedom?" I ventured.

"I can't call it freedom," she shot back, letting rare vulnerability crack her features. "There's a feeling of loneliness. After six p.m. I don't know where to go."

When Sheetal said this I recalled some research I had seen from nearby Bangalore, where a 2012 study of transgender mental health had been commissioned following thirty-nine "unnatural deaths" in the *hijra* community over eighteen months, fifteen of which were suicides.[16] An astonishing 32 percent of the informants surveyed said they had considered suicide in the previous month. These figures tallied with those from other parts of the world, and there had always been high suicide rates in *hijra* communities. But something had shifted in recent years, I was told by Manohar Elavarthi, the head of the organization that commissioned the research. Elavarthi believed the suicide figures had spiked because of the "psychological stress" of the human rights era. "The speed at which you change does not match the speed at which societies change." He cited specific examples from Bangalore, where *hijras* had struck out on their own. "But then they find themselves out there, cut off from their families, cut off, too, from the *jamaath* [the *hijra* society], totally isolated. They can't cope."

The way Sheetal coped was—despite her education and upward mobility—by remaining within the *jamaath*. She was one of the youngest *nayaks* in India, and one of the best-educated. She had national ambitions, too. When we met in the bar of a Chennai airport hotel in 2015, she was in transit back to Pondicherry after a national meeting of transgender leaders in Delhi, to discuss the implementation of the NALSA judgment. She was doing an increasing amount of travel, she told me, and she made much of her position as a reformer of what she believed was a very necessary system.

She spoke of herself in the third person: "You can't expect every leader will be like Sheetal. Older people are getting money from their daughters. Sheetal's not like that because now the new generations are coming up and are not willing to be a slave." Sheetal believed the *jamaath* to be more necessary than ever: "If *jamaath* is not there, they'll be free to go and fight with the public, to make nonsense. In *jamaath* if something like that comes up, we call them [to order], to make correct. If they don't listen, we take them out of *jamaath*." Her biggest achievement, she said, was that she had intervened successfully to stop *hijras* begging from shops in Pondicherry, thus engendering more respect for them. When I asked how they earned their living instead, though, she was vague.

Through her gender identity Sheetal had lost any prospects of a conventional career—and her family. In compensation for the former, she found the NGO world and AIDS entrepreneurship, at which she excelled. And in compensation for the latter, she worked the *jamaath*. This meant even taking a break from her career path in the AIDS world to apprentice herself to a guru in Bombay for four years, begging and hustling.

Why?

"When I come out, who is going to care for me?" she responded, somewhat aggressively. "This is not Melbourne or Sydney, yaah?"

SHEETAL HAD A THIRD JOB, besides running SCOHD and running the local *hijras* and *kothis*.

She was ward manager in a hospital.

A few years earlier, Pondicherry's Mahatma Gandhi Medical College & Research Institute decided to set up a transgender-care clinic. The institute was one of India's top medical schools, and by 2016 its clinic would be the first full-spectrum trans health facility in the country: its first vaginoplasty patient was one of its own doctors, a brilliant young anesthetist named Sameera Jahagirdar, who had been instrumental in setting up the facility.

But the first step had been to develop a formal relationship with the local *hijra* community, and as the local boss, Sheetal was the broker. At Sheetal's insistence, the hospital hired four transgender women from the community: these, unsurprisingly, included Sheetal herself, who as well as being appointed a ward manager was given the responsibility for community outreach.

It was through Sheetal that the medical school conducted its first research into Pondicherry's transgender community, in 2016: a study of the urogenital complications arising out of botched surgeries. Of the fifty-five examined, at least six had such serious problems that they would succumb to renal failure if these were not corrected. "You can only imagine the pain and shame these girls live with every day," the doctor Sameera Jahagirdar said to me.

I had first met Sameera with her "hubby" Karthick in 2013, at a café in Pondicherry's French colonial quarter. She had only recently started hormone treatment: she wore low-key androgynous clothing—jeans and a white *kurta*—and was beginning to grow out her hair, around a lively moon face. She was warm and willowy and unaffected, medically precise about her gender transition but also emotionally fluent. Two years later, when I went to visit her at the hospital, she greeted me in a white coat with her hair pulled back into workmanlike ponytail; when she removed the coat you could see the bumps of her new breasts growing beneath her men's collared shirt.

She was still "Sameer-Sir" at work, although many of her colleagues knew the score.

Karthick, a few years younger, was definitely a "hubby" rather than a *panthi*. He had his own well-paid job in publishing, and the couple had met each other's families, who had come around to accepting them as a couple. They even wore wedding rings, exchanged in a private ceremony attended by both fathers, one a schoolmaster, the other a journalist.

Sameera was of that small elite of Indian transgender women whose opportunities and self-awareness meant that they bypassed, or even defined themselves against, the *hijra* identity. Sameera had discovered her gender identity through literature, online, and then in medical libraries: this meant that she had internalized the Western notion of "transgender," of rights and of biomedical transition, before even considering whether she might be a *hijra*. If she had been of another class or another generation, she told me, her only option would have been to join the *jamaath*. Instead, she said, "LGBTQI is my *jamaath*." She was an active member of Orinam, the Chennai-based activist organization, and her few close friends were made through the group. Joining Orinam was "a very conscious decision. I thought, I need a support system, a community, and it can't be the *jamaath*. I was worried about the social status, scared about the stigma [around being a *hijra*]. That's not for me. I'm a doctor!"

Sameera acknowledged that she had been wary when Sheetal first came to work at the hospital: she still harbored a residual fear of *hijras*. Nonetheless, she came to value Sheetal's presence. The *nayak*'s bluntness opened doors for hospital staff to understand—and ask questions about—the doctor's own transition. And Sheetal worked tirelessly to make sure that transgender patients were given due care and respect across the hospital's services.

FOR HER PART, Sheetal loved the work at the hospital: "People respect me. They call me Madam. I'm coping well with the job."

I asked about Sameera.

"Oh, I *love* him. You are free with him, to come to talk to him." But Sheetal worried that "he's not coming out [as transgender], that's the problem." This was before Sameera's surgery, and Sheetal did not commit to the feminine names or pronouns for her new colleague: "I want to hire Sameer for my office as a part-time doctor, but he won't come. A lot of things, he can't do, because he is not out."

But when I spoke to Sameera in 2017—I was not able to pin Sheetal down again, despite much trying—the relationship had soured. It seemed that Sheetal struggled to abide by the hospital's hierarchy, in which Sameera had authority over her. Sameera complained that Sheetal thought of the hospital as part of her domain and had set herself up as the gatekeeper between the transgender community and the hospital, filtering who could present themselves for its medical services.

For Sameera it was a case study in culture clash; the difference between the way the feudal *hijra* society operated and the way a modern institution such as a gender-care facility in a hospital needed to function. Sheetal's inability to adapt was a harbinger of the difficulties to come, Sameera worried, as the country with the world's largest enumerated population of transgender people moved into the gender order of the modern world.

By 2019, the two seemed to have made their peace: "I've moved on," Sameera told me. Indeed: she was running health-care camps in Rajasthan, participating in an online video series being made in Hyderabad, and planning to move with Karthick to Australia, to specialize in intensive care.

IN 2019, SAMEERA was still listed by her male name on the hospital website. But among colleagues and patients—where she now ran the intensive care unit—she was now "Ninety-five percent Sameera-Madam." There had been some hairy moments, though: not from staff but from patients or more often their families, who sometimes leered at her or even—in one instance—groped her: "When I took the family off to the counseling room this one *goonda* from the village kept his hand on my butt, he squeezed it, pinched, it, rubbed his finger right up my ass. Inside my ICU, with my nurses and junior doctors just standing there. He had the cheek even to do a flying kiss to me. I lost my mind there! I gave him a nice, tight slap! Everyone saw!"

Just as I had with the *kothi* Mohana after her harassment during the Mayana Kollai festival in Devanampattinam, I asked Sameera whether this would have happened were she a cisgender woman. Was she not, now, just experiencing what happened to girls and women in India all the time? "Yes, sure, on the street," she responded, after chewing on the question for a while. "But a woman in authority? Never." We went on to talk about how, as she put it, "It is taken for granted that you are available [sexually] if you are a feminine boy. You're *supposed* to get sexually harassed, even beaten." She reflected on her own childhood, where she had been teased a lot for her effeminacy, and she isolated, with surgical precision, the "insult, but joy" of being derided and desired at the same time. "I hated it, but I also felt good about it. You're different. And as different, you're treated as bad. But you want it. You want the attention. That's where the [internal] conflict starts. That's how the mind gets divided. 'I'm *supposed* to be like this.'" She could have been describing the *kothis* of Devanampattinam.

In 2015, the priestess Sivagami told me she had been referred to the Transgender Care Clinic by Sheetal, and was talking to the psychologist there about having surgery.

I was astounded.

Sivagami had been so adamant the last time I visited that she would not do so. Now she was considering it because of peer pressure, and a feeling that she would not otherwise gain the requisite respect from the broader *hijra* community: "Anyway, I have no children. Who is going to look after me when I am old, if not my own daughters?" But she felt torn: priestly power is signified by a bare male chest, the hairier the better, and this was her vocation. She had been praying for guidance for months.

According to the *hijra* code you ascend to a certain godliness—and attain a higher level of honors—when you are emasculated: the burial of your severed organ in the ground confirms that you have the power to confer fertility on others. In fact, when Sheetal and I had spoken about her own surgery, she told me she had done it primarily for the sake of honor: "So many people expected it of me. They call me Mom but when I go to *jamaath* they make fun of me. They make fun of my daughters and granddaughters too, because their *guru* is not a true transgender." No one had demanded the surgery of Sheetal, she insisted, it was just that "we don't get the respect until it happens." She owed it not just to herself, but to her daughters, too, and she described it as a survival strategy rather than something arising out of an internal need.

Certainly, the services now available to Sivagami at the shining new hospital in Pondicherry were much better than those she would have been forced to endure in a Bombay backstreet twenty years previously, and this might have explained her change of heart. She decided to proceed: "Only surgery will make the reason of my birth meaningful, as 'a woman's heart in a man's body.'"

Still, she would not undergo any breast augmentation or take hormones, so that she could maintain the masculine chest required to perform *poojas*. She had discussed this with the psychologist and with Sheetal, and they had both agreed this was her best solution. Thus would she embody her own particular and somewhat unique gender: she would have a male upper torso and a female lower one.

Such permutations seemed increasingly possible in the era of transgender rights, which was ventilating India's age-old *hijra* community with notions of personal autonomy.

Lakshaya, a generation younger, was mainlined to these notions through the Internet and her activism, and was finding her own singular path, too: "Cutting my penis will not make me more of a woman. I am a woman already."

ON MARCH 31, 2017, Lakshaya was asked by Sheetal to be master of ceremonies at the International Transgender Day of Visibility event in Pondicherry. The event was attended by the chief minister, and many senior officials and politicians, too. My heart swelled as I looked at the photographs: there was my Devanampattinam girl at the podium, in a Western-style pink dress that was stylish but conservative; it covered her arms and was fastened at the collar, and had a row of big metal buttons down the front. Perhaps Pondicherry was distant enough from the village for Lakshaya to wear women's attire in public; perhaps she was coming to enjoy dressing as a woman if done on her own terms. Her hair was short, but with her trademark sassy bangs, and she had costume jewelry in her ears that matched the buttons on her dress.

The pride that swept over me, looking at the images, reminded me of how I had felt watching Tiwonge Chimbalanga mesmerize the audience at the Colours of Cape Town fund-raiser for LGBTI refugees in Cape Town, in 2015. There had been an uncomfortable edge to my pride with Aunty Tiwo; an anxiety that I was falling into the savior complex so often critiqued as one of the pitfalls of the Pink Line. I had paid for her to work two days a week at PASSOP, the LGBTI refugee organization, and this seemed to have helped pull her out of alcoholism and into purpose. I had tried, similarly, but unsuccessfully, to fund Michael Bashaija's education in Uganda before he fled the country, and come to his rescue a few times in Kenya, too.

In India there had not been that dynamic with anyone, least of all Lakshaya, who was immensely proud: she refused even to take payment for the significant work she did as my Devanampattinam fixer. I gifted her, instead, with a fridge, a housewarming present for her new home. My role seemed closer to some kind of mentorship: we had spent many hours with her, my interpreter Lavanya and I, helping her think about her future. I had brought her to Pondicherry to meet the doctor Sameera, for example, in the hope that this would inspire her to think about a professional career, and I had introduced her fulsomely to my own LGBT connections in Chennai.

Lakshaya attracted my attention among the Devanampattinam *kothis* because she was *moving*: it seemed to me that by following her flight I could track progress along and across the Pink Line in India. And here she was in a hall in Pondicherry, introducing the chief minister no less! I heard that her wits had actually saved the day when the guest of honor had misguidedly referred to transgender people as "handicapped," and the crowd had threatened to walk out in protest. Lakshaya found a way to pacify the audience without offending the chief minister: "If we are handicapped," she said in beautiful Tamil, "it is because we have been made to be handicapped by friends, and family, and neighbors. Yes, sir, you are correct. We are in that way handicapped indeed."

Later, over Skype, Lakshaya beamed as she told me the story: "I had to clarify things there and then, so I did it in a very correct way. I earned a lot of respect from people because of it! A friend from Chennai even said I could be a journalist in the future!"

IN THAT SAME Skype conversation, in late 2017, I asked Lakshaya what was going on in her life.

She did not say anything, but clapped flat palms together in that way that *hijras* do.

Was she telling me she had become a beggar?

She explained: "The last nine months of my life have been the worst in my life. Sheetal moved me to a bigger job in Pondicherry, and I became mentally disturbed because of the in-fighting. For a while I thought I might kill myself. So I quit."

Perhaps Lakshaya had been promoted above her ability. Or, conversely, perhaps this very ability had put her in conflict with *hijras* more senior than her in the *jamaath*,but whose access to resources she now controlled. One way or the other, she had become a casualty of precisely the construction of the *kothi* identity that scholars and activists warned against. She had ridden high on the wave of AIDS funding and then crashed. She was a *kothi* Icarus.

"I'm more peaceful now," she insisted. "I can sleep."

Had she looked for other work?

She had taken a job at a private company, but had only lasted a couple of days: "I sensed people were looking at me, talking behind my back." There was another offer on the table, stocktaking at a heavy-motorvehicle company, but she would get only four thousand rupees a month for that—about sixty dollars—and her debts on the new house were triple that. And so, yes, she had taken to begging: "I've been able to support myself, and to take care of the interest on my house." She easily earned twelve thousand rupees a month by working only three or four days a week.

What about her principles? Her deal with her mother?

"I wear a sari to do a job, Mark. It's simply my situation." She managed it by traveling fifty kilometers to another town to work, where people did not know her. She acknowledged that she was in a bind: too girly to work a regular job, too manly to work the *hijra* job. "Pant-shirt is a far more comfortable dress. You don't have to stuff your breasts and wear a bra. And if I have a little bit of hair, the shopkeepers shout, 'Why so manly?' So I have to pluck each and every hair on my face." Of course, she wore a wig when working, which elicited comment from other working girls: "'Why don't you have your own hair?' But I can't grow my hair long, because when I go back home I am a *kothi*, back in pant-shirt." So, yes, she said, "it's difficult, but I endure it, because I just think of my family."

On workdays she would leave Cuddalore early in pant-shirt, her feminine attire stashed in a little bag. She would travel with another *kothi*; they had found a place to change once there. Usually, they managed to change back before the return journey, but sometimes, if they were at risk of missing the last bus, they would be forced to return in their saris: "If the bus driver sees a TG on the bus, he leaves the light on so you can't sleep. Even so, it's better, because drunk people are always traveling, and they take advantage."

This was nothing, though, compared to the harassment she received on the job for having her male genitals intact. This came "from members of my own community, because there's always discrimination against those of us who have not had the surgery," and also from the shopkeepers she begged from. "Men reach down to touch your penis, 'You're not operated! You're a male, not a transgender! Go away and have your surgery and then come back!'"

I breathed deeply before asking my next, obvious, question.

"You know me, Mark. I'm someone who doesn't believe a reproductive organ should decide gender identity." She used these very words in Tamil: she was a quick study. "But there's constant pressure coming from the community, and that is making me feel unfulfilled as a *kothi* anymore. The pressure makes me fear that it's in the future for me [to have the surgery]."

"That's devastating to hear, Lakshaya," I said. I wanted to cry.

She registered my emotion and gave a smile that flickered across the Skypewaves, as if to reassure me—and perhaps herself: "All these thoughts happen when I'm tying up a sari and walking around in one. Doing the job. But once I get home, the moment I remove my wig, I remove these thoughts also."

Later in the conversation, she said: "I don't have to answer to anyone when doing this job. I answer to myself."

Lavanya, my interpreter, took her on: "You have choices, Lakshaya!" But Lakshaya stuck to her guns: "It's not a choice. It's my situation."

MOHANA HAD COME with Lakshaya to talk to me over Skype.

It turned out she had a "situation," too. She was getting married.

This, from the All-India Pass, the queen of Devanampattinam, the one who said she could never be with a woman. *What?*

"I'll be able to manage it. I'll be able to have a child. It's not complicated. Every man and woman do it. Why can't I?" What about her *panthi*?

"He will also get married. Then people will stop bugging us. We can still meet."

My interpreter Lavanya, a strong feminist, rose to the challenge: "And if your wife has relationships outside the marriage, how will you feel?"

"She won't. Women don't do that."

"How typical for you to think like that!" said Lavanya. "Maybe you are a man after all."

"I have my parents," Mohana said. "I have to respect them. To give them happiness and satisfaction."

Lavanya was not letting go: "What about *her* parents?"

"I will do nothing to dishonor them," Mohana said. "Every man has to live with this."

Did Lavanya translate that correctly? Was Mohana calling herself a "man"?

LAVANYA WAS AN old hand in the Tamil Nadu nonprofit world. She scratched around, and found Lakshaya a job.

And so when we next were in touch, in early 2018, Lakshaya told me she was working for Internet Saathi, a project of Google India and Tata, devoted to "bridging the online gender divide in rural India," according to its website, by training women in digital literacy in three hundred thousand villages across India.[17] By August 2018 Internet Saathi had benefited seventeen million women in the country, *Forbes India* reported.[18] A few thousand of these were in three Tamil Nadu districts, where Lakshaya now coordinated teams of "women ambassadors" to do outreach and training according to the template developed by the AIDS organizations.[19]

What a perfect job for someone who had once empowered herself in this way, making the world bigger by going online.

Lakshaya was happy, doing really well in her job. She traveled a lot now, but such was the new world of work that she could do much of it in the home she had made with her mother, along the beach in Devanampattinam, which she could now afford to keep, given her stable income.

ON SEPTEMBER 6, 2018, the Indian Supreme Court gave its judgment repealing Section 377 of the Indian penal code and decriminalizing homosexuality. I was alerted to this, fittingly, by my correspondent in Devanampattinam: "Waiting for a Historical moment," wrote Lakshaya in English in a Facebook status update on the morning the judgment was expected.[20] Then, three hours later, she posted the banner "Love is Love …," and a meme: a map of India fashioned out of a rainbow flag with the hashtag "#LGBT legalized."[21]

"Our ability to recognize others who are different is a sign of our own evolution," said one of the four judges, D. Y. Chandrachud, in an erudite and humane judgment that took into its sweep a century of law, from the Oscar Wilde trial to Trinidad and Tobago's decriminalization of homosexuality five months earlier.[22] With citations ranging from Leonard Cohen to Eve Kosofsky Sedgwick (one of the founders of queer theory), Judge Chandrachud set the bar globally for jurisprudence about sexual orientation and gender identity. He acknowledged the primary remedy the court sought to give—to restore to queer people "the simple right as human beings to live, love and partner as nature made them," decades overdue—but wanted to demonstrate, too, how the Indian constitution could be used to forge "true equality" by "questioning prevailing notions about the dominance of sexes and genders."

India's chief justice Dipak Misra articulated similar aspirations in his main judgment: to end discrimination, particularly toward the country's huge transgender population, would be nothing less than "the herald of a New India."[23] Judge Misra wrote, at length, about how the "stigma, oppression and prejudice" experienced by "transgenders" had to be "eradicated," and he urged all Indians to "stand up and speak up" against any such discrimination; he also praised the community itself for "their formidable spirit, inspired commitment, strong determination and infinite hope." Only once transgender people were liberated from "a certain bondage indescribable in words" would "the LGBT community" have the "equal rights" guaranteed to them in the Constitution.

Judge Misra opened his ruling with Goethe: "I am what I am, so take me as I am."[24] This had, of course, been refracted through *La Cage aux Folles* and Gloria Gaynor into a global gay anthem. Without even having read the judgment, Lakshaya could riff on it in a little poem she published in Tamil, on Facebook, on the day it was handed down:

My love
My gender identity

I don't need any law that is going to question me
And push people into fear… .
I look forward to a new beginning.[25]
*#LGBTIQ+ #IPC [Indian Penal Code]_377 #NO_GOING_*
BACK

THREE MONTHS LATER, in December 2018, Lakshaya lost her job: Internet Saathi's funding cycle in Tamil Nadu had come to a close. She was back to begging, at least until she could find another job.

Mohana was not yet married.

The priestess Sivagami had not yet had her surgery.

ON IT GETTING BETTER

ON JANUARY 26, 2019, nine years after Tiwonge Chimbalanga stood in the dock to be charged with "carnal knowledge against the order of nature" in Malawi[1] and nearly five years since I had first visited her at her home-in-exile, I went back to see her. I had not been to Tambo Village in a while, and—my deadlines looming—I had the notion of ending this book where it began: back in South Africa, twenty kilometers along the shore from my Cape Town home, in Aunty's two-room shack.

It was a Saturday afternoon, the day after month-end payday, and I was anxious about what I might find. The streets, indeed, were teeming: large groups picnicking in the park across from Aunty's house; kids skittering between slow-moving cars while adults sat out on the street, some drinking the Black Labels fished out of Aunty's fridge for eighteen rand ($1.30) a bottle. As I pulled up outside Aunty's, three young men were leaning against the empty vegetable stall, now a bar counter it seemed, drinking beer out of easy-to-hide tot glasses.

Aunty was standing with them, delighted to see me, and seemingly sober. Her skin was radiant, without either the silvery sheen of base or the blear of *babelas*, as South Africans call a hangover. Her breasts were now pronounced, beneath a woven black top, and she was wrapped in patterned local Nguni cloth rather than her usual "Nigerian" attire. Benson was at her side, as ever, and he seemed sober, too: Aunty told me they had taken to drinking red wine rather than beer, as this was healthier.

I had not visited for about two years, and the shack was shabbier than I remembered it, the big table replaced by a battered Formica desk. The rather random collage of snapshots and clippings had given way to framed portraits of Aunty and Benson, such as the ones I had carried to Malawi, set in a straight line quite high up on the walls. The effect, given the portraits' Elysian studio backgrounds, was of the couple looking down onto their corporeal selves, less glamorous for sure, but seemingly more healthy and stable than I had ever known them.

As we chatted, there was the gentle percussion of customers tapping on the security gate, wanting to swap their empty beer bottles for full ones out of the fridge. Still, Aunty said, her earnings were meager because the margins were so small and she did not have enough capital to buy more cases of beer wholesale. She complained about her poverty: she was still working at PASSOP, the refugee organization, as a paid "volunteer," where she earned three thousand rand—about two hundred dollars—a month, far below the minimum wage.

PASSOP was now run by a fellow Malawian, a man named Victor Mdluli, and he had become Aunty's latest guardian angel—although she could not quite accept that he was her boss rather than the other way around. Like all those who had looked after her since her arrest nine years previously, Mdluli found Aunty to be "a whole bunch of work," he told me: recently, she had stormed into the German foundation who funded her, raising hell over a late payment. Still, Mdluli understood Aunty's history; he spoke her language, and he really valued her at PASSOP. "Aunty Tiwo really does work hard, and she has a big heart," he told me—even if this heart had to be managed. Aunty, it turned out, had taken to offering new asylum seekers shelter in her shack, sharing her space and her food with them until they found their feet, but several had reported back about the strings attached: she would hit on them.

As we sat in the shack that Saturday afternoon, Aunty gushed about how happy she now was. "Everyone knows Aunty," she said. "Everyone loves Aunty." Another tap on the security gate; another exchange of bottles: "You see, they all supporting me."

What about the police, I asked. Her business was illegal after all.

"No problems! They love me. Even today they come round. 'Aunty, any problems, call us.'"

Aunty painted a picture of herself now as a leader of those very Malawians in Tambo Village who had once scorned and even assaulted her. I imagined there was some truth to it: "If any Malawian has a problem, they can come to Aunty. Not just Malawian. Xhosa, too. *Anyone*. I try to help." On my previous visit, I had heard how Benson's brothers, devout Muslims, had come over one afternoon to remove him from Aunty's satanic influence: "*Moffie! Moffie! Moffie!*" they had shouted at her, using the South African word for "faggot." Benson had refused to leave with them and his furious brothers had beaten him so badly that Aunty's landlord had rushed out to separate them and see the assailants off.

How were things with Benson's family now, I asked?

"They *love me*!" She beamed as she told the story, in her way, of how she had helped one of Benson's brothers, just arrived from Malawi, obtain a newcomer's letter, the first step toward refugee status. The brother had met her at PASSOP's office, and had reported back to the family that she was a person of substance, with a desk and a computer and influence. Aunty was now thick with Benson's sister, who brought all her problems to her door. "No more *moffie, moffie, moffie!* Now I am family to them. I help with everything." The help included small handouts—thirty rand here, fifty rand there—when larders were bare, as they often were. Benson's kin apparently visited often; of course, being Muslims, when they did they drank only Coke.

What thrilled Aunty even more was a visit she had just received from a distant relative who now lived nearby. His daughter was getting married soon and he wanted Aunty to be there, to represent the Chimbalangs: "I am chief 's daughter, you know."

IN SEPTEMBER 2010, a few weeks after Aunty was pardoned following Ban Ki-Moon's mercy mission to Malawi, a fifteen-year-old teenager hanged himself in in Greensburg, Indiana. His name was Billy Lucas, and his family reported that he had suffered years of torment at school from other kids who assumed he was gay. In the following weeks, three other such deaths were reported in the United States, including that of Tyler Clementi, an eighteen-year-old Rutgers freshman who jumped to his death off the George Washington Bridge after a video of him kissing a man was posted online by his roommate.

When the journalist Dan Savage put up a link to a report on the Lucas suicide, a reader commented that he wished he could have had five minutes with the kid, to tell him "it gets better."[2] Most of us who went through some form of shame or humiliation as teens, for being queer or gay or gender nonconforming or trans or just different, know this to be true. And so Savage had the brainwave for what would become a wildly successful social media campaign, featuring celebrities recording videos scripted to give hope to queer youth. Savage encouraged people to post their own videos, and by 2019, the It Gets Better Project had collected and disseminated over sixty thousand stories. According to its home page, the project inspired "people across the globe to share their stories and remind the next generation of LGBTQ+ youth that hope is out there and it will get better."[3]

"It Gets Better" became an inspirational meme through the decade, a mantra for the expanding global LGBT movement. If the "long arc of the moral universe" bent toward justice, as Martin Luther King Jr. famously said (quoting the theologian Theodore Parker), then surely that arc was a rainbow and justice would be served to queer people, too?

"It Gets Better" suggests an ever-advancing temporal frame: the world was moving inexorably closer to accepting or even embracing queer and trans people as equals: any resistance along the Pink Line was to be understood as a setback, or pushback, along the way. This forward motion twined, powerfully, with the ever-expanding spatial frames of migrancy and urbanization: it would get better, so many desperate people hoped, *somewhere else*.

Certainly, by 2019, the Pink Line was oscillating, if not quite fading away. In May 2019, the World Health Organization finally adopted the ICD-11, depathologizing transgender identity. The same month, Taiwan became the first country in Asia in which same sex couples could marry—but in Africa, the Kenyan High Court ruled against the decriminalization of homosexuality. Still, something had shifted in Kenya, as it had in India through a decriminalization campaign a decade previously: the queer movement had new allies, and queer Kenyans were now a visible and increasingly accepted part of the country's urban middle class.

In January 2019, Angola followed Africa's other large former Portuguese colony, Mozambique, and unilaterally decriminalized homosexuality. And after Belize and Trinidad and Tobago, lawsuits were being prepared by activists in four other Caribbean countries: Dominica, Saint Vincent and the Grenadines, Barbados—and even Jamaica. Getting better was slow work: in June 2019, a credible biennial survey, commissioned by the largest Nigerian LGBT organization, showed that only 60 percent of Nigerians would throw out a queer family member, as opposed to 83 percent in 2017.[4] And only 70 percent thought LGBT people should be jailed, down from 90 percent in 2017.

Back in my part of the world, the Botswana High Court decriminalized homosexuality a month after the Kenyan court failed to do so. The plaintiff was a young man named Letsweletse Motshidiemang, who had filed the case as a twenty-one-year-old university student, with the help of a law professor. Interviewed at the time of the judgment, Motshidiemang's words echoed Aunty's: in the small rural village where he was reared, "people knew I was different, but I was surrounded by people who loved me. I was never taught to hate myself." That job was done by something else: "It was the laws."

The Botswana judgment came two years after Ricki Kgositau's victory, in the same court, in her suit to have the gender marker changed on her driver's license. As in neighboring South Africa, in Kenya, and in several Latin American countries, activists were following a deliberate approach: it *could* get better, if rights were fought for incrementally, as courts and the societies they adjudicated got used to the changing world.

In Kenya, the judgment had actually cited a 2003 Botswana decision: "The time has not yet arrived to decriminalize homosexual practises."

The Botswana judge, Michael Leburu, offered his riposte: "As society changes, the law must evolve."[5]

EVERYWHERE IN MY travels for this book, I saw examples of "It Gets Better" activism: from the video journals of transgender men like Liam in the United States, to Elena Klimova's Dyeti-404 project in Russia, initiated in reaction to the violent homophobia triggered by that country's anti-propaganda legislation. When Klimova was banned from VKontakte, she set up her own website. When she was found guilty of contravening the law, she simply paid the fine and carried on providing a platform for isolated young people to share stories and find community online. Along the way she attracted other adults, such as Pasha's girlfriend Alya, who became an online counselor with the project. I met several young people, on my trips to Russia, for whom it had got better, thanks to Dyeti-404.

In Egypt, in 2013, I met a kid who called himself Juelz, a teenager from a provincial city, who was found by family with his male lover. His head was shaved and he was dragged through town tied to a horse cart, and then locked in a room for a month, beaten daily. He wanted to kill himself but he kept himself alive by posting "It Gets Better videos," he told me, on YouTube via his cell phone, advising others in similar situations. It did get better for Juelz: he qualified as a lawyer, stayed defiantly out of the closet, and was planning when we last spoke, in 2018, to join his boyfriend in the United States.

In the United States, an increasing number of parents—such as the mother Dee, to whom I spoke about her transitioning child—held this new form of online activism responsible for misleading their own confused teenage girls, by associating "getting better" with transitioning to masculinity, rather than dealing with underlying depression. And sometimes, flicking through these online testimonials they did seem to me to represent the solipsism of the selfie generation, scripted in self-affirmation boilerplate. But it was fascinating to track the way "the personal is the political," the maxim of my own generation, had morphed into the notion that sharing one's story was itself transformative, even redemptive.

At the end of the nineteenth century, when Europeans started naming sexual behavior, people also started thinking differently about their bodies and how they shared them, because of the way private behaviors became public identities. Now, a century later, thanks to the Social Media Revolution, not only did notions of privacy recede even further, but identities became individual and subjective rather than collective and "objective." As a journalist and a biographer I had always held that the best way to understand change was to tell people's stories; now a younger generation was challenging me to see how telling one's story—becoming visible, sharing resources and experiences—could actually *effect* social and political change. This was Harvey Milk reloaded for the digital age: not simply, "Gay brothers and sisters, you must come out!" but, "Say how you got here, and how you feel about it, and inspire others to do the same!"

Of course, if you were an asylum seeker, like Aunty or Michael or Maha, then telling your story had a very specific currency: it bought your ticket to refugee status in another country. But why did the people in this book, across the world, choose to tell their stories *to me*, to be read *by you*?

In some instances, they changed their minds mid-process. Although I could not have been more delighted with the outcome, Fadi had not been my first choice in Israel/Palestine: Nabil, the gay man harassed by the Shin Bet in Ramallah, had made it to Canada and did not want to revisit the past; Khader, whom I had also met in my first visit to the country, blew me off when I came back. Perhaps Khader was tired of telling his story; perhaps, like Liam in Ann Arbor, he wanted to tell it for himself; perhaps he just didn't take to me. Luckily, others did: once I was actually doorstopping poor Zaira in Guadalajara, she felt she had to come and meet me, and to bring the family with her. It turned out well, but then she disappeared again. So, too, did Maha in Amsterdam, and Pasha in Moscow: people move on, or don't want to revisit traumas. How strange it must be for them, then, to later see their narratives set in print, arrested at a particular moment, often a difficult one.

But beyond these interpersonal dynamics—or shifts in peoples' lives—there were strong common reasons why the people in this book chose to share so much of their time, and lives, with me and thus with you. Much of it had to with their sense of themselves as activists, in having taken a stand to move not only their lives but also a situation forward. Pasha understood herself as a victim of a new form of fascism—a potent notion in her part of the world—and she wanted the world to know about it. Maha felt it was important that the experiences of Arab lesbians become part of the LGBT narrative. Fadi was passionate about the world understanding what it meant to be Palestinian and gay in Israel. Lakshaya felt, increasingly as our relationship developed, that her perspective had to be heard in the new debates about transgender rights in India. And—even if there had been tragedy, such as in Pasha's case—they were all proud of what they had done. They were attracted to the idea of being acknowledged, and even affirmed, not just for what they had been through, but for who they were. Of being *heard*.

This puts a very particular responsibility on my shoulders. "What will the benefit be for *us*?" asked the fisherman Mohana, bluntly, at that first meeting at the temple in Devanampattinam, when I suggested that they might invite me into their lives. Lakshaya shushed her—she was already an activist and understood the power of networks and publicity—but I was grateful, then and always (even if sometimes exasperated), for this kind of reminder about the transactive element of my work. I was assiduous in tempering expectations, but of course they were there: from Pasha, the hope that publicity would influence her fight to get Yarik back; from Aunty and Michael, the hope that it would draw attention to her, and much-needed financial support. That telling their stories, through me, would help it get better.

As I write these final words, in September 2019, Michael's social media posts are upbeat, but I know that he no longer has access to a state grant, now that a year has passed since his arrival in Canada. Is he okay? Does he have a job, and has his very unsatisfactory housing situation improved? I don't know: he is not responding to my messages at the moment. I cannot say with any certainty that it will get better for him, even though I encouraged him with these words the last time we spoke, and offered him strategies to help make it so: "Give it time," I told him. I had been consoling him with such words since I first met him, in Kampala, on the day he was to go to court to testify against the assailant who kidnapped and tortured him. I hope he is able to look at his life now, five years later, and feel that it *has* got better.

Maya, in Amsterdam, was not able to say so for certain, last time we spoke.

I cannot say that it will get better for Lakshaya either, now that she is out of a job again. And so, once more, she has to clap and beg and maybe even lift the sari she is compelled to wear. She has a CV now, and some good references: hopefully these will open the path to another job, but if they do not, will she succumb to the destiny she worked so valiantly to escape? In many ways her battle to be herself mirrors those of the non-binary kids I met, like Sean, across the world in Ann Arbor. But unlike Sean, Lakshaya has no safety net. Like Aunty and like Michael, her poverty—let alone her gender identity—makes it hard to predict whether things will get better.

Aunty scrapes a few rand off each bottle of beer she sells, and supports an unemployed man—and now it seems his family, too—on meager earnings that are by no means secure. In March 2019 her funding from the German foundation dried up, and I found myself digging into my pockets again to keep her working at PASSOP for another month, justifying it to myself as a contribution to Aunty out of my royalties. Then I found out that Aunty's other erstwhile benefactor, the older British gay man, had arranged a job for her in a gardening program for homeless people, and that she had hustled a loan under false pretenses from her new employers on day one; she had blown it in a weekend-long bender, not showing up to work the following Monday. By September, PASSOP had found another grant for her, but I cannot say that it will get better for her, no matter how much I try to help, given how labile she is, how deeply she has fallen into the dependency trap, how violent life can be in her world.

I had been so relieved to find her healthy and happy after that visit in January 2019 that I had all but sung myself home along the False Bay Shore. I so want it to get better. As I set out to craft these final pages about the Pink Line, I realized how invested I was myself—a gay man exactly Dan Savage's age—in the redemptive (or at the very least ameliorative) energy of the global LGBT rights movement of the early twenty-first century. I wanted that long arc to bend already—not just politically, but narratively, too. If I wasn't going to chronicle the disappearance of the Pink Line, at least I was going to offer stories of triumph over it, or resilience in the face of it. Or of resolution, an impossibility.

WOULD IT HAVE got better for Pasha had she found a way to suppress her transgender identity—or had it not been suggested to her at all via the waves of the Information Revolution?

Would it have got better for Michael had his American benefactor *not* sent him the funds to flee to Nairobi?

Would it have got better for Zaira, and for her relationship with Martha, had she just gone to Mexico City to get her registered as Sabina's other's parent?

Would it have got better for Maha had she stayed in her beloved Cairo rather than moving to Amsterdam, a place she came to loathe, even if being in Cairo meant living in the closet?

Would it have got better for Aunty had she been compelled to find her way in the world without the net that Amnesty International laid out for her, a net that became a trap?

Would it have got better for Rose had she resisted the temptation to transition, and stayed off the testosterone? Or resisted the temptation to de-transition?

How much worse would it really be for Lakshaya if she went off to beg in a sari each day—and even perhaps had the surgery—but became stable enough, financially, to pay off her debts and keep her beautiful home on the beach?

On we could go.

Such questions might help us understand the choices faced by people along the Pink Line, but to attempt to answer them would be the province of fiction: this book leads us only where its protagonists have chosen—or been compelled—to take us. And my distance from them—I am not in their heads, nor they in mine—makes it impossible for me to adjudicate on their lives. Sometimes they have told me whether it has got better, sometimes not. I cannot say it for them. But I can say something, for certain: things have changed, for all of them.

This is what strikes me most about the people I met: just how dynamic they are; how far they have all moved, in just one generation, away from the norms that defined their families and cultures for decades, even for centuries. They have all made choices that would have been unimaginable just a generation earlier, and in so doing they have not only shifted their lives dramatically, but their cultures and societies, too.

This is as true for Riot Youth kids of Ann Arbor as it is for the *kothis* of Devanampattinam: they are forging gender identities for themselves in ways unimaginable—and unfathomable—for their parents. So, too, in different ways, Maha in Cairo and Fadi in Jaffa, the products of both the Digital Revolution and the Arab Spring, a first generation of Arabs to claim sexual orientation as an identity, and to invent a new language for it.

Like Maha in Egypt, Zaira in Mexico was a beneficiary of the women's movement: this alone opened both women's horizons, and made it possible to think of lives and families without men. In Guadalajara, Zaira put it clearly to me: the advances in rights culture, not to mention reproductive technology, gave her options that did not exist for earlier generations. But like everyone in this book, she lived in a borderland, an interregnum, presented with new possibilities but unable, yet, to realize these possibilities in the real world. Hence her activism: the *amparo*, insisting that the law recognize her new family.

Pasha's transgender identity and Michael's gay identity were sharpened—perhaps even formed—by the contentions taking place around them, in Russia and Uganda respectively, these two frontline states along the Pink Line, and the conflicts into which they were forced: with a spouse, in Pasha's case, and with parents, in Michael's.

In another time, Michael might have expressed his sexuality on the down-low, as people with homosexual inclinations have in his culture for generations. Or, unable to do so because of his gender nonconformity, he might have found himself even more at risk, as a teenager—drugs, alcohol—than he was as a runaway and later a refugee.

In another time, Pasha might have stuck with masculinity, but this might, as she told me, have killed her.

We are forged by our contexts and, of course, we make our contexts, too. When thinking about Aunty's options, though, I am struck by the way her identity remained remarkably consistent. The world saw her as "bewitched," and then "gay," and then "transgender," and then "LGBTI." She could, and would, take on these labels—particularly the last one—if she needed to. But there was something eternal and immutable about how she saw herself, never mind how the world threw at her.

This challenged my own understanding of gender as a construct. She did not "become" a woman, as Simone de Beauvoir writes in *The Second Sex*.[6] She was one.

THE PERSONAL JOURNEY I HAVE TAKEN, in the years I have been working on this book, has taken me across my own internal Pink Lines, into new territories of empathy, of knowledge, and of self-knowledge, too.

As a child in my first year at primary school in Johannesburg, where the boys and girls were separated at break time, I struggled to compete physically with my own kind and usually found myself playing alone. I have written, before,[7] about how, on one particular day, I must have been lingering around the runnel of sorts that formed the boundary between the two sides of the playground—my reverie might have even carried me across the boundary—when a teacher pounced, and gave me a firm lecture about where I belonged on the gender binary. I learned a valuable lesson: if I was going to fit in, I needed to appear to accept the boundaries set for me. Transgressions had to be underground or in the ether, beyond the patrol of adults.

But what if, as a little boy, I had been teleported to the Bay Area in the second decade of the twenty-first century, and because of repeated runnel-transgression had landed up in the consulting room of, say, the child psychologist Diane Ehrensaft? Would I have been turned into a little girl because I harbored fantasies involving my mother's wardrobe and didn't like the rough play of boys? Or would I have been told it was okay to be "gender-creative" and developed a whole new identity beyond the gender binary? What would I have become?

When I met Diane Ehrehsaft, I told her such thoughts made me a little panicky. She nodded sagely: "I think you're relieved that you grew up in simpler times because you *knew* who you were. If, somewhere in your consciousness, you had been conflicted or ambivalent, you might feel differently now." Still, she said to me, "I have to ask, are we overwhelming the kids in any way with all these extended possibilities? It's a lot easier to walk around in a box than to have no boundaries."

In truth, the panic I was feeling was not as strong as the intrigue that developed, within me, during the years I researched and wrote this book: I began to wonder about my own gender identity, and the paths not taken. To the extent that I had been somewhat effeminate as a boy, was it because I was attracted to other boys, and therefore thought I needed to be girlish to get their attention? Or did I become "gay"—a tribal identity that has never seemed quite adequate—because I needed to belong *somewhere*, and heterosexual masculinity was not quite capacious enough? I never thought I was a girl, but there were certainly times when I wished I were one, imagining myself in the arms of a pimpled Lothario rather than having to pass a ball to him on the sports field. What if it had been okay to cross over that runnel, or even—God forbid—dwell in its ambiguity, turning that seemingly impenetrable border between the genders into a borderland that could hold me?

As I write these words, I find myself teleporting the six-year-old child on the runnel somewhere else, to Devanampattinam in the early twenty-first century.

My destiny is clear: I am a *kothi*.

Thinking about this, I remember the historian Saleem Kidwai's words, about how *kothi* could be an oppressive identity, as opposed to the liberating, it-gets-better ones of gay or transgender. Reflecting on the lives of Lakshaya and the crew at the temple, I can see this, of course. I would not want to trade places. And yet my experiences with the *kothis*, and with everyone else I have met on this journey, have taught me a lesson about the limitations of the "It Gets Better" mantra, no matter its power. It posits a one-way generational traffic flow between older people in "freer" environments, and younger people in more constrained ones; between Lakshaya and me, for example. It suggests the forward motion—the ineluctable progress promised by liberal democracy—that comes with *growing up*. It suggests that Uganda and Egypt and India and Mexico might "mature" into the kind of societies, with the kind of freedoms, that are found in Western Europe or North America.

Such a world view restricts one from seeing people in other places—with other experiences, in other circumstances—as equal. It does not allow for what I, an older white gay professional from

South Africa educated in the United States, might learn from my experiences in other places: from Tambo Village just across the bay; from Devanampattinam all the way across the Indian Ocean; from my experiences with people young enough to be my children, still trying to figure out the things that have long been resolved for me. Maybe parents come to know this, but I am not one. And I have changed, thanks to this book. I no longer walk around in the certain box of my masculinity, and I find that immensely liberating.

The first time I met Lakshaya was actually not at the temple, but at a meeting that had been convened for me at the offices of the AIDS organization where she worked, in November 2012. According to the new global script, the introductory go-around consisted of name, pronoun, and sexual orientation or gender identity.

"I am Mark," I said. "He, him, his." And before I knew it: "*Kothi.*"

It felt great to say so.

Cape Town, September 2019

NOTES

I have cited only direct quotes from secondary sources, data from surveys, or information not easily found through an internet search. A selected bibliography follows, in "Further Reading."

EPIGRAPH

1. James Baldwin, *The Devil Finds Work: An Essay* (New York: Vintage International,2011), e-book, 178.

AUTHOR'S NOTE

1. Kwame Anthony Appiah, "Go Ahead, Speak for Yourself," *The New York Times*, 10 August 2018.

PROLOGUE: A DEBT TO LOVE

1. Caroline Somanje, "Gays Engage!," *The Nation* (Malawi), 28 December 2009.
2. Andy Rice, "Malawian Gay Couple's Beautiful Thing, and Its Ugly Consequences," *Daily Maverick* (South Africa), 9 June 2010.
3. Ibid.
4. *The Advocate*, 27 November 2018.
5. David Paternotte, "Blessing the Crowds: Catholic Mobilizations Against Gender in Europe," in S. Hark and P. Villa (eds), *AntiGenderismus: Sexualität und Geschlecht als Schauplätze aktueller politischer Auseinandersetzungen*, (Bielfeld: Transcript Verlag, 2015).
6. William Clarke, "France Least Tolerant Country in Western Europe of Homosexuals," *The Telegraph* (United Kingdom), 17 May 2013.
7. Justin McCarthy, "Two in Three Americans Support Same-Sex Marriage," Gallup (United States), 23 May 2018.
8. Kaya Genç, "Sex Changes in Turkey," *The New York Review of Books* (United States), 28 June 2018; Human Rights Watch, *Audacity in Adversity LGBT Activism in the Middle East and North Africa* (United States), 16 April 2018.
9. The Editorial Board, "Trump's Heartless Transgender Military Ban Gets a Second Shot," *The New York Times* (United States), 28 March 2018.

1. THE WORLD'S PINK LINES

1. Speech by Barack Obama, "Remarks by President Obama and President Sall of the Republic of Senegal at Joint Press Conference," The White House, 27 June 2013.
2. Poll, "Marriage," Gallup (United States), 2018.
3. "Watch Unreleased Footage of Obama's Phone Call to James Obergefell on the Night of the Supreme Court's Same-Sex Marriage Decision," *The Washington Post* (United States), 16 August 2016.
4. Reuters, "Barack Obama Applauds Supreme Court Decision on Gay Marriage," NDTV (India), 26 June 2013.
5. Amnesty International, *Senegal: Land of Impunity* (United Kingdom), 2010.
6. United States Department of State, *Senegal 2012 Human Rights Report*, Country Reports on Human Rights Practices for 2012, 2012.
7. Jim Watson, "DOMA Decision a 'Victory for American Democracy,'" ABC News Radio, 27 June 2013.

8. "Remarks by President Obama and President Sall of the Republic of Senegal at Joint Press Conference," The White House, 27 June 2013.
9. Christiane Grefe and Ulrich Ladurner, "Investiert in Afrika und wir teilen den Profit," *Zeit Online* (Germany), 2 April 2014.
10. Andrew Foxall, "From Evropa to Gayropa: A Critical Geopolitics of the European Union as Seen from Russia," *Geopolitics* (30 December 2017), 3.
11. Lester Feder, "The Russian Plot to Take Back Eastern Europe at the Expense of Gay Rights," *BuzzFeed News* (United States), 9 November 2013.
12. Speech by Vladimir Putin, "Presidential Address to the Federal Assembly," Kremlin, 12 December 2013.
13. Speech by Vladimir Putin, "Meeting of the Valdai International Discussion Club," Kremlin, 19 September 2013.
14. Max Bearak, "Theresa May Criticized the Term 'Citizen of the World,' but Half the World Identifies That Way," *The Washington Post* (United States), 5 October 2016.
15. Ryan Teague Beckwith, "Read Donald Trump's Speech on the Orlando Shooting," *Time* (United States), 13 June 2016.
16. J. Lester Feder, Addie Schulte and Kim Deen, "The Man Who Taught Donald Trump to Pit Gay People Against Immigrants," *BuzzFeed News* (United States), 3 July 2018.
17. Ibid.
18. Timothy Snyder, *The Road to Unfreedom: Russia, Europe, America* (London: Bodley Head, 2018), 101.
19. Sarah Wildman, "Marine Le Pen Wants to Protect France's LGBTQ Community—but Opposes Same-Sex Marriage," *Vox*, 5 May 2017.
20. "Europe's Anti-immigrant Parties Are Becoming More Gay-Friendly, Partly as a Way to Bash Muslim Immigrants," *The Economist* (United Kingdom), 5 July 2018.
21. Rebecca Staudenmaier, "Gay in the Af D: Talking with LGBT Supporters of Germany's Populist Party," Deutsche Welle (Germany), 17 March 2017.
22. Thomas Rogers, "Gays Really Love Germany's Racist, Homophobic Far Right Party," *Vice* (United States), 11 May 2017.
23. Shaun Walker, "Ikea Removes Lesbian Couple from Russian Edition of Magazine," *The Guardian* (United Kingdom), 21 November 2013.
24. "Play Actors," *Special Correspondent*, produced by Novaya Kompaniya 2013, Moscow: All-Russia State Television and Radio Broadcasting

Company VGTRK, 12 November 2013, www.youtube.com/watch?v=MYIWgduByfw.

25. Ibid.
26. Ibid.
27. Ibid.
28. Laurie Essig, *Queer in Russia: A Story of Sex, Self, and the Other* (Durham: Duke University Press, 1999), 6.
29. Ogala Emmanuel, "No Going Back on Criminalizing Same-Sex Marriage in Nigeria—Mark," *Premium Times* (Nigeria), 7 January 2013.
30. Full text of Dr Mahathir's speech, *The Star Online* (Malaysia), 20 June 2003.
31. "Cardinal Responds to U.N.'s Criticism of Africa's Social Policies," *National Catholic Register* (United States), 21 February 2012.
32. Roula K halaf, "Iran's 'Generation Normal,' " *Financial Times* (United Kingdom), 29 May 2015.
33. "Iran's Supreme Leader: Libidinous Act of Gay Marriage Signals the Stampede of Human Values," translated by Hossein Alizadeh, 6 March 2014, available in Farsi: www.leader.ir/fa/speech/11526.
34. Kate Lamb, "Why LGBT Hatred Suddenly Spiked in Indonesia," *The Guardian* (United Kingdom), 22 February 2017.
35. Opening speech by Viktor Orbán, Second Budapest World Congress of Families, 25 May 2017, miniszterelnok.hu.
36. Courtney Weaver, "God's TV, Russian Style," *Financial Times* (United Kingdom), 16 October 2015.
37. Claire Provost, "'This Is a War': Inside the Global 'Pro-family' Movement Against Abortion and LGBT Rights," *openDemocracy* (United Kingdom), 6 June 2017.
38. Ibid.
39. "Chinese Cyberchiefs Preach Net Sovereignty in Moscow," *China Digital Times* (China), 27 April 2016.
40. Hannah Ellis Petersen, "China Bans Depictions of Gay People on Television," *The Guardian* (United Kingdom), 4 March 2016.
41. Heba Kanso, "Amid Egypt's Antigay Crackdown, Gay Dating Apps Send Tips to Stop Entrapment," Reuters News (United Kingdom), 23 October 2017.
42. Maryana Torocheshnikova, "Nevidimye Deti [Invisible Children]," Radio Liberty (United States), 2 February 2015.

43. "UN: General Assembly Statement Affirms Rights for All," Human Rights Watch, 18 December 2008.
44. "Understanding of LGBT Realities 'Non-existent' in Most Countries, Says UN Expert," UN News, 12 June 2019.
45. Andrew Kohut et al., Pew Research Center, *The Global Divide on Homosexuality: Greater Acceptance in More Secular and Affluent Countries*, 4 June 2013 (United States).
46. Robert Wintemute, "From 'Sex Rights' to 'Love Rights': Partnership Rights as Human Rights," in Nicholas Bamforth (ed.), *Sex Rights*, (Oxford: Oxford University Press, 2005), 186–224.
47. Kohut et al., *The Global Divide on Homosexuality*.
48. "The World Factbook: Country Comparison: Distribution of Family Income—Gini Index," Central Intelligence Agency.
49. C. Sutherland et al., Human Sciences Research Council, *Progressive Prudes: A Survey of Attitudes Towards Homosexuality & Gender Non-conformity in South Africa*, 2016 (South Africa: Human Sciences Research Council).
50. Mark Gevisser, "Mandela's Stepchildren: Homosexual Identity in Post-apartheid South Africa," in Peter Drucker (ed.), *Different Rainbows*, (London: Gay Men's Press, 2000), 111–19.
51. Ibid.
52. B. Roberts et al., Human Sciences Research Council, *Sexual Orientation and Gender Identity (SOGI): Tabulation Report Based on the 2015 Round of the South African Social Attitudes Survey (SASAS)*, 2016 (South Africa: Human Sciences Research Council).
53. Ibid.

2. AUNTY'S STORY

1. Bob Roehr, "How Homophobia Is Fuelling Africa's HIV Epidemic," *The BMJ*, No. 340 (2010), x.
2. *Two Men and a Wedding*, directed by Sara Blecher (2011, Johannesburg, Real Eyes Films).
3. Perez Hilton, "The Power of Madonna! Malawi Releases Gay Couple After Madge Protests!," perezhilton.com, 31 May 2010.
4. R. Levitan (HIAS), 2018, personal communication.
5. UNHCR, 2008, *UNHCR Guidance Note on Refugee Claims Relating to Sexual Orientation and Gender Identity*, Refworld.

6. Sharita Gruberg, "Obama Administration Makes Refugee Program More LGBT-Inclusive," Centre for American Progress, 30 October 2015.
7. Council of Europe, *Discrimination on Grounds of Sexual Orientation and Gender Identity in Europe*, 2nd ed., 2012 (France: Council of Europe Publishing).
8. Ian Willoughby and Alexis Rosenzweig, "EU Says Czech 'Arousal' Test for Gay Asylum Seekers Could Violate Human Rights Convention," Radio Praha (Czech Republic), 9 December 2010.
9. Allison Liu Jernow, *Sexual Orientation, Gender Identity and Justice: A Comparative Law Casebook* (Switzerland: International Commission of Jurists, 2011), 287–88.
10. Sabine Jansen, "Introduction: Fleeing Homophobia, Asylum Claims Related to Sexual Orientation and Gender Identity in Europe," in Thomas Spijkerboer (ed.), *Fleeing Homophobia: Sexual Orientation, Gender Identity and Asylum*, (USA and Canada: Routledge, 2013), 4.
11. UNHCR, "Guidelines on International Protection No 9: Claims to Refugee Status Based on Sexual Orientation and/or Gender Identity …," 23 October 2012.
12. Robert Booth, "Judge Rejected Asylum Seeker Who Did Not Have Gay 'Demeanour,'" *The Guardian*,21 August 2019.
13. Jamie Grierson, "Home Office Refused Thousands of LGBT Asylum Claims, Figures Reveal," *The Guardian*,2 September 2019.
14. As quoted in Ryan Richard Thoreson, "Troubling the Waters of 'a Wave of Homophobia': Political Economies of Anti-queer Animus in Sub-Saharan Africa," *Sexualities* 17, 1–2 (2014), 41.
15. Franz Fanon, *Black Skin, White Masks* (London: Pluto Press, 2008), 139.

3. A NEW GLOBAL CULTURE WARS?

1. Michele K. Lewis and Isiah Marshall, *LGBT Psychology: Research Perspectives and People of African Descent* (United States: Springer Science+Business Media, 2011), 145.
2. Jeffrey Gettleman, "Americans' Role Seen in Uganda Anti-Gay Push," *The New York Times* (United States), 3 January 2010.
3. Aiden Pink, "Massachusetts GOP Candidate Blames Holocaust on Gay Nazis," *The Forward* (United States), 13 May 2018.
4. Kapya Kaoma, *Globalizing the Culture Wars: U.S. Conservatives, African Churches, and Homophobia*, Political Research Associates, 2009 (United States).

5. Heidi Beirich, Evelyn Schlatter and Leah Nelson, *Dangerous Liaisons: The American Religious Right and the Criminalization of Homosexuality in Belize*, Southern Poverty Law Center, 2013 (United States).
6. James Kassaga Arinaitwe, "How US Evangelicals Are Shaping Development in Uganda," Al Jazeera (Qatar), 25 July 2014.
7. Jeff Sharlet, "Jesus Plus Nothing: Undercover Among America's Secret Theocrats," *Harper's Magazine*, March (2003), 53– 64.
8. Jeff, Sharlet, "Straight Man's Burden: The American Roots of Uganda's Anti-gay Persecutions," *Harper's Magazine*, September (2010), 44.
9. Andrew Sullivan, "Rick Warren and Uganda's Looming Gay Genocide," *The Atlantic* (United States), 7 December 2009.
10. Graeme Reid, "US Court Dismisses Uganda LGBTI Case, but Affirms Rights," Human Rights Watch (United States), 7 June 2017.
11. Beirich, Schlatter, and Nelson, *Dangerous Liaisons: The American Religious Right & the Criminalization of Homosexuality in Belize*, Southern Poverty Law Center, Montgomery, Alabama July 2013.
12. "Stirm Strikes Back at SPLC," 7 News Belize (Belize), 29 July 2013.
13. Adele Ramos, "Churches Call for Referendum on Sodomy Law," *Amandala* (Belize), 28 November 2014.
14. Extremist group information summary, "World Congress of Families," Southern Poverty Law Center.
15. Description of the World Congress of Families activities, "Exposed: The World Congress of Families," Human Rights Campaign, June 2015.
16. Hannah Levintova, "How US Evangelicals Helped Create Russia's Anti-gay Movement," *Mother Jones* (United States), 21 February 2014.
17. Miranda Blue, "Globalizing Homophobia, Part 3: A New Life for Discredited Research," Right Wing Watch (United States), 4 October 2013.
18. Levintova, "How US Evangelicals Helped Create Russia's Anti-Gay Movement."
19. *National Catholic Register*, "Poland's Ruling Party Leader Praises Polish Archbishop for LGBT Opposition," 19 August 2019.
20. Reuters, "Poland's Kaczynski Condemns Gay Pride Marches as Election Nears," 18 August 2019.
21. Transcription, "Lords Hansard text for 25 October 2012," British Parliament, 25 October 2012.
22. Peter Ackroyd, *Queer City: Gay London from the Romans to the Present Day* (London: Chatto and Windus, 2017), 42.

23. Alok Gupta, "This Alien Legacy: The Origins of 'Sodomy' Laws in British Colonialism," in Corinne Lennox and Matthew Waites (eds), *Human Rights, Sexual Orientation and Gender Identity in the Commonwealth,* (London: Human Rights Consortium, Institute of Commonwealth Studies, 2013), 85 and 94.
24. Fumbuka Ng'wanakilala, "Tanzania Stands Firm on Aids-Gay Rights Spat with UK," Reuters (United Kingdom), 4 November 2011.
25. "Statement on British 'Aid Cut' Threats to African Countries That Violate LBGTI Rights," *Pambuzuka News* (Kenya and United Kingdom), 27 October 2011.
26. Museveni Comments on AntiHomosexuality Bill, "Uganda: Ambassador Credentialed; Gets Earful on Antihomosexuality Bill," WikiLeaks, 28 January 2010.
27. Elias Biryabarema, "Ugandan President Signs Anti-gay Bill, Defying the West," Reuters (United Kingdom), 24 February 2014.
28. "Fundamentalists in Pakistan protest LGBT pride event at US embassy …," MPact Global Action for Gay Men's Health and Rights (United States), 5 July 2011.
29. *Kandahar Pride*, produced by Cpl Casimir Krul (Afghanistan: AFN Afghanistan, 2013), online clip.
30. Jasbit K. Puar, *Terrorist Assemblages: Homonationalism in Queer Times* (Durham and London: Duke University Press, 2007).
31. Sarah Schulman, "Israel and 'Pinkwashing,'" *The New York Times* (United States), 22 November 2011.
32. Joseph Massad, "Re-orienting Desire: The Gay International and the Arab World," *Public Culture* 14, No. 2 (Spring 2002), 363.
33. "Nigerian President Signs Antigay Bill into Law," Reuters (United Kingdom), 13 January 2014.
34. Christiane Grefe and Ulrich Ladurner, "Investiert in Afrika und wir teilen den Profit," *Zeit Online* (Germany), 2 April 2014.
35. "Cardinal Responds to U.N.'s Criticism of Africa's Social Policies," *National Catholic Register* (United States), 21 February 2012.
36. Andriy Maymulakhin, Olexandr Zinchenkov, and Andriy Kravchuk, Nash Mir (Our World) Gay and Lesbian Centre, *Ukrainian Homosexuals and Society: A Reciprocation*, 2007 (Kiev), 69.
37. Kapya Kaoma, *Globalizing the Culture Wars*, 2009.
38. David W. Virtue, "Anglican Communion Future Unclear: Realignment Yes, Schism Now Unlikely," Church of the Word, 27 September 2004.

39. Rahul Rao, "Global homocapitalism," *Radical Philosophy* 194, No. 1 (November/December 2015), 45.

4. MICHAEL'S STORY

1. The text of (void) Anti-Homosexuality Act 2014, "Uganda LBGTI Resources," Rights in Exile Program.
2. "Resettlement is not a Human Right, It is a Privilege—UNHCR to Ugandan LGBTI Refugees in Kenya," *Kuchu Times* (Uganda), 1 April 2015.
3. Ibid.
4. "Uganda: Anti-homosexuality Act's Heavy Toll," Human Rights Watch (United States), 14 May 2014.
5. Rahul Rao, "Remembering Mwanga: Same-Sex Intimacy, Memory and Belonging in Postcolonial Uganda," *Journal of Eastern African Studies* 9, No. 1 (2015), 2 and 6.
6. James Wasula, "Africans Must Join Hands and Fight Homosexuality," *New Vision* (Uganda), 12 June 2005.
7. *Rolling Stone* (Uganda), 2–9 October 2010.
8. "Uganda Court Orders Anti-gay Paper to Shut: Group," Reuters (United Kingdom), 2 November 2010.
9. David Smith, "Ugandan Minister Shuts Down Gay Rights Conference," *The Guardian* (United Kingdom), 15 February 2012.
10. Quoted in Joanna Sadgrove et al., "Morality Plays and Money Matters: Towards a Situated Understanding of the Politics of Homosexuality in Uganda," *Journal of Modern African Studies* 50, No. 1 (2012), 121 and 109.
11. Ibid., 124–25.
12. Crowdfunding page, "Rescue Fund to Help LGBT People Escape Africa," Indiegogo.
13. Melanie Judge, "'Rescuing' Gay People from Africa Is No Answer to Homophobic Laws," *The Guardian* (United Kingdom), 6 March 2014.
14. Update posted by Michael Bashaija, Facebook, 9 September 2018.
15. Update posted by Michael Bashaija, Facebook, 10 September 2018.
16. Updates posted by Michael Bashaija, Facebook, 21 September, 3 October, 6 October, 28 October, 30 October, 11 November and 17 November, 2018.
17. AFP, "Kenya Court Refuses to Decriminalise Homosexuality," ENCA (South Africa), 25 May 2019.

5. THE PINK LINE THROUGH TIME AND SPACE

1. Faith Karimi and Nick Thompson, "Uganda's President Museveni Signs Controversial Anti-gay Bill into Law," CNN (United States), 25 February 2014.
2. Michel Foucault (translated from the French by Robert Hurley), *The History of Sexuality* (New York: Pantheon Books, 1978), 23.
3. Susan Stryker, *Transgender History: The Roots of Today's Revolution*, 2nd ed. (New York: Seal Press, 2017), 56.
4. John D'Emilio, "Capitalism and Gay Identity," in Henry Abelove, Michèle Aina Barale, and David M. Halperin (eds), *The Lesbian and Gay Studies Reader*, (New York and London: Routledge, 1993), 467–78.
5. Stryker, *Transgender History*, 50.
6. "Play Actors", *Special Correspondent*, produced by Novaya Kompaniya (2013), Moscow: All-Russia State Television and Radio Broadcasting Company VGTRK, 12 November 2013, www.youtube.com/watch?v=MYIWgduByfw.
7. *Navtej Singh Johar & Ors. versus Union of India thr. Secretary Ministry of Law and Justice*, Writ Petition (Criminal) No. 76 of 2016.
8. Akshay Khanna, *Sexualness* (New Delhi: New Text, 2014), 2.
9. "Introduction," in Arvind Narrain and Alok Gupta (eds), *Law Like Love: Queer Perspectives on Law*, (New Delhi: Yoda Press, 2011), xxvi.
10. Arturo Sánchez García, "The Happy Judicialization of Sexual Rights: Abortion and Same Sex Marriage in Mexico" (PhD dissertation, *Kent Law School*, October 2014), 128–29.
11. Official City of Buenos Aires page on LGBT scene and its history, "Diverse Buenos Aires," buenosaires.gob.ar.
12. Richard Florida, *The Rise of the Creative Class* (New York: Basic Books, 2002).
13. Richard Florida, "Gay-Tolerant Societies Prosper Economically," *USA Today* (United States), 30 April 2003.
14. As quoted in Dennis Altman and Jonathan Symons, *Queer Wars* (Cambridge, United Kingdom: Polity Press, 2016), 95.
15. Stryker, *Transgender History*, 46–48.
16. Chioma Igbokwei, "HIV Epidemic Looms," *The Sun* (Nigeria), 19 August 2017.
17. Human Rights Watch, "Lebanon: Entry Ban Follows Gender, Sexuality Conference," 27 August 2019.
18. Ahval News, "U.S. Providing over $20 Million to Ankara LGBT Organisation—Interior Minister," 4 September 2019.

6. MAHA AND AMIRA'S STORY

1. Shereen El Feki, *Sex and the Citadel: Intimate Life in a Changing Arab World* (New York: Anchor Books, 2014), 218.
2. Human Rights Watch, *In a Time of Torture: The Assault on Justice in Egypt's Crackdown on Homosexual Conduct*, March 2004 (United States).
3. Brian Whitaker, "Homosexuality on Trial in Egypt," *The Guardian* (United Kingdom), 19 November 2001.
4. Human Rights Watch, *In a Time of Torture*, March 2004.
5. Scott Long, "Entrapped! How to Use a Phone App to Destroy a Life," *A Paper Bird*, 19 September 2015.
6. Howard Schneider, "Cultural Struggle Finds Symbol in Gay Cairo: Arrests of 52 Men Reflect Tension Between Islamic Traditionalists, Secularists," *The Washington Post* (United States), 9 September 2001.
7. Human Rights Watch, *In a Time of Torture*.
8. Ibid.
9. Admin7Crimes, "More Than 274 LGBTQ Victims of Egypt's Ongoing Repression" *Erasing 76 Crimes*, 17 November 2016.
10. J. Lester Feder, "LGBT Egyptians Go into Hiding as Regime Cracks Down," *BuzzFeed News* (United States), 23 September 2014.
11. Ibid.
12. Liam Stack, "Gay and Transgender Egyptians, Harassed and Entrapped, Are Driven Underground," *The New York Times* (United States), 10 August 2016.
13. "Egyptian Gays Living in Fear Under Sisi Regime," *News24* (South Africa), 2 January 2015.
14. Scott Long, "New Arrests of Alleged Trans and Gay People in Cairo," *A Paper Bird*, 1 March 2015.
15. www.youtube.com/watch?v=nstpKSb5 dQs&f bclid=IwAR0oBWIxU6f URPjsu9p_4m TGW2Y_mXO_SU1EAK1L69A-0Bhg3OlDsoDgg8U, accessed 2017, dead link.
16. J. Lester Feder, Addie Schulte, and Kim Deen, "The Man Who Taught Donald Trump to Pit Gay People Against Immigrants," *BuzzFeed News* (United States), 3 July 2018.
17. Event page posted by "SEHAQ, Queer Refugees Group," "In the memory of Ehab," Facebook, 11 August 2018.
18. Noah Martin, "'We Need Freedom': Sehaq, the Party Space for Amsterdam's Queer Refugees," *The Guardian*,31 July 2019.

7. PINK FOLK-DEVILS

1. "Hamed Sino Applauds Rainbow Flat at Cairo Concert," ScoopEmpire (Egypt), 19 March 2016.
2. Human Rights Watch, *Audacity in Adversity: LGBT Activism in the Middle East and North Africa*, 16 April 2018 (United States).
3. United Nations Assistance Mission for Iraq, *Report on Human Rights in Iraq: January to June 2012*, October 2012 (Baghdad: UNAMI Human Rights Office and Office of the High Commissioner for Human Rights).
4. Human Rights Watch, *"They Want Us Exterminated": Murder, Torture, Sexual Orientation and Gender in Iraq,*17 August 2009 (United States).
5. Ibid.
6. "Iran's Supreme Leader Says "There Is No Worse Form of Moral Degeneration Than Homosexuality," OutRight Action International, 27 May 2016.
7. Correspondence from Neela Ghoshal, Human Rights Watch, to the author, 27 November 2018.
8. Amrou Al-Kadhi, "As a Gay Man Born in Iraq, I Know That Western Intervention Is to Blame for the Murder of LGBT Iraqis," *The Independent* (United Kingdom), 5 July 2017.
9. Stanley Cohen, *Folk Devils and Moral Panics: The Creation of the Mods and Rockers*, 3rd ed. (United Kingdom: Routledge, 2011), 1; in Gilbert Herdt, *Moral Panics, Sex Panics: Fear and the Fight Over Sexual Rights* (New York: New York University Press, 2009).
10. Gayle S. Rubin, "Thinking Sex: Notes for a Radical Theory of the Politics of Sexuality," in Henry Abelove, Michèle Aina Barale, and David M. Halperin (eds), *The Lesbian and Gay Studies Reader*, (New York and London: Routledge, 1993), 25; in Herdt, *Moral Panics, Sex Panics*.
11. Rictor Norton, "The Gay Subculture in Early Eighteenth-Century London," in *The Gay Subculture in Georgian England*, online publication, updated 23 May 2013.
12. Ibid.
13. Ibid.
14. Michael Neilson, "Gays and Lesbians Feel Heat of Discrimination and Prejudice in Indonesia," *The Sydney Morning Herald* (Australia), 27 February 2016.
15. Human Rights Watch, *"These Political Games Ruin Our Lives": Indonesia's LGBT Community Under Threat*, 10 August 2016 (United States).

16. "Indonesia: Vice Presidential Candidate Has Anti-rights Record," Human Rights Watch, 10 August 2018.
17. Tom Boellstorff, "Against State Straightism: Five Principles for Including LGBT Indonesians," E-International Relations, 21 March 2016.
18. Tom Boellstorff, "The Emergence of Political Homophobia in Indonesia: Masculinity and National Belonging," *Ethnos* 64, No. 4 (2004), 465.
19. Timothy Snyder, *The Road to Unfreedom: Russia, Europe, America* (London: The Bodley Head, 2018), 132.
20. Full text of Dr. Mahathir's speech, *The Star Online* (Malaysia), 20 June 2003.
21. Speech by Vladimir Putin, "Presidential Address to the Federal Assembly," Kremlin, 12 December 2013.
22. David K. Johnson, "America's Cold War Empire: Exporting the Lavender Scare," in Meredith L. Weiss and Michael J. Bosia (eds), *Global Homophobia: States, Movements, and the Politics of Oppression*, (Illinois: University of Illinois Press, 2013), 56 –57.
23. Ibid., 62– 63.
24. Owen Matthews, "Vladimir Putin's New Plan for World Domination," *The Spectator* (United Kingdom) 22 February 2014.
25. Graeme Reid, *"Traditional Values": A Potent Weapon Against LGBT Rights*, Human Rights Watch (United States), 6 November 2017.
26. Masha Gessen, "The Gay Men Who Fled Chechnya's Purge," *The New Yorker* (United States), 3 July 2017.
27. Yelena Milashina, "Honor Killings: How the Ambitions of a Famous LGBT Activists Reawakened Ancient Terrifying Customs in Chechnya", *Novaya Gazeta*, 1 April 2017.
28. Gilbert Herdt, *Moral Panics, Sex Panics: Fear and the Fight Over Sexual Rights* (New York: New York University Press, 2009), 32.
29. Russian LGBT Network and Yelena Milashina (translated by Evgeny Belyakov), Доклад о фактах преследования ЛГБТ в регионе Северного Кавказа [*Report on Facts of Persecution of LGBT People in the Region of North Caucasus*], 2017 (St. Petersburg), 4.

8. PASHA'S STORY

1. Transcript of hearings: Pasha's civil suit against Yulia (translated by Evgeny Belyakov, from the files of Pasha Captanovska), Lyubertsy City Court, 4–5 August 2016.
2. Ibid.

3. Decision on Pasha's lawsuit (translated by Evgeny Belyakov, from the files of Pasha Captanovska), Lyubertsy City Court, 25 November 2016.
4. "Psychological Assessment of a Child: Psychological Assessment 1488/a," *Federal Medical Research Center on Psychiatry and Narcology of the Ministry of Health of Russian Federation* (translated by Evgeny Belyakov, from the files of Pasha Captanovska), 9 December 2014.
5. Ibid.
6. Update posted by Pasha Captanovska, Facebook, 10 August 2014.
7. Ibid.
8. Update posted by Pasha Captanovska, Facebook, 12 August 2014.
9. Russian Federation: Federal Law No. 436—FZ of 2010, On Protection of Children from Information Harmful to Their Health and Development, 29 December 2010.
10. Update posted by Pasha Captanovska, Facebook, 27 January 2013.
11. Paul Vale, "Russian Lawmaker Proposes Bill to Deny Homosexual Parents Custody of Their Own Children," *HuffPost* (United Kingdom), 5 September 2013.
12. "Russia: Silencing Activists, Journalists Ahead of Sochi Games," Human Rights Watch(United States), 7 August 2013.
13. Fiona O'Brien, "Sochi 2014: Russian Anti-gay Stance Exaggerated, Says Lesbian Ski-Jumper," *The Sport Review* (United Kingdom), 9 February 2014; Andrew Higgins, "Facing Fury Over Antigay Law, Stoli Says 'Russian? Not Really,'" *The New York Times* (United States), 7 September 2013.
14. Speech by Vladimir Putin, "Meeting of the Valdai International Discussion Club," Kremlin, 19 September 2013.
15. Roland Oliphant, "Putin Says Gay Visitors to Sochi Olympics Must 'Leave Children Alone,'" *The Telegraph* (United Kingdom), 17 January 2014.
16. *Young and Gay in Putin's Russia*, part 1/5, written and performed by Johnny White (2014, Vice Media), video, 5:14, 13 January 2014, www.youtube.com/watch?v=AZ _aSl3ktjg.
17. Human Rights Watch, *License to Harm: Violence and Harassment Against LGBT People and Activists in Russia*, 15 December 2014 (United States).
18. Masha Gessen and Joseph Huff-Hannon, (eds), *Gay Propaganda: Russian Love Stories* (New York: OR Books, 2014), 19–25.
19. Hayes Brown, "A Gay Couple Had to Flee Russia for the Crime of Caring for Their Adopted Children," *BuzzFeed*, 12 August 2019.

20. "Russia: Court Hearing Against LGBT Group," Human Rights Watch (United States), 2 April 2015.
21. "Global Attitudes Toward Transgender People," IPSOS, 29 January 2018.
22. "Play Actors," *Special Correspondent,* produced by Novaya Kompaniya (2013, Moscow: All-Russia State Television and Radio Broadcasting Company VGTRK, video, 1:11:57, www.youtube.com/watch?v=MYIWgduByfw.

9. GENDER-THEORY PANIC

1. David Paternotte, "Blessing the Crowds: Catholic Mobilizations against Gender in Europe," in S. Hark and P. Villa (eds), *Anti-Genderismus: Sexualität und Geschlecht als Schauplätze aktueller politischer Auseinandersetzungen*, 2015), 130.
2. See Sonia Corrêa, David Paternotte, and Roman Kuhar, "The Globalisation of Anti-gender Campaigns," *International Politics and Society*, 31 May 2018.
3. Kira Cochrane, "From Mary Wollstonecraft to Queer Theory," *The Guardian* (United Kingdom), 24 December 2008.
4. As quoted in Sarah Bracke and David Paternotte, "Unpacking the Sin of Gender," *Religion and Gender* 6, No. 2 (2016), 143.
5. "Pope Francis: Who Am I to Judge Gay People?," BBC News (United Kingdom), 29 July 2013.
6. Speech by Pope Francis, "Meeting with the Polish Bishops: Address of His Holiness Pope Francis," The Holy See, 27 July 2016.
7. Éric Fassin, "Gender and the Problem of Universals: Catholic Mobilizations and Sexual Democracy in France," *Religion and Gender* 6, No. 2 (2016), 176 –77.
8. German Lodola and Margarita Corral, "Support for Same-Sex Marriage in Latin America," in Jason Pierceson, Adriana Piatti-Crocker, and Shawn Shulenberg (eds), *Same-Sex Marriage in Latin America: Promise and Resistance*, (Lanham: Lexington Books, 2013), 43.
9. Uki Goñi, "Defying Church, Argentina Legalizes Gay Marriage," *Time* (United States), 15 July 2010.
10. Mario Pecheny, Daniel Jones, and Lucía Ariza, "Sexual Politics and Religious Actors in Argentina," *Religion and Gender* 6, No. 2 (2016), 212.
11. Adrian Carrasquillo, "Pope Francis, Argentina's President Kirchner Have a History of Contentious Battles," NBC News (United States), 14 March 2013.

12. Melissa Chernaik and Lisa Grove, Grove Insight, *Review of Existing Research on Marriage 2004 to 2009: Report by Grove Insight for Freedom to Marry* (United States: Freedom to Marry).
13. *Channel 4 News*, "Colm Tóibín: Catholic Church 'Neutered' on Gay Marriage," produced by ITN (2015, London: BBC), video, 4:22, 20 May 2015, www.youtube.com/watch?v=b-3LDyltfs8.
14. Sorcha Pollak, "Australian Campaign for Marriage Equality Follows Irish Model," *The Irish Times* (Ireland), 24 September 2017.
15. Results of Survey, Australian Bureau of Statistics, Australian Marriage Law Postal Survey, 2017; Shirleene Robinson and Alex Greenwich, "How the Yes Campaign Was Successful: Thank You, Internet," *HuffPost* (Australia), 24 November 2017.
16. "Brazil's Classrooms Become a Battleground in a Culture War," *The Economist* (The Americas), 29 November 2018.
17. Anna Jean Kaiser, "Call for Students to Film 'Biased' Teachers Brings Brazil's Culture Wars to the Classroom," *The Guardian* (United Kingdom),3 May 2019
18. Sumaira F.H., "Brazil's Bolsonaro Acts to Stop Spread of 'Gender Ideology' in Schools," *UrduPoint*,3 September 2019.
19. Sonia Corrêa, "The Brazilian Presidential Election: A Perfect Catastrophe?," Sexuality Policy Watch; Isabela Oliveira Kalil, "Emerging Far-Right in Brazil: Who Are Jair Bolsonaro's Voters and What They Believe," *Centre for Urban Ethnography* 3 (2018), 22.
20. Gustavo Gomes da Costa Santos, "How an Anti-LGBT Agenda Helped Secure Bolsonaro's Election Victory," *Public Seminar*, 29 November 2018.
21. Nicholas Casey, "Colombian Opposition to Peace Deal Feeds Off Gay Rights Backlash," *The New York Times* (United States), 8 October 2016.
22. As quoted in Ana Campoy, "A Conspiracy Theory About Sex and Gender Is Being Peddled Around the World by the Far Right," *Quartz* (United States), 4 November 2016.
23. José Fernando Serrano Amaya, "La tormenta perfecta: Ideología de género y articulación de públicos," *Revista Latinoamericana Sexualidad Salud y Sociedad*, No. 27 (2017), 149–71.
24. Gloria Careaga-Pérez, "Moral Panic and Gender Ideology in Latin America," *Religion and Gender* 6, No. 2 (2016), 251–55.
25. Summary of violence against trans and gender-diverse people worldwide, "TDoR 2016 Press Release," Transgender Europe, 9 November 2016.

26. Sam Cowie, "Violent Deaths of LGBT People in Brazil Hit All-Time High," *The Guardian* (United Kingdom), 22 January 2018.
27. Report, "Judith Butler Attacked in Brazil: A Briefing," Sexual Policy Watch, 11 January 2018.
28. Judith Butler, *Gender Trouble: Feminism and the Subversion of Identity* (New York: Routledge, 1990).
29. Jay Prosser, *Second Skins: The Body Narratives of Transsexuality* (New York: Columbia University Press, 1998).
30. Éric Fassin, "Gender and the Problem of Universals: Catholic Mobilizations and Sexual Democracy in France," *Religion and Gender* 6, No. 2 (2016), 176.
31. Miranda Blue, "Globalizing Homophobia, Part 3: A New Life for Discredited Research," Right Wing Watch (United States), 4 October 2013.
32. Hannah Levintova, "How US Evangelicals Helped Create Russia's Anti-gay Movement," *Mother Jones* (United States), 21 February 2014.
33. Erica L. Green, Katie Better, and Robert Pear, "'Transgender Could Be Defined Out of Existence Under Trump Administration," *The New York Times* (United States), 21 October 2018.
34. Ryan T. Anderson and Roger Severino, "3 Ways Conservative Lawmakers Should Fight Obama's Bathroom Directive," *The Daily Signal* (United States), 23 May 2016.
35. *National Catholic Register*, "Poland's Ruling Party Leader Praises Polish Archbishop for LGBT Opposition", 19 August 2019.
36. Speech by Viktor Orbán, "Prime Minister Viktor Orbán's speech at the 27th Congress of Fidesz—Hungarian Civic Union," miniszterelnok.hu, 12 November 2017.
37. Ibid.
38. Isabela Oliveira Pereira da Silva, "Gênero, política e religião nos protestos contra Judith Butler," *Nexo Jornal* (Brazil), 21 November 2017.

10. ZAIRA AND MARTHA'S STORY

1. "Primera boda gay en GDL," video, 14 December 2013, www.youtube.com/watch?v=_4MK4ZItv5s.
2. Ibid.
3. "GDL Noticias—Pareja de mujeres se une en legítimo matrimonia," Televisa Guadalajara, 14 December 2013, www.youtube.com/watch?v=T8C3aA4gcaM.

4. Correspondence from Francisco Robledo to the author, 16 May 2017.
5. *No Dress Code Required* (*Etiqueta no rigurosa*), documentary, directed by Cristina Herrera Borquez (2017, Mexico: La Cleta Films)
6. "Paternidad asumida con amor desde la homosexualidad," *Laguna* (Mexico), 21 April 2017.
7. United States Census Bureau, *Same-Sex Couple Households: American Community Survey Briefs*, 2011 (United States: U.S. Department of Commerce).
8. "Todas las familias, todos los derechos: la petición de los asistentes a la marcha gay en la CDMX," *Animal Politico* (Mexico), 25 June 2016.
9. María De Las Heras, *Matrimonio gay en México: con mayor en contra*, 2010.
10. "Apoyan legalizar las uniones gay en el país; 25%cree que afecta los valores morales," *Excélsior* (Mexico), 23 May 2016.
11. "ONGs de Aguascalientes exhiben a sacerdotes inducir voto a favor del PAN" (translated by Juliete Cabeza), ADNPolitico (Mexico), 10 June 2016.
12. "Este es el discurso completo que dio amlo en el zócalo," Expansión (Spain), 10 July 2018.

11. PINK DOLLARS, GLOBAL GAY

1. Website homepage, Atlantis Events.
2. Colleen Curry and Olivia Katrandjian, "Gay Cruise Passengers 'Weren't Trying to Put on Show,'" ABC News (Australia), 24 March 2012.
3. "Couple Returns from Gay Cruise to Address Public Sex Allegations," KESQ (United States), 26 March 2012.
4. Dennis Mayer and John Hart, "Exclusive: Gay Couple Arrested on Atlantis Events Cruise Tell Their Side of the Story," *Queerty*, 16 May 2012.
5. "St. Jean Says Anti-social Behavior, Homosexuality Bigger Than Imagined," *Dominca News Online* (Dominica), 6 September 2012.
6. Human Rights Watch, *"I Have to Leave to Be Me": Discriminatory Laws Against LGBT People in the Eastern Caribbean*, March 2018 (United States).
7. "Paradise Lost: The Plight of LGBT People in the Eastern Carribean," Human Rights Watch(United States), 21 March 2018.
8. "BTA: 'Bill Poses Threat to Success of Tourism,'" *Bernews* (Bermuda), 12 December 2017.

9. Rick Morgan and Ryna Ruggiero, "Cruise Line Carnival Corp. Joins the Fight Against Bermuda's Same-Sex Marriage Ban," CNBC (United States), 3 April 2018.
10. Owain Johnston-Barnes, "BTA on Pride: The Message Went Out," *The Royal Gazette* (Bermuda), 4 September 2019.
11. Terence Tange, "George Clooney: Brunei Boycott over Gay Death Penalty 'Warning Shot' to Malaysia, Indonesia," *Malaymail* (Malaysia), 14 May 2019.
12. "Mahathir: Beware of the West," Al Jazeera (Qatar), 19 June 2003.
13. "Play Actors," *Special Correspondent*, produced by Novaya Kompaniya (2013, Moscow: All-Russia State Television and Radio Broadcasting Company VGTRK), www.youtube.com/watch?v=MYIWgduByfw.
14. Tom Phillips and Anna Jean Kaiser, "Brazil Must Not Become a 'Gay Tourism Paradise,' Says Bolsonaro," *The Guardian*, 26 April 2019.
15. Chloe Govan, "Brunei LGBT community Living in Fear Despite Sultan's Death Penalty Reprieve," *The Telegraph*, 10 May 2019.
16. "Transcript: Obama's Remarks on Supreme Court Ruling on Same-Sex Marriage," *The Washington Post* (United States), 26 June 2015.
17. Hope King, "Corporate America Celebrates Gay Marriage Decision," CNN Business (United States), 26 June 2015.
18. Patrick Kulp, "The Best Reactions by Major Companies to the Historic Gay Marriage Decision," *Mashable* (United Kingdom), 26 June 2015.
19. "Target's Same-Sex Registry Ad Praised by LGBT Advocacy Bloggers," *HuffPost* (United States), 26 July 2012.
20. In Jon Binnie, *The Globalization of Sexuality* (London; Thousand Oaks, CA; New Delhi: Sage Publications, 2004), 59.
21. Ibid., 61.
22. Dennis Altman, "On Global Queering," *Australian Humanities Review*, 2 (1996).
23. "Heineken Launches New Global Brand Campaign; First Film, "The Entrance," an Online Hit," Heineken, 18 January 2011.
24. Akhil Katyal, "The Double Game of Sexuality: Idioms of Same Sex Desire in Modern India" (PhD dissertation, SOAS, University of London, 2011), 112.
25. Dennis Altman, "Gay Identities in Southeast Asia," in *Different Rainbows*, ed. Peter Drucker (London: Gay Men's Press, 2000), 150.
26. Mark Weiss, "Israeli Firms to Back Strike over Surrogacy Exclusion," *The Irish Times* (Ireland), 20 July 2018.

27. Lee Walzer, *Between Sodom and Eden: A Gay Journey Through Today's Changing Israel* (New York: Columbia University Press, 2000), 179.
28. Allison Kaplan Sommer, "Why the Battle for Gay Rights in Israel Passes Through Parenthood, Not Marriage," *Haaretz* (Israel), 22 July 2018.
29. Noga Tarnopolsky, "Debate over Surrogacy Draws Tens of Thousands of Israelis into the Streets," *Los Angeles Times* (United States), 23 July 2018.

12. FADI AND NADAV'S STORY

1. *Oriented*, directed by Jake Witzenfeld (Conch Studios, 2015), available on Netflix.
2. Ibid.
3. Tamara Traubmann, "Drag Against the Occupation," *Haaretz* (Israel), 27 February 2008.
4. Max Blumenthal, "Israel Cranks Up the PR Machine," *The Nation* (United States), 16 October 2013.
5. Sarah Schulman, *Israel/Palestine and the Queer International* (Durham: Duke University Press, 2012), 117.
6. Update posted by Fadi Daeem, Facebook, 28 May 2016.
7. Sarah Schulman, "A Documentary Guide to Pinkwashing," *HuffPost* (United States), 2 February 2016.
8. Sarah Schulman, "Israel and 'Pinkwashing,'" *The New York Times* (United States), 22 November 2011.
9. Aeyal Gross, "Pinkwashing Debate: Gay Rights in Israel Are Being Appropriated for Propaganda Value," *Haaretz* (Israel), 10 June 2015.
10. Aeyal Gross, "The Politics of LGBT Rights in Israel and Beyond: Nationality, Normativity, and Queer Politics," *Columbia Human Rights Law Review* 46, No. 2 (2015), 85.
11. Update posted by Nadav Kain, Facebook, 18 April 2016.
12. Video posted by Nadav Kain, Facebook, 30 May 2016.
13. "Gay Israel," Israel Ministry of Foreign Affairs, 19 July 2018.
14. Harriet Sherwood, "Israeli Military Accused of Staging Gay Pride Photo," *The Guardian* (United Kingdom), 13 June 2012.
15. Yaakov Katz, "40% of IDF's Gay Soldiers Suffer Abuse," *The Jerusalem Post* (Israel), 16 August 2011.
16. Maggie Sager, "Palestinian Queer Activists Challenge the 'Pinkwashing' of the Israeli Occupation," alQaws for Sexual & Gender Diversity in Palestinian Society, 16 February 2011.
17. "Three-Quarters of Jewish Israelis Support Same-Sex Unions: Poll," i24News (Israel), 6 January 2016.

18. Lena Odgaard, "Gay Pride Parade in Holy Jerusalem," Al-Monitor (United States), 31 July 2013.
19. Quoted in Alisa Solomon, "Viva la Diva Citizenship: Post-Zionism and Gay Rights," in Daniel Boyarin, Daniel Itzkovits, and Ann Pellegrini. (eds), *Queer Theory and the Jewish Question*, (New York: Columbia University Press, 2003), 156.
20. Gross, "The Politics of LGBT Rights," 94.
21. Ibid., 106.
22. "20,000 Attend Tel Aviv Rally for Gay Club Victims," *The Jerusalem Post* (Israel), 8 August 2009.
23. Aeyal Gross, "Harvey Milk Was Here," *Zeek* (United States), 25 October 2009.
24. Gil Z. Hochberg, "Introduction: Israelis, Palestinians, Queers: Points of Departure," *GLQ: A Journal of Lesbian and Gay Studies* 16, no 4. (2010), 495.
25. Ibid., 494.
26. Jeffrey Heller, "Israeli Gays' Safe Haven Turns Deadly," Reuters, 2 August 2009.
27. "Bibi Netanyahu Statement on the Orlando Terror Attack," video, 2:37, 15 June 2016, www.youtube.com/watch?v=7FBqTgNb5MA.
28. Hochberg, "Introduction: Israelis, Palestinians, Queers," 514.
29. James Kirchik, "Sarah Schulman's Pinkwashing Op-Ed Is Nonsense," *Tablet Magazine* (United States), 29 November 2011.
30. Lecture transcript, Haneen Maikey and Ramzi Kumsieh, "Resister au Pinkwashing-au cœur du mouvement queer arabe," (Paris), March 21, 2012.
31. "Any Palestinian Is Exposed to Monitoring by the Israeli Big Brother," *The Guardian* (United Kingdom), 12 September 2014. Charles A. James, "Israeli Army's Gay Soldiers Must Stop Persecuting Gay Palestinians," *Haaretz* (Israel), 23 September 2014.
32. "You Should Be Ashamed of Supporting Israel, Hamas Tells West," *Haaretz* (Israel), 28 October 2010.
33. "Palestinian Authority Bans Events by Local LGBTQ+ Organisation," *The New Arab*,19 August 2019
34. Amira Hass, "Shin Bet Inquiry: Did the Israeli Slip His Gay Palestinian Lover into the Country Illegally?," *Haaretz* (Israel), 28 May 2012.
35. Yossi Klein, "The Horrors of Being Gay, Pal- estinian and Refugee," *The New Republic* (United States), 20 August 2002.

36. Michael Kagan and Anat BenDor, Tel Aviv University's Public Interest Law Program (PILP), *Nowhere to Run: Gay Palestinian Asylum-Seekers in Israel*, April 2008 (Israel).
37. *The Invisible Men*, directed by Yariv Mozer (2012; Mozer Films and LEV Pictures), documentary film.
38. Kathleen Peratis, "For Gay Palestinians, Tel Aviv is Mecca," *The Forward* (United States), 24 February 2006.
39. Kagan and Ben-Dor, *Nowhere to Run*.
40. *Oriented*, dir. Witzenfeld.
41. Ibid.
42. Ibid.
43. Ibid.
44. Ibid.
45. "Yasmine Hamdan / La Mouch (Tribute Video)" video, 4:08, 25 January 2013, www.youtube.com/watch?v=x1BVhbDw5jI.
46. "Adonis-Sawt L Madini (Tribute Video)," video, 3:13, 14 April 2013, www.youtube.com/watch?v=RuEsvOC2hVs.
47. Mathew Schultz, "'We're Fighting Two Fights Here': Being Gay and Palestinian in Israel," *Vice* (United States), 29 November 2015.
48. "Adonis-Sawt L Madini (Tribute Video)," video, 3:13, 14 April 2013, www.youtube.com/watch?v=RuEsvOC2hVs.

13. THE TRANSGENDER CULTURE WARS

1. David Cameron, "Conservative Party Conference Speech," BBC (United Kingdom), 5 October 2011.
2. Charlotte Alter, "First Family: The Unlikely, Untested and Unprecedented Campaign of Mayor Pete Buttigieg," *Time* (United States), 2 May 2019.
3. "Biden Surging Among Democrats in Presidential Race, Quinnipiac University National Poll Finds; U.S. Voters Support Wealth Tax, Oppose Free College," Quinnipiac University Poll, 30 April 2019.
4. Pete Buttigieg, "South Bend Mayor: Why Coming Out Matters," *South Bend Tribune* (United States), 16 June 2015.
5. Martin Duberman, *Has the Gay Movement Failed?* (Berkeley: University of California Press, 2018).
6. Joseph G. Kosciw, Emily A. Greytak, Adrian D. Zongrone, Caitlin M. Clark, and Nhan L. Truong, GLSEN, *The 2017 National School Climate Survey*, 2018 (New York: GLSEN).
7. *National LGBT Survey: Summary Report*, Government Equalities Office, 2018 (United Kingdom).

8. Workplace Equality Program Team, Human Rights Campaign, *Corporate Equality Index 2018: Rating Workplaces on Lesbian, Gay, Bisexual, Transgender, and Queer Equality*, 2018 (Washington, D.C.: Human Rights Campaign).
9. April Guasp, Anne Gammon, and Gavin Ellison, Stonewall, *Homophobic Hate Crime: The Gay British Crime Survey 2013*, 2013 (United Kingdom).
10. Katy Steinmetz, "The Transgender Tipping Point," *Time* (United States), 29 May 2014.
11. Katy Steinmetz, "America's Transition," *Time* (United States), 9 June 2014.
12. Ibid., 38–46.
13. Ibid.
14. Seth Adam and Matt Goodman, "Number of Americans Who Report Knowing a Transgender Person Doubles in Seven Years, According to New GLAAD Survey," GLAAD, 17 September 2015.
15. Human Rights Campaign and Trans People of Color Coalition, *A Time to Act: Fatal Violence Against Transgender People in America 2017*, 2017 (Washington, D.C.: Human Rights Campaign).
16. Claire Zillman, "Changing Genders at Work: Inside the Fortune 500's Quiet Transgender Revolution," *Fortune* (United States), 13 July 2015.
17. Webpage, "Interactive Map: Clinical Care Programs for Gender-Expansive Children and Adolescents," Human Rights Campaign.
18. Johanna Olson-Kennedy, "Referrals to the Center for Transyouth Health and Development by Year," CHLA Center for Transyouth Health and Development, 2018
19. Webpage, "The Gender Service background, funding and program logic," The Royal Children's Hospital, Melbourne, Australia.
20. Gender Identity Research and Education Society (GIRES), *The Number of Gender Variant People in the UK—Update 2011*, 2011 (United Kingdom).
21. Susan Stryker, *Transgender History: The Roots of Today's Revolution*, 2nd ed. (New York: Seal Press, 2017), 66.
22. *Who Knows Best?*, documentary, directed by Alex Berk and John Conroy (2017, London: BBC 2).
23. Jesse Singal, "How the Fight over Transgender Kids Got a Leading Sex Researcher Fired," *The Cut*, 7 February 2016.
24. Molly Hayes, "Doctor Fired from Gender Identity Clinic Says He Feels 'Vindicated' After CAMH Apology, Settlement," *The Globe and Mail* (Canada), 7 October 2018.

25. Polly Carmichael, "GIDS Keynote: Intercom Trust Conference, Plymouth," Gender Identity Development Service,26 November 2017, https://drive.google.com/file/d/16D2m4dRWCTZ WfQ029tFb962JKZhaQGDn/view.
26. Dani Heffernan, "The APA Removes 'Gender Identity Disorder' from Updated Mental Health Guide," GLAAD, 3 December 2012.
27. Holly B. Kozee, Tracy L. Tylka, and Loren Bauerband, "Measuring Transgender Individuals' Comfort with Gender Identity and Appearance: Development and Validation of the Transgender Congruence Scale," *Psychology of Women* 36, 2 (2012), 181.
28. "Argentina Adopts Landmark Legislation in Recognition of Gender Identity," OutRight Action International, 8 June 2012.
29. Evan Urquhart, "Gatekeepers vs. Informed Consent: Who Decides When a Trans Person Can Medically Transition?," *Slate* (United States), 11 March 2016.
30. Hadley Freeman, "Sport Can Help to Clarify the Trans Debate," *The Guardian* (United Kingdom), 6 March 2019.
31. Government Equalities Of fice and the Rt. Hon. Penny Mordaunt MP, "Government Announces Plans to Reform Process of Changing Legal Gender," Gov.uk, 3 July 2018.
32. "Who Decides Your Gender?," *The Economist* (United Kingdom), 27 October 2018.
33. Helen Joyce, "The New Patriarchy: How Trans Radicalism Hurts Women, Children—and Trans People Themselves," *Quillette* (Australia), 4 December 2018.
34. Richard Köhler, "Implementation of Legal Gender Recognition Procedures Based on Self-Determination in Malta, Norway, Denmark, Argentina, and Ireland with a Focus on Fraudulent Intents and Repeated Decisions," TGEU, 11 January 2017.
35. Nick Duffy, "Transphobia and Homophobia Are Inextricably Linked," *The Economist* (United Kingdom), 13 July 2018.
36. Ibid.
37. Joyce, "The New Patriarchy."
38. Andrew Surma, "Fliers Distributed Throughout Grass Lake Opposing Transgender Bathroom Rule," *MLive* (United States), 8 September 2017; News 10, "Local Mother of Transgender Child Speaks Out," Wilx News 10 (United States), 30 October 2017.
39. Update posted by Tammy Marie, Facebook, no date supplied, from correspondence with Terri Tuttle Neely.

40. Jonathan Shorman and Hunter Woodall, "Kansas GOP Votes to 'Oppose All Efforts to Validate Transgender Identity,'" *The Wichita Eagle* (United States), 18 February 2018.
41. Update posted by Tammy Gerlach, Facebook, no date supplied, from correspondence with Terri Tuttle Neely.
42. Catherine E. Lhamon and Vanita Gupta, "Dear Colleague Letter on Transgender Students," U.S. Department of Justice and U.S. Department of Education, 13 May 2016.
43. "Vice President Joe Biden: Transgender Discrimination 'Civil Rights Issue of Our Time,'" Transgender Law Center, 31 October 2012.
44. *State of Texas v. United States*, 7.16-cv-54-O, (District Court Northern District of Texas Wichita Falls Division, 2016).
45. Tony Perkins, "ADF Takes Highland in Bathroom Fight," Family Research Council, 20 September 2016.
46. Speech by Pope Francis, "Meeting with Priests, Religious Seminarians and Pastoral Workers: Address of His Holiness Pope Francis," The Holy See, 1 October 2016.
47. Perkins, "ADF Takes Highland."
48. Julian Borger, "Trump Administration Wants to Remove 'Gender' from UN Human Rights Documents," *The Guardian* (United Kingdom), 25 October 2018.
49. *R.G. & G.R. Harris Funeral Homes, Inc. v. EEOC & Aimee Stephens*, ACLU, 24 October 2018.
50. Erica L. Green, Katie Better, and Robert Pear, "'Transgender Could Be Defined out of Existence Under Trump Administration," *The New York Times* (United States), 21 October 2018.
51. Webpage, "WOLF v. U.S.," WoLF.
52. Ibid.
53. Tim Fitzsimons, "Conservative Group Hosts Anti-transgender Panel of Feminists 'from the Left,'" NBC News (United States), 30 January 2019.
54. Stryker, *Transgender History*, 131.
55. Janice Raymond, *The Transsexual Empire: The Making of the She-Male* (Boston: Beacon Press, 1979).
56. Germaine Greer, *The Whole Woman* (New York: Anchor Books, 2000).
57. Josh Gabbatiss, "London Pride: Anti-trans Activists Disrupt Parade by Lying Down in the Street to Protest 'Lesbian Erasure,'" *The Independent* (United Kingdom), 7 July 2018.
58. Ibid.

59. Jonny Best, "Please Join Us in Asking Stonewall to Reconsider Its Transgender Policies and Approach," iPetitions.com, 2019.
60. "WoLF vs US: Frequently Asked Questions," Women's Liberation Front website, February 2019.
61. As quoted in Luke Feltham, "'Necessary Discrimination': CAS Rejects Caster Semenya's Appeal," *Mail & Guardian* (South Africa), 1 May 2019.
62. Martina Navratilova, "The Rules on Trans Athletes Reward Cheats and Punish the Innocent," *The Times* (United Kingdom), 17 February 2019.
63. Katelyn Burns, "Caster Semenya and the Twisted Politics of Testosterone," *Wired* (United States), 11 May 2019.
64. Ockert de Villiers, "Semenya Starts Legal Battle Against IAAF: 'I Am a Woman and I Am Fast,'" *IOL* (South Africa), 19 June 2018.
65. Parker Marie Molloy, "Equality Michigan Petitions Michfest to End Exclusionary Policy," *The Advocate* (United States), 29 July 2014.
66. Ruth Padawer, "When Women Become Men at Wellesley," *The New York Times* (United States), 15 October 2014.

14. THE RIOT YOUTH STORIES

1. Post by Liam Kai, Twitter, 18 June 2014.
2. Post by Liam Kai, Twitter, 2 June 2014.
3. Jay Prosser, *Second Skins: The Body Narratives of Transsexuality* (New York: Columbia University Press, 1998), chapter 2.
4. Henry Rubin, *Self-Made Man: Identity and Embodiment among Transsexual Men* (Nashville: Vanderbilt University Press, 2003).
5. Ibid., 11.
6. Tey Meadow, *Trans Kids: Being Gendered in the Twenty-First Century* (Oakland: University of California Press, 2018), 215.
7. Stephen Rosenthal, "Approach to the Patient: Transgender Youth: Endocrine Considerations," *Journal of Clinical Endocrinology & Metabolism* 99, No. 12 (2014), 4379–89.
8. Meadow, *Trans Kids*, 75.
9. YouTube video description, "Dr. Medalie performs FtM peri areolar mastectomy procedure with purse string closure," 24 January 2011. https://www.youtube.com/watch?v=h1UealCPtnU.
10. Post by Liam Kai, Twitter, 4 July 2014.
11. Post by Liam Kai, Twitter, 4 July 2014.
12. Information document, "GSA Court Victories: A Quick Guide for Gay Straight Alliances," American Civil Liberties Union, 2015.

13. GenderFluid Support, "Gender Master List," Tumblr, 2019.
14. "Gay and Transgender Youth Homelessness by the Numbers," Center for American Progress, 21 June 2010.
15. National Center for Transgender Equality (NCTE), *Report of the 2015 U.S. Transgender Survey*, 2016.
16. Leslie Feinberg, *Stone Butch Blues* (Sydney: ReadHowYouWant, 1993).
17. *Transgender Kids: Who Knows Best?*, dir. Berk and Conroy.
18. Jesse Singal, "When Children Say They're Trans," *The Atlantic* (United States), July/August 2018.
19. Sara Solovitch, "When Kids Come in Saying They Are Transgender (or No Gender), These Doctors Try to Help," *The Washington Post* (United States), 21 January 2018.
20. Meadow, *Trans Kids*, 78.
21. James M. Cantor, "How Many Transgender Kids Grow Up to Stay Trans?" *PsyPost*, 30 December 2017.
22. Charlie Kiss, "The Idea That Trans Men Are 'Lesbians in Denial' Is Demeaning and Wrong," *The Economist* (United Kingdom), 3 July 2018.
23. "GIDS Referrals Increase in 2017/18," The Tavistock and Portman NHS Foundation Trust (United Kingdom), 17 May 2018.
24. Johanna Olson-Kennedy, "Referrals to the Center for Transyouth Health and Development by Year," CHLA Center for Transyouth Health, 2018.
25. Worriedmom, "The Lost Generation Strikes Back," 4thWaveNow, 5 May 2017; Inga Berenson, "How Has the UK Become a Police State? (And Has Twitter Become Its Informant?)," 4thWaveNow, 22 March 2018.
26. Lisa Littman, "Rapid-Onset Gender Dysphoria in Adolescents and Young Adults: A Study of Parental Reports," *PLOS One* 13, No. 8 (2018).
27. "New Study out of Finland: Girls with Gender Dysphoria Have Many Other Mental Health Issues," 4thWaveNow, 23 May 2015.
28. Lisa Marchiano, "Misunderstanding a New Kind of Gender Dysphoria," *Quillette*, 6 October 2017.
29. Lisa Marchiano, "Layers of Meaning: A Jungian Analyst Questions the Identity Model for Trans-Identified Youth," 4thWaveNow, 25 September 2016.
30. Avgi Saketopoulou, "Minding the Gap: Race and Class in Clinical Work with Gender Variant Children," *Psychoanalytic Dialogues* 21, No. 2 (2011), 1233–43.
31. In Margaret Talbot, "About a Boy," *The New Yorker* (United States), 18 March 2013.

32. Anonymous, "No Menses, No Mustaches: Gender Doctor Touts Non-binary Hormones & Surgery for Self-Sacrificing Youth," 4thWaveNow, 4 August 2017.
33. Ibid.
34. World Professional Association for Transgender Health, *Standards of Care for the Health of Transsexual, Transgender, and Gender Nonconforming People*, 7th ed., 2011.
35. "Who Decides Your Gender?," *The Economist* (United Kingdom), 27 October 2018.
36. "Transgender Politics Focuses on Who Determines Someone's Gender," *The Economist* (United Kingdom), 25 October 2019.
37. Paul Preciado, *Testo Junkie* (New York: Feminist Press, 2013), 55.
38. In Talbot, "About a Boy."
39. Virginia Goldner, "Trans: Gender in Free Fall," *Psychoanalytic Dialogues* 21, No. 2 (2011), 166 and 165.
40. Susan Stryker, *Transgender History: The Roots of Today's Revolution*, 2nd ed. (New York: Seal Press, 2017), 1.
41. Donna Haraway, *Simians, Cyborgs and Women: The Reinvention of Nature* (London: Routledge, 1991), 180.
42. Laura Jacobs, "Posthuman Bodies, Posthuman Selves," in Genny Beemyn, *Transgender History in the United States*, a special unabridged version of a book chapter from *Trans Bodies, Trans Selves*, ed. Laura Erickson-Schroth, 41– 42, https://www.umass.edu/stonewall/sites/default/files/Infoforandabout/transpeople/genny_beemyn_transgender_history_in_the_united_states.pdf.
43. Johanna Olson-Kennedy, "Referrals to the Center for Transyouth Health and Development by Year," CHLA Center for Transyouth Health, 2018.
44. Francesca Mari, "GenderBender," *Texas Monthly*, March 2016; Colt Keo-Meyer, "Infographics," coltkeo-meier.com.

15. THE WORLD'S NEW PINK LINE

1. Morgan Jerkins and Meredith Talusan, "Writing, Trans Identity, Race, and All the Poetry: An Interview with Meredith Talusan," *The Toast* (United States), 23 April 2015.
2. Andrea Long Chu, "On Liking Women," *n+1*, winter 2018.
3. Andrew Kohut et al., Pew Research Center, *The Global Divide on Homosexuality: Greater Acceptance in More Secular and Affluent Countries*, 4 June 2013 (United States).

4. Mark Gevisser, "Ang Ladlad Party Brings Beauty Parlours and Gay Pageants out to Vote in Philippines," *The Guardian* (United Kingdom), 12 May 2013.
5. Mikee Nuñez-Inton, "ILGA Meets ... Mikee Into," International Lesbian, Gay, Bisexual, Trans and Intersex Association, 26 August 2015.
6. Mikee Nuñez-Inton, "The *Bakla* and Gay Globality in Chris Martinez's *Here Comes the Bride*," *Intersections: Gender and Sexuality in Asia and the Pacific* 38, August 2015.
7. Robert Beachy, *Gay Berlin: Birthplace of a Modern Identity* (New York: Alfred A. Knopf, 2014), xvii.
8. Edward Carpenter, *The Intermediate Sex: A Study of Some Transitional Types of Men and Women* (Berlin: TGS Publishing, 2009).
9. "The Legality of Gender Change," *National Geographic*, 2016.
10. Eugene K. Chow, "China's Complicated Approach to Transgender Rights," *The Diplomat* (Japan), 23 October 2017.
11. Michael Taylor, "Trans Chinese Teens Forced into 'Conversion Therapy'—Study," Thomson Reuters Foundation News,6 September 2019.
12. Meredith Talusan, "Why I Chose Thailand for My Gender Reassignment Surgery," *Condé Nast Traveler* (United States), 13 June 2018.
13. Digital map, "Criminalisation and Prosecution of Trans People," TGEU, 2019.
14. *Quincy Mc Ewan et al and Society Against Sexual Orientation Discrimination (SASOD) vs. The Attorney General of Guyana, [2018] CCj 30 (AJ)*, Caribbean Court of Justice, 2018.
15. "Kano State Prostitution and Other Immoral Acts (Prohibition) Law 2000," in Philip Ostein, *Sharia Implementation in Northern Nigeria, 1999–2006: A Sourcebook*, Vol. III, (Ibadan, Nigeria: Spectrum Books, 2007), 207.
16. Elnathan John, "The Keeper of Secrets," in *Safe House: Explorations in Creative Nonfiction*, ed. Ellah Wakatama Allfrey (Toronto: Dundurn, 2016), 109–28.
17. "Mahathir: Beware of the West," Al Jazeera (Qatar), 19 June 2003.
18. "Najib: LGBTs, Liberalism, Pluralism Are Enemies of Islam," *The Malaysian Insider* (Malaysia), 19 July 2012.
19. Presentation by Christophe Broqua and Marine Geoffrion, "*Góor-jiggéen* and *Kodjo-besia*: The Resignification of Two Categories from Gender to Sexuality in Senegal and Ghana," International Association for the Study

of Sexuality, Culture and Society (IASSCS) Xth International Conference, Dublin, Ireland, 17–20 June 2015.

20. Nkunzi Zandile Nkabinde, *Black Bull, Ancestors and Me: My Life as a Lesbian Sangoma* (Johannesburg: Jacana Media, 2009).
21. Emilienne Malfatto and Jelena Prtoric, "Last of the Burrnesha: Balkan Women Who Pledged Celibacy to Live as Men," *The Guardian* (United Kingdom), 5 August 2014.
22. Jenny Nordberg, "Afghan Boys Are Prized, So Girls Live the Part," *The New York Times*, 20 September 2010.
23. Genny Beemyn, *Transgender History in the United States*, a special unabridged version of a book chapter from *Trans Bodies, Trans Selves*, ed. Laura Erickson-Schroth, 7, https:// www.umass.edu /stonewall / sites /default /files / Infoforandabout /transpeople/genny_beemyn_transgender_history_in_the_united_states.pdf.
24. As quoted in Human Rights Watch, *Rights in Transition: Making Legal Recognition for Transgender People a Global Priority*, 2011 (United States).

16. THE KOTHI STORIES

1. As quoted in Akshay Khanna, *Sexualness* (New Delhi: New Text, 2014), 161.
2. Gayatri Reddy, *With Respect to Sex: Negotiating Hijra Identity in South India* (Chicago and London: University of Chicago Press, 2005), 26.
3. A. Revathi, *The Truth About Me: A Hijra Life Story* (New Delhi: Penguin Books India, 2010).
4. M. D. Muthukumaraswamy, "When Graveyards Throb with Life and Women Power," *The Times of India* (India), 17 March 2016.
5. Lawrence Cohen, "The Kothi Wars: AIDS Cosmopolitanism and the Morality of Classification," in *Sex in Development: Science, Sexuality, and Morality in Global Perspective*, eds. Vincanne Adams and Stacy Leigh Pigg (Durham and London: Duke University Press, 2005), 291.
6. Update posted by Lakshaya, translated from Tamil by Lavanya Keshavraj for the author, Facebook, no date.
7. Khanna, *Sexualness*, 54.
8. Ibid., 71.
9. Ibid., 343.
10. Ruth Vanita and Saleem Kidwai, eds., *Same-Sex Love in India: Readings from Literature and History* (New York and Basingstoke: Palgrave, 2001).
11. Update posted by Lakshaya, translated from Tamil by Lavanya Keshavraj for the author, Facebook, no date.

12. Ministry of Social Justice and Empowerment, *Report of the Expert Committee on the Issues Relating to Transgender Persons* (India), 27 January 2014.
13. Chaitanya Mallapur, "Why New Bill Meant to Benefit Transgender People Is Termed Regressive," IndiaSpend,22 August 2019.
14. Lok Sabha, Transgender Persons (Protection of Rights) Bill, 2019, bill No. 169 of 2019, 15 July 2019.
15. Update posted by Lakshaya, translated from Tamil by Lavanya Keshavraj for the author, Facebook, 22 April 2013.
16. Sumit Dutta et al., *Addressing Mental Health Needs Among Male Born Sexual Minorities*, April 2014 (India: Karnataka Health Promotion Trust).
17. Homepage, "Bridging the Online Gender Divide in Rural India," Internet Saathi.
18. Monica Bathija, "Internet Saathi: Improving digital literacy among women," *Forbes India* (India), 7 August 2018.
19. Webpage, "Our Values in Action," Internet Saathi.
20. Update posted by Lakshaya, translated from Tamil by Lavanya Keshavraj for the author, Facebook, 6 September 2018.
21. Update posted by Lakshaya, translated from Tamil by Lavanya Keshavraj for the author, Facebook, 6 September 2018.
22. *Navtej Singh Johar & Ors. vs Union of India*, Writ Petition (Criminal) No. 76 of 2016. Supreme Court of India, 6 September 2018.
23. Ibid.
24. Ibid.
25. Update posted by Lakshaya, translated from Tamil by Lavanya Keshavraj for the author, Facebook, 6 September 2018.

EPILOGUE: ON IT GETTING BETTER

1. Andy Rice, "Malawian Gay Couple's Beautiful Thing, and Its Ugly Consequences," *Daily Maverick* (South Africa), 9 June 2010.
2. Tara Parker-Pope, "Showing Gay Teenagers a Happy Future," *The New York Times* (United States), 22 September 2010.
3. Homepage, "Welcome to the It Gets Better Project," It Gets Better Project.
4. Initiative for Equal Rights and Vivid Rain, "Social Perception Survey on Lesbian, Gay, Bi-sexual and Transgender Persons Rights in Nigeria," June 2019.

5. Ryan Lenora Brown, "In Historic Shift, Botswana Declares Homosexuality Is Not a Crime," *The Christian Science Monitor* (United States), 11 June 2019.
6. Simone de Beauvoir, *The Second Sex* (New York: Vintage Books, 1974), 301.
7. Mark Gevisser, *Lost and Found in Johannesburg: A Memoir* (New York: Farrar, Straus and Giroux, 2014), 77.

FURTHER READING

BY MARK GEVISSER

These are essays and reports I published on the subject of the Pink Line before this book's publication. Some of the chapters in this book were first published, in different form, in these pieces. They are all available on www.markgevisser.com.

"House of Rainbow: LGBT Rights Balanced on the Pink Line," *Griffith Review* 59, January 2018. Also published as "House of Rainbow: The New Pink Line Dividing the World," *The Guardian*, 3 March 2018.

"Walking Girly in Nairobi," in *Safe House: Explorations in Creative Nonfiction*, edited by Ellah Wakatama Allfrey. Toronto: Dundurn, 2016. Also published as "Love's

Runaway's: The Gay Ugandans Forced into Exile," *The Guardian*, 18 May 2016.

"LGBT Power Surge: Why Russia, Uganda and Other Repressive States Are Fighting a Losing Battle Against Sexual Freedom," *Foreign Policy*, December 2015.

"The Transgender Woman Fighting for Her Right to See Her Son," *The Guardian*, 12 November 2015.

"Engendered: The Trans Community Is Coming Out and Bringing with It a Depth of Understanding of What It Means to Be Human," *The Nation*, 6 April 2015. "Self-Made Man," *Granta* 129, 2015.

"Kanaga's Choices: Queer and Transgender Identity in the Digital Age," Global Information Society Watch, 2015.

"Homosexuality and the Global Culture Wars," *Boldly Queer, African Perspectives on Same-Sex Sexuality and Gender Diversity*, edited by Theo Sandfort, Fabiene Simenel, Kevin Mwachiro, and Vasu Reddy. The Hague: Hivos, 2015.

"Love in Exile," *The Guardian*, 27 November 2014.

"Ang Ladlad Party Brings Beauty Parlours and Gay Pageants out to Vote in Philippines," *The Guardian*, 12 May 2013.

OTHER READING

Ackroyd, Peter. *Queer City: Gay London from the Romans to the Present Day*. London: Vintage, 2017.

Ahmed, Sara. *Strange Encounters: Embodied Others in Post-coloniality*. London: Routledge, 2000.

Aizura, Aren Z., et al., eds. "Decolonizing the Transgender Imaginary," *Transgender Studies Quarterly* (2014) 1 (3). Akshay Khanna. *Sexualness*. New Delhi: New Text, 2014.

Altman, Denis. "AIDS and the Globalization of Sexuality," *Social Identities*, Vol. 14, 2008.

Altman, Dennis. "On Global Queering," *Australian Humanities Review*, 2 (1996). Altman, Dennis. *Global Sex*. Chicago and London: University of Chicago Press, 2001.

Altman, Dennis, and Jonathan Symons. *Queer Wars*. Cambridge, United Kingdom: Polity Press, 2016.

Amar Paul. *The Security Archipelago: Human-Security States, Sexuality Politics, and the End of Neo-liberalism*. Durham, NC: Duke University Press, 2014.

Appiah, Kwame Anthony. *Cosmopolitanism: Ethics in a World of Strangers*. New York and London: Norton, 2006.

Appudurai, Arjun. *Modernity at Large: Cultural Dimensions of Globalization*. Minneapolis: University of Minnesota Press, 2000.

Beachy, Robert. *Gay Berlin: Birthplace of a Modern Identity*. New York: Alfred A. Knopf, 2014.

Beemyn, Genny. *Transgender History in the United States*, a special unabridged version of a book chapter from *Trans Bodies, Trans Selves*, edited by Laura Erickson-Schroth. https://www.umass.edu/stonewall/sites/default/files/Infoforandabout/transpeople/genny_beemyn_transgender_history_in_the_united_states.pdf.

Binnie, Jon. *The Globalization of Sexuality*. London; Thousand Oaks, CA.; New Delhi: Sage Publications, 2004.

Blue, Miranda, "Globalizing Homophobia, Parts 1–4," Right Wing Watch, 4 October 2013.

Bob, Clifford. *The Global Right Wing and the Clash of World Politics*. New York: Cambridge University Press, 2010.

Boellstorff, Tom, "The Emergence of Political Homophobia in Indonesia: Masculinity and National Belonging," *Ethnos* 64, No. 4 (2004), 465–86.

Boellstorff, Tom. *The Gay Archipelago: Sexuality and Nation in Indonesia*. Princeton: Princeton University Press, 2005.

Bornstein, Kate. *Gender Outlaws: The Next Generation*. New York: Seal Press, 2010. Bornstein, Kate. *My New Gender Workbook: A Step-by-Step Guide to Achieving Peace Through Gender Anarchy and Sex Positivity*. New York: Routledge, 2013.

Bracke, Sarah, and David Patternotte, eds. "Habemus Gender! The Catholic Church and 'Gender Ideology,' *Religion and Gender* 6, No. 2, 2016.

Butler, Judith. *Gender Trouble: Feminism and the Subversion of Identity*. New York: Routledge, 1990.

Butler, Judith. *Undoing Gender*. New York: Routledge, 2004. Chiang, Howard, ed. *Global Encyclopedia of Lesbian, Gay, Bisexual, Transgender, and Queer (LGBTQ) History*. New York: Gale, 2019.

Chu, Andrea Long. "On Liking Women," *n+1*, Winter 2018.

Cohen, Lawrence. "The Kothi Wars: AIDS Cosmopolitanism and the Morality of Classification." In *Sex in Development: Science, Sexuality, and Morality in Global Perspective*, edited by Vincanne Adams and Stacy Leigh Pigg. Durham, NC, and London: Duke University Press, 2005.

Corbett, Ken. *Boyhood: Rethinking Masculinities*. New Haven: Yale University Press, 2009.

Corrales, Javier, and Mario Pecheny. *The Politics of Sexuality in Latin America: A Reader on Lesbian, Gay, Bisexual and Transgender Rights*. Pittsburgh: University of Pittsburgh Press, 2010.

Currah, Paisley, and Susan Stryker, eds. *TSQ: Making Transgender Count* 2 (1). Durham, NC: Duke University Press, 2015.

De la Dehesa, Rafael. *Queering the Public Sphere in Mexico and Brazil: Sexual Rights Movements in Emerging Democracies*. Durham, NC, and London: Duke University Press, 2010.

D'Emilio, John, "Capitalism and Gay Identity." In The Lesbian and Gay Studies Reader, edited by Henry Abelove, Michèle Aina Barale, and David M. Halperin. New York and London: Routledge, 1993.

Drucker, Peter. *Different Rainbows*. London: Gay Men's Press, 2000.

Duberman, Martin, Martha Vicinus, and George Chauncey, eds. *Hidden from History: Reclaiming the Gay and Lesbian Past*. New York: Penguin, 1989.

Duberman, Martin. *Has the Gay Movement Failed?* Berkeley: University of California Press, 2018.

Dutta, Aniruddha, "Legible Identities and Legitimate Citizens: The Globalization of Transgender and Subjects of HIV-AIDS Prevention in Eastern India," *International Feminist Journal of Politics*, Vol. 15, 2013.

Dutta, Aniruddha, and Raina Roy, "Decolonizing Transgender in India: Some Reflections" *TSQ* 1, No. 3, August 2014.

Ehrensaft, Diane. *The Gender Creative Child: Pathways for Nurturing and Supporting Children Who Live Outside Gender Boxes*. New York: The Experiment, 2016.

El Feki, Shereen. *Sex and the Citadel: Intimate Life in a Changing Arab World*. New York: Anchor Books, 2014.

Epprecht, Mark. *Heterosexual Africa? The History of an Idea from the Age of Exploration to the Age of AIDS*. Athens, Ohio: Ohio University Press, 2008.

Epprecht, Mark. *Hungochani: The History of a Dissident Sexuality in Southern Africa*. Montreal: McGill-Queen's Press, 2004.

Essig, Laurie. *Queer in Russia: A Story of Sex, Self, and the Other*. Durham, NC: Duke University Press, 1999.

Fassin, Éric, "The Rise and Fall of Sexual Politics in the Public Sphere: A Transatlantic Contrast," *Public Culture* 18, No. 1, 2006.

Feinberg, Leslie. *Stone Butch Blues*. Sydney: ReadHowYouWant, 1993.

Foucault, Michel. Trans. Robert Hurley. *The History of Sexuality*. New York: Pantheon Books, 1978.

Garcia, J. Neil C. *Philippine Gay Culture: Binabae to Bakla, Silahis to MSM*. Quezon City, Philippines: UP Press, 2008.

Gaudio, Rudolf. *Allah Made Us: Sexual Outlaws in an Islamic African City*. Malden, MA: Wiley-Blackwell, 2009.

Gessen, Masha, and Joseph Huff-Hannon, eds. *Gay Propaganda: Russian Love Stories.* New York: OR Books, 2014.

Goldner, Virginia, "Trans: Gender in Free Fall," *Psychoanalytic Dialogues* 21, No. 2 (2011), 159–71.

Gross, Aeyal, "The Politics of LGBT Rights in Israel and Beyond: Nationality, Normativity, and Queer Politics," *Columbia Human Rights Law Review* 46, No. 2 (2015), 81–152.

Gupta, Alok, "This Alien Legacy: The Origins of 'Sodomy' Laws in British Colonialism." In Human Rights, Sexual Orientation and Gender Identity in the Commonwealth, edited by Corinne Lennox and Matthew Waites. London: Human Rights Consortium, Institute of Commonwealth Studies, 2013.Halberstam, J. Jack. *Gaga Feminism: Sex, Gender and the End of the Normal.*Boston: Beacon Press, 2013.

Halberstam, J. Jack. *Trans**. Oakland: University of California Press, 2018.

Herdt, Gilbert. *Moral Panics, Sex Panics: Fear and the Fight over Sexual Rights*. New York: New York University Press, 2009.

Hoad, Neville. *African Intimacies: Race, Homosexuality and Globalization*. Minneapolis: University of Minnesota Press, 2007.

Hoad, Neville, "Arrested Development, or The Queerness of Savages: Resisting Evolutionary Narratives of Difference," *Postcolonial Studies* 3:2 (2000), 133–58.

Hoad, Neville, Karen Martin, and Graeme Reid, eds. *Sex and Politics in South Africa*. Cape Town: Double Storey, 2005.

Hochberg, Gil, ed. "Queer Politics and the Question of Palestine/Israel," *GLQ: A Journal of Lesbian and Gay Studies* 16, No. 4. (2010), 493–663.

Human Rights Watch. *Audacity in Adversity LGBT Activism in the Middle East and North Africa*. 16 April 2018. United States.

Human Rights Watch. *Fear for Life: Violence against Gay Men and Men Perceived as Gay in Senegal*. 2010. Human Rights Watch. *"I Have to Leave to Be Me": Discriminatory Laws Against LGBT People in the Eastern Carribean*. March 2018. United States.

Human Rights Watch. *In a Time of Torture: The Assault on Justice in Egypt's Crackdown on Homosexual Conduct*. March 2004. United States. Human Rights Watch.

License to Harm: Violence and Harassment Against LGBT People and Activists in Russia. 15 December 2014. United States.

Human Rights Watch. *Rights in Transition: Making Legal Recognition for Transgender People a Global Priority*, 2011.

Human Rights Watch. *"These Political Games Ruin Our Lives": Indonesia's LGBT Community Under Threat*. 10 August 2016. United States.

Human Rights Watch. *"They Want Us Exterminated": Murder, Torture, Sexual Orientation and Gender in Iraq*. 17 August 2009. United States. Jernow, Allison Liu. *Sexual Orientation, Gender Identity and Justice: A Comparative Law Casebook*. Switzerland: International Commission of Jurists, 2011.

John, Elnathan, "The Keeper of Secrets." In Safe House: Explorations in Creative Nonfiction, edited by Ellah Wakatama Allfrey. Toronto: Dundurn, 2016.

Joyce, Helen, "The New Patriarchy: How Trans Radicalism Hurts Women, Children—And Trans People Themselves," *Quillette*, Australia, 4 December 2018.

Kaoma, Kapya. Political Research Associates. *Colonizing African Values: How the US Christian Right Is Transforming Sexual Politics in Africa*. 2012, United States.

Kaoma, Kapya. Political Research Associates. *Globalizing the Culture Wars: U.S. Conservatives, African Churches, & Homophobia*. 2009. United States.

Katyal, Akhil. *The Doubleness of Sexuality: Idioms of Same-Sex Desire in Modern India*. New Delhi: New Text, 2016.

Kollman, Kelly, "Same-Sex Unions: The Globalization of an Idea," *International Studies Quarterly* (2007) 51, 329–57.

Kuhar, Roman, and David Paternotte. *Anti-gender Campaigns in Europe: Mobilizing Against Equality*. London and New York: Rowman & Littlefield, 2017.

Levintova, Hannah. "How US Evangelicals Helped Create Russia's Anti-gay Movement," *Mother Jones*, United States, 21 February 2014.

Long, Scott, "Anatomy of a Backlash: Sexuality and the 'Cultural' War on Human Rights," Human Rights Watch, 2005.

Long, Scott, "Unbearable Witness: How Western Activists (Mis)recognize Sexuality in Iran," *Contemporary Politics* 15: 1 (2009), 119–36.

Martel, Frederic. *Global Gay: Comment la revolution gay change le monde*. Paris: Flammarion: 2013.

Massad, Joseph A. *Desiring Arabs*. Chicago: University of Chicago Press, 2007. Massad, Joseph, "Re-orienting Desire: The Gay International and the Arab World," *Public Culture* 14, No. 2 (Spring 2002), 361–85.McBee, Thomas Page. *Man Alive: A True Story of Violence, Forgiveness and Becoming a Man*. San Francisco: City Lights, 2014.

McBee, Thomas Page, "Self-Made Man #1–#32," column, *The Rumpus*, 2012–2015. Meadow, Tey. *Trans Kids: Being Gendered in the Twenty-First Century*. Berkeley: University of California Press, 2018.

Mock, Janet. *Redefining Realness: My Path to Womanhood, Identity, Love & So Much More.* New York: Atria Books, 2014.

Morris, Jan. *Conundrum*. London: Faber & Faber, 2010.

Narrain, Arvind, and Ghautam Bhan. *Because I Have a Voice: Queer Politics in India*. New Delhi: Yoda Press, 2005.

Narrain, Arvind, and Alok Gupta. *Law Like Love: Queer Perspectives on Law*. New Delhi: Yoda Press, 2011.

Nealy, Elijah C. *Trans Children and Youth: Cultivating Pride and Joy with Families in Transition*. New York: W. W. Norton & Company, 2017.

Nelson, Maggie. *The Argonauts*. Minneapolis: Graywolf Press, 2016.

Nkabinde, Nkunzi Zandile. *Black Bull, Ancestors and Me: My Life as a Lesbian Sangoma*. Johannesburg: Jacana Media, 2009.

Norton, Rictor. "The Gay Subculture in Early Eighteenth-Century London," in *The Gay Subculture in Georgian England*, on-line publication, updated

23 May 2013. Parker, Richard. *Beneath the Equator: Cultures of Desire, Male Homosexuality and Emerging Gay Communities in Brazil.* New York: Routledge, 1999.Paternotte, David, "Blessing the Crowds: Catholic Mobilizations Against Gender in Europe." In Anti-Genderismus: Sexualität und Geschlecht als Schauplätze aktueller politischer Auseinandersetzungen, edited by S. Hark and P. Villa. Bielfeld: Transcript Verlag, 2015.

Patternote, David, "Global Times, Global Debates? Same Sex Marriage Worldwide," *Social Politics: International Studies in Gender, State & Society* 22, No. 4 (winter 2015), 653–74.

Paternotte, David, and Manon Tremblay, eds. *The Ashgate Research Companion to Lesbian and Gay Activism*. London: Ashgate, 2015.

Pepper, Rachel, ed. *Transitions of the Heart: Stories of Love, Struggle and Acceptance by Mothers of Transgender and Gender Variant Children*. Jersey City: Cleis Press, 2012.

Plemons, Eric. *The Look of a Woman: Facial Feminization Surgery and the Aims of Trans-Medicine*. Durham, NC: Duke University Press, 2017. Preciado, Paul. *Testo Junkie*. New York: Feminist Press, 2013.

Prosser, Jay. *Second Skins: The Body Narratives of Transsexuality*. New York: Columbia University Press, 1998.

Puar, Jaspir K., "Global Circuits: Transnational Sexualities in Trinidad," *Signs* 26, No. 4 (summer 2001), 1039–65.

Puar, Jasbir K. *Terrorist Assemblages: Homonationalism in Queer Times*. Durham, NC, and London: Duke University Press, 2007.

Rao, Rahul, "Global Homocapitalism," *Radical Philosophy* 194, No. 1 (November/ December 2015), 38–49.

Rao, Rahul, "Queer Questions," *International Feminist Journal of Politics*, 2014.

Rao, Rahul, "Re-membering Mwanga: Same-Sex Intimacy, Memory, and Belonging in Post-colonial Uganda," *Journal of Eastern African Studies* 9, No. 1 (2015), 1–19. Reddy, Gayatri. *With Respect to Sex: Negotiating Hijra Identity in South India*. Chicago and London: University of Chicago Press, 2005.

Reid, Graeme. *How to Be a Real Gay: Gay Identities in Small-town South Africa*. Scottsville: UKZN Press, 2013.

Revathi, A. *The Truth About Me: A Hijra Life Story*. New Delhi: Penguin Books India, 2010.

Rose, Jacqueline, "Who Do You Think You Are?," *London Review of Books*, 5 May 2016.

Rubin, Gayle S., "Thinking Sex: Notes for a Radical Theory of the Politics of Sexuality." In *The Lesbian and Gay Studies Reader*, edited by Henry Abelove, Michèle Aina Barale, and David M. Halperin. New York and London: Routledge, 1993.

Rubin, Henry. *Self-Made Men: Identity and Embodiment Among Transsexual Men*. Nashville: Vanderbilt University Press, 2003.

Sadgrove, Joanna, Robert M. Vanderbeck, Johan Andersson, Gill Valentine, and Kevin Ward, "Morality Plays and Money Matters: Towards a Situated Understanding of the Politics of Homosexuality in Uganda," *Journal of Modern African Studies* 50, No. 1 (2012), 103–29.

Saketopoulou, Avgi, "Minding the Gap: Race And Class In Clinical Work With Gender Variant Children," *Psychoanalytic Dialogues* 21, No. 2 (2011), 1233– 43. Sánchez García, Arturo, "The Happy Judicialization of Sexual Rights: Abortion and

Same-Sex Marriage in Mexico," PhD dissertation, Kent Law School, Canterbury, U.K., October 2014.

Sandfort, Theo, Fabiene Simenel, Kevin Mwachiro, and Vasu Reddy. *Boldly Queer: African Perspectives on Same-Sex Sexuality and Gender Diversity*. The Hague: Hivos, 2015.

Schulman, Sarah. *Israel/Palestine and the Queer International*. Durham, NC: Duke University Press, 2012.

Sedgwick, Eve Kosofsky. *Epistemology of the Closet*. Berkeley: University of California Press, 1991.

Serano, Julia. *Excluded: Making Feminist and Queer Movements More Inclusive*. New York: Seal Press, 2013.

Serrano-Amaya, José Fernando, "La tormenta perfecta: Ideología de género y articulación de públicos," *Revista Latinoamericana Sexualidad Salud y Sociedad*, No. 27 (2017), 149–71.

Sharlet, Jeff, "Straight Man's Burden: The American Roots of Uganda's Anti-gay Persecutions," *Harper's Magazine*, September (2010), 36–48.

Snyder, Timothy. *The Road to Unfreedom: Russia, Europe, America*. London: Bodley Head, 2018.

Solomon, Alisa, "Viva la Diva Citizenship: Post-Zionism and Gay Rights." In *Queer Theory and the Jewish Question*, edited by Daniel Boyarin, Daniel Itzkovits, and Ann Pellegrini. New York: Columbia University Press, 2003.

Solomon, Andrew. *Far from the Tree: Parents, Children and the Search for Identity.* New York: Scribner, 2012 Stryker, Susan. *Transgender History: The Roots of Today's Revolution*, 2nd ed. New York: Seal Press, 2017.

Stryker, Susan, and Stephen Whittle. *The Transgender Studies Reader*. New York: Routledge, 2006.

Stryker, Susan, and Aren Aizura, eds. *Transgender Studies Reader*, Vol. 2. New York: Routledge, 2013.

Stychin, Carl F, "Same-Sex Sexualities and the Globalization of Human Rights Discourse, *McGill Law Journal* (2004) 49.

Tamale, Sylvia, ed. *African Sexualities: A Reader*. Cape Town, Dakar, Nairobi, and Oxford: Pambuzuka Press: 2011.

Thoreson, Ryan Richard. *Transnational LGBT Activism: Working for Sexual Rights Worldwide*. Minneapolis and London: University of Minnesota Press, 2014. Thoreson, Ryan Richard, "Troubling the Waters of 'a Wave of Homophobia': Political Economies of Anti-queer Animus in Sub-Saharan Africa," *Sexualities* 17, 1–2 (2014).

Travers, Ann. *The Trans Generation: How Trans Kids (and Their Parents) Are Creating a Gender Revolution*. New York: NYU Press, 2018.

Valentine, David. *Imagining Transgender: An Ethnography of a Category*. Durham, NC, and London: Duke University Press, 2007.

Van Klinken, Adriaan, and Ezra Chitando. *Public Religion and the Politics of Homosexuality in Africa*. London and New York: Routledge, 2016.

Vanita, Ruth, and Saleem Kidwai. *Same-Sex Love in India: Readings from Literature and History*. London: Palgrave, 2000.

Weber, Cynthia. *Queer International Relations: Sovereignty, Sexuality and the Will to Knowledge*. Oxford: Oxford University Press, 2016.

Weiss, Meredith L., and Michael J. Bosia. *Global Homophobia: States, Movements, and the Politics of Oppression*. Illinois: University of Illinois Press, 2013.

Whitaker, Brian. *Unspeakable Love: Gay and Lesbian Life in the Middle East*. London: Saqi Books, 2008.

Wintemute, Robert, "From 'Sex Rights' to 'Love Rights': Partnership Rights as Human Rights." In *Sex Rights*, edited by Nicholas Bamforth. Oxford: Oxford University Press, 2005.

ACKNOWLEDGMENTS

This book would not have been possible without the Open Society Fellowship I was awarded, and the support I received from Leonard Benado, Steve Hubbell, Bipasha Ray, and their team. The team working on LGBT rights at Open Society generously helped develop the concept of this book, and made invaluable introductions: I thank, in particular, Michael Heflin, Maxim Anmegichean, Greg Czarnecki, Ian Southey-Swartz, Nguru Karugu, Giselle Kasim, and Joy Chua. Joel Bedos, Graeme Reid, and Carla Sutherland helped conceptualize this book and made more invaluable introductions; so, too, did Julie Dorf and Mark Bromley of the Council for Global Equality, who also brought me to a conference to begin thinking about these ideas, and invited me to engage activists at several meetings they convened.

An invitation to present at the Hivos African Same-Sex Sexualities and Gender Diversity Conference in Nairobi in 2014 gave me the opportunity to assemble the big ideas of this book, and a commission from Commonwealth Writers assisted me with the East African research. Commissions from *Granta* and *The Guardian* enabled further research in the United States, India, and Southern Africa; I am grateful to Sigrid Rausing, Jonathan Shainin, and Clare Longrigg for their invaluable editorial insights, too. A critical burst of thinking and writing happened during a residency at Bellagio in March 2018; I am indebted to the Rockefeller Foundation for having selected me, to Pilar Palaciá for the glorious sanctuary, and to my fellow residents—in particular Jody Heymann, Robin Gorna, and Doug Hattaway—for their insights.

Graeme Reid's team at Human Rights Watch—and those who came before them, under Scott Long—have set the standard for documenting the goings-on along the Pink Line: the archive they have generated is indispensable. I wish to thank, in particular, Kyle Knight and Ryan Thoreson, and especially Neela Ghoshal, for her commitment to helping me (and Michael Bashaija) in East Africa. Lester Feder's *BuzzFeed* reports from the Pink Line have also been invaluable; I thank him, too, for his collegiality. Conversations with other scholars and activists working on these issues have also helped frame the ideas of the book: Sonia Corrêa, Scott Long, David Patternote, Eric Plemons, and Rahul Rao have been particularly generous with their time and insights. Thanks, too, to Justus Eisfeld, Maria Margaronis, the late Joel Nana, Fernando Serrano Amaya, Jessica Stern, and Muthoni Wanyeki. Daniel Wolfe and Richard Elovich will not remember it, but the spark for this book was a conversation at their house in Brooklyn in 2011, when Richard slipped me his copy of Arjun Appadurai's *Modernity at Large* in response to my inchoate ramblings.

There is no way a project of this scope could have been undertaken without the generosity, hospitality, and expertise of friends, colleagues, and strangers across the world. In Cape Town I thank Victor Mdluli, Guillane Koko, and the devoted team at PASSOP; in Malawi I thank Gift Trapence and Dunker Kamba; in Uganda, Richard Lusimbo, Adrian Jjuuko, and Sean Mugisha; in Senegal, Djiadji Diouf and Mariam Armesen; in Nigeria, Jide Mcauley, Jude Onwambor, and Cheikh Traore.

In Egypt, Scott Long provided introductions, analysis, and warm hospitality, and Tarek al-Moustafa, my researcher and interpreter, was a brilliant sounding board and a networker extraordinaire. Others who helped with interpreting were Ahmed Awadallah, Ramy Youssef, and Noor Sultan. Thank you, too, to Azza Sultan, Paul Amar, and others I cannot name.

In Israel and Palestine, Sarah Schulman and Elle Flanders made vital introductions for me, as did Aeyal Gross, a sure guide through this complex country. Eve Guterman was an invaluable researcher and translator. Thanks, too, to Rawda Morcos, Amira Hass, and Louise Bethlehem. I am indebted to Jake Witzenfeld, the director of *Oriented*, who introduced me to Fadi, and gave me access to his film transcripts.

I could not have done my work in Russia without the brilliant Evgeny Belyakov, my researcher and interpreter, another networker extraordinaire. I also thank Margret Satterthwaite, Constantin Yablonskiy, Evgeny Byrgyn, and Alfred Miniakhmetov who helped with interpreting; Tatiana Vinnichenko and Rakurs for hosting me in Arkhangelsk, and Polina Sevchenko and Coming Out St. Petersburg for hosting me there. Anastasia Smirnova and Maria Kozlovskaya of the Russian LGBT Network introduced me to Pasha, and were of great help, too, in schooling me in the issues, as were Andrei and Yael Demedetskiy, and Masha Gessen.

In Mexico, I thank Julieta Cabeza Blum, my smart and wonderful researcher, translater, interpreter, and food guide. Andres Carrillo Marrot did interpreting for me, too; Ricardo Baruch and d Arturo Sánchez García offered invaluable background research. Miguel Angel Ochoa suggested I meet Zaira and Martha and made the introductions; Rodrigo Cruz did additional research on Mexico and Latin America; Alex Ali Mendez, Alehli Ordonez, and Rex Wockner were much-needed resources on the law in Mexico.

In the U.S., my introduction to the Riot Youth kids was through Laura Wernick: I am indebted to her, and to the devoted team then in place at the Neutral Zone in Ann Arbor, in particular Lori Roddy and Jonah Thompson. Will Sherry hosted me at Spectrum at the University of Michigan, and Alex Kulick was my Ann Arbor researcher and fixer. Further research was conducted for me by Alexander Pines and Mel Ferrara. The following people played vital roles in assisting, enlightening, and connecting me: Joel Baum, Diane Ehrensaft, Jamison Green, Esther Kaplan, Tey Meadow, Rachel Pepper, Eric Plemons, Asa Radix, Andrew Solomon, and Herb Schreier. Several Riot Youth alumni, in particular Milo Inglehart, were generous with their time and insight.

In the Philippines, my trip was facilitated by Ging Cristobal. I could not have done the work there were it not for the generosity of Leo Chiang and Johnny Symons, who took me on board the shoot for their documentary, *Out Run*.

I would not have met the *kothis* of Devanampattinam nor been able to write about them without the assistance of three extraordinary people: my friend Vikram Doctor, a patient informant and razor-sharp sounding board for all the years of this project; L 'Ramki' Ramakrishnan of Orinam, an equally patient political and intellectual guide in Tamil Nadu; and Levanya Keshavraj, my researcher and interpreter, who urged me to get out of the city and then became my constant conduit to the village. Our visits, with my friend the photographer Candace Feit and our driver Saravanan, were an undoubted highlight of my time on the Pink Line. I thank Vikram Sundarraman for additional research and interpreting. Others who have helped, in and about India, include Vinay Chandran, Alok Gupta, Sameera Jahargirdar, Saleem Kidwai, Arvind Narrain, Siddharth Narrain, Akshay Khanna, and Aniruddhan Vasudevan.

I would like to thank the following friends, colleagues, and strangers for reading and commenting on part or all of the manuscript: Tarek al-Mustafa, Ricardo Baruch, Robert Beachy, Louise Bethlehem, Sonia Corrêa, Leena Dallasheh, Maggie Davey, Vivek Divan, Vikram Doctor, Julie Dorf, Peter Gevisser, Ran Greenstein, Aeyal Gross, Alok Gupta, Alfred LeMaitre, Scott Long, Julia Martin, Claire Messud, Philip Miller, David Paternotte, Eric Plemons, L Ramakrishnan, Ira

Sachs, Yana Sitnikova, Andrew Solomon, Carol Steinberg, Jonny Steinberg, and Martine Taub.

Four friends, in particular, have coaxed this book into being, with their encouragement and their reading of drafts of the manuscript, and their wise counsel: Jessica Dubow, Damon Galgut, Philip Miller, and Ellah Wakatama Allfrey, who played a hands-on role as unofficial editor, too. I am indebted beyond words to them. Claire Anderson, Evgeny Belyakov, and Mel Ferrara fact-checked the manuscript and compiled the endnotes: they were a formidable finish-line team.

David Godwin's counsel was wise and acute: I remain forever grateful for this over the past decade. Much thanks, too, to Sarah Chalfant, Rebecca Nagel, and Alba Ziegler-Bailey from the Wylie Agency. At Farrar, Straus and Giroux I have had the extraordinary good fortune to be in the hands of a double act, Ileene Smith and Jackson Howard. I'm am deeply grateful to Ileene for her belief in my work and her wisdom about publishing; to Jackson for his insight, commitment, and passion in the editing and making of this book. Chandra Wohleber copyedited this book with precision and insight, and Alex Merto dressed it in startling brilliance. To them and to everyone else at FSG I am immensely grateful. Jonathan Ball Publishers remain my South African home; as ever, I thank Jeremy Boraine and his team. Thank you, too, to Helen Conford and her team at Profile Books in London for the passion and skill they have brought to *The Pink Line*.

I do not write books quickly or effortlessly, something to which my closest friends and family will attest. I am grateful to all—you know who you are—for the way you care for me, hold me, inspire me. First, last, and always, more than ever this time for his love, wisdom, and support: Dhianaraj Chetty.

Finally, I thank all who were willing to trust me enough to talk to me: those, of course, who will meet in these pages, but equally those who, because of space and time and other random considerations, I have not been able to write about here. Please know that the efforts you made with me were not in vain: you have illuminated and transformed me with your stories, even if they are not represented here. I hope I can do you justice elsewhere, and that you continue doing justice, too. The long arc bends …

ABOUT THE AUTHOR

Photo: Fiona McPherson

Mark Gevisser's previous books include *Lost and Found in Johannesburg: A Memoir* and *A Legacy of Liberation: Thabo Mbeki and the Future of the South African Dream*, which was published in South Africa as *Thabo Mbeki: The Dream Deferred*, and won the country's premier nonfiction award, the Alan Paton Prize, in 2008. As a journalist, commentator and essayist he has written for publications including *The New York Times*, *The Guardian*, *Granta*, *The New York Review of Books*, *The Nation*, *The Wall Street Journal*,and the *Los Angeles Times.* His feature-length film *The Man Who Drove with Mandela* won the Teddy Award for Best Documentary at the Berlin Film Festival in 1999, and he has curated exhibitions about South African history and society in his native Johannesburg. He has been an Open Society Fellow and a Rockefeller Resident at Bellagio, and has taught narrative nonfiction at universities and in workshops. He was born in Johannesburg in 1964 and educated at Yale, and now lives in Cape Town with his partner.